Teaching Young Adult Literature

Teaching Young Adult Literature

Edited by
Mike Cadden,
Karen Coats, and
Roberta Seelinger Trites

The Modern Language Association of America
New York 2020

Printed in the United States of America

Library of Congress Cataloging-in-Publication Data

Names: Cadden, Michael, editor. | Coats, Karen, 1963- editor. | Trites, Roberta Seelinger, 1962- editor.
Title: Teaching young adult literature / edited by Mike Cadden, Karen Coats, Roberta Seelinger Trites.
Description: New York : The Modern Language Association of America, 2020. | Series: Options for teaching, 10792562 ; 50 | Includes bibliographical references.
Summary: "Offers pedagogical techniques for teaching classic and contemporary young adult (YA) literature and texts about growing to adulthood. Addresses issues of selecting classroom texts, building cultural awareness, responding to censorship, and reading both emotionally and critically. Gives syllabus suggestions for undergraduate and graduate courses in literature, education, and library science"—Provided by publisher.
Identifiers: LCCN 2019055255 (print) | LCCN 2019055256 (ebook) | ISBN 9781603294584 (hardcover) | ISBN 9781603294553 (paperback) | ISBN 9781603294560 (EPUB) | ISBN 9781603294577 (Kindle)
Subjects: LCSH: Young adult literature—Study and teaching (Higher) | Young adult literature—History and criticism.
Classification: LCC PN1008.8 .T43 2020 (print) | LCC PN1008.8 (ebook) | DDC 808.06/8—dc23
LC record available at https://lccn.loc.gov/2019055255
LC ebook record available at https://lccn.loc.gov/2019055256

Options for Teaching 50
ISSN 1079-2562

Cover illustration of the print and electronic editions: Minji Kim, *Image Making*, 2018

POD 2021 (first printing)

Published by The Modern Language Association of America
85 Broad Street, Suite 500, New York, New York 10004-2434
www.mla.org

Contents

Mike Cadden, Karen Coats, and Roberta Seelinger Trites

Introduction

Young adult literature, which is literature written for and marketed to teenagers, has gained an unprecedented readership in recent years. For example, in the week of 7 July 2014, eight of the top twenty-five sellers on the *USA Today* best-seller list were YA novels ("Best-selling Books"). Following the overwhelming success of the Harry Potter series, *The New York Times* created its own best-seller list for YA novels, in a gesture that appeared to elevate but actually segregated YA novels from non-YA best sellers. In 2012, *Publisher's Weekly* reported that as much as fifty-five percent of the YA literature sold in the United States was bought by adults—and those adults reported that seventy-eight percent of the time they were purchasing YA books for their own use, not to give to teenagers ("New Study"). By 2017, estimates of adults purchasing YA literature had risen to seventy percent of total YA sales ("Book Publishing"). Clearly, the YA market is a vibrant and vital sector of the publishing industry. Meanwhile, many state legislatures, responding to accrediting agencies, have mandated courses in YA literature for their preservice education candidates. Specifically, the national accrediting agency for future teachers of English, the National Council of Teachers of English (NCTE), includes as their "first element" in content knowledge "being knowledgeable about" YA literature ("NCTE/NCATE Standards").

While scholarship about YA literature itself has increased in sophistication in the last two decades and YA literature has become established as a genre relevant to MLA members and their students, there remains a gap in scholarship surrounding the literary pedagogy of YA literature at the postsecondary level. This volumes seeks to address that gap. Our goal is to help those who are teaching college courses in YA literature think about creative and innovative ways to teach the many types of narratives considered to be YA literature. We also demonstrate how YA literature can be incorporated into classes that are not focused solely on adolescent literature. In the process, we interrogate the complex issues that inform the pedagogy of YA literature.

Definitions

The concept of adolescence was not widely theorized in the United States until the early twentieth century, when G. Stanley Hall's work in *Adolescence* helped synthesize several centuries of thought about the difference between becoming an adult and being one. Hall observed that older children increasingly remained in school rather than shouldering adult responsibilities and developing mature habits of duty and discipline by entering the workforce, and so his depiction of adolescence as a time of Sturm and Drang "was a response to late nineteenth-century fears of overcivilization, emasculation, and degeneration" (Mintz 196). In other words, teenagers no longer employed in the workforce ostensibly had too much time to focus on their emotions and the effects of maturation. Although based in evolutionary theories about development, Hall's work began the process of identifying adolescence as a social construct—that is, as a group identity that links people according to social perceptions of their shared characteristics—in this case, age. Those interested in the broader context of adolescence as a historical phenomenon will find helpful works by Kenneth Kidd, Joseph Kett, John Neubauer, and Leerom Medovoi.

Because adolescence has not been a recognized stage of life development in every era or in every culture, it remains an open and fruitful subject with which to engage students in discussions of their own perceptions of the concept. Perhaps the simplest definition of *adolescence* is that posited by the psychologists Richard M. Lerner and Laurence Steinberg: adolescence is "the second decade of life" (x). When we refer to "adolescents," we tend to follow this definition. Clearly, though, the ages eleven through fourteen are something of a gray area with regard to YA literature. The American Library Association's John Newbery Award, for instance, considers any literature for children up to age fourteen as a children's book, while its Michael L. Printz Award for Excellence in Young Adult Literature goes to books intended for readers age twelve to eighteen. We also recognize that current social constructions of adolescence assume it to be a stage of life characterized by the transition from childhood to adulthood, but because economic conditions in the United States and Canada in the twenty-first century have increased young adults' financial dependence on their parents, adolescence now, for many people, extends into their twenties. This well may be a factor in YA literature's increasing relevance to college students. Rarely are older teenagers and those in their early twenties committed to permanent careers or homes or intimate relationships, many of their friendships are transitional, and few will remain permanently in the role of student. As Karen Coats puts it, adolescence "is defined by its state of flux and impermanence. Adolescence is a phase someone goes through" ("Young Adult Literature" 325).

One standard definition of YA literature is "anything that readers between the approximate ages of twelve and eighteen choose to read either for leisure reading or to fill school assignments" (Nilsen et al. 3). Even this broad definition, however, fails to take into account the marked increase in texts produced for older adolescents in recent decades. Thus, throughout this volume, we define YA literature as texts written or produced for adolescents and marketed directly to teens, while the term *adolescent literature* can be thought of as the broader category of all literature about the stage of maturation from childhood into adulthood, a definition that includes texts from *Romeo and Juliet* to the latest teen dystopia. As Mike Cadden notes, YA literature shares with children's literature the quality of being named for its reading audience, rather than its content ("Genre" 310). Adolescent literature, on the other hand, includes adolescence as a content topic but is not necessarily written only for a teen audience. Furthermore, the publishing industry tends to distinguish "middle grade" novels (for students in middle school) from YA novels (grades 9–12), and has recently adopted the term *new adult* to refer to novels marketed to people in their late teens and early twenties—legal adults who may not yet self-identify as fully adult. In this volume, the term *YA literature* refers to all texts marketed to teen readers but excludes those books that are specifically marketed to middle graders, which are usually considered alongside children's literature.

In defining YA literature in terms of the marketplace, we are acknowledging that publishers frequently have the power to determine whether a book about an adolescent is intended for adults or teenagers. For example, Sapphire's *Push* was widely read by teenagers but ended up on *The New York Times* best-seller list for adult trade fiction following the success of the film adaptation in 2010. Novels marketed to teenagers, such as *The Book Thief* and *The Hunger Games*, appeared in distinct categories for young readers in the same week ("Best Sellers"). *Teaching Young Adult Literature* focuses on the college-level pedagogy that surrounds texts marketed to teenagers.

History and Development of Young Adult Literature

Historically, literary works about adolescence have emerged from multiple intellectual strands. In this section, we identify some of the literary, philosophical, and economic factors that eventually led to the establishment of YA literature as a distinct literary category. Michael Cart's *Young Adult Literature: From Romance to Realism* provides a compelling and more extensive history of YA literature than space allows here (3–20). Readers interested in a complete time line of YA publishing history can find it in *Literature for Today's Young Adults* (Nilsen et al. 47–82).

Stories about maturation have fascinated people for centuries, as has the subject of shaping young minds through education. The European Enlightenment's emphasis on education, however, brought increased attention to the workings of the adolescent mind. Steven Mintz contrasts two influential schools of educational theory in the Enlightenment era: that which holds children to be the "repository of virtues" in a given society and that which emphasizes how "malleable" children are (11). Conduct books, for example, generally assumed that children needed to be instructed in socially acceptable behaviors (Armstrong 5–6). Two important philosophers to react against this "repository" school of thought were John Locke, who, in *Some Thoughts Concerning Education* (1693), wrote about influencing how young people learn and grow, and Jean-Jacques Rousseau, whose philosophies—articulated perhaps most clearly in *Emile* (1762)—advocated for a specific educational philosophy founded in the discovery of the natural world. John Morgenstern links this increasing interest in education with literacy, the rise of the middle class, and the expansion of the novel as a creative form. He claims that increased literacy inspired by such philosophers as Locke and Rousseau changed the nature of childhood in two ways: "First, the social reality of childhood changed as, more and more, childhood became associated with institutionalized schooling in literacy. Second, the nature of adult subjectivity changed as a gap opened between the literacy of adults and children, a gap that children's literature has been invited to fill" (65). To fill this gap, authors such as John Newbery, Maria Edgeworth, and Mary Wollstonecraft penned stories intended to stimulate young readers' literacy and critical thinking skills. Indeed, in *A Vindication of the Rights of Woman* (1792) Wollstonecraft also pushed back against those educational theorists who focused exclusively on educating boys, while a more conservative historian of the novel, such as Clara Reeve, in *The Progress of Romance* (1785), aligned with traditionalists in insisting that young girls read only romances that are morally uplifting. All these theorists demonstrate an increasing fascination with the malleability of the young mind. Even adherents to the idea of children as repositories of social values, such as the conservative advocates of the Sunday School Movement of the late eighteenth century, understood that, through literacy, growing children can be influenced for good or ill.

During the Romantic era, attention came to be fixed upon the primacy of the human mind and its malleability as it matures from childhood to adulthood. With *Wilhelm Meister's Apprenticeship* (1795–96), Goethe crafted the first in a long line of bildungsromans—that is, the novel of spiritual *Bildung*, or moral development. William Wordsworth's extended narrative in *The Prelude* (1805) also demonstrates many features of a traditional bildungsroman and focuses on the interior growth of one individual's mind, from childhood into productive adulthood. Manfred Engel defines the bildungsroman as being focused on the Germanic concept of *Bildung* as "a process of organic or quasi-organic development" that leads a novel to focus on "character" and "development," not on any "process of social or biological determination but a process of formation" (265–66). Variants of the bildungsroman include the *Entwicklungsroman* ("the novel of development" that stops short of full maturation), the *Erziehungsroman* ("the novel of education" or upbringing), and the *Künstlerroman* ("the novel of artistic development"); they all focus on the interior or spiritual growth of one character (Engel 265). Contemporary criticism of YA literature is historically rooted in the scholarly criticism of the bildungsroman and its variants; scholars of the bildungsroman were the first to firmly establish a critical interest in the interior life of a maturing adolescent.

Jerome Buckley identifies the component parts of a traditional bildungsroman as involving a boy growing up in a rural setting who feels repressed by his parents, especially his father, and who escapes to the city, where he has first a debasing and then an exalting romantic relationship. By the novel's end, he has found a place in society in which he can productively work and love (18–23). Buckley offers *David Copperfield* (1849–50), *Great Expectations* (1860–61), *Jude the Obscure* (1895), and *The Way of All Flesh* (1903) as notable British examples of the genre. *Sons and Lovers* (1913) and *The Portrait of the Artist as a Young Man* (1916) fit the traditional genre of the Künstlerroman with a male protagonist.

Patricia Meyer Spacks expands the category of the bildungsroman to include novels about female maturation. Likewise, Elizabeth Abel, Marianne Hirsch, and Elizabeth Langland, early feminist literary critics, criticize the traditional, patriarchal definitions of the bildungsroman and Künstlerroman. Typical examples of the bildungsroman with a female protagonist include *Jane Eyre* (1847) and *Little Women* (1868–69). Annis Pratt and Barbara White contrast the novel of female development to the bildungsroman's pattern of preparing girls for the marriage market; they believe bildungsromans too often demonstrate a girl "growing down," out of her rebelliousness and into social conformity, rather than "growing up" (14). Literary critics including Ralph A. Austin, Olga Bezhanova, Tobias Boes, Katherine Dalsimer, Esther Kleinbord Labovitz, and Geta Leseur have also complicated a genre traditionally seen as Anglo-European by applying frameworks of race, ethnicity, embodiment, orientation, and nationality to the bildungsroman. Although novels about maturation from childhood to adulthood typically focus on the growth of one individual's mind, the infinite diversity of human experience allows for a wide variety of bildungsromans that describe what it means to grow up in different ethnicities or nationalities or religions, what it means to grow up with a differently abled body, what it means to grow up queer, what it means to grow up cisgender or trans, or what it means to grow up oppressed by migration status, economic deprivation, or a political state.

During much of the nineteenth century, many bildungsromans would have had readers ranging from young people to adults because "children and childhood were less segregated from adults and adulthood" (Clark 16). Nevertheless, during that century, a complex array of novels about adolescence written specifically *for* adolescents began to emerge—in part because of increased attention to educational philosophy and in part because of the Romantic interest in the bildungsroman and the interior life and growth of the individual. Additionally, in Great Britain in the nineteenth century, an emphasis on educating a (white) population to become colonialists led to the popularization of school stories and adventure novels by such authors as Thomas Hughes, Captain Frederick Marryat, Mary Martha Sherwood, Robert Louis Stevenson, and G. A. Henty. While the school stories and adventure tales that flourished in Great Britain were also being published in North America, two authors in particular from the United States, Louisa May Alcott and Mark Twain, demonstrated that audiences were also eager to buy novels that indoctrinated young minds into reformist ideologies, including ideas that would gain prominence in the progressive era, such as universal suffrage and mandatory education. Both Alcott and Twain were influenced by the most prominent American Romanticist of the nineteenth century, the transcendentalist Ralph Waldo Emerson, and his interest in childhood and the life of the mind validated both Twain's and Alcott's interests in writing about young people (Trites, *Twain* 4–5). Once Alcott and Twain proved how lucrative it could be to write ideologically driven bildungsromans that could be marketed to the young, many such novels followed from authors in North America, including *A Boy's Town* (1890), *Rebecca of Sunnybrook Farm* (1905), *Anne of Green Gables* (1908), *A Girl of the Limberlost* (1909), and *Daddy-Long-Legs* (1912).

The Progressive Era's reformist strand of adolescent literature was particularly notable in North American novels about adolescent experiences, such as *Maggie: A Girl of the Streets* (1893), *The Red Badge of Courage* (1895), *Sister Carrie* (1900), and *The Call of the Wild* (1903). Although these novels were written for adult audiences, many teenagers read them and experienced how these novels call attention to oppressive social structures even while they affirm the economic status quo. Another strand of reformist novels that focuses on how oppressive racial structures affect the adolescent experience exploded during the late Harlem Renaissance with such narratives as *Their Eyes Were Watching God* (1937), *Black Boy* (1946), and *Invisible Man* (1952). Narratives about youth and maturation had thus proved to be a profitable genre in North America before World War II. These stories about adolescence were influenced by a wide range of traditions, including the Enlightenment's emphasis on the malleability of young minds, Romanticism's interests in the individual mind, and Progressivism's commitment to reformism.

Two significant developments during the Great Depression shaped novels for adolescents. First, adult unemployment led teenagers unable to find jobs to remain in high school; constrained from becoming producers in the economy, these young adults instead became consumers (Mintz 236–37; Cart 5). Second, booksellers innovated new ways to lower the cost of books by selling literary paperbacks. With the advent of Penguin Books in the United Kingdom in 1935 and Pocket Books in the United States in 1939, literary fiction became more affordable to a wider audience—including to adolescents. Penguin capitalized on the popularity of paperbacks among its young readers by creating an imprint dedicated to children's literature, Puffin Picture Books, in 1938 (Trubek). Scholastic Books, founded as a newsletter in 1920, branched into schools with children's book clubs in 1948 and made paperback books widely available to teenagers by the 1950s ("Our History"). Perhaps the best known examples of novels about adolescence that were widely read in paperback form by teenagers are two post–World War II novels: *The Catcher in the Rye* (1951) and *To Kill a Mockingbird* (1960).

Indeed, World War II proved to be the most significant turning point in the history of YA literature. Mary Hilton and Maria Nikolajeva assert that "[w]riters who had survived the war as children and young adults themselves began to reject the sentimental tradition and the invisibility of teenage interiority in twentieth-century literature for the young"; they also point to the powerful impact Anne Frank's diary had on postwar readers (6). Additionally, because of the expanding postwar economy, the purchasing power of adolescents in North America significantly increased (Mintz 285–86). An entire marketing culture began to cater to teenagers' interests in music, clothing, movies—and books. Maureen Daly's *Seventeenth Summer* (1942) is often regarded as the first novel specifically marketed to teenagers (Hunt 4). What were then referred to by librarians as juvenile novels, published in the 1940s and 1950s, included series fiction, sports fiction, and romances. In 1957, the American Library Association established the Young Adult Services Division as a separate division from children's services (Starr). Publishers began to designate novels as Young Adult when they discovered they could market novels directly to teenagers. The postwar zeitgeist and the Cold War ideology that led to the space race in the 1950s also influenced sophisticated developments in science fiction and fantasy literature that metaphorically addressed fascism, such as *A Wrinkle in Time* (1962), the Dark Is Rising series (1965–77), the Tripods series (1967–88), and *A Wizard of Earthsea* (1968). This last book is also clearly influenced by the civil rights movement, given the author's careful attempts to craft multicultural characters. In fact, the civil rights movement spurred the publishing industry to recognize that young people have specific interests and needs that certain types of intellectually honest novels written for teenagers could meet. The Council on Interracial Books for Children, founded in 1965 and inspired by the Black Arts Movement, influenced authors such as Rosa Guy, Virginia Hamilton, Sharon Bell Mathis, and Walter Dean Myers to write intricate multicultural narratives for teen readers. Additionally, the earliest novels to emerge from increased attention to rebellious teen voices were designated YA. They include *It's Like This, Cat* (1964), *The Outsiders* (1967), *The Pigman* (1968), and *I'll Get There: It Better Be Worth the Trip* (1969). Although *I'll Get There* does not address gay sexuality in ways that resonate with contemporary sensibilities, it was noteworthy for its honesty about same-sex desire. While some early YA novels, such as *It's Like This, Cat*; *The Outsiders*; and *Teacup Full of Roses* (1972), explore the difficult issues that confront teenagers in urban settings, others, such as *Mr. and Mrs. Bo Jo Jones* (1968), *My Darling, My Hamburger* (1969), and *Go Ask Alice* (1971) are cautionary tales about heteronormative sexuality or drugs or both.

Interest in the psychological and social complexity of teenagers continued in the 1970s with YA novels such as *The Chocolate War* (1974) and *Roll of Thunder, Hear My Cry* (1976). Experimental YA fiction also emerged in the 1970s and 1980s; novels like those in the Stone Book series (1976–78), *Breaktime* (1978), and *Weetzie Bat* (1989) demonstrated that teen readers were willing to grapple with postmodern narrative structures and characterizations. The 1980s also saw increased attention to the gay and lesbian community and stark social issues such as homelessness and AIDS. By the 1990s, YA literature was a firmly established sector of the publishing industry, but the publication of J. K. Rowlings's Harry Potter series exploded the field, stimulating interest in particular in speculative fictions written in a series format, including the gothic supernatural (e.g., the Twilight series), the dystopic (e.g., the Hunger Games series), the post-apocalyptic (e.g., the Maze Runner series), and cyborg novels (e.g., the Cinder series). Additionally, the memoir has found its place in the teaching of adolescent literature, in part because of the Common Core's push to expose students to more nonfiction and in part because of the proliferation of excellent recent memoirs marketed to teenagers, such as Jacqueline Woodson's *Brown Girl Dreaming* (2014) and John Lewis's tripartite graphic narrative *March* (2013–16).

While some critics, like Ruth Graham, may believe that the proliferation of YA literature in the twenty-first century represents a downturn in the public's reading tastes, the fact nevertheless remains that, by 2014,

YA publishing had reached an all-time high ("U.S. Publishing Industry's Annual Survey"). Furthermore, throughout the twenty-first century, many colleges and universities have acknowledged the intellectual diversity of YA literature by including in their curricula courses that recognize the legitimacy of YA literature as a sophisticated barometer of contemporary social life and as a field that contains, innovates, and has the potential to energize the study of multiple literary forms and genres.

The following factors, then, are part of the historical context for the increased production of YA literature and its inclusion in postsecondary pedagogy: Romanticism's interest in the growth of the individual mind (an interest that still has not waned in the twenty-first century), ongoing didactic interest in manipulating adolescents to believe specific morals and ideologies, the increased profitability involved in selling books to teenagers and schools, the civil rights movement and the ways it empowered young people to reject the status quo, teenagers' increased market share as consumers, and interest among postsecondary educators in training future teachers and literary scholars to teach this influential genre. The YA audience has provided authors and publishers the opportunity to create complex works of art, ranging from the novel in poem form to the graphic narrative, and the opportunity to mass-produce popular though perhaps derivative series, such as the Twilight series and the Divergent series.

Review of Criticism about Young Adult Literature

It is a staple of American literary studies to define literature in terms of adolescence—as when Hemingway famously claims that all American novels descended from one about adolescence, *Adventures of Huckleberry Finn* (22). Leslie Fiedler even asserts that canonical American novels are "at home in the children's section of the library" and that they are often about development because the authors themselves keep writing about their own childhoods, unwilling to grapple with the allure of sexuality and admit their adult responsibilities: "Our greatest novelists, though experts on indignity and assault, on loneliness and terror, tend to avoid treating the passionate encounter of a man and woman, which we expect at the center of a novel. Indeed, they rather shy away from permitting in their fictions the presence of any full-fledged, mature women . . ." (24). Similarly, Julia Kristeva argues, in her psychoanalytic study of the classic liberal-humanist novel, "The Adolescent Novel," that the traditional novel is concerned with growth. With an eye toward the YA novel, however, Coats complicates Kristeva's claim, recognizing several categories of novels that defy this description, including existential and postmodern novels and the series book ("Young Adult Literature" 320). In other words, although literary critics may have a long history of evaluating the concept of adolescence in literature—and literature as adolescent—criticism that theorizes YA literature is a fairly recent phenomenon. For example, Caroline Hunt observed only in 1996 that very little theorization of YA literature existed (4–5).

By 1999, however, several critics had begun to theorize YA literature as a whole. Coats has identified how Bakhtinian dialogics inform much of that early literary criticism about YA literature, especially because Bakhtin emphasizes the ideological nature of literature—as do a great many of the critics who have theorized YA literature in terms of genre ("Young Adult Literature" 317). For example, one of the first full-length studies of the YA novel, Robyn McCallum's *Ideologies of Identity in Adolescent Fiction*, focuses on the dialogic construction and representation of the adolescent self in YA literature. Coats finds a similar dialogic tension inherent in *Disturbing the Universe*, in which Roberta Seelinger Trites takes a Foucauldian approach to analyzing adolescents' relations to power structures ("Young Adult Literature" 318). Rejecting bildungsroman-influenced criticism that defines YA literature solely in terms of growth, Trites argues that negotiating such power structures as social institutions and the biological imperatives of sex and death affect the maturation of many characters in YA fiction. Early work in the narrative theory of the YA novel also relies on Bakhtin, as when Cadden identifies the ethical first-person narrator of a YA novel to be the one who exposes the unavoidable irony of an adult author creating a teenaged narrator. Cadden also praises those novels that balance the top-down relationship of an adult narrator speaking through a constructed teen narrator with a double-voiced discourse that exposes the text's ideologies ("Irony" 146–47). Some of the first scholars to theorize YA literature were thus involved in identifying how ideological structures surrounded the "interconnection, multiple perspectives, and mutuality" in novels written for teenagers (Coats, "Young Adult Literature" 319).

In another theoretical strand, one that is psychoanalytic and yet still inflected with ideological concerns, Coats provocatively makes use of Kristeva's concept of abjection as a critical method for interrogating the YA novel. Much of the alienation and social isolation in YA literature can be understood through this concept. Coats identifies as a staple of YA literature the scapegoated outsider observing human interactions "with equal parts longing and disdain" from the periphery or social rim of the teenager's social group ("Young Adult Literature" 319). She identifies *The Outsiders* as perfectly named in that it identifies adolescence as a human condition defined by how adults have abjected teenagers to outsider status in order to keep the social body "clean and proper" (*Looking Glasses* 149). Additionally, Kidd relies on Kristeva to historicize adolescent literature, arguing that the Kristevan model helps explain how "the construction of vulnerable subjectivity" (140) in contemporary YA literature is a literary "turn or stage in the genre's larger evolution" (176). Kidd traces the psychological development of adolescent literature through three phases:

> First, the articulation of adolescence in psychological as well as literary terms, beginning with Hall; second, the literary-psychological-ethnographic framing of a problem interior in and around the notion of "identity" and by way of explorations of gender and sexuality; and third, the transformation of that interior into a "young adulthood" at once confident and highly vulnerable, in such a way that adolescent literature begins to overlap with the literature of trauma. (139)

Kidd and Coats thus both place adolescent and YA literature within psychological structures.

Another strand of YA criticism strives to queer traditional age-based structures. Nikolajeva has coined a term useful to both children's literature and YA criticism: *aetonormativity*. Using the Latin prefix for "age" (*aeto*), the term suggests how norms are based in age (*Power* 8). Nikolajeva claims that adolescent literature queers traditional age-based norms, just as queer theory queers heteronormativity (6–10). Because YA literature frequently makes use of Bakhtinian concepts of the carnivalesque to empower teens—often inverting adult norms of power—aetonormativity is a concept that can help critics identify issues of empowerment for both characters in and readers of YA literature.

Hilton and Nikolajeva argue that the turbulence of adolescence serves as a metaphor for the tempestuous second decade of the twenty-first century: "Through sympathetically portraying the alienated pains and pleasures of adolescence, through *enacting* adolescence with all its turmoil, writers bring young readers face to face with different forms of cultural alienation itself: the legacy of colonialism, political injustice, environmental desecration, sexual stereotyping, consumerism, madness, and death"

(1). Hilton and Nikolajeva's argument provides one more explanation for the exploding popularity of YA literature in the twenty-first century.

Although Hilton and Nikolajeva identify a broad range of YA literary topics, from "the legacy of colonialism" to "death," like many critics of YA literature, notably Trites in *Disturbing the Universe*, they recognize sexuality as a key component of the genre: "If political instability in the search for identity can be mapped onto the process of adolescent maturation, then sexual awakening and hormonal turmoil is also a marker of the disjunction between child and adolescent" (12). Kathryn James and Victoria Flanagan are among the critics who investigate sexuality as one of the major topics of adolescent literature. Hilton and Nikolajeva, like Lydia Kokkola and Kerry Mallan, include issues of performativity, queerness, orientation, gender identity, and cross-dressing in their studies of sexuality in YA literature, while Michael Cart and Christine Jenkins more specifically chart the historical trajectory of depictions of LGBTQ+ characters and their allies. Sexuality and gender identity are not defining criteria of YA literature, but they have attracted the interest of a number of critics. Given that many of these critics operate outside the United States, their perspectives on sexuality in YA literature may have escaped the straitening impulse of the American evangelical tradition as well as the still ongoing Victorian-Romantic impulse to protect supposedly innocent children from what many censorship-oriented adults view as the corrupting nature of sexuality.

Deflecting the tendency to focus on sexuality as a defining feature of YA literature, Coats invites critics to evaluate YA literature in terms of ethics and ideas when she distinguishes between books with open and closed moral universes. She argues "that a book that has . . . a closed moral universe, that is, a plot line that features punishment for the wicked and reward for the good, is more likely to be preadolescent, whereas a book that calls that moral universe into question . . . is clearly YA" ("Young Adult Literature" 322). Moreover, Claudia Mills asserts that ethical criticism can be employed "to encourage sensitivity, not to silence conversation but to stimulate it" (8). The intellectual trends that have fostered the emergence of YA literature since World War II have done exactly that: these literary works encourage readers to think about the ethical relation between individuals and their worlds, between individuals and their embodiment, between peoples and their epistemological frameworks, and between peoples and sociopolitical structures. Taken as a whole, YA literature invites readers to question every aspect of their moral universe.

The Structure of This Volume

Teaching YA Literature explores a range of issues from the theoretical to the practical. We thus divide the volume into three sections: theories about YA literature, discussions of its genres, and assignments to be used in the college-level classroom.

Part I: Theories, Themes, and Issues

The first part of this volume, "Theories, Themes, and Issues," addresses teaching some of the most frequently theorized aspects of YA literature. The essays in this part are organized around the shifts involving emotions, identity, conflicts, and maturation that surround adolescence as a time of transition. This section concludes with essays that explore censorship and teaching cross-culturally.

Michelle Ann Abate's "Young Adult Literature, Literary Theory, and Emotionalism" begins this section, calling attention to both the YA novel as an art form and the way the genre's reliance on "powerful emotions" opens up opportunities for interpretation through multiple types of critical theory. Relying on S. E. Hinton's *The Outsiders* and Isabel Quintero's *Gabi, A Girl in Pieces*, Abate demonstrates how having her students focus their study on emotion in YA literature allows them to read YA literature for both its content and its implications, drawing them into a more open and complex relation with theory itself.

In "Contemplating Childhood and Adolescence in Elie Wiesel's *Night*," Lee Talley discusses Wiesel's Holocaust memoir as an antibildungsroman working within the bildungsroman tradition. The Holocaust itself, however, serves to dispel Romantic illusions about childhood innocence and adult experience. Talley demonstrates how *Night* can be effectively used in the classroom to push students to question the binary construct of childhood-adulthood while increasing their understanding of the Holocaust.

With "Youth, Transnationalism, Identity: Young Adult Literature and World Literature," Melek Ortabasi opens a cluster of essays in this section about identity. Ortabasi's essay focuses on how the bildungsroman establishes "narrative norms" that have been applied to stories that construct and narrate the colonization of groups in the Eastern and Southern Hemispheres. Moreover, Ortabasi demonstrates how these novels—from Germany, Argentina, Russia, Iran, and Senegal—are frequently engaged in the work of colonial expansion and resistance to it.

Carey Applegate interrogates what it means to be a black- or brown-skinned youth in the urban United States in "Say Their Names: Complicating the Single-Story Narrative of City Kids." She relies on Chimamanda Adiche's concept of the single story to problematize the frequent characterization of youth of color as "thugs," and she offers important counter-readings that examine racism as a recurring problem in YA literature.

In "Embracing Discomfort and Difference in the Teaching of Young Adult Literature," Ebony Thomas writes an autobiographical teaching memoir about how her intersectionalities as an African American woman have influenced the organization of her classes. She, too, writes about the danger of the single story, and she describes how she asks students to think about the metaphors they use in order to disrupt students' conventional thinking, particularly in terms of moving from conversations about otherness to discussions about how our "collective humanity" influences all of us.

Amy Cummins continues the discussion of race and adolescence in "Teaching Texas Borderlands Young Adult Literature," in which she describes how she uses Latinx literature from the Texas borderlands, where she teaches. Cummins offers a compelling argument for meeting the needs of specific student populations with local literatures. Her essay also serves as an excellent reference guide for those seeking nonmainstream Latinx narratives for their students.

Margaret Noodin, Donna Pasternak, Laurie Barth Walczak, and Michael Zimmerman are a group of Wisconsin educators who explore Native American YA literature in terms of its cultural models. They have worked at the Indian Community School of Milwaukee, and their perspectives working with both high school and college students provide helpful directions to faculty members seeking to learn more about teaching Native American YA literature.

With "A Girls' Studies Approach to Young Adult Literature," Katie Kapurch opens the cluster on gender theory in the study of YA literature. Kapurch defines the pedagogy of girls' studies in terms of understanding how girls are "active creators of culture" and how feminine adolescence is socially constructed rather than being defined entirely by biological sex and age. She pairs *The Outsiders* with a cultural reading of the release of the rock album *With the Beatles* to demonstrate how "girlishness" is not only about female youth. The cluster continues with Livia Antony and Padma Baliga's exploration of how to teach gender in the context of multicultural and transnational literature in "'Re-Presenting' Gender in Multicultural

Young Adult Literature." The essay pairs gender-oriented narratives from India and Japan to provide feminist readings of two Japanese manga narratives and an Indian film and graphic novel.

Angel Daniel Matos provides an essay about how important gender and gender identity, sexuality, and orientation are to the workings of YA literature in "Subverting Normative Paradigms: Teaching Representations of Gender and Queerness in Young Adult Literature." He explores the critical discourse, texts, and sources that best enable students to have discussions about gender, sexuality, and queerness. Melanie Goss explores queerness from a different perspective in "Teaching Transgressive Texts," discussing what it means to teach narratives about mental health, mental illness, and gender. She focuses on Beatrice Sparks's *Go Ask Alice*, Patricia McCormick's *Cut*, and Laurie Halse Anderson's *Wintergirls* in order to challenge how students think and write about controversial topics like self-harm.

Jon M. Wargo and Laura Apol write about decolonizing students' imaginations in "But I Can't Use This in a *Classroom*! Teaching Risky/ Risqué Young Adult Literature." They are uniquely qualified, as professors in colleges of education, to assess the concerns preservice teachers have about teaching controversial YA literature. Wendy J. Glenn adds to this cluster about controversial literatures in "Addressing School Censorship in the Young Adult Literature Course." She squarely addresses the problems and prevalence of censorship in K–12 schools and provides information about how to arm future teachers with the ability to deal with would-be censors.

S. Patrice Jones shifts the focus of this section to teaching YA literature in a variety of courses, departments, and institutions. She considers what English departments, education departments, and schools of library science and information have to offer the study of YA literature. Billie Jarvis-Freeman then advocates for the use of YA literature in general education. In "Surveying the Fiction: Teaching Young Adult Literature across the Curriculum," she demonstrates how YA literature can be effectively incorporated into a course on the history and literature of Western civilization. Finally, Helma van Lierop-Debrauwer's "Literary Education That Crosses Borders" describes how YA literature is used in college classrooms in the Netherlands, while Justyna Deszcz-Tryhubczak analyzes the instruction of college students in Wrocław, Poland. Combined, these two essays offer international perspectives on the field.

Together, the essays in this section emphasize some of the most fascinating and controversial issues, including emotions, maturation, identities, sexuality, mental health, censorship, and transnationality, involved in the teaching of YA literature.

Part II: Genres and Forms

The second part of this volume focuses on the genres and forms that are either dominant or specialized within the larger category of young adult literature. These nine essays fall into three clusters. The first group of three essays deals with speculative and fantastic literature—genres that have always been popular in the young adult category.

In "Teaching Young Adult Science Fiction," Farah Mendlesohn observes that what is considered good science fiction writing often contradicts critics' assumptions about what is important in young adult literature. This essay asks readers to consider the tension between speculative fiction and young adult literature's respective foci. Speculative fiction challenges the reader to deal with abstraction and fact gathering, in contrast with what Mendlesohn says is YA literature's demand that readers develop empathy for characters. Her goal is to provide a review of those writers who offer readers texts that contemplate solutions to worlds gone wrong. She offers a reading curriculum that provides students with a real sense of what science fiction is and does.

Elizabeth Marshall's focus in "Representations of Youth, Schooling, and Education in Dystopian Young Adult Novels" discusses a narrower but fundamental set of texts of constant interest and relevance to young adult readers: texts that represent school in dystopic ways. Marshall draws on a number of genres: classic novels, picture books, elementary readers, young adult literature, and film. A primary goal of her course is to invite students to understand the difference between the terms and ideas of *schooling* and *education*, and she encourages students to question what it means to be educated. Marshall posits that dystopian YA novels advance political ideologies about education, from curriculum to assessment.

The last essay in this cluster is Mary Bricker's "Teaching Genre: Fairy Tales and Their Retellings in Young Adult Literature." Bricker's class focuses on the fairy tales of the Brothers Grimm and the remakes targeting a young adult audience. She finds that it is the students' basic familiarity with the tales that provides a solid basis for critical thinking about textual interventions and inventions that engage the mechanics of popular culture's interest in retellings. Carefully prepared, multistep presentations on fairy tale retellings allow students in Bricker's course to draw from multiple subgenres of young adult literature, including science fiction, fantasy, realism, and historical fiction. Students research origins, authorial adaptations, strategies for endings, and character design.

The second cluster of essays focuses on strategies for representing reality in young adult fiction. In Mary Adler's "The Story behind the Story: A Cross-Text, New Historicist Approach to Historical Fiction," the focus is on authorial influence in historical fiction. Adler invites her students to read actively and challenge the "grand narrative" of history as presented in textbooks. She concentrates on war fiction because of its proclivity to create a single-voiced representation of events for young people. Through discussions of war novels that offer various points of view, narrative structures, and authorial positions, students begin to see the strategies used to represent history. Through this study, students face narrative representations of conflict and death, and they find opportunities for self-reflection that build empathy and understanding.

In "Taking a Second Look at First-Person Narration in Young Adult Realistic Fiction," Cathryn Mercier describes her course on contemporary realistic fiction for young adults in which she studies first-person narration as a tool to foster identification. The work of both Joanne Brown and Jonathan Culler, among others, provides students a contingent description rather than a firm definition of the idea of realism as a basis for critical discussion, and over thirty recent novels and graphic narratives provide subjects for narratological analysis. By the end of the course, students connect ideas of subjectivity, realism, and diverse critical approaches to draw conclusions about the nature of young adult realism.

In the final essay in this cluster, "Peritext and Pedagogy: Supporting Critical Thinking through Young Adult Nonfiction," Don Latham and Melissa Gross describe a course in which students are provided a model for assessing standard elements in a genre that they are usually not invited to question: peritext. How does the peritext—the extratextual features of a book, as defined by Gérard Genette—offer clues for student inquiry? By focusing on two award-winning nonfiction accounts, students learn how to examine the periphery of the text and how different books reveal different things. Students review author biography, author notes, source notes, references, bibliography, suggested readings, and image credits in order to evaluate the relative credibility of a work.

The last of the three clusters in part II examines form rather than genre. In "Teaching the Young Adult Verse Narrative" Coats invites us to consider the special challenges raised by verse narrative, a form that combines poetry, narrative, and sometimes drama. Verse narrative, Coats contends, is more difficult to navigate than other literary forms and challenging to teach. Coats considers how to choose verse narrative to use in particular contexts, how to approach the poetic in the form, and how to theorize the form using contemporary cultural theory.

Gwen Athene Tarbox argues for a special consideration of comics, now an essential form in YA literature. "Integrating Comics into an Undergraduate Young Adult Literature Course" provides a foundation in YA comics theory and approaches the study of YA comics as separate from the study of children's picture books and YA prose novels. Tarbox's class examines the comics form's relation to content—the contradictions between words and images; the ways panels and borders dictate how meaning is created; and how race, gender, and ethnicity are impossible to ignore in these novels.

The last essay in this section is a study of film. Meghann Meeusen's "Teaching Adolescent Film: A Cultural-Historical Activity-Theory Approach" pays attention to the many remakes of popular stories through the medium of film in particular. Using cultural-historical activity theory, Meeusen helps students "conceptualize the contextual and material factors inherent to the production and reception of adolescent film adaptations." This approach merges the study of narrative structure and production elements and also acknowledges the role of culture and history. Meeusen's YA film pedagogy demands the examination of the contexts of production and critical reception.

Part III: Assignments

Teaching YA texts to college students affords special pleasures and opportunities that arise out of the connections between the subject matter and the students approaching it. These books reflect and contextualize many past and current concerns of students, and thus the most effective assignments are those that allow students to reflect on and theorize their own experiences, make engaged connections with one another through the texts, and bring in cultural artifacts that flesh out the contexts of the texts in multimodal ways. The slight distance between the ages of the characters and the ages of the students also offers unique opportunities for students to think about themselves in retrospect, specifically interrogating the ways young people are represented and what cultural meanings are placed upon them. This section offers detailed suggestions for assignments and approaches that capitalize on the special affordances YA literature offers for engaged, participatory learning.

The first two essays in this section focus on how to marry students' social skills with the learning goals of a literature classroom. Both methods explored in these essays produce greater gains in both self-awareness and perspective taking. Melissa Sara Smith, in "Theorized Storytelling: A Tool for Practicing Reader-Response Criticism," offers a way to transform a practice that emerges organically in most YA literature courses. She argues that students are often motivated to tell their own stories because they relate to young adult characters. Instructors can capitalize on this tendency by guiding students in formal critiques of their own stances as narrators and inviting them to imagine themselves as characters. Ultimately, such a practice teaches them to read fictional texts more analytically. Roxanne Harde, in "Team-Based Learning and Young Adult Literature," argues that team-based learning is an especially effective approach to use with texts that engage with sexual and racial violence. She demonstrates how students committed to teams develop relationships of trust and accountability and, as a result, avoid making easy interpretations and unquestioned assumptions. They come away with deeper learning and a greater appreciation of perspectives other than their own.

The next three essays in this section offer alternatives to traditional research paper assignments in ways that capitalize on the distinctive possibilities of YA literature. Beverly Lyon Clark and two of her former students, Camille Buffington and Eric Esten, explain in their essay, "On Curating Online Anthologies: Not the Traditional Term Paper," the process of researching and putting together a set of materials that contextualizes a YA text. They provide detailed instructions on how to support students in the process of collecting a variety of multimodal sources and resources and of curating a well-designed online anthology. The assignment not only expands students' knowledge of the text but also provides them with a valuable introduction to the emerging field of digital humanities. Virginia Zimmerman has also developed a creative alternative to the traditional research paper, which she explains in "The Young Adult Critical Edition Project." Noting that most YA texts do not have critical editions, she tasks students with creating one, including all the elements one might find in a professionally produced edition. In collecting biographical and contextual information as well as criticism, students gain experience in writing, research, and evaluating sources while becoming experts on the text itself. Jan C. Susina's "Sound Tracks of Our Lives: Mix Tapes and Playlists in the Young Adult Literature Classroom" points to the prevalence of entertainment media in teenagers' lives and demonstrates how the development of playlists related to YA novels enhances both self-understanding and understanding of the texts through transmedial engagement.

The final two essays in this section focus on a particular cultural ideology relevant to YA literature. In "The Politics of Realism: Interdisciplinary Explorations of Adolescent 'Storm and Stress,'" Katherine Bell describes how she asks students to interrogate traditional concepts of adolescence, specifically as they relate to cultural fears and mechanisms of the control and regulation of youth, through cultural artifacts related to YA texts. Lauren Byler zeros in on the representation of girls in YA texts. In "Teaching Young Adult Girls' Books: Why Bother?" Byler troubles student perceptions of the signifiers and valuations that attach themselves to the term *girl*. By adopting a long historical arc and reading primary fictional and nonfictional texts alongside challenging theoretical ones, Byler asks students to consider the "political risk in overlooking the power of the artlessness attributed to girls and books associated with them."

Indeed, there is much political risk in overlooking YA texts in general, but there is even more to be gained by finding ways to engage students in productive conversations about how these texts shine a light on their own lives as well as on the culture at large. With the activities and methods described in the essays that follow, instructors can reap the benefits of the inherent social connections between YA literature and young adult readers.

Works Cited

Abel, Elizabeth, et al. *The Voyage In: Fictions of Female Development.* UP of New England, 1983.

Armstrong, Nancy. *Desire and Domestic Fiction: A Political History of the Novel.* Oxford UP, 1987.

Austin, Ralph A. "Struggling with the African Bildungsroman." *Research in African Literatures*, vol. 46, no. 3, 2015, pp. 214–31.

"Best Sellers." *The New York Times*, 3 Jan. 2010, www.nytimes.com/best-sellers-books/2010-01-03/overview.html.

"Best-Selling Books." *USA Today.* www.usatoday.com/entertainment/books/best-selling/week/2014/28/.

Bezhanova, Olga. *Growing Up in an Inhospitable World: Female Bildungsroman in Spain*. Asociación de Literatura y Cultura Femenina Hispánica, 2014.
Boes, Tobias. *Formative Fictions: Nationalism, Cosmopolitanism, and the Bildungsroman*. Cornell UP, 2012.
"Book Publishing: Young Adult and New Adult Book Markets." *The Balance*, www.thebalance.com/the-young-adult-book-market-2799954.
Buckley, Jerome Hamilton. *Season of Youth: The Bildungsroman from Dickens to Golding*. Harvard UP, 1974.
Cadden, Mike. "Genre as Nexus: The Novel for Children and Young Adults." Wolf et al., pp. 302–13.
———. "The Irony of Narration in the Young Adult Novel." *Children's Literature Association Quarterly*, vol. 25, no. 3, 2000, pp. 146–54.
Cart, Michael. *Young Adult Literature: From Romance to Realism*. American Library Association, 2010.
Cart, Michael, and Christine Jenkins. *The Heart Has Its Reasons: Young Adult Literature with Gay/Lesbian/Queer Content, 1969–2004*. Scarecrow, 2006.
Clark, Beverly Lyon. *Kiddie Lit: The Cultural Construction of Children's Literature in America*. Johns Hopkins UP, 2003.
Coats, Karen. *Looking Glasses and Neverlands: Lacan, Desire, and Subjectivity in Children's Literature*. U of Iowa P, 2004.
———. "Young Adult Literature: Growing Up, In Theory." Wolf et al., pp. 315–29.
Dalsimer, Katherine. *Female Adolescence: Psychoanalytic Reflections on Works of Literature*. Yale UP, 1986.
Engel, Manfred. "Variants of the Romantic Bildungsroman." *Romantic Prose Fiction*, edited by Gerald Gillespie et al., John Benjamins, 2008, pp. 263–95.
Fiedler, Leslie. *Love and Death in the American Novel*. 1960. Dalkey Archive Press, 2003.
Flanagan, Victoria. *Into the Closet: Cross-Dressing and the Gendered Body in Children's Literature and Film*. Routledge, 2008.
Graham, Ruth. "Against YA." *Slate Book Review*. The Slate Group, 5 June 2014, www.slate.com/articles/arts/books/2014/06/against_ya_adults_should_be_embarrassed_to_read_children_s_books.html.
Hall, G. Stanley. *Adolescence: Its Psychology and Its Relations to Physiology, Anthropology, Sociology, Sex, Crime, Religion, and Education*. Appleton, 1904. 2 vols.
Hemingway, Ernest. *The Green Hills of Africa*. 1935. Scribner, 1953.
Hilton, Mary, and Maria Nikolajeva. *Contemporary Adolescent Literature and Culture: The Emergent Adult*. Ashgate, 2012.
Hunt, Caroline. "Young Adult Literature Evades the Theorists." *Children's Literature Association Quarterly*, vol. 21, no. 1, 1996, pp. 4–11.
James, Kathryn. *Death, Gender, and Sexuality in Contemporary Adolescent Literature*. Routledge, 2009.
Kett, Joseph F. *Rites of Passage: Adolescence in America, 1790 to the Present*. Basic Books, 1977.

Kidd, Kenneth. *Freud in Oz: At the Intersections of Psychoanalysis and Children's Literature.* U of Minnesota P, 2011.

Kokkola, Lydia. *Fictions of Adolescent Carnality: Sexy Sinners and Delinquent Deviants.* John Benjamins, 2013.

Kristeva, Julia. "The Adolescent Novel." *Abjection, Melancholia, and Love: The Work of Julia Kristeva*, edited by John Fletcher and Andrew Benjamin, Routledge, 1990, pp. 8–23.

Labovitz, Esther Kleinbord. *The Myth of the Heroine: The Female Bildungsroman in the Twentieth Century: Dorothy Richardson, Simone de Beauvoir, Doris Lessing, Christa Wolf.* Peter Lang, 1987.

Lerner, Richard M., and Laurence Steinberg. *Handbook of Adolescent Psychology.* 2nd ed., Wiley, 2004.

Leseur, Geta. *Ten is the Age of Darkness: The Black Bildungsroman.* U of Missouri P, 1995.

Mallan, Kerry. *Gender Dilemmas in Children's Fiction.* Palgrave, 2009.

McCallum, Robyn. *Ideologies of Identity in Adolescent Fiction: The Dialogic Construction of Subjectivity.* Garland, 1999.

Medovoi, Leerom. *Rebels: Youth and the Cold War Origins of Identity.* Duke UP, 2005.

Mills, Claudia. Introduction. *Ethics and Children's Literature*, edited by Mills, Ashgate, 2014, pp. 1–12.

Mintz, Steven. *Huck's Raft: A History of American Childhood.* Harvard UP, 2004.

Morgenstern, John. "The Rise of Children's Literature Reconsidered." *Children's Literature Association Quarterly*, vol. 26, no. 2, 2001, pp. 64–73.

"NCTE/NCATE Standards for Initial Preparation of Teachers of Secondary English Language Arts, Grades 7–12." *NCTE*, Oct. 2012, www.ncte.org/library/nctefiles/groups/cee/ncate/approvedstandards_111212.pdf.

Neubauer, John. *The Fin-de-Siècle Culture of Adolescence.* Yale UP, 1992.

"New Study: 55% of YA Books Bought by Adults." *Publisher's Weekly*, 13 Sept. 2012, www.publishersweekly.com/pw/by-topic/childrens/childrens-industry-news/article/53937-new-study-55-of-ya-books-bought-by-adults.html.

Nikolajeva, Maria. *Power, Voice, and Subjectivity in Literature for Young Readers.* Routledge, 2009.

Nilsen, Alleen Pace, et al. *Literature for Today's Young Adults.* 9th ed., Pearson, 2012.

"Our History." *Scholastic*, www.scholastic.com/aboutscholastic/history.htm.

Pratt, Annis, and Barbara White. "The Novel of Development." *Archetypal Patterns in Women's Fiction*, by Pratt, Indiana UP, 1981, pp. 13–37.

Spacks, Patricia Meyer. *The Adolescent Idea: Myths of Youth and the Adult Imagination.* Basic Books, 1981.

Starr, Carol. "Brief History of the Young Adult Services Division." *American Library Association*, www.ala.org/yalsa/aboutyalsa/history/briefhistory.

Trites, Roberta Seelinger. *Disturbing the Universe: Power and Repression in Adolescent Literature.* U of Iowa P, 2000.

———. *Twain, Alcott, and the Birth of the Adolescent Reform Novel.* U of Iowa P, 2007.

Trubek, Anne. "How the Paperback Novel Changed Popular Culture." *Smithsonian*, 30 March 2010, www.smithsonianmag.com/arts-culture/how-the-paperback-novel-changed-popular-literature-11893941/?no-ist.

"U.S. Publishing Industry's Annual Survey Reveals $28 Billion in Revenue in 2014." *Business Wire*, www.businesswire.com/news/home/20150611005182/en/U.S.-Publishing-Industrys-Annual-Survey-Reveals-28.

Wolf, Shelby A., et al., editors. *Handbook of Research on Children's and Young Adult Literature.* Routledge, 2011.

Part I

Theories, Themes, and Issues

Michelle Ann Abate

The Effect of Affect: Young Adult Literature, Literary Theory, and Emotionalism

At Ohio State University, I regularly teach a graduate course titled Literary Theory and Literature for Children and Young Adults. The students enrolled represent a diverse array of academic fields and levels of familiarity with the subject matter. For instance, my class includes students from the master's and doctoral programs in English as well as Teaching and Learning. In addition, it has students who have studied literary theory in their previous undergraduate or graduate coursework and others who are encountering this material for the first time.

For the primary readings of the various theoretical schools under consideration, I use the collection *Literary Theory: An Anthology*, edited by Julie Rivkin and Michael Ryan. Meanwhile, as common texts for our class to practice applying the theoretical lenses that we were examining, I select one example of three types of books for young readers: a picture book, a middle-grade narrative, and a work of YA literature. My intention with these selections is to incorporate narratives that target different age ranges, feature different subject matters, and make use of different literary aesthetics. That said, one of these genres regularly moves to the forefront of the course: YA literature. The narrative belonging to this category is the one that students are repeatedly most interested in talking about in relation to literary theory. Week after week, regardless of which critical approach is under consideration, the YA text that I have chosen to use for the class is the one that students routinely use to explore what that particular lens permitted us to see, learn, or discover about a text, as well as what limitations arise by analyzing a narrative in this particular manner.

This essay explores the reasons fueling the attraction and appeal that YA literature has for my students. Why are so my many members of my class drawn to these narratives as they examine theoretical approaches ranging from formalism, structuralism, and psychoanalysis to postcolonialism, narratology, and new historicism? How much of this allure can be attributed to the specific YA book's characters, plot, and writing style, and how much can be linked to the genre as a whole? What does the prominence that these texts consistently have for my students say about the relation that these narratives possess with literary theory? Much has been written over the years about what literary theory can teach us about YA literature. The discussion that follows reveals what YA literature can teach us about literary theory.

Young Adult Literature and Literary Theory

Literary critics commonly bifurcate narrative analysis into two general practices: what they call reading "with the grain" or "against the grain" of a text. As Lois Tyson explains about the former practice, "When we read with the grain of a literary work, we interpret the work the way it seems to invite us to interpret it" (7). An example of this act would be examining Judy Blume's *Are You There, God? It's Me, Margaret* in light of feminist theory or Angie Thomas's *The Hate U Give* from the standpoint of critical race theory. By contrast, when critics read against the grain, they "analyze elements in the text of which the text itself seems unaware" (Tyson 7). An example of this phenomenon would be analyzing *Are You There, God?* in the context of postcolonial theory or *The Hate U Give* through the framework of posthumanism. While these approaches are not wholly antithetical to the events in these narratives, they don't immediately spring to mind as ones that play a significant role in these texts.

Both past and present works of YA literature support the application of numerous literary theories. For example, the text that is commonly seen as inaugurating the genre, S. E. Hinton's *The Outsiders*, spotlights the family hardships, personal difficulties, and physical violence experienced by a group of working-class youths—subjects that readily lend themselves to the theoretical lenses of Marxism, psychoanalysis, gender studies, and cultural materialism. Isabel Quintero's *Gabi, a Girl in Pieces* likewise examines a wide array of topics, themes, and issues. The summary of the book provided by the publisher provides an overview: "Gabi Hernandez chronicles her last year in high school in her diary: college applications, Cindy's pregnancy, Sebastian's coming out, the cute boys, her father's meth habit, and the food she craves." Given these narrative threads, *Gabi* invites the with-the-grain approaches of critical race theory, feminism, queer theory, and postcolonialism. Meanwhile, the book's diary format, combined with how often Gabi engages in metacommentary that calls attention to herself as the narrator, readily supports the approaches of structuralism, postmodernism, and narratology.

That said, both *The Outsiders* and *Gabi* contain narrative events that permit various against-the-grain readings. Comments in *Gabi* such as "I was sitting in the back of the bus today, watching the old retarded couple making out (like usual)" (16) invite an examination from the standpoint of critical disability studies. Likewise, the numerous poems that Gabi writes in her journal—and thus shares with readers—lend themselves to formalist as well as psychoanalytic approaches. *The Outsiders* can also be read in a variety of against-the-grain ways. For instance, the tender, loving, and demonstrative way that Ponyboy and his fellow greasers interact with one other provide the basis for examining the novel with queer theory. Similarly, the numerous references to popular musicians such as Elvis, movie stars like Paul Newman, and books like *The Carpetbaggers* encourage a cultural studies approach. Finally, the recurring use of Robert Frost's bucolic poem "Nothing Gold Can Stay" opens up the possibility of reading Hinton's text from the perspective of ecocriticism. In this way, YA literature offers a rich site for the exploration of literary theory. These novels are compelling works of aesthetic art, and they are also equally rich sites for a variety of interpretive methods.

Theoretical Criticism and Emotional Detachment

While YA books such as *The Outsiders* and *Gabi* support myriad theoretical approaches, I contend that these narratives constitute such popular choices with the students in my course for reasons other than their analytical agility. The powerful appeal that YA literature possesses in my class has its root in the nature of literary theory and the textual criticism that arises from it.

Anyone who has ever taught a course on literary theory—or even just attempted to include aspects of these approaches into the classroom—knows that many students dislike and often even openly resist the subject. The reasons for this stance are multifold. First and perhaps foremost, "students at all levels remain confused by much of this jargon-riddled discipline, which seems to defy their understandings" (Tyson xiii). That said, classroom antipathy for literary theory goes beyond the often inaccessibility of its writing style. As Tyson has observed, students resist literary theory out of a "fear of losing the intimate, exciting, magical connection with literature that is our reason for reading in the first place." The abstract, philosophical nature of much literary theory "doesn't seem to connect with our love of literature, let alone with the everyday world we live in" (1). Individuals read books to be moved, to lose themselves in a great story, and to encounter different people, places, and emotions. Literary theory seems wholly antithetical to those motivations, experiences, and pleasures. On the contrary, "it seems that theory's purpose must be to take us into some abstract, intellectual realm" (1).

Because literary theory forms the basis for literary criticism, this stance carries over to textual analysis. As Rita Felski has observed, there is not merely a disciplinary avoidance of but a professional judgment levied against scholars who disclose having an affective connection to a narrative. Critics do not wish to be "tarred with the brush of subjective or emotional response" (4). Instead, textual analysis is supposed to exist in a realm above or beyond emotion. Critical analysis and personal affect are positioned as incompatible, oppositional, and mutually exclusive. After all, any untrained reader can gush that he or she loved a certain book, but it takes a specially trained critic to articulate why a book is aesthetically, culturally, and intellectually important. For this reason, literary criticism, at least since the Russian formalists in the 1920s, has required a certain level of "critical detachment" (6). This stance signals professionalism and, with it, intellectual rigor or, at least, academic seriousness (47). By being emotionally reserved, a critic conveys that his or her analysis is not being clouded by feelings. Moreover, given the way in which intellectualism and emotionalism are positioned as adversarial, literary criticism often takes aim at emotional responses, demonstrating that they are naive, misguided, and unsophisticated. "[T]he smartest thing," Felski reports, that a literary critic "can do is to see through the deep-seated convictions and heartfelt attachments of others" (15–16). For this reason, the primary role of literary critics for generations has been "the critic-as-ironist who 'stands back' from a text in order to defamiliarize it via the knowing equanimity of her gaze" (7).

As a consequence, together with being discouraged by the often jargon-laden rhetoric of literary theory, students are disheartened by the way that it requires them to adopt what Felski refers to as a detached "critical mood" (6). In order to engage in narrative analysis, students must refrain from any public display of their passion for literature, their enjoyment of plot, and their affection for characters. Phrased in a different way, they must ironically abandon much of what they love about books, reading, and storytelling in the first place. Critical analysis requires them to "guard against any risk of deep involvement, absorption, or immersion in their object, priding themselves on their stoicism and lack of susceptibility to a text's address" (54). Borrowing a phrase from the French philosopher Paul Ricoeur, Felski calls this method of criticism a "*hermeneutic of suspicion*" (1). As she goes on to explain, "These practices combine, in differing ways, an attitude of vigilance, detachment, and wariness (*suspicion*) with identifiable conventions of commentary (*hermeneutics*)" (3). When combined, these practices produce a situation where "critics read against the grain and between the lines; their self-appointed task is to draw out what a text fails—or willfully refuses—to see" (1). In this way, not only are critics required to be emotionally guarded, but they are also expected to view texts in the same way, approaching them with wariness "rather than openness, aggression rather than submission, irony rather than reverence" (21). Instead of deepening their connection to literature, theoretical interpretation demands that they sever it. "Purged of obvious signs of affect and attachment," Felski observes, "the temperature of critique is cool rather than hot" (74).

The Centrality of Affect in Young Adult Literature

In *Literature for Today's Young Adults*, Kenneth L. Donelson and Alleen Pace Nilsen articulate some of the signature traits of YA literature. Together with discussing features such as the use of first-person narration and the fast pacing of the plots, they also mention how these texts are infused with "strong emotions." In the words of Donelson and Nilsen, YA narratives do not attempt to control, contain, or suppress human feeling; on the contrary, they "appeal to the same powerful emotions of adolescence—love, romance, sex, horror, and fear." The duo goes on to elaborate: "These strong emotions are best shown through a limited number of characters and narrative events and language that flows naturally while still presenting dramatic images" (30). This feature is not simply a common trait in YA literature but a central one that Donelson and Nilsen list as one of the defining characteristics of the genre. "Successful Young Adult Novels Deal with Emotions That Are Important to Young Adults," they announce as their seventh and final hallmark (35).

While the students in my literary theory course were, of course, drawn to titles like *The Outsiders* or *Gabi* because of their interesting characters, compelling plots, and excellent writing, I contend that students also found these works appealing test cases for the various interpretive lenses that we were studying because of the affect that permeates these novels. In keeping with the signature features of the genre as a whole, *The Outsiders* does not recoil from powerful emotions. On the contrary, these elements occupy the forefront of the narrative. Over the course of the text, Ponyboy experiences a wide range of emotions, from fear, love, and excitement to frustration, hope, and despair. Furthermore, the narrator-protagonist routinely announces, names, and calls attention to his affective state. Indeed, even though *The Outsiders* is commonly touted as inaugurating the gritty style of new realism for YA literature, the book teems with emotionalism. Both Ponyboy and his fellow greasers, for example, are very affectionate with one another, verbally as well as physically. In one scene, for example, the fourteen-year-old narrator says about Johnny, "He was crying. I held him like Soda had held him the day we found him lying in the lot" (74). Even the seemingly hardened hoodlum Dally Winston reveals his softer side. "'Johnny,' Dally said in a pleading, high voice, using a tone I had never heard from him before, 'Johnny, I ain't mad at you. I just don't want you to get hurt. You don't know what a few months in jail can do to you. Oh, blast it, Johnny, . . . you get hardened in jail. I don't want that to happen to you. Like it happened to me . . ." (90). Later, Ponyboy realizes "Johnny was the only thing Dally loved" (152). Ponyboy is equally candid about the frustration, anger, and injustice that he and his fellow greasers feel in light of their socioeconomic situation and the hardships that arise from it. As Ponyboy says about his older brother, "Darry's gone through a lot in his twenty years, grown up too fast" (2), and then, even more sympathetically a few pages later, "[Darry's] just got more worries than somebody his age ought to" (17).

Quintero's *Gabi* likewise explores a wide range of affective states. Moreover, the emotions that the narrator-protagonist experiences occupy a central component of the text. Akin to the period of adolescence itself, they range from ecstatic highs to crushing lows, sometimes in the space of just a few moments. From conflicts with her mother and problems with her friends to worries about getting into college and the difficulties connected to her father's meth addiction, Gabi's life is never dull or mundane. The opening entries that span July 24–29 form a poignant case in point. In the space of just those five days, Gabi writes in her diary about myriad issues that elicit an equally wide array of emotions: she tells us about her birth to an unwed mother and her maternal family's disapproving reaction; she muses about her hopes and fears regarding the impending school year; she shares her love for hot wings—and then also shares how she has gotten diarrhea from eating them; she documents her close friend's disclosure that she is pregnant; she likewise recalls the time when another friend told her that he was gay; throughout, Gabi often contemplates about what it means to hail from a Mexican family living in the United States (7–13). Gabi's writing about these issues is always emotionally frank and verbally direct. A passage that appears on the opening page of the book forms a representative example:

> Every time I go out with a guy, my mom says, "Ojos abiertos, piernas cerradas." Eyes open, legs closed. That's as far as the birds and the bees talk has gone. And I don't mind it. I don't necessarily agree with that whole wait-until-you're-married crap though. I mean, this is America and the twenty-first century, not Mexico one hundred years ago. But, of course, I can't tell my mom that because she'll think I'm bad.
>
> Or worse: trying to be White. (7)

Because emotions play such a central role in young adult narratives like *The Outsiders* and *Gabi*, they must also play a central role in consideration of these novels. Unlike other genres of literature, YA literature cannot be viewed in an emotionally detached way. On the contrary, the affect that the characters experience—and, by extension, the emotions that reading about their lives evokes in the audience—need to remain part of the discussion. For this reason, YA books like *The Outsiders* and *Gabi* resist and even reject the emotional distance that has long been required of literary criticism that is rooted in theory. Maintaining a cool, detached, and even stoic affective stance is simply not possible when it comes to discussing YA novels. Emotions are too fundamental to the plot, characters, and events of these narratives.

In this way, YA literature can be seen as an antidote and even corrective to the dissatisfaction, disappointment, and even frustration that many students experience about the dispassionate stance that is a prerequisite of critical engagement. In the closing section of *The Limits of Critique*, Felski wonders: "What would it mean to halt this critical machinery for a moment?

To treat experiences of engagement, wonder, or absorption not as signs of naïveté or user error but as clues to why we are drawn to art in the first place?" (179–80). Indeed, as Felksi says even more poignantly earlier in her discussion about the moratorium that literary criticism places on expressions of emotion, "Why are we so hyperarticulate about our adversaries and so excruciatingly tongue-tied about our loves?" (13). Literary critics were drawn to being literary critics in the first place because they had a passion for books. Why, when they engage in analysis, do we require them to disavow the love that they have for literature and the feelings that good storytelling evokes?

YA literature demonstrates the beneficial effects of keeping affect in literary criticism. Books like *The Outsiders* and *Gabi* not only allow emotions to remain in the realm of theoretical analysis; they require it. After all, as Felski goes on to point out, "Works of art do not only subvert but also convert; they do not only inform but also transform—a transformation that is not just a matter of intellectual readjustment but one of affective realignment as well (a shift of mood, a sharpened sensation, an unexpected surge of affinity or disorientation)" (17). YA literature has long engaged in this practice. In many ways, in fact, this axiom—that books not only change the way that readers cognitively think but also how they emotionally feel—is one of the principles on which the genre was founded. In examples ranging from Robert Cormier's *The Chocolate War*, Laurie Halse Anderson's *Speak*, and Walter Dean Myers's *Monster* to Gene Luen Yang's *American Born Chinese*, Benjamin Alire Sáenz's *Aristotle and Dante Discover the Secrets of the Universe*, and Thomas's *The Hate U Give*, YA literature is known for showcasing marginalized groups, overlooked sociocultural issues, and taboo personal and political subjects in order to raise awareness, spark conversation, and cultivate understanding. While these texts address a wide array of different issues—school bullying, rape, racism, xenophobia, homophobia, police brutality—they have one feature in common: they cultivate an emotional connection between readers and their characters to generate empathy.

YA novels offer a vivid demonstration of the affordances rather than the limitations of keeping emotion in critical theory. Books like *The Outsiders* and *Gabi* reveal how affect and analysis can and even should be positioned as mutually beneficial rather than mutually exclusive. In the words of Felski once again, "Works of art . . . can trigger passionate attachments and sponsor new forms of identification, subjectivity, and perceptual possibility" (17). While literary criticism written about books for adults try to overlook, obfuscate, and even ignore this fact, YA literature does not allow it to be forgotten. In so doing, the genre has at least as much to offer literary theory as literary theory has to offer it, and perhaps more so.

Works Cited

Anderson, Laurie Halse. *Speak*. 1999. Square Fish, 2011.

Blume, Judy. *Are You There, God? It's Me, Margaret*. 1970. Atheneum, 2014.

Cormier, Robert. *The Chocolate War*. 1974. Ember, 2004.

Donelson, Kenneth L., and Alleen Pace Nilsen. *Literature for Today's Young Adults*. Pearson, 2005.

Felski, Rita. *The Limits of Critique*. U of Chicago P, 2015.

Hinton, S. E. *The Outsiders*. 1967. Penguin, 1995.

Myers, Walter Dean. *Monster*. Amistad, 1999.

Quintero, Isabel. *Gabi, a Girl in Pieces*. Cinco Puntos Press, 2014.

Rivkin, Julie, and Michael Ryan, editors. *Literary Theory: An Anthology*. 2nd ed., Blackwell, 2004.

Sáenz, Benjamin Alire. *Aristotle and Dante Discover the Secrets of the Universe*. Simon and Schuster, 2012.

Thomas, Angie. *The Hate U Give*. HarperCollins, 2017.

Tyson, Lois. *Critical Theory Today: A User-Friendly Guide*. 2nd ed., Routledge, 2006.

Yang, Gene Luen. *American Born Chinese*. First Second, 2006.

Lee A. Talley

Contemplating Childhood and Adolescence in Elie Wiesel's *Night*

Since Elie Wiesel's *Night* is frequently given to younger readers, and since most of my students want to teach in New Jersey, a state that requires students to learn about the Holocaust and genocide, I teach the memoir in my section of an adolescent literature course. Teaching *Night* within the context of adolescent or YA literature recontextualizes the memoir in significant ways and helps students better understand the ideological construction and changing history of childhood. Although my students are familiar with Anne Frank and some have even read *Night* before, they have neither yet apprehended how children and teenagers suffered during the Holocaust nor contemplated how young people's experiences were different from adults'. Teaching them Susan Rubin Suleiman's concept of the 1.5 generation thus forms the center of my pedagogical work.

Connecting the larger history of childhood to this text and then reading the memoir through the lens of the bildungsroman, as well as the text's publishing history, elucidate the importance of readers' most basic skill—close reading—to illuminate how power operates even unintentionally. Ultimately, *Night* enables students to problematize Romantic models of growth and development, which sustain beliefs in childhood innocence and adult experience; to apprehend darker parts of children's history during World War II as well as the publishing industry's anti-Semitism; and to come to terms with the discomfiting realization that individuals in specific historical moments can lack autonomy.

Within the context of a literature course largely focused on coming of age, *Night* trenchantly interrogates the bildungsroman, a literary form—along with the Entwickslungroman—we have been discussing since the first day of class (see Trites, esp. 9–10). Wiesel certainly "comes of age" by the end of the text, but the final image of him seeing his reflection in a mirror as a "corpse . . . contemplating me" (115) problematizes not only his growth but the very genre itself. Indeed, there is "no better example of the bildungsroman turned inside out and upside down" (Vanderwerken 57). Readers can no longer fit *Night* into more comfortable readings of the Holocaust that focus on a "universal, human story" or stress individual strength and the generosity of those who helped people survive.[1] Moreover, the 2006 edition of *Night*—with a new preface by Wiesel that includes passages from his earlier and angrier Yiddish version of the memoir, Marion Wiesel's superior translation of François Mauriac's foreword, and Wiesel's 1986 Nobel Peace Prize acceptance speech—facilitates more complex ways of thinking about the Holocaust, childhood, and adolescence.[2]

During the classes in which we discuss *Night* and the next text we read, Art Spiegelman's *Maus* (both the 1986 and 1991 editions), I work to help students become, and ideally remain, comfortable with the challenges of "learn[ing] from—as opposed to about—history" (Britzman 119). The Holocaust requires accepting the reality of extraordinary human cruelty to other people, including children. I encourage students to be as receptive as possible to knowledge that radically unsettles clichés about growing from difficulty and loss and remind them in more colloquial terms of one of Deborah Britzman's most potent claims: "the adult's desire for a stable truth, in its insistence upon courage and hope, shuts out the reverberations of losing and being lost" (134). Holding on to the difficult knowledge of just how much Wiesel and millions of others suffered and lost is, for some, "terrorizing" (2). Thus, I consciously imagine our Holocaust classes in Winnicottian ways, and I work to create a holding environment safe enough for this type of difficult learning to take place.

I frame my classes with the history of Wiesel's writing *Night* (Seidman; Weissman), but I add Suleiman's concept of the 1.5 generation. Suleiman distinguishes children who survived the Holocaust from adults who survived by carefully explicating how children experienced persecution but lacked a fully adult understanding or agency. She further explains that if we understand adult survivors of the Holocaust to be first-generation survivors and their children to be the second generation, then child Holocaust survivors constitute the 1.5 generation. I then guide students in key close readings of the text and paratextual materials accompanying the 2006 edition to aid them in apprehending how children and young adults were particular victims of these atrocities. My aim is to move future teachers beyond the boxed sets given to them when they teach, to make all students more comfortable with the challenges of real learning, and to help students appreciate the importance of paratextual spaces they often ignore: dedications, prefaces, forewords, and afterwords. These narrative frames drive home the text's insights on the legacy of the Holocaust for child and teenage survivors.

I begin with a PowerPoint that highlights Suleiman's main points and her claim that the 1.5 generation's experience of "premature bewilderment and helplessness" coincided with "premature aging[:] having to act as an adult while still a child," pairing her argument's central points with photographs of Jewish children in ghettos and concentration camps (277). In a class focused on coming of age and the beliefs we have about childhood, adolescence, and adulthood, Suleiman's articulation of the challenges facing young people are particularly pertinent. For the majority of students, this is the first time they have seen images of young people's suffering during World War II, and we closely read the images I have curated alongside her claims.[3] The fact that only eleven percent of European Jewish children were still alive in 1945 quickly and devastatingly personalizes abstract statistics about the Holocaust (Suleiman 278). This figure is made all the more chilling by quick classroom math: of the thirty-five students in the class, only about four would have survived—and even fewer if we use the grimmer estimate from the United States Holocaust Museum of 6.25% ("Plight").

I focus on three of Suleiman's main points: the historical and geographical specificity of European Jewish children's experience; the developmental model she uses to explain the wide range of responses to these formative experiences, including children's relation to language and responsibility; and her privileging of literary works as the ideal site for readers to understand survivors' experiences. Students appreciate the sensible and subtle developmental schema Suleiman lays out to comprehend the varied nature of children's experiences: children "too young to remember" (infancy to age 3); children "old enough to remember but too young to understand" (ages 4–10); and those "old enough to understand but too young to be responsible" (ages 11–14) (281). The distinction Suleiman makes of older children's use of "abstract words appropriately and with understanding as well as a vocabulary to name the experience that the younger child lacks" is especially useful (282). Crucially, she defines adulthood as "the state where one is both capable of naming one's predicament and [being] responsible for acting on it in some considered way," combining the important power of naming with agency.[4] Suleiman defines responsibility as "having to make choices (and act on those choices) about their own or their family's actions in response to catastrophe," facilitating our return to one of the class's themes, language and power, from a different and importantly applied perspective (283).

Her work with language, however, extends beyond the significance of a young person's ability to employ accurate and subtle words to articulate complex feelings or experiences. Suleiman suggests there is a "privileged place for the literary in the narratives of (child) survivors," explicating "literary" as "the kind of work on language and thought that produces the complex understanding of self and world, both on the part of the writer and the reader" (291). Not only does Wiesel's 2006 edition of *Night* enable students to see this, but the powerful and subtle differences between translations drive this point home extraordinarily well. As our subsequent discussions reveal, the differences between the 1986 Stella Rodway translation, which includes a preface by Robert McAfee Brown as well as the foreword by François Mauriac, and the 2006 translation are significant indeed. The newer edition, which Marion Wiesel translated from the original French much more ably, cuts Brown's preface to include one by Elie Wiesel and adds his Nobel Prize acceptance speech as a type of afterword.

I distribute a handout with passages culled from the first twelve pages of both editions for students to fill out, discussing the first two and then having small groups fill out the rest of the sheet so that they can see at a glance just how potent the subtle differences in translation are. In all future class discussion and in any paper they may write, they are expected to cross-reference passages they believe significant with the older edition. I require students to buy the new edition and recommend they buy a print version of the older edition, though they can download free versions online. All students bring some version of both editions for class discussion. We begin with Rodway's description of Moishe as being "very poor and liv[ing] humbly" (1). By contrast, the Marion Wiesel version describes him as "poor and liv[ing] in utter penury" (3). The Romantic mystic of the first volume, whom one could assume chose to live "humbly," becomes a much more obviously liminal figure who lives in grinding poverty. We then discuss how the newer translation both adds and removes passive constructions to illuminate the terrible choices people had as well as those who had power in these circumstances. Passive descriptions of what the Nazis did in the first edition are transformed into more active and accurate verbs. For example, the Rodway translation explains how "one day they expelled all the foreign Jews" (3), while the 2006 version states that "one day all foreign Jews were expelled from Sighet" (6). The passive voice underscores the Jews' powerlessness. Later, Rodway describes how "before three days had passed, German army cars had appeared in our streets" (7). Marion Wiesel's version instead stresses the speed with which the Nazis arrived and uses the active voice to amplify their power: "in less than three days, German Army vehicles *made* their appearance on our streets" (9, emphasis added). The final example on the handout pushes students to think about cultural context, for the Rodway edition describes "the Saturday before Pentecost" (10), a phrase Marion Wiesel corrects to "some two weeks before Shavuot" (12). Few students know what either Pentecost or Shavuot is, and they need to be guided to understand how framing an event in terms of a Christian calendar would have been irrelevant (and even insulting) to a devout Jew. Once students understand the Judeo-Christian context of the words and the appropriate religious calendar associated with each, they are able to contemplate the cultural framing of the text and the ways the older edition was marketed to a much more Christian (and anti-Semitic) readership.[5] Although we do not discuss the paratextual materials that day, I signal how they will want to attend to the Christian imagery and framing of Brown's preface and Mauriac's foreword to the older edition.

We then analyze the text thematically to read the memoir as a type of bildungsroman: notions of childhood and adulthood and images of mentors, guides, and father figures provide meaning in *Night*. After dividing the class into teams—with two sets exploring each theme competitively—and mapping their findings as well as discussing key passages, we bring these elements together in our discussion of whether *Night* works as a bildungsroman. I then guide them toward a reading, using their textual evidence, which invariably supports David L. Vanderwerken's claims that *Night* inverts the bildungsroman with its final scene to assert that it is an antibildungsroman. Interrogating the bildungsroman returns us to Roberta Seelinger Trites's work, which has formed the intellectual center of the course, but fleshes out the specifics of how surviving the Holocaust warps the trajectory of growth and development to or toward adult citizenship so familiar in adolescent literature.

Indeed, Wiesel's understanding of his own reflection as a "corpse . . . contemplating me" and his reminder that "the look in his eyes as he gazed at me has never left me" illuminate Wiesel's uncanny estrangement from his skeletal teenage self at the end of the war in that moment, as well as how that part of him is ineluctably bound up with who he is today (115). What is more, the newer materials appended to the memoir enlarge the primary text to include more children and young people. *Night*'s dedication now invokes the memories of Marion Wiesel's family and explicitly his little sister, Tzipora, as well as his parents, while the preface and Nobel Prize speech extend the memoir's musings on childhood. We learn, for example, of Tzipora's "vanishing," "a beautiful, well-behaved little Jewish girl with golden hair and a sad smile, murdered with her mother the very night of their arrival" (ix). When he writes of the personal and political importance to "preserve a record of the ordeal I endured as an adolescent, at an age when one's knowledge of death and evil should be limited to what one discovers in literature" (vii), both of Wiesel's narrative frames contrast his lived experience with the types of knowledge my students are appropriately discovering in books. Similar to key passages in the memoir proper, at very important moments, Wiesel dissociates himself from the narrative, writing of himself—or a universal witness or survivor—in the third person (e.g., "Deep down, the witness knew then, as he does now, that his testimony would not be received" [ix]). These portions of the text make clear at a formal level both the terrible challenges of testifying as well as the continued sense of disbelief at the chance involved in survival. He closes the preface with one of those moments, writing how "[t]he witness has forced himself to testify. For the youth of today, for the children who will be born tomorrow. He does not want his past to become their future" (xv).

Marion Wiesel's subtler translation of Mauriac's foreword amplifies the importance of children's deaths during the Holocaust. The Rodway version passively describes how "trainloads of little children . . . were to be fuel for the gas chamber and the crematory" (viii), whereas the Marion Wiesel translation describes these young victims in ways that magnify their humanity and the tragedy of their loss: these "trainloads of small children . . . were destined to feed the gas chambers and crematoria" (xviii). She transforms the fact of their death from inanimate "fuel" to an end involving a dreadful destiny and one last action, feeding. Given adults' responsibility to feed the young, this final description is full of even more pathos.

Wiesel writes for a future he sees embodied in children, a sentiment echoed in a devastating and empowering moment of his Nobel speech, where he imagines his childhood self asking, "[W]hat have you done with my future, what have you done with your life?" He replies to that boy by explaining how he has "tried to keep memory alive," invoking the very first version of *Night* by echoing its title in his discussion of how the world could remain silent (118), and broadening the scope of his speech to include more contemporary political struggles. Before he thanks the Nobel Committee, he summons "the young Jewish boy wondering what I have done with his years" and lets everyone know "it is in his name that I speak to you and that I express to you my deepest gratitude as one who has emerged from the Kingdom of the Night" (120). By calling forth his child self and letting his audience know that it is in "his name" that he speaks and writes, students are reminded of how one does not grow up and leave one's child or teenage self behind. Wiesel summons the image of youth to remind us of both the atrocities he experienced early in his life and his lifelong commitment to honor his adolescent suffering and survival.

The 2006 memoir proper and the materials that frame it foreground the adolescent, calling attention in devastating ways to how children are akin to adults in certain situations. Suleiman's concept of the 1.5 generation opens up this text, while the new edition's paratextual materials potently call up the child he was. Indeed, *Night* elucidates just how often people do not bother to uphold the distinction that Marah Gubar rightfully urges us to rethink and remember: that in certain situations there is a dreadful kinship between adult and child because other portions of their identity override the age-based one. The examples we use in this part of the discussion could include the Syrian refugee crisis and the way Muslim and African American boys are imagined as terrorists and thugs before they are seen as children.

Ideally, *Night* has profoundly interfered with students' narratives about the Holocaust and appropriately added another complicating layer to their understanding of childhood and adolescence. *Night* trenchantly illuminates how the distinction between child and adult overlooks adolescence, an important liminal state that appropriately complicates one of many binary oppositions that organize so much of how we think, while fleshing out the importance of making careful age-based distinctions in certain situations. Ultimately the 2006 text's liminal spaces—its dedication, preface, foreword, and inclusion of Wiesel's Nobel Prize acceptance speech—push us to interrogate the importance of Wiesel being part of the 1.5 generation and the particular tragedy of Jewish children and young people's suffering during the Holocaust. This is a stark contrast to the two Christian frames of the Rodway edition. The more appropriately translated 2006 edition illuminates the terrible lack of power European Jews—whether adult or child—had in Nazi-controlled ghettos and concentration camps, the chance involved in survival, and the ways this one teenager grew up and labored to give meaning to the rest of his life. Although the memoir proper is an antibildungsroman, the new edition's paratextual materials amplify the importance of youth while making clear that the boy, Elie Wiesel, grew to become a powerful and eloquent adult, indebted to his adolescent experience, and an important world citizen.

Notes

1. For more on Frank's diary and this phenomenon, see Britzman, pp. 121–25.

2. See Seidman for analysis of the Yiddish version and its important differences from the English one. For ideas about how to incorporate both into class discussion, see Weissman.

3. I find that analyzing photographs helps students see how individual children responded differently to their situations. Likewise, moving from concepts and prose they find challenging to images, which are emotionally difficult yet ostensibly easier to read, is an effective way of assisting, in this case, sophomore-level students at a public comprehensive university, many of whom are not English majors, in thinking more abstractly and theoretically about these issues.

4. This is a particularly potent articulation of adulthood that connects with other texts we have read, such as Anderson's *Speak*, and it prepares students for Spiegelman's *Maus* as well.

5. On the reception of *The Diary of Anne Frank*, see Britzman; Prose. On the Christian nature of the Rodway edition, see Seidman.

Works Cited

Anderson, Laurie Halse. *Speak*. Penguin/Putnam, 1999.

Britzman, Deborah. *Lost Subjects, Contested Objects: Toward a Psychoanalytic Inquiry of Learning*. State U of New York P, 1998.

Gubar, Marah. "Risky Business: Talking About Children in Children's Literature Criticism." *Children's Literature Association Quarterly*, vol. 38, no. 4, Winter 2013, pp. 450–57.

Prose, Francine. *Anne Frank: The Book, the Life, the Afterlife*. Harper Perennial, 2010.

Seidman, Naomi. "Elie Wiesel and the Scandal of Jewish Rage." *Jewish Social Studies*, vol. 3, no. 1, Autumn 1996, pp. 1–19.

Spiegelman, Art. *Maus: A Survivor's Tale. And Here My Troubles Began*, no. 2, Pantheon Books, 1991.

———. *Maus: A Survivor's Tale. My Father Bleeds History*, no. 1, Pantheon Books, 1986.

Suleiman, Susan Rubin. "The 1.5 Generation: Thinking About Child Survivors and the Holocaust." *American Imago*, vol. 59, no. 3, Fall 2002, pp. 277–95.
Trites, Roberta Seelinger. *Disturbing the Universe: Power and Repression in Adolescent Literature.* U of Iowa P, 2000.
United States Holocaust Museum. "Plight of Jewish Children." *Holocaust Encyclopedia*, www.ushmm.org/wlc/en/article.php?ModuleId=10006124.
Vanderwerken, David L. "Wiesel's *Night* as Anti-Bildungsroman." *Modern Jewish Studies*, vol. 7, no. 4, 1990, pp. 57–63.
Weissman, Gary. "Questioning Key Texts: A Pedagogical Approach to Teaching Elie Wiesel's *Night*." *Teaching the Representation of the Holocaust*, edited by Marianne Hirsch and Irene Kacandes, Modern Language Association of America, 2004, pp. 324–36.
Wiesel, Elie. *Night.* Translated by Marion Wiesel, Hill and Wang / Farrar, Straus and Giroux, 2006.
———. *Night.* Translated by Stella Rodway, Bantam Books, 1986.

Melek Ortabasi

Youth, Transnationalism, Identity: Young Adult Literature and World Literature

The detailed description for my upper-division world literature seminar, which focuses on transnational youth, reads as follows:

> Most of us would agree that a variety of factors conspire to define our experiences of youth. The modern texts we will read in this course all feature young characters dealing with the "storm and stress" often associated with coming of age. Nevertheless, each protagonist's quest for an adult identity is framed by very different cultural contexts. Through our readings, which speak of—and to—young people, we will explore how literature itself has helped shape the stories we tell about the process of growing up. By engaging with the diverse realities in which these young literary characters negotiate their places in the world, you may come to a fuller understanding of what "growing up" means to you.

While the course is not billed as a YA literature course, the primary texts are all fictionalized biographies or literary memoirs about the experience of growing up, a common theme very much shared with popular YA literature. The main goal of the course, as the description above makes clear, is to question, challenge, and develop a cultural conception—"coming of age"—that is often, problematically, assumed to be universally shared. As I developed the course, I sought to build a culturally aware, comparative, and theoretically grounded way of teaching the coming-of-age narrative to undergraduate students. Like all other courses in the World Literature Program at Simon Fraser University, the syllabus draws readings from all over the world and prioritizes texts in translation. The diversity of voices represented in the syllabus allows the class to challenge the idea of homogeneity of experience as well as trace the powerful transnational currents of cultural and literary influence that have shaped narrative quests for adulthood in many parts of the world.

This "world" approach to literary writing about the coming-of-age experience is a relatively rare one, as a survey of university-level syllabi and the pedagogical literature on this popular YA theme will attest. This is not surprising, since the YA genre, a particularly Anglo-American category, is a relatively recent phenomenon and an outgrowth of the post–World War II teen culture boom. Furthermore, not all cultures define books for youth or coming of age in the same way: in Germany, for example, YA would be recognizable to Americans under the label of "Jugendbücher" ("youth books") as opposed to "Kinderbücher" ("children's books"); however, fantasy is often differentiated from a more psychologically realistic or historical coming-of-age account, which might instead be labeled "Adoleszenzroman" ("adolescent novel"). In Japan, there is no label an anglophone reader might recognize on sight. However, if you were a teenager wandering into one of the ubiquitous bookstores in Tokyo, you would likely head to the "raito noberu" ("light novel") section. When I asked an editor at a prominent Japanese children's books publisher about the term *YA*, she laughed and said it would never fly in Japan because the English phrase calls up associations with pornography for Japanese speakers! In other words, many cultural examples exist in which the YA label is not affixed to writing that shares more or less the same purpose in terms of target audience.

I therefore focus instead on what is still a large subgenre of YA in North America and an internationally well-established genre for young people who are no longer children but not yet adults: the coming-of-age novel, or bildungsroman. In selecting texts for this course, then, I operated on an extended definition of *YA*. The choice of the bildungsroman aligns with the longer history of moral and entertaining writing for youth within the context of modernity, and the Romantic bildungsroman embodies deeply personal questions that motivate readers of YA books even today:

What does it really mean to be an adult? What sort of person do I want to become, and how will I get there?

Because these questions are central to the emergence of the YA coming-of-age narrative, my course begins with an unconventional historical reading of Johann Wolfgang von Goethe's groundbreaking antibildungsroman, *Die Leiden des jungen Werther* (*The Sorrows of Young Werther*), which grounds our study in what youth literature says *about* youth and coming of age. Here I set the parameters for the main questions the class will pursue over the course of the semester:

> What do literary texts say about how youth is culturally, politically, and historically defined? How do we read for that?
> How do definitions of literary genre and style travel and shift in various traditions or contexts to make space for YA, and the coming-of-age story in particular, as a modern literary category?
> Given how youth culture (including literature) is shared transnationally through various media and interlingual translation, how can these stories let us think about its effect on the lives of actual young people in different places and times?

Werther works well in answering these questions not just as a historical and "reputable" literary foundation but also as the YA media sensation that it was: the social panic surrounding the text, and the passion with which young people devoured it, is well-known.[1] Further, Werther's "sorrows" describe the social and cultural pressures on young people to grow up by focusing on the resulting psychological fallout. Finally, it presents the coming-of-age story in truncated form, in a way that challenges social norms: Werther fails to grow up, but by doing so passionately and dramatically, he becomes the YA antihero most young readers would recognize today.

To demonstrate in a clearly direct way the power of an influential YA text like *Werther* and how its message is both reproduced and challenged over time, the class moves on in the fourth week or so to Ulrich Plenzdorf's 1972 adaptation and parody *Die neuen Leiden des jungen W* (*The New Sufferings of Young W*), which features a similarly disaffected young protagonist named Edgar, this time living in the German Democratic Republic (GDR). The parallels with Goethe's novella are obvious in terms of the plot (an unrequited love in a love triangle); Edgar's dissatisfaction with conforming to social norms; and his eventual failure to succeed on his own terms. In a clever deployment of intertextuality, Edgar even accidentally encounters and reads a coverless, discarded version of *Werther*, to the end ironically unaware that the book is a well-known and respected German classic.

The contrasts between Goethe and Plenzdorf are apparent, however, which underlines the need for close reading and a comparative approach: in Plenzdorf's story—widely regarded as a protest novel—the protagonist is already dead. Speaking from the afterlife directly to readers, Edgar offers a poignant and only partially self-aware critique of himself and society. In principle, he respects the communist regime of the GDR but can only inarticulately and pointlessly rebel against the social homogeneity and predictability it demands. Ultimately, the social protest Plenzdorf's text offers is more ambiguous than Goethe's, since the text remains unclear about whether readers should consider Edgar's death accidental or suicidal.

Like Goethe's text, *New Sorrows* made a big splash, spawning public discussion groups on a national scale and engaging particularly young people in the GDR, who were passionately invested in the protagonist's struggles.[2] Because of their clear kinship, *Werther* and his late twentieth-century echo provide an ideal starting point to explore how a genre can grow and transform over time and space—even when the chain of influence is indirect.

By week six of the semester, as I begin to introduce texts beyond the European canon, I ask students to keep in mind two points: first, the bildungsroman, and the story it tells about youthful identity, is itself a dominant cultural form that has done much to colonize the modern literary consciousness of the global East and South.[3] As such, it assumes a particular set of narrative norms, which include the young protagonist's *resistance* to norms. Second, these fictionalized coming-of-age narratives often portray emerging adult identities that are framed by engagements with and resistance to pervasive and often oppressive foreign cultures. Because these newer texts inherit the focus on the individual distinctive to the Romantic tradition, readers witness the young protagonists growing up and doing so with a keen awareness of the foreign influences acting upon their struggle to come of age. The intimacy of the personal narrative vantage point that distinguishes the genre also raises the general question the class and I pose for ourselves with each subsequent text: how does this coming-of-age story reinterpret, in a literary fashion, ideas of youth in its own historical and cultural context?

In the weeks remaining in the semester, we generally explore six more culturally diverse coming-of-age narratives paired according to three major transnational, youth-related themes. Below, I cover each theme and how to begin a dialogue between the paired texts in the context of that theme. (There are, of course, other possible themes, such as youth and sex, immigrant youth, and youth and world pop culture.)

Political Youth

Ernesto "Che" Guevara's account of his youthful travels throughout South America in 1952, *Diarios de motocicleta* (*The Motorcycle Diaries*), and Sofya Kovalevskaya's fictional exploration of a well-to-do Russian girl's political awakening, *Nigilitska* (*Nihilist Girl*), explore the theme of youthful upheaval and resistance in a political context. Both texts explore a young person's growing awareness of the problems in his or her own society: Guevara travels the continent, setting the stage for his political future as he casually observes firsthand the reality of socioeconomic, cultural, and ethnic disparities in Latin America. In a more traditional narrative arc, Kovalevskaya's protagonist, Vera, graduates from a sheltered, willful ignorance to becoming a committed follower of philosophy and nihilist ideology; she finally assumes the life of a dissident in the growing political turmoil of late-nineteenth-century Russia.

A key word guiding our comparison of these narratives is *awakening*—a common analogy for both coming of age as well as gaining political awareness—which manifests quite differently in the texts. In *The Motorcycle Diaries*, Ernesto is a young, adventurous medical student, not the complicated, conflicted figure who later became "Che." However, by closely comparing Guevara's text with the 2004 movie based on the book, students learn how foreknowledge of the iconic author's future compels many readers, including the makers of the film, to project that future onto this engaging but largely nonpolitical travel account.

Nihilist Girl also poses a contrast between a young, naive figure and the radical political revolutionary she later becomes, although in this narrative we witness the transformation. For Vera, political awakening and identity formation are one and the same, but the haphazard way in which it unfolds places her future in jeopardy. A love affair with a much older tutor is not a good model for female self-development and political awakening, the novel suggests, since the novel ends with the increasingly defiant young protagonist having made the bold but rash decision to marry a political dissident to save his life. Readers never find out what happens after Vera boards the train to Siberia, where her soon-to-be husband has been exiled, but the prognosis is grim.

Interestingly, the political theme itself becomes a topic of discussion, since most students are somewhat taken aback at the activist passion of both protagonists, which is a telling sign of our own time and place; many students seem unaware that youthful revolutionaries have long been stock literary figures. The students' surprise is mirrored by the texts' fascination with and uneasiness surrounding the political involvement of youth. Implicit in *The Motorcycle Diaries* and overt in *Nihilist Girl* is a glorification of the youthful passion of the protagonist and, at the same time, trepidation about the social and personal consequences thereof. Both texts suggest to young readers that while acquiring political awareness is a mark of growing up, there are many potential dangers associated with plunging into the politically complex adult world equipped with only the headlong enthusiasm of youth.

Postcolonialism and Youth

Vera and Ernesto ultimately choose to resist social norms at their own peril, but the two young women in the autobiographical texts we encounter next learn the hard way that their very presence violates social norms. Marjane Satrapi's *Persepolis* and Ken Bugul's *Le baobab fou* (*The Abandoned Baobab*) feature fictionalized versions of the authors' younger selves who are transplanted to cultural contexts hostile to their ethnic and linguistic otherness. Marjane, whose parents send her to Vienna alone in an effort to protect their headstrong young daughter from the increasingly repressive Iranian regime, and Ken, an ambitious young Senegalese woman who accepts a scholarship for further study in Belgium, are rule breakers from the beginning. But even a strong sense of self-identity cannot protect these young women from the transnational fallout of empire and colonialism and the racial hierarchies that result from them.

Striking for their unsparing criticism of European society and unstinting description of the personal mental suffering it caused, both memoirs are unconventional but convincing examples of postcolonial texts. Written in a colonial language (both are translated from the French), they relate the experience of young women who, despite having received a Western education in their home countries, find themselves rejected by the society from which that education originates. Instead, the Europeans project stereotypes on these young women: with Ken, her blackness makes her a sexualized object sought out by white men for consumption;

in Marjane's case, Europeans dismiss and criticize her, assuming her to be ignorant. Although Marjane and Ken react very differently to this discrimination, they both find their sense of self so decimated that they experience depression and suicidal thoughts. Most students agree that these texts vividly depict the particular fragmentation of self that postcolonial critics like Homi Bhabha and others have described.

As coming-of-age stories, however, they add another dimension to the question of postcolonial identity and do so in contrasting ways. In Satrapi's memoir, as we trace her life from childhood to young adulthood, it becomes clear that Marjane's strong family support network, her intellectual tenacity, and her passion for social justice are the features that allow her to reach adulthood. Marjane is portrayed as critical of the status quo even as a small child, and she imparts a strong sense that she would have persevered regardless of the cultural obstacles put in her way. This self-possessed young woman finds a strong contrast in Ken, who is painfully aware of being the unwanted child of a fourth wife in a traditional polygamous Wolof family. The beneficiary of a questionable colonial education that serves to alienate her from her community, she regards going to Belgium as the logical way forward. Once there, however, Ken is rejected again and sexually exploited because she is black. At one point she slides into prostitution and is bluntly informed of her appeal by an unattractive white Belgian client: "Ah! You Black women, you're divine" (73). By embracing the role of the exotic African woman, however, she loses herself so completely that readers do not know by the end of the narrative whether she will ever be able to assume a self-identity she can accept. Although we know that Ken writes her own story, the coming-of-age narrative itself is truncated, refusing to give readers any expected closure. By either satisfying or rejecting our expectations, these texts offer nuanced and compelling descriptions of growing up as a transnational, postcolonial subject.

Youth and World Pop Culture

Our final pairing of texts launches into less serious territory but still addresses the question of how the coming-of-age process can be affected by transnational forces. Looking back on the pop culture scene of about forty years ago, Mikael Niemi's *Populärmusik från Vittula* (*Popular Music from Vittula*) features a series of fictionalized vignettes inspired by the author's childhood and youth in northern rural Sweden of the 1960s and '70s, while Ryu Murakami's *Shikusutii nain* (*Sixty-Nine*) chronicles the year 1969 in a sleepy Japanese coastal town as experienced by a teenager, Kensuke, who closely resembles the author. Both works are well-known domestically: *Sixty-Nine* has a good amount of exposure because of Murakami's general popularity in Japan, especially with young people, and *Popular Music* hit a particular chord with the public, becoming a best seller that is now familiar to most Swedes both young and old. With their nostalgic and humorous tone, both narratives say much about how young people consume and appropriate popular culture, using it to define both themselves and others.

While adolescent protagonists seeking to ride the latest wave of popular culture–fueled peer pressure are nothing new in YA, these short novels stand out because both boys feel left behind because of where they live. Growing up self-consciously in rural areas of "minor" countries, Murakami's and Niemi's alter ego protagonists give new meaning to the adolescent trope of feeling "uncool." Their keen sense of national and global marginalization is engendered by the presence of mass media in their lives, which induces in them a desire to imitate what they see. When Matti, Niemi's protagonist, sees Elvis on TV for the first time as a little boy, he is starstruck. Seeking to emulate America's first mega pop star, he takes up air guitar and parrots the English lyrics even though he has no idea what they mean. Seventeen-year-old Kensuke, always sensitive to the edgy and cool, works hard to copy the behavior of the contemporary student protesters in Tokyo and elsewhere, but the "barricade" he eventually organizes at his high school is ultimately for show: it is not really in protest of anything.

Postcolonial theory—in particular the concept of mimicry—lends itself well to explaining why these teenage boys aspire to foreign popular culture, but it does not fully explain how they relate to it. Imitation, as any developmental psychologist will tell us, is also an important method by which children and adolescents build their identities. By experimenting with new concepts and ideas, the young protagonists are not only reacting to the foreign but are proactively translating it into their own reality.[4] Colorfully described in both novels is how Kensuke and Matti adapt the global to the local, actively and selectively curating their experience of cultural hybridity. Matti continually appropriates rock and roll for his own uses regardless of its original meaning (which he cannot understand anyway), for example by comparing it at one point to the force and sound of the ice breaking apart on the river in the spring (74). Kensuke, for his part, aggressively inhabits his self-made Japanese high school world, in love with Western rock and roll and experimental film on the one hand, while completely uninterested in the American naval base that dominates his harbor town on the other. For both young men, world pop culture is not just a dominant force acting upon their lives but a local tool of resistance and a way of growing into the larger world.

As educators have noted, "young adult literature [is] an illuminative guide not only for individual self discovery but for understanding along *communal*, societal lines" (Garcia 129). In an increasingly globalized world, both the individual and society have become sites of linguistic and cultural intersectionality. This is patently true of the diverse students in my Vancouver classroom: the vast majority come from a family where English is not the only language spoken, and many of them are either immigrants or the children of immigrants. A critical reading of world coming-of-age narratives, with their emphasis on protagonists growing up in complex worlds, is an excellent means for students to develop a nuanced understanding of their own.

Most rewarding, perhaps, is when the students experience precisely what the course description predicts: a personal connection to the texts that helps frame their own coming of age. One student, a young man from rural British Columbia, was struck by how much he identified with the experience of small-town life described in Niemi's *Popular Music*. A young woman whose family had come to Canada from Colombia could not wait to share the "coolness" of Murakami's *Sixty-Nine* with her cousins who still live there. Clearly, these narratives spoke to the young adults in my classroom, sparking a sense of the familiar as well as the excitement of gaining a new perspective on it.

Notes

1. A suicide notice in *The New York Times* as late as 1910 continues to assign blame: "Goethe's *Die Leiden des jungen Werther*, 136 years after it was written, is still claiming its victims" ("Sorrows").

2. "Throngs of enthusiasts flocked to the theaters to see the play and to the bookstores to buy the novel. The years 1972 and 1973 were marked by an almost constant discussion, not just in GDR literary circles, but in the GDR populace at large, of Plenzdorf's work" (Wilcox viii).

3. The novel itself and its subgenres have been discussed as a Western form with a wide range of influence. See, for example, essays treating the adoption of the genre in various regions in Moretti.

4. For example, recent studies of fan fiction, a simultaneously imitative and creative form of pop culture popular among teens, show that writing in the genre "can play an important role in the development of young people's literacies and identities" (Dunkels et al. 92).

Works Cited

Bhabha, Homi K. *The Location of Culture.* Routledge, 1994.

Bugul, Ken. *The Abandoned Baobab: The Autobiography of a Senegalese Woman.* Translated by Marjolijn de Jager, U of Virginia P, 2008.

Dunkels, Elza, et al., editors. *Youth Culture and Net Culture: Online Social Practices.* Information Science Reference, 2011.

Garcia, Antero. *Critical Foundations in Young Adult Literature: Challenging Genres.* Sense, 2013.

Goethe, Johann Wolfgang von. *The Sorrows of Young Werther.* Translated by Burton Pike, Modern Library, 2004.

Guevara, Ernesto "Che." *The Motorcycle Diaries: A Journey around South America.* Verso, 1996.

Kovalevskaya, Sofya. *Nihilist Girl.* Translated by Natasha Kolchevska with Mary Zirin, Modern Language Association, 2001.

Moretti, Franco, editor. *The Novel. History, Geography, and Culture*, vol. 1, Princeton UP, 2006.

Murakami, Ryu. *Sixty-Nine.* Translated by Ralph F. McCarthy, Kodansha International, 2005.

Niemi, Mikael. *Popular Music from Vittula.* Translated by Laurie Thompson, Seven Stories Press, 2004.

Plenzdorf, Ulrich. *The New Sufferings of Young W.* Waveland Press, 1996.

Satrapi, Marjane. *The Complete Persepolis.* Pantheon Books, 2007.

"The Sorrows of Werther." *The New York Times*, 21 Sept. 1910, timesmachine.nytimes.com/timesmachine/1910/09/21/105091480.pdf.

Wilcox, Kenneth P. Introduction. *The New Sufferings of Young W.*, by Ulrich Plenzdorf, Waveland Press, 1996, pp. v–xii.

Carey Applegate

Say Their Names: Complicating the Single-Story Narrative of City Kids

In a single month in 2017, three unarmed fifteen-year-old black boys were killed by police. In all three cases, the initial reports from officers significantly changed with the introduction of new evidence, in the form of either video recordings or coroner's reports. We don't know exactly what happened in any of these deaths, but the facts, as reported by the police, don't add up (King). These reports, of course, evoke memories of other young black men, particularly Trayvon Martin and Mike Brown, whose deaths stirred a broader public consciousness about violence targeted at people of color by people in positions of authority. The killing of eighteen-year-old Brown, the grand jury decision not to indict Officer Darren Wilson, and the related protests in Ferguson, Missouri, and around the United States, for example, served to only confirm the role of racism in the justice system for people who were still reeling from the death of Martin. In reporting on Brown's death, many news outlets relied on an overly simplified narrative of good versus evil, describing the police officer in heroic terms and using stereotypes and grainy, threatening images to characterize Brown as violent and, certainly, "no angel" (Eligon). We have heard echoes of this story over and over again. It is the story of numerous people of color—particularly black men and boys—being killed by people in power—particularly police officers—and then being demonized in the media after their deaths. Jordan Davis. Tamir Rice. Aura Rosser. Meagan Hockaday. Cameron Tillman. Philando Castile. Sandra Bland. Eric Garner. Freddie Gray. Michelle Cusseaux. Tanisha Anderson. And, as of this month, Jayson Negron, Darius Smith, and Jordan Edwards.

This narrative about black and brown youths—that they are dangerous thugs, that they are uneducated, that they need to be saved—has been woven into much of the public discourse around urban education and education reform. In many education films and discussions around education reform, black and brown students are seen through a deficit lens and their teachers, many of whom are white females, are expected to become saviors who will lead their students away from lives of hardship and despair. This narrative is so popular that it has become what Chimamanda Adichie calls a "single story"; in other words, when people who are not part of this community consider the lives of individuals in this community, they have this one expectation of them: that they are poor, uneducated, probably violent, almost definitely involved in gangs, and in need of saving. For obvious reasons, this is inherently problematic; it not only impacts teaching and learning in urban schools, but it has also shaped a dangerous popular discourse about what it means to be young and brown-skinned in the United States today. For future teachers, especially those wishing to teach in city schools, it is important for them to recognize and deconstruct the teacher-savior narrative and, more important, its related messages about students in these schools. As a teacher-educator and English education scholar-activist, I decided that one of my goals in teaching the class City Kids, City Schools using popular texts would be to work with my students, many of whom will become teachers themselves, to interrogate this narrative.

Conceptualization

My goal in this essay, and with the City Kids, City Schools class outlined below, is to model strategies for helping my predominantly white college students to recognize and celebrate black and brown youths—often coded as "urban students" or "city kids"[1]—as individuals with agency, complex lives, and nuanced relationships beyond the stereotypes and tropes that we see so often in popular texts and public discourse. One of my hopes is for my students from our predominantly white university to walk away from this class armed with counternarratives that challenge systems of racism and oppression that are often unquestioned by people in positions of power.

Course Assignments, Readings, and Narratives

This course was divided into three teaching units: City Kids, City Teachers, and City Schools. While each unit incorporated a variety of texts, the City Kids segment focused primarily on YA "problem" literature featuring urban students: Jason Reynolds's *When I Was the Greatest*, Angela Johnson's *The First Part Last*, Simone Elkeles's *Perfect Chemistry*, Todd Strasser's *Can't Get There from Here*, G. Neri's *Yummy*, and Coe Booth's *Kendra* and *Tyrell*. Supplemental texts included films, poetry, TED Talks, nonfiction articles and essays, memes, character sketches, and other digital sources. In addition, I often shared stories of different students whom I had taught during my time as a high school English teacher, and we Skyped with a retired elementary school teacher who had twenty years of teaching experience in three different city schools. Grades were based on in-class activities (including participation, reading responses, and quizzes), three short critical response papers, and a final project or paper.

Since the class itself was framed through an education lens, I had the students begin the semester by writing about their impressions of urban education. I collected these papers, skimmed them to get an overall sense of what the students believed coming into the class, gave individuals credit for completing them, and put them in a file folder and did not look at them again until the end of the semester. For their last critical response paper, I gave students the option to use their initial writing pieces and their work in the class to trace the development of their thinking about city kids and city schools throughout the semester.

At the beginning of the City Kids segment, most of the students' responses about urban education were driven by stereotypes. In order to move beyond these stereotypes, we had to first look at what was driving them. Since most students were familiar with teacher-savior movies like *Freedom Writers*, we started with that as our cultural touch point. We watched a *Mad TV* sketch called "Nice White Lady" and talked about how the students were portrayed and why those depictions were funny (or not), and then we watched Kiri Davis's short documentary *A Girl Like Me*, in which she replicates the 1940s black and white doll test and explores the internalized racism that many young black women face today. The students and I used these texts, along with discussions around coded language and double-consciousness, to frame our activities for the unit. As we moved through inquiry activities, whole-class discussions, book groups, in-class writing, peer revisions, and formal textual analysis, students began to interrogate their assumptions. Each class session, students were challenged to complicate their perceptions of students in teacher-savior narratives. By the end of the class, most students were invested in the stories beyond the stereotypes—something that came through in their last critical response paper.

One of my very basic goals for this class was for my students to feel connected to the characters, to have empathy for them, and to visualize their narratives beyond the books. In order to make this more personal for them, I gave them at least one book club session for every four classes. Students picked questions they wanted to discuss from a list of fifteen, and I often found them returning to questions that I hoped they would select: How realistic was the characterization? Would you want to meet any of the characters? Did you like them? Hate them? If one (or more) of the characters made a choice that had moral implications, would you have made the same decision? Why? Why not? If you were casting this book for a movie, who would you cast in the main roles? Why? These book clubs gave students an opportunity to discuss the books casually, to get a sense of the characters and the plot, and to understand the book on a more personal level.[2]

Once students had read and discussed at least two YA novels—for example, *Yummy* and *When I Was the Greatest*, which were the first two books that I taught during the semester—we watched Adichie's "The Danger of a Single Story" TED Talk and then used that talk as a catalyst for discussion, with these guiding questions: What is the "single story" that we hear about city kids? What is our default understanding of their lives? What do they do or not do, say or not say? Where do the narratives that we've read or watched over the past few weeks reinforce that story? Where do they challenge and add to that story? Throughout the rest of the unit, in all of our discussions about texts related to adolescents, these were some of the core questions that pushed us to better understand the portrayals of city kids and how they related to what we were seeing on the news and in other venues.

As we looked at different dimensions of how city kids were depicted, one of the most interesting classroom activities asked each group of students to examine a different adolescence-based gang memoir/narrative and analyze its paratext and epitext. Students were asked to conduct mini-inquiry projects to answer the following questions: How do we read the cover and the "guts" of this book? Where would we shelve it in a bookstore? In a library? In a classroom? To whom is this book marketed? Why? How can we tell? Beyond the book itself, what other kinds of marketing materials exist? What messages are being sent about city kids just through this book's paratext and epitext? Depending on whether the book was classified as fiction or nonfiction, students made different observations about the ideologies presented by the text's paratext and epitext. They often found that the fictional texts were heavily romanticized—literally: they often involved a budding romance between the main character and a "softer" character in order to make the main character more accessible. The nonfiction narratives tended to focus on building the mythology of the monster, feeding into a single story of hypermasculinity and violence. Gang narratives studied during this activity included *Tyrell*, *Perfect Chemistry*, *Yummy*, Sanyika Shakur's *Monster: The Autobiography of an L.A. Gang Member*, Reymundo Sanchez's *My Bloody Life: The Making of a Latin King*, and Dashaun "Jiwe" Morris's *War of the Bloods in My Veins: A Street Soldier's March Toward Redemption.*

The last couple of activities for this unit helped students to further make connections between what they were reading about in their YA novels, what they were discussing and theorizing in class, and the related current events unfolding in the news. We ended the unit with *Between the World and Me*, in which Ta-Nehisi Coates uses the conceit of writing a letter to his teenage son to help him understand how to navigate a racist United States in the wake of police brutality and other racial injustices. This personal narrative, which was inspired by James Baldwin's *The Fire Next Time*, is a call to action, an awakening for a new generation and new allies. Before we began discussing this book as a class, students started with an open inquiry project where they researched locations, histories, movements, terms, and other topics referenced in the book that they wanted to learn more about. On this day, I shared memories of my students who had been lost to violence, we explored the #iftheygunnedmedown Twitter hashtag, and I modeled the kinds of questions that I use during my own research process. For this particular mini-inquiry session, some of the sample topics included: #blacklivesmatter, media coverage of black shooting victims (versus white shooters), colorism, Howard University, and "The Mecca." This activity excited and energized students, and it gave them great connections for our big-picture discussions.

One of the most powerful activities—always during the last week of this unit—asked students to do a close reading of parts of the transcript from the *State of Missouri v. Darren Wilson* trial, to examine the specific cognitive metaphors that Wilson uses to describe Brown—not to come to any conclusions about guilt or innocence but to analyze the language used. What they decided was that there was potential bias present in his testimony. For example, Wilson described Brown as "intense . . . aggressive . . . like a demon" (406);[3] together, we teased this metaphor out and examined the implications of it in the context of the killing. As we wrapped up our discussion, my students and I made connections back to the YA literature and supplemental texts that we had been reading.

Teaching this class and this content in our current environment is both challenging and rewarding. In future iterations of this course, I plan to incorporate Angie Thomas's *The Hate U Give*, Ava DuVernay's documentary *13th*, and texts from Black Lives Matter and other activist communities. It is easy sometimes for students to get lost in the texts, to see the characters' lives as reflective of individual challenges and choices, and to make personal connections between themselves and the individual characters. However, as we see time and time again, the tensions that are revealed in the texts that we study are influenced by institutional structures and, in turn, part of shaping our understanding of and interactions with the world around us. Helping students engage in those conversations early on in order for them to understand structural conflicts and the institutional systems at work—and, yes, to become better advocates and stronger, more conscientious allies—is at the heart of what this class is designed to do.

Notes

1. In this essay I use these terms interchangeably. In the class, however, I tended to use *city kids* in order to establish an expectation of nuance that isn't always granted with the term *urban students*, which has become increasingly used as coded language. *City kids* was also more in line with one of our texts and the eponym for our class, *City Kids, City Schools: More Reports from the Front Row* (Ayers et al.).

2. Whenever we had book clubs, we always held Socratic seminars during the next class, with the intention of moving students into deeper critical thinking. While the book clubs asked students to relate to characters on a personal level and invest in the books, Socratic seminars demanded that students deeply analyze the current text and make connections between texts and previous discussions.

3. Wilson also remarked that during the struggle with Brown, he felt like a "five-year-old holding onto Hulk Hogan" (*State* 393).

Works Cited

Adichie, Chimamanda Ngozi. "The Danger of a Single Story." *TED*, 2009, www.ted.com/talks/chimamanda_adichie_the_danger_of_a_single_story .html.

Ayers, William, et al., editors. *City Kids, City Schools: More Reports from the Front Row*. The New Press, 2008.

Booth, Coe. *Kendra*. Push, 2010.

———. *Tyrell*. Push, 2007.

Coates, Ta-Nehisi. *Between the World and Me*. Spiegel and Grau, 2015.

Eligon, John. "Michael Brown Spent Last Weeks Grappling with Problems and Promise." *The New York Times*, 24 Aug. 2014, www.nytimes.com/2014/08/25/us/michael-brown-spent-last-weeks-grappling-with-lifes-mysteries.html.

Elkeles, Simone. *Perfect Chemistry*. Walker, 2009.

"#iftheygunnedmedown." *Twitter*, 1 June 2017, twitter.com/hashtag/iftheygunnedmedown?lang=en.

Johnson, Angela. *The First Part Last*. Simon and Schuster Books for Young Readers, 2010.

King, Shaun. "Three Unarmed 15-Year-Old Boys Killed by U.S. Cops in One Month—But Only One Case Saw Much-Needed Coverage." *New York Daily News*, 31 May 2017, www.nydailynews.com/news/national/king-cops-kill-3-unarmed-teens-month-1-sees-coverage-article-1.3210259.

Morris, Dashaun "Jiwe." *War of the Bloods in My Veins: A Street Soldier's March Toward Redemption*. Scribner, 2008.

Neri, G. *Yummy: The Last Days of a Southside Shorty*. Illustrated by Randy DuBurke, Lee and Low Books, 2010.

"Nice White Lady." *Mad TV*. *YouTube*, uploaded by Klaustrophobic, 12 July 2007, www.youtube.com/watch?v=ZVF-nirSq5s.

Reynolds, Jason. *When I Was the Greatest*. Atheneum Books for Young Readers, 2015.

Sanchez, Reymundo. *My Bloody Life: The Making of a Latin King*. Chicago Review Press, 2000.

Shakur, Sanyika. *Monster: The Autobiography of an L.A. Gang Member*. Grove Press, 2004.

State of Missouri v. Darren Wilson. Grand jury transcript, 20 Aug. 2014. *The New York Times*, 24 Nov. 2014, graphics8.nytimes.com/newsgraphics/2014/11/24/ferguson-assets/grand-jury-testimony.pdf.

Strasser, Todd. *Can't Get There from Here*. Simon and Schuster Books for Young Readers, 2010.

Thomas, Angie. *The Hate U Give*. Balzer and Bray, 2017.

Ebony Elizabeth Thomas

Embracing Discomfort and Difference in the Teaching of Young Adult Literature: Notes toward an Unfinished Project

Encouraging our students to embrace discourses of difference should be one of the goals of YA literary pedagogy. When I have created curricula in my classes to align with this goal, Shaobo Xie's essay "Rethinking the Identity of Cultural Otherness" has been a mentoring text for me. In it, Xie positions difference as a "counterhegemonic strategy, a way of mobilizing, activating discursive agency or energy," in order to strive toward decolonized education (8). I keep in mind Eve Tuck and K. Wayne Wang's prescient warning that decolonization is not a metaphor. Today's best YA literature raises questions that implore our students to consider selves, worlds, themes, and positions that are unsettling, uncomfortable, and incommensurable. How, then, might we embrace this discourse of difference—sometimes welcomed, sometimes discomforting—in our pedagogy?

When teaching literature for youth and young adults, many educators do so with the ultimate intent of creating ethical and literate citizens for a global, multicultural twenty-first-century society. Students in YA literature classes at colleges and universities are important advocates who can introduce diverse texts to their future students, patrons, and family and community members as teachers, librarians, and reading or literacy specialists. Furthermore, in addition to diversifying the literature that young people read, as the demographics of our classrooms, schools, and society shift, the application of critical lenses that are multicultural, diverse, decolonizing, and humanizing to all texts for youth and young adults will become even more essential (Botelho and Rudman). Some students of the social-media generation are bringing their own critical lenses into our courses, while others are invested in nostalgia and more traditional ways of reading texts. As instructors of students coming from many different perspectives, it is our task to encourage discursive pluralism in our courses, even if this means leaning into pedagogies of discomfort (Zembylas and Boler) in the hope that creative tension, as Martin Luther King, Jr., noted in his famous letter from Birmingham jail, can eventually lead to equity, justice, and social change.

Despite the compelling need to encourage our students to embrace discourses of difference in today's YA literary and cultural landscape, getting all on board with this goal can be difficult. New and experienced instructors wonder how to engage and motivate their students as readers. In turn, college and university students often wonder about the scope of YA literature for young people and how it relates to their own lived experiences as adolescents. Out of these teaching and learning concerns, a number of challenges emerge: the danger of a single text, a fraught cultural climate, and identity conflicts (among students as well as between students and their instructors). I explore each of these challenges below.

Problem 1: The Danger of a Single Text

For more than thirty years, annual reports from the University of Wisconsin's Cooperative Children's Book Center have revealed deep and persistent inequities in the number of books for children and young adults featuring characters of color and native characters ("Publishing Statistics"). This inequity may be perpetuated by, among other factors, the ways that YA literature has traditionally been taught. The experiences of peoples from nondominant groups are sometimes represented through the use of a single text, often a novel per group being represented. This sends a tacit message to preservice teachers, librarians, and community members that youth and young adults from nondominant and marginalized communities are less valuable than others and that their experiences are monolithic. Beginning productive conversations about diversity in YA literature must start with placing diverse literature on the syllabus—beyond a single novel or two.

Some students may resist this diversification of the syllabus, finding it politically correct or feeling that it dredges up uncomfortable topics. Others may feel that it does not go far enough, especially if their identities are not mirrored in the text. This is consistent with what I have found in my research on high school students' literary choices; for instance, at one suburban school, students from all backgrounds resisted text selections that dealt with race, and when compelled to read a passage fraught with racial tension, from LouAnne Johnson's *My Posse Don't Do Homework* (adapted as the 1995 film *Dangerous Minds*), they treated it as a discursive minefield (Thomas, "We Always"). I concluded the following:

> The literature in our curriculum is often weighted with dilemmas of race, ethnicity, and other aspects of identity for which there is little productive discourse. Students receive implicit messages that conflicts must be resolved, despite the fact that we live in a world with many pressing conflicts and few politically viable solutions. Furthermore, it is not often emphasized to students that conflict resolution sometimes results in the positions of some people being ignored, subjugated, or suppressed; that not all conflicts are resolvable; and that multiple, even contradictory, points of view about even the most contentious topics are possible. (172)

The discourse of difference does not become easier when YA literature moves from high schools to colleges and universities. As Xie observes, "All these new conceptions of otherness shock us into a renewed perspective on the relationship of self and other. They point to the complexity and multipositionality of identity, reformulating the issue of identity as a matter of difference" (2). The course encourages this renewed perspective long before the unit when we discuss text selection issues.

Problem 2: A Fractured Culture

Another significant challenge that arises comes from discourse on themes, topics, and situations deemed controversial within our fractured culture, such as (but certainly not limited to) racial and gender differences, sexual orientation, religious diversity, and disabilities. That significant conflicts arise in facilitated discussions is unsurprising. Classroom conversations about fraught topics mirror similarly fraught conversations in our broken society, which can be uncomfortable under the best of circumstances. In my research on dilemmas about race talk during literary lessons in high school English classrooms, I have found such talk to be rife with difficulty, leading to dilemmatic conversations, disconnections, and ultimately disengagement from the literature under study (Thomas, "Dilemmatic Conversations"). Pushing through our discomfort with conflict in these instances is essential.

Given today's contentious campus climate, I do not have one-size-fits-all solutions that will work in every YA literature course. In previous scholarship, I have proposed three solutions for high school English teachers that may be useful for my faculty colleagues: cultivating greater awareness of instructional discourse and actions, self-study of one's instructional practices, and using digital tools. A growing body of literature for K–12 teachers and others who work with children and teens can help them better structure talk and interaction across difference. Although postsecondary faculty may not find such resources germane to the teaching of adults, becoming more aware of what we say and do during conflict-laden moments and how we say and do it may be helpful, as might be journaling, recording with permission, or observation of lessons. Front-loading tense conversations around controversial literature through the use of courseware is another possibility: curating a class blog, requiring discussion posts on a message board, or uploading online resources representing different points of view may help students think through their positions. Once classroom talk is structured in ways that foster empathy and greater understanding, the mirrors, windows, and doors of multicultural children's and YA literature can become a key site for the work of equity and justice in our time (Bishop ix). This is more than just lofty rhetoric: it is attainable praxis.

Problem 3: Identity Conflicts

I consider myself quite fortunate. I have had the privilege of teaching and learning from students who are deeply invested in and committed to tackling one of the major social justice and ethical issues of our time: inequities in public and private education in the United States. My students' diverse backgrounds, rich experiences, intellects, and thirst for knowledge and societal transformations inspire me. The vast majority of my students are primed to embrace the discourse of difference in my YA literature courses, pressing through any discomfort that they might be experiencing.

However, another challenge that I faced initially when I transitioned from high school to university teaching was managing my identities and social subjectivities to maximize student comfort with me as their professor.

For instance, it was not effective for me as a young African American professor without an Ivy League background and with a black, urban, working-class midwestern accent to simply tell my students they needed to diversify their texts or they were not serving students well. My first few classes did not respond well to these demands. Some resented my discourses of difference, questioning whether I was qualified to be in my position at all. This was distressing to me after many years of successful teaching at the K–12 level. Each semester, I took students' qualitative feedback to heart and made many changes so that I could accommodate their needs, raise their comfort levels, and help them feel safe. However, even while providing as much safety and comfort as I can, the work of justice remains central to my philosophy as an educator.

Conflicts in my courses during those early years were not just limited to some students questioning my competence (Wilson). Reading diverse YA literature and graphic novels brought up interpersonal conflicts among students as well. Some students objected to reading Cris Beam's transgender YA novel *I Am J*, claiming that it was "too graphic." Others disliked G. Neri and Randy DuBurke's *Yummy: The Last Days of a Southside Shorty* because of how the story of the young black protagonist was narrated. These objections sometimes went beyond the realm of debate and moved into students feeling harmed by their classmates. Reflecting on those tough semesters, I can see that YA literature of difference brings our real-life differences into sharp relief. Thus, the work of diversifying both our syllabi and instruction goes beyond beliefs and dispositions toward equality. It is messy, difficult work that has real-world implications. Moreover, the specificity of the challenges differs according to the identities and social subjectivities of the people in the classroom—professors and students.

Toward Humanizing Stories: Strategies That Make a Difference

Solution 1: A Critical Multicultural Lens: Diversifying the Metaphors We Read By

Given these three challenges, I have changed the way that I teach YA literature, media, and culture. First, I disrupt the single text and lens. One way that I have done this is by inviting students to view Chimamanda Ngozi Adichie's influential TED Talk, "The Danger of a Single Story," during or before our first regular class session. I do not ask students to complete a formal assignment. They journal and take notes during their viewing, and we discuss the talk afterward. This forestalls some of the disquietude students feel as we explore ways that canonical YA literature may spin captivating tales but also are problematic when issues of difference are considered.

The next step is to invite them to rethink the metaphors that they read by. This is quite different from adopting a theoretical lens, such as feminist or Marxist theory, and applying it to the text. Before students are invited to delve deep into textual criticism, as a black feminist scholar, I ask them to connect the text to self. That is because our purposes for selecting, evaluating, teaching, and assessing YA literature are different in education courses than they are in English literature classes that focus on texts. As future middle and high school English teachers, course participants will be teaching students who most certainly will be connecting the texts they are reading to their developing self-identities and social subjectivities. If students in my course are disconnected from their own reader responses, instead privileging certain interpretations or purporting objectivity before understanding how difference influences the ways that we are positioned vis-à-vis narrative, then their own students may be less motivated and engaged in literature lessons as a result.

Critical multiculturalism is but one way to begin considering the unfinished project that is the discourse of difference. A critical multicultural lens can be applied to any text for children or young adults, whether it's a book, article, comic, short story, poem, photograph, or film. Although poststructural in nature, critical multiculturalism stands in contrast to other kinds of ideological criticism in that it is

> a pedagogy of difference [that] seeks not simply to invert dependent hierarchies of domination, but rather to inflect the central categories and assumptions of Western rationality towards a displacement of their oppressive political effects. Conflict is not described as a monolinear struggle between the oppressed and the oppressors but as a struggle for spaces of hegemonic rupture out of which new democratizing possibilities may be won and new articulations of identity may be constructed. (McLaren 286)

Unlike feminist theory and Marxism, which propose alternative metanarratives to dominant ones (e.g., masculinity; class privilege), critical multicultural approaches to literature are pliable enough for a convergence of identities—and narratives—to coexist in the YA curriculum and the classroom.

I have found Maria José Botelho and Masha Kabakow Rudman's *Critical Multicultural Analysis of Children's Literature* to be capacious enough to use across my courses. The textbook begins with the chapter "Metaphors We Read By," which inspires conversation and was itself inspired by another book, *Metaphors We Live By* (Lakoff and Johnson). As Botelho and Rudman note, "Critical multicultural analysis focuses on the reader as the midwife of meaning. The theoretical constructs of discourse, ideology, subjectivity, and power lead the reader to locating how the power relations of class, race, and gender are exercised in text" (3). Understanding how readers make sense of diversity, difference, and power is a key function of teaching YA literature today.

What are the metaphors we read by? This is a question I pose each fall to myself and my YA literature students, many of whom will be the language arts educators of the future. This invitation prompts us to think about not only what we read and why we are reading it but also what happens during the reading process itself. In the first chapter of *Critical Multicultural Analysis*, my students encounter critical questions inspired by the Australian educator Nathalie Wooldridge that we spend the balance of the semester thinking about. These questions expose some of these previously hidden "metaphors we've been reading by" all our lives. Wooldridge asks readers to consider the norms, the perspectives, and the demographics of who are being presented and how they are presented. She also asks the following:

> Who is silenced (and heard) here?
> Whose interests might best be served by this text?
> What ideological positions can you identify?
> What are the possible readings of this situation/event/character? How did you get to that reading?
> What moral or political position does a reading support? How do particular cultural and social contexts make particular readings available (e.g., who could you not say that to)? How might it be challenged? (qtd. in Botelho and Rudman 4)

Asking these questions helps preservice and in-service teachers, as well as other students in the classroom, discuss how critical literary curricula that humanizes instead of divides us from each other might be beneficial to schools and society. They position stories for young adults as more than exploration of issues but also as a potential location for humanization. Shifting conversations about diversity in stories from a dialectic of otherness and minoritization to a dialogue that defines and describes our collective humanity at a time when the population of school-aged children and adolescents are becoming much more diverse is vital.

Solution 2: Taking Action: Fostering the Discourse of Difference in the World

Shifting the discourse of difference from a focus on oppositional otherness toward a dialogue that defines and describes our collective humanity is important. Instead of viewing stories as a site of unyielding struggle, I see stories as a potential location for humanization. To that end, my graduate students and I began our @HealingFictions Twitter account in January 2016, wherein we recommend the best in diverse children's and YA literature every day at noon. As of this writing, we have more than one thousand followers and have recommended more than six hundred books. Our work has been part of conversations about youth activism and education through digital media. Furthermore, our annual list of best books for young readers, sparked by a suggestion from the Penn Graduate School of Education communications director Kat Stein, continues to gain traction within the publishing world.

We hope to expand these initial efforts into a major Web site for advocacy and research on diverse children's literature, media, and culture called the *Humanizing Stories Initiative*, featuring book recommendations, essays, columns on critical issues in the field, and resources for teachers, librarians, publishing industry professionals, families, and communities. Additionally, we plan to use the initiative to collect survey and interview data on responses to literature and media for children, youth, and young adults and hope to eventually expand into a major initiative for the study of diversity in youth literature, media, and digital cultures.

Toward Embracing Discourses of Difference

In his 2016 Jefferson lecture, Ken Burns asserted that "the humanities help us understand almost everything better—and they liberate us from the myopia our media culture and politics impose upon us." Burns's words signal a longing for the power of the collective human narrative, as unifier and cultural mediator, to knit the whole of the nation and the world together toward a single purpose. If, as Burns warns, the culture wars of the present have "manufactured a false dialectic just to accentuate *otherness*," this leads us to the uncomfortable question of why the current cultural and political landscape is marked with struggle. Is it really the culture wars that have manufactured this "false dialectic," or has the discourse of difference simply illuminated the perspectives and imaginations of the other—in other words, the rest of us? Examining the literary landscape and popular culture today, there are few places where this struggle over narrative and meaning are present in such sharp relief as in YA literature, media, and culture.

Unless we confront nostalgia, white supremacy, settler colonialism, and cis/heteropatriarchy in the texts that we provide for each successive generation, we will find the social change that we seek to be elusive. As Xie asserts:

> The politics of difference must, therefore, be conceived as an unfinished project. . . . For all kinds of people who are socially, politically, and ethnically marginalized to claim legitimacy and sovereignty, they have to assert themselves as unassimilable and unsubsumable. They owe their discursive power to critiquing, interrogating, and unsettling the repressive imperial total system of social life. (9)

What helps me invite my current students to join the unfinished project of embracing difference is not only through analyzing the use of metaphors to characterize the landscape of YA literature and media but also through dreaming alongside them about the possibilities for the YA literature of the future.

Works Cited

Adichie, Chimamanda Ngozi. "The Danger of a Single Story." *TED*, 2009, www.ted.com/talks/chimamanda_adichie_the_danger_of_a_single_story.html.

Bishop, Rudine Sims. "Mirrors, Windows, and Sliding Glass Doors." *Perspectives*, vol. 6, no. 3, 1990, pp. ix–xi.

Botelho, Maria José, and Masha Kabakow Rudman. *Critical Multicultural Analysis of Children's Literature: Mirrors, Windows, and Doors.* Routledge, 2009.

Burns, Ken. "Ken Burns: Jefferson Lecture." *National Endowment for the Humanities*, 2016, www.neh.gov/about/awards/jefferson-lecture/ken-burns-biography.

Lakoff, George, and Mark Johnson. *Metaphors We Live By.* U of Chicago P, 2003.

McLaren, Peter. *Schooling as a Ritual Performance: Toward a Political Economy of Educational Symbols and Gestures.* Rowman and Littlefield, 1999.

"Publishing Statistics on Children's Books about People of Color and First/Native Nations and by People of Color and First/Native Nations Authors and Illustrators." *Cooperative Children's Book Center School of Education*, ccbc.education.wisc.edu/books/pcstats.asp. Accessed 2 Apr. 2018.

Thomas, Ebony Elizabeth. "Dilemmatic Conversations: Some Challenges of Culturally Responsive Discourse in a High School English Classroom." *Linguistics and Education*, vol. 24, no. 3, Sept. 2013, pp. 328–47.

———. "'We Always Talk about Race': Navigating Race Talk Dilemmas in the Teaching of Literature." *Research in the Teaching of English*, vol. 50, no. 2, Nov. 2015, pp. 154–76.

Tuck, Eve, and K. Wayne Wang. "Decolonization Is Not a Metaphor." *Decolonization: Indigeneity, Education, and Society*, vol. 1, no. 1, 2012, pp. 1–40.

Wilson, Sherrée. "They Forgot Mammy Had a Brain." *Presumed Incompetent: The Intersections of Race and Class for Women in Academia*, edited by Gabriella Gutiérrez y Muhs et al., Utah State UP, 2012, pp. 65–77.

Xie, Shaobo. "Rethinking the Identity of Cultural Otherness: The Discourse of Difference as an Unfinished Project." *Voices of the Other: Children's Literature and the Postcolonial Context*, edited by Roderick McGillis, Garland, 2000, pp. 1–16.

Zembylas, Michalinos, and Megan Boler. "Discomforting Truths: The Emotional Terrain of Understanding Difference." *Pedagogies of Difference: Rethinking Education for Social Justice*, edited by Peter Pericles Tryfonas, RoutledgeFalmer, 2003, pp. 110–36.

Amy Cummins

Teaching Texas Borderlands Young Adult Literature

To teach Texas borderlands literature is to participate in the necessary cultural work of incorporating Mexican American voices into school curricula, choice reading, and YA literature scholarship. I approach the pedagogy of Texas borderlands literature from my perspective as a white faculty member who teaches the course Children's and Adolescent Literature at the University of Texas, Rio Grande Valley, located in deep south Texas. This essay details reasons for my pedagogical choices, descriptions of methods, and selected themes in this literature. I reflect primarily on my course unit about the contemporary Rio Grande Valley (RGV) authors Viola Canales, David Rice, Xavier Garza, René Saldaña, Jr., and David Bowles.

The approaches described in this essay hold particular importance for colleges and universities designated as Hispanic-serving institutions (HSIs), defined as institutions in the United States (including Puerto Rico) that have at least twenty-five percent full-time Latina/o student enrollment, with sixty-four percent of the Latina/o college students enrolled in the 2015–16 academic year ("Hispanic-Serving Institutions"). Reading Texas borderlands YA literature, which means reading Mexican American and

Tejana/o YA literature, holds value for readers in all regions. Readers gain insight, find connections, and take pleasure through reading about characters and situations functioning variously as mirrors, windows, and doors into experiences both familiar and new (Bishop ix). Jamie Campbell Naidoo explains, "*Everyone* is the target audience for culturally diverse books," as a reader "does not have to be from a particular cultural group to appreciate a book that celebrates and informs about a specific culture" (56).

My inclusion of RGV authors is also informed by place-conscious education, which immerses students in local heritage, culture, and landscapes. Place-conscious or place-based educators resist the ways schooling can be placeless and isolated from the world. As Saldaña says, "Start with where you know—not *what*, but *where*; in other words, start with that which is closest" ("Writing" 689). Embedding local material and regional examples enhances students' memory and application of course concepts. Place-conscious education values region and may include culturally responsive pedagogy.

Culturally responsive pedagogy is modeled at my university by Stephanie Alvarez through her work with the Mexican American studies program. For the Cosecha Voices project, university students recorded and publicly shared their experiences in migrating and working in agriculture; the assignments led "to the affirmation and celebration of experiences once silenced," creating student confidence as well as connections with their heritage (Alvarez and Martínez 229). Analyzing life experiences through academic study can "open up space for students to articulate their histories and lived experiences within their classroom" (Gonzales 127). For example, Diana Noreen Rivera's course on the Brownsville author Américo Paredes also exemplifies both place-conscious and culturally responsive methods.

As Miguel Guajardo, Francisco Guajardo, and Edyael Del Carmen Casaperalta show in their community-based learning approach in the RGV, culturally responsive teaching values storytelling, ethnography, and family histories; in community relationships, the local partners are treated as equals (Guajardo et al. 3). Young adults gain empowerment to know themselves, to succeed in school and attend college, and to help others gain academic success as well. Culturally responsive teaching can be practiced not only by teachers who share aspects of identity with students but also by teachers from social, cultural, and economic backgrounds different from their students; this type of teaching builds bridges across cultural differences.

In my classes, I acknowledge my white background and other aspects of my identity that reveal who I am and that affect how I read the world. I actively work against the tendency toward "racial unawareness, avoidance or dominance" that can lead to white faculty members "reproducing white hegemony" in universities (Charbeneau 658). I must work deliberately to ensure that the voices of my university students are heard and nurtured. My interpretations of Texas borderlands literature did not develop in isolation without my students, who are from this region and bring linguistic expertise, firsthand experience, and cultural intuition. The student population at my university is ninety percent Hispanic, primarily Mexican American. We build meanings collaboratively. Self-doubts about readiness to teach can be useful, prompting humility and ongoing education. Being out of one's comfort zone prompts valuable reflection.

Building cultural awareness is particularly urgent for faculty teaching courses targeted to preservice educators. Existing textbooks used in schools undermine teachers' efforts for an inclusive and culturally relevant curriculum; however, YA courses, often required in teaching degree plans, inform future generations of English language arts educators. For example, Jessica Tovar-Hilbert's research on eighth grade literature anthologies adopted in Texas reveals that, from 2001 to 2011, "cultural representation for Hispanic students increased less than 2%," and "Hispanic authors represented 8.92% of the authorship in 2001 and 10.26% in 2011." School curricula need to supplement these numbers with texts targeted to young adults that speak to their family experiences. Education research finds that bilingual adolescents respond to English literacy learning as "a much more appealing activity if viewed as supportive of their Latina/o identity" (Jiménez 995).

William Broz established the importance of the "funds of knowledge" approach to the teaching of Mexican American YA literature (83). Household funds of knowledge come from areas such as business, medicine, agriculture, ranching, farming, mining, construction, repair, household management, and religion. Understanding that students have meaningful expertise from their home lives, Broz shows how teachers in reader-response classrooms can use their appreciation of funds of knowledge "to select some of the texts for students to read and interpret for which students' cultural knowledge is a useful interpretive tool" (84). Broz demonstrates how Mexican American cultural values of *familismo* ("family"), *respeto* ("respect"), *curanderismo* ("folk medicine and faith"), religion, and collectivism appear in novels such as *The Jumping Tree*, by Saldaña, and *The*

Tequila Worm, by Viola Canales (86). Broz influenced and mentored many teachers in the RGV, including me.

The RGV is a delta on the north of the Rio Grande River and includes Hidalgo, Willacy, Starr, and Cameron Counties. As I discuss in an article I wrote with Amelia Sanchez and Christine Severn, the best-known writers for young adults who hail from the RGV are Canales, Bowles, Saldaña, Rice, and Garza (Cummins et al.). All these authors were born between 1957 and 1970. They are supportive of one another and of community literacy efforts in the RGV, where each visits regularly. In my children's and YA literature class, we read three books by RGV writers, and different texts appear in a separate course on pedagogy. Of course, the Texas-Mexico borderlands region includes authors in addition to those highlighted here; for example, faculty can assign YA novels by Mexican American authors such as Guadalupe García McCall, Diane Gonzales Bertrand, Diana López, E. E. Charlton-Trujillo, Joe Jiménez, Rubén Degollado, Daniel García Ordaz, Christopher Carmona, Katelynn Renteria, and Rene S. Perez.

The five contemporary YA authors from the RGV mentioned above have received critical attention and recognition, including prestigious book awards. Each author holds at least one graduate or professional degree. Canales, from McAllen, Texas, worked in law and government service and now teaches law part-time at Stanford University. YA books by Canales include *The Tequila Worm* and its Spanish translation, a short-story collection, and a bilingual poetry collection. Bowles, from Donna, Texas, worked as a public school teacher and a district coordinator for bilingual and ESL students before joining the faculty at the University of Texas Rio Grande Valley. Bowles's YA books include *They Call Me Güero: A Border Kid's Poems* and the Garza Twins fantasy series, starting with *The Smoking Mirror* and *Feathered Serpent, Dark Heart of Sky: Myths of Mexico.* Saldaña, from Peñitas, now lives in Lubbock, Texas, where he is a professor of education at Texas Tech University. His YA books include three novels, three collections of stories, and a coedited collection of stories, poetry, and photographs, *Juventud: Growing Up on the Border* (Saldaña and Garza-Johnson). Rice, from Edcouch-Elsa, lives primarily in Austin, Texas, where he is a substitute teacher, film producer, and cultural entrepreneur. Rice has published three YA collections of stories, beginning with *Give the Pig a Chance*, the book that began the boom in youth writing from the RGV. Garza, an author and artist from Rio Grande City, lives in San Antonio, Texas, where he teaches art to middle school and college students.

Garza's bilingual books for early adolescents include three collections of short stories and the novel series that opens with *Maximilian and the Mystery of the Guardian Angel: A Bilingual Lucha Libre Thriller.*

I teach *The Tequila Worm* first to establish the centrality of this material to YA literature. Emphasizing Mexican American YA literature provides a counternarrative to the dominant discourse many students have already experienced, according to Ruth Quiroa. She analyzed publishing trends from 1993 to 2010 and identified positive themes and negative stereotypes; I teach excerpts from Quiroa's essay in every class. *The Tequila Worm* also establishes the idea of the "Chicana feminist bildungsroman" and influenced later authors (Cummins and Infante-Sheridan 18).

Within the opening unit, Writers from the Rio Grande Valley, I provide slideshows introducing selected RGV authors, including biographical information, book covers and illustrations, and topics crossing multiple books. The introductions, updated each semester to reflect new achievements, demonstrate that these significant authors merit scrutiny. This unit emphasizes regional pride as well as knowledge, and it includes consciousness-raising about the accomplishments of people from this region.

Topics portrayed in books from the RGV allow for pairing in thematic units with other YA literature. Some common elements include recognizable, local settings; portrayals of young adults within both immediate and extended families, including elders, as well as in age-peer groups; storytelling and *leyendas* ("legends"); religious practices and beliefs; portrayals of Mexican American cultural traditions such as the game *lotería*, the music genre *pachanga*, and *lucha libre* ("wrestling"), among others; *mestizaje*, which refers to the blending of European and American Indian languages and cultures; cultural icons and touchstones in regional history; coming of age and developing a sense of self; duty to family and community; migrations and border life; and questions of moving away from home.

Education remains a particularly prominent topic in YA literature by Mexican American authors. I use the term *academic agency* to describe "the actions of asserting one's right to education, gaining access to formal education, and using education for self-chosen purposes" (Cummins 43). This theme appears in novels such as Canales's *The Tequila Worm*, Martinez's *The Smell of Old Lady Perfume*, McCall's *Under the Mesquite*, Bertrand's *Trino's Time* and *The F Factor*, Saldaña's *The Jumping Tree* and *A Good Long Way*, Ashley Hope Pérez's *What Can't Wait*, and Isabel Quintero's *Gabi, a Girl in Pieces.* Having readers consider portrayals of teaching and learning, both in school and domestic settings, provides students an opportunity for self-analysis and literary analysis.

School and education are highly valued in Mexican American culture. Studies have documented the roles of parents and siblings in Latina/o students' school success. Robert Jiménez finds that "students provided many examples of how their parents were involved in their literacy learning," such as with funds to buy books, trips to the library, guidance in learning to read, and "consejos or advice they had received from their fathers" for literacy education (991). Being part of "mutually supportive family situations" supports literacy learning as well as character development (990). Parents play a vital role in *educación*, which "refers to the family's role in inculcating in children a sense of moral, social, and personal responsibility and serves as a foundation for all other learning" (Valenzuela 23).

Thus, an inclusive concept of education encompasses *educación*, fusing academic aspects with ethical or moral aspects of learning. Angela Valenzuela states that "though inclusive of formal academic training, *educación* additionally refers to competence in the social world, wherein one respects the dignity and individuality of others" (23). Gilda Ochoa states that *educación* connotes not only academics but "the whole person—how one behaves and interacts." Teachers who want to bridge home and school milieus could not only understand and convey subject matter but also build "self-confidence, kindness, and respect" (193). I assert that *educación* involves curriculum and methods; it is part of culturally responsive teaching. In other words, *educación* is not in opposition to academic education but is crucial to it.

Representing another perspective, Margaret Cantú-Sánchez identifies how growing up within an "anglocentric school system" creates "an education/educación split" in which Mexican American students find that "their cultural and academic identities and epistemologies split and contradict one another" (44). Cantú-Sánchez incorporates culturally relevant literature in her secondary and postsecondary English teaching, asking students to respond to the texts with their own views and to write about "the dilemmas encountered by protagonists of our texts, while drawing on their own life experiences." Cantú-Sánchez fosters in her students a productive "confrontation that signals the beginning of a *mestizaje*" of belief systems: "Rather than continue such methodologies that separate my student's cultural epistemologies from those of school, I invite them to do just the opposite" (45). In her criticism of conventional education, Cantú-Sánchez honors the influence of the Chicana feminist philosopher Gloria

Anzaldúa, author of *Borderlands / La frontera*. Anzaldúa—who graduated with English teacher certification from a college that later became part of the university where I work—began her teaching career in the local Pharr–San Juan–Alamo school district. She describes how, in 1971, she was supplementing the curriculum with texts by Chicana/o authors, and despite being "reprimanded and forbidden to do so" by her principal, she persisted and still "slipped in" the texts (82). Echoes of this situation remain a half century later. However, a sign of change is that in this same school district, all the incoming sixth graders in summer 2017 read *The Tequila Worm* by Canales.

Because teaching literature is teaching writing, students in a YA literature course frequently compose in response to texts. Assignments in my course include daily in-class writings that reflect on the readings; personal literacy narratives in which students describe influences on their development as readers and writers in any language; alternative book reports, graphic responses, or book trailers requiring artistic and visual responses to books; literary analysis essays; peer response workshops; and group projects in which class members plan activities for teaching the book at a targeted grade level and covering specific state standards. Online students complete discussion boards, blogs, or wikis.

An important assignment in my unit on RGV writers is the analytical and experiential essay. This assignment requires the student to compare personal or family experiences with aspects of one of the first two books in the course. This work draws awareness to the fact that readers and learners bring their own experiences to texts; literature is not read in a vacuum but is part of life. By reflecting on their own experiences and making text-to-self connections, students gain a greater understanding of growing up. I do not assume that students have had experiences similar to those depicted in the books, but students can compare and contrast real life to fiction. Sharing of the material is also part of our process, and class members voluntarily read aloud papers to the class. Students engage well with this assignment and submit excellent work. I see how students care deeply about the quality and expressiveness of their writing when analyzing personal experiences and connecting course content with their lives.

Projects, assignments, and discussions in my course invite students to develop their interpretations, compare their lived experiences with published texts, and tell their own stories. As ethnic studies research shows, the sooner students can center their education around lived experiences, the better. Some class members go on to teach the authors studied in the course and to create new borderlands literature through their own writing.

Secondary and college students in any region deserve the opportunity to read, discuss, and share interpretations about Texas borderlands literature. Themes such as education and *educación* can make an impact on future teachers. While I hope that faculty teaching YA literature at all institutional types will incorporate works by south Texas authors and other Mexican American writers, it is especially urgent for faculty and students at HSIs to read these texts and add to the conversation about them.

Works Cited

Alvarez, Stephanie, and José Luis Martínez. "*La palabra, conciencia, y voz*: Tato Laviera and the Cosecha Voices Project at the University of Texas Pan American." *The AmeRícan Poet: Essays on the Work of Tato Laviera*, edited by Stephanie Alvarez and William Luis, Hunter College Center for Puerto Rican Studies, 2014, pp. 204–36.

Anzaldúa, Gloria. *Borderlands / La frontera: The New Mestiza*. 1987. Aunt Lute Books, 2007.

Bertrand, Diane Gonzales. *The F Factor*. Arte Público Press, 2010.

———. *Trino's Time*. Arte Público Press, 2001.

Bishop, Rudine Sims. "Mirrors, Windows, and Sliding Glass Doors." *Perspectives*, vol. 6, no. 3, 1990, pp. ix–xi.

Bowles, David. *Feathered Serpent, Dark Heart of Sky: Myths of Mexico*. Cinco Puntos Press, 2017.

———. *The Smoking Mirror*. IFWG Publishing, 2015.

———. *They Call Me Güero: A Border Kid's Poems*. Cinco Puntos Press, 2018.

Broz, William J. "Funds of Knowledge and Mexican American Cultural Values in MA YAL." *Young Adult Literature and Adolescent Identity across Cultures and Classrooms: Contexts for the Literary Lives of Teens*, edited by Janet Alsup, Routledge, 2010, pp. 83–98.

Campbell Naidoo, Jamie. "The Américas Award, Cultural Competence, and the Politics of Publishing." *The Américas Award: Honoring Latino/a Children's and Young Adult Literature of the Americas*, edited by Laretta Henderson, Lexington Books, 2016, pp. 49–56.

Canales, Viola. *The Tequila Worm*. Wendy Lamb Books, 2005.

Cantú-Sánchez, Margaret. "In/Civilities of the American Classroom: A Clash between a Chicana Teacher and an Anglocentric School System." *El Mundo Zurdo 5: Selected Works from the 2015 Meeting of the Society for the Study of Gloria Anzaldúa*, edited by Domino Renee Perez et al., Aunt Lute Books, 2016, pp. 41–48.

Charbeneau, Jessica. "White Faculty Transforming Whiteness in the Classroom through Pedagogical Practice." *Race, Ethnicity, and Education*, vol. 18, no. 5, 2015, pp. 655–74.

Cummins, Amy. "Academic Agency in YA Novels by Mexican American Women Authors." *Gender(ed) Identities: Critical Rereadings of Gender in Children's and Young Adult Literature*, edited by Tricia Clasen and Holly Hassel, Routledge, 2017, pp. 42–58.

Cummins, Amy, and Myra Infante-Sheridan. "Establishing a Chicana Feminist Bildungsroman for Young Adults." *New Review of Children's Literature and Librarianship*, vol. 24, no. 1, 2018, pp. 18–39.

Cummins, Amy, et al. "Legends in the Making: Contemporary Writers for Children and Young Adults from the Rio Grande Valley of South Texas." *The Dragon Lode*, vol. 37, no. 1, 2018, pp. 9–15.

García McCall, Guadalupe. *Under the Mesquite.* Lee and Low Books, 2011.

Garza, Xavier. *Maximilian and the Mystery of the Guardian Angel: A Bilingual Lucha Libre Thriller.* Cinco Puntos Press, 2011.

Gonzales, Leslie D. "The Horizon of Possibilities: How Faculty in Hispanic-Serving Institutions Can Reshape the Production and Legitimization of Knowledge within Academia." *Hispanic-Serving Institutions: Advancing Research and Transformative Practice*, edited by Anne-Marie Núñez et al., Routledge, 2015, pp. 121–35.

Guajardo, Miguel, et al. "Transformative Education: Chronicling a Pedagogy for Social Change." *Anthropology and Education Quarterly*, vol. 39, no. 1, Mar. 2008, pp. 3–22.

"Hispanic-Serving Institutions (HSIs): 2015–2016." *Excelencia in Education*, Mar. 2017, www.edexcelencia.org/research/hispanic-serving-institutions-hsis-2015-16. Accessed 10 May 2017.

Jiménez, Robert T. "Literacy and the Identity Development of Latina/o Students." *American Educational Research Journal*, vol. 37, no. 4, 2000, pp. 971–1000.

Martínez, Claudia Guadalupe. *The Smell of Old Lady Perfume.* Cinco Puntos Press, 2008.

Ochoa, Gilda L. *Learning from Latino Teachers.* Jossey-Bass, 2007.

Pérez, Ashley Hope. *What Can't Wait.* Carolrhoda Lab, 2011.

Quintero, Isabel. *Gabi, a Girl in Pieces.* Cinco Puntos Press, 2014.

Quiroa, Ruth. "Promising Portals and Safe Passages: A Review of Pre-K–12 Latino- and Latina-Themed Literature." *Diversity in Youth Literature: Opening Doors through Reading*, edited by Jamie Campbell Naidoo and Sarah Park Dahlen, American Library Association, 2013, pp. 45–62.

Rice, David. *Give the Pig a Chance and Other Stories.* Bilingual Press, 1996.

Rivera, Diana Noreen. "Third Space Resistance in Américo Paredes' *With His Pistol in His Hand*: A Defense of Nuevo Santander." *Recovering the U.S. Hispanic Literary Heritage*, edited by Donna M. Kabalen de Bichara and Blanca López de Mariscal, vol. 9, Arte Publíco Press, 2014, pp. 17–40.

Saldaña, René, Jr. *A Good Long Way.* Arte Publíco Press, 2010.

———. *The Jumping Tree.* Dell Laurel-Leaf, 2001.

———. "Writing, Teaching, and Researching: An Interview with René Saldaña, Jr." By David Moore, *Journal of Adolescent and Adult Literacy*, vol. 53, no. 8, May 2010, pp. 688–90.

Saldaña, René, Jr., and Erika Garza-Johnson, editors. *Juventud: Growing Up on the Border.* VAO Publishing, 2013.

Tovar-Hilbert, Jessica. "An Analysis of Authors, Content, and Genres of Hispanic-Related Selections in Adopted Eighth Grade Literature Anthologies in Texas, 2001–2011." Texas Association for Literacy Education Conference, Corpus Christi, Texas, 11 Feb. 2017. Poster.

Valenzuela, Angela. *Subtractive Schooling: U.S.-Mexican Youth and the Politics of Caring.* State U of New York P, 1999.

Margaret Noodin, Donna L. Pasternak, Laurie Barth Walczak, and Michael Zimmerman, Jr.

Language, Identity, and Social Reality in Twenty-First-Century American Indian Young Adult Fiction

There has never been anything easy about leaving childhood. For young adult readers caught in the space between youth and adulthood, good fiction can be a place to learn and explore alternate endings and problems not yet encountered or a reflection of a self that seems alone in the world. In a postsecondary setting, it can be especially difficult for older readers to understand which contemporary texts are authentic, important, and worthy of critical examination. If the face, family, or web of teen challenges is centered in American Indian culture, few books come close to reality. Yet literacy, writing skills, and the ability to think critically about narrative are clearly connected to competency at all ages. Thus, it is important that educators seeking to impact the overall success of American Indian youth, and those scholars wishing to understand how to evaluate American Indian fiction, have a solid introduction to contemporary literature for American Indian young adults.

Ways to introduce American Indian YA fiction in the twenty-first century include expanding notions of diversity, moving beyond standard texts, recognizing local context, and considering how indigenous languages contribute to literacy. Students can benefit from reading stories of the multiracial urban, suburban, and rural American Indian diaspora. In classrooms where American Indian students are sometimes the majority and sometimes not even present in the school, teachers can guide young readers as they encounter American Indian characters in a broader historical, social, political, and cultural context.

Beyond the Canon: Making Text Selection Meaningful

Teacher educators in the University of Wisconsin–Milwaukee School of Education discovered many teacher candidates for K–12 classrooms struggle with selecting texts, even for themselves, whether for pleasure or for academic reading. Like many students, the teacher candidates Donna Pasternak teaches have been assigned texts in almost every English class they have ever taken from kindergarten through college. When students complete their reading interest surveys on the first day of class, many of them indicate that they read what they are given (if they even read those assigned texts at all, as some sheepishly confess to her). This situation is highly problematic, as these future teachers will be designing reading programs and teaching English sometime in the near future without any explicit skills with which to identify and select quality literature—literature, in this case, that does not objectify American Indians or their experiences. Assigning or suggesting quality texts can also be highly problematic for unsophisticated readers when the author of a text explores critical issues or attempts self-effacing humor that includes stereotypes for literary reasons, such as in the YA novels *Crazy Horse's Girlfriend*, by Erika T. Wurth, and *If I Ever Get Out of Here*, by Eric Gansworth.

To support future teachers as they select and critically analyze the texts they assign, suggest, or teach, Donna and her colleagues designed a 200-level course that can serve as the introduction to children's and YA literature required by most teacher education programs (although all students can enroll in this course to satisfy their humanities requirement). The purpose of the course is to help teacher candidates analyze contemporary texts to discern if selections are authentic, important, and worthy of critical examination, while also ensuring these teacher candidates can support their future students to be critical readers who understand literary study enough to identify the ways that many texts for children and adolescents "reproduce and reinforce racial and ethnic hierarchies" (Hintz and Tribunella 345) through cultural appropriation, as well as to think critically about issues of authenticity and accuracy, authorship and ownership, audience, perspective, reclamation, and artistic freedom and ethical responsibility.[1]

The class is organized as a reading workshop following Nancie Atwell's design from *In the Middle: New Understandings about Writing, Reading, and Learning*. The classwork engages the students in minilessons about literary study, book talks, teacher and peer conferencing, and small- and large-group activities while they read different texts, which they have been taught to select, on a preassigned topic, theme, or genre (Atwell 87–299). Held in an active learning space that socializes learning through inquiry and collaboration, which has been determined to significantly impact teaching and learning and to empower students,[2] the course, at first encounter, acts as a model of literary study that moves away from the transmission model of lecture, recitation, and seatwork many of these students have experienced in their K–16 education. The course content differs from most traditional university-level literary study because class meetings are spent discussing different texts and making comparisons in whole- and small-group meetings, reading silently and documenting primary texts, and making critical observations about texts in their reading journals.[3]

Early in the class, students examine their texts for present cultural models. They respond to a series of questions to analyze their selections and to understand key terms and controversies while reading texts:

> What cultural models does the narrator or implied author present in the text?
> How and to what extent does the narrator or implied author reify or critique the cultural models in the text?
> How and to what extent does the narrator or implied author invite the reader to take up or critique the cultural models in the text?
> Who does this text assume I am?
> What cultural models do I bring to the text?
> How and to what extent do the cultural models I bring to the text align or conflict with the cultural models presented by the narrator or implied author?
> What are the social and political implications of the reification or critique of the cultural models at work in the text?

It is through activities such as these that teacher candidates learn to select quality literature that not only connects to their own lives and interests but also develops the same selection skills in future students. After all, if readers are not engaged readers, they will never be readers at all.

Reading without Walls in the Middle School English Language Arts Classroom

Since the graphic novelist Gene Luen Yang—a Printz Award winner, a two-time National Book Award nominee, a 2016 MacArthur Fellow, and the Library of Congress National Ambassador for Young People's Literature—issued the Reading without Walls Challenge, the word *wall* has become imbued with complicated political, social, and racial meaning in the United States. As the current political climate has called attention to literal, symbolic, and figurative walls, young people potentially hear messages of separation. Walls, whether real or imaginary, divide Americans in the contemporary cultural climate.

Yang's suggestion that young people read without walls so as to get outside their comfort zone offers an alternative to this division. On his Web site, Yang asks students to read a book "about a character who doesn't look like or live like" them, a book about a topic unfamiliar to them, or a book in a format that they "don't normally read for fun." The challenge presents an opportunity for readers to not just hang a mirror or install a window on the wall, but to raze the wall with the two cornerstones of successful English language arts education: voice and choice. Students empowered with voice and choice can indeed move beyond their comfort zones and perhaps envision a different classroom, community, and country.

As the eighth grade American studies English teacher at an independent, coeducational, college preparatory pre-K–12 school in the Milwaukee area, Laurie Walczak begins the school year with Yang's award-winning contemporary classic of YA literature, the graphic novel *American Born Chinese*, launching her class with discussions of the essential question: what does it mean to be American? Yang's Reading without Walls Challenge pushes the conversation, as students choose their own books to read and relate them to the essential question, if applicable.

One of the novels Laurie's students usually discover in their search for books for the Reading without Walls Challenge is Sherman Alexie's *The Absolutely True Diary of a Part-Time Indian*, which received the National Book Award. Published around the same time as *American Born Chinese*, Alexie's semiautobiographical, illustrated novel shares similar themes and consistently appears on book lists with Yang's graphic novel. Laurie's students often read and enjoy *The Absolutely True Diary*: students pass the middle school library's multiple copies among one another, and some students go on to read Alexie's other works.

While Laurie appreciates that her students embrace *The Absolutely True Diary*, ask challenging questions, and engage in meaningful dialogue inspired by Yang and Alexie, Laurie finds that students frequently do not move beyond Alexie to other American Indian voices in YA literature. Although there is an abundance of books by American Indian authors, students frequently do not recognize Alexie's novel as just one voice from the Spokane–Coeur d'Alene community. Thus, Laurie sees her challenge as to provide more options for readers.

The We Need Diverse Books (WNDB) grassroots organization and its social media presence proves extremely useful for teachers and students alike in a learning environment where voice and choice are supported and respected and comfort zones are eschewed. WNDB's mission—"Putting more books featuring diverse characters into the hands of all children"—makes for a powerful tool in encouraging students to read books by or about native people (diversebooks.org). Indeed, in WNDB's 2017 Summer Reading Series, several such books were recommended alongside more commonly known authors and texts. For example, for readers of *Will Grayson, Will Grayson*, a novel about gay identity by John Green and David Levithan, WNDB suggests *If I Ever Get Out of Here*, by the Onondaga author Eric Gansworth, explaining that both books "feature teens whose difficult lives are somehow, somewhat alleviated by the power of good music." Similarly, *House of Purple Cedar*, by the Oklahoma Choctaw Tim Tingle, is proposed for readers who enjoyed *One Crazy Summer*, by the African American author Rita Williams-Garcia, because "in both, main characters learn about community and family history, and how that history relates to the oppression they experience every day." If students like superhero comic books, WNDB recommends *The Outside Circle*, by Patti LaBoucane-Benson, because "both are memorable graphic titles featuring bad guys gone good." For poetry readers who choose anthologies such as *Poetry Speaks: Who I Am*, WNDB offers *Dreaming in Indian: Contemporary Native American Voices*, because "both are stunning, poetic anthologies designed to give teens a voice."

Whereas Alexie's *Absolutely True Diary* may be a starting place for students' voice and choice, helping them discover other books not only puts more diversity of American Indian literature in their hands but may also urge them to confront their own discomfort, seek more stories different from their own, and resist divisive social forces. Other sources of information about the many national indigenous storytelling traditions can begin to map pathways to understanding American Indian YA literature as more than a tribal melting pot—resources that would serve future and in-service teachers as well as their students.[4]

National Languages and Identities Diversified and Revitalized

Every modern classroom is a microcosm of knowledge production with many intersections of understanding. Teachers and students recombine old facts with new views and continue the human tradition of storytelling. As students encounter the personal and communal identities of American Indian YA literature, they need to read beyond binary distinctions, beyond diversity as it is usually described, and beyond static representation of tribes and sovereign nations. Titles that enter the classroom as the only representation of Native America can be read as part of a much larger network of literary styles and languages. Breaking down the canon also requires building up new notions of indigeneity that include authentic literary, artistic, and linguistic practices. Native authors have always been "reinventing the enemy's language," as Joy Harjo and Gloria Bird explain in their book of the same title. Teachers in the Great Lakes region say in Ojibwe, one of the many indigenous languages still used today, "*gidiniwewidamomin maamwibimaadiziyang oma akiing mii igo ezhi-gikenimdizoyaang gaye gikenimiyangidwa*" ("the sounds of our language as we live together on earth are the way we know ourselves and are known by others"; Noodin 131; Noodin's trans.).

Several well-known American Indian YA authors have moved beyond English, as they "claim narrative authority" through use of indigenous language and linguistic patterns (Bradford 336). For example, the Birchbark House series by Louise Erdrich introduces hundreds of Ojibwe words through interjections and rephrasing in Ojibwemowin. Characters add to the main plot by referring to and speaking English, French, and Ojibwe as the area south of Lake Superior slowly becomes part of the United States. And while the novel is mostly in English, the hundreds of Ojibwe words illustrate the collision between cultures, often revealing the way some ideas never fully translate from one language to another. For instance, Nokomis tells living, evolving *aadizookanag*, while Dedey shares factual, contemporary *dibaajimowinan*. Both words mean "story," which can lead to discussions of diverse understandings of genre and the difference between fiction and nonfiction. The Birchbark House series also invites discussion of storytelling protocols, allowing for conversations about authorship, copyright, and dissemination.

In the spring of 2016, the Ojibwe language instruction at the Indian Community School of Milwaukee began to incorporate written texts as part of the curriculum for grades two through eight. The same titles are also used at the University of Wisconsin–Milwaukee with first- and second-semester students who are just beginning to learn the language. Published by Wiigwaas Press in Minneapolis, Minnesota, the monolingual books provide insight into Ojibwe culture and narrative production, teaching students syntax, grammar, and traditional storytelling methods through texts constructed by contemporary elders and teachers. Many of the scenarios depicted in the stories are eloquently articulated in the target language as well as illustrated by Ojibwe authors to assist with the understanding of how the story moves along.

There are several benefits to having these resources at one's disposal. In the elementary grades, the books provide excellent practice for the children as they slowly sound out each syllable to gain proper phonemic use and bolster their acquisition of the characters in the Roman alphabet. At the college level, the books serve the same purpose as students are introduced to unfamiliar consonant clusters and a writing system unlike anything they will likely have encountered in the past. In contemporary Ojibwe language teaching, many schools and teachers utilize the Fiero double vowel system of writing, which was developed by Charles Fiero in the 1950s and is patterned after the Roman orthography. Many of the same sounds are present in both languages, with a few contrasting exceptions. Reading in both languages early in the learning process supports acquisition of all the sound variations. In grades four and five, the texts allow children with previous exposure to the stories to build on their reading and comprehension skills and to begin developing critical thinking skills in an Ojibwe cultural context. In the middle school years, the confidence of the students gradually increases, and students are able to use the stories as models for original stories of their own. At the college level the stories serve as a platform for linguistic analysis as they begin to notice patterns of word and sentence formation.

Over the course of the calendar year, as the monolingual Ojibwe texts have been utilized in the classroom, there have been several cases of individual achievement. Perhaps the most striking examples have been in the second grade, where the enthusiasm and perseverance of young readers are rewarded by the creation of a literary setting equivalent to what they encounter in their English reading classroom. Within the context of language revitalization, this linguistic and cultural parity is a significant achievement.

As is evident from the experiences teaching American Indian YA literature in this essay, how professors and teachers approach this literature across educational levels and teaching situations is challenging but important work indeed. Bringing texts to students, as either representations of their culture or representations of cultures that contrast with their own, can help students and teachers move beyond Alexie's popular, but singularly satiric, view. There is a rich storytelling tradition in American Indian literature through which varied indigenous groups across the United States have been explored. These texts can work together to highlight and support indigenous languages as vibrant and active. American Indian YA literature aligns with contemporary American literary traditions and also enhances or reaffirms a reader's understanding of native cultures, language, and context. Reading stories about the multiracial urban, suburban, and rural American Indian diaspora invites students and their teachers to understand critically a complex literature that challenges the walls that separate us as well as relates the stories that connect us all in this nation where each voice has a story to tell.

Notes

1. See Hintz and Tribunella, pp. 358–72.

2. See Fecho; Freire; Golub; Jennings and Smith; Mitchell and Christenbury; Pasternak, "Combat Ready"; and Soter et al.

3. See Applebee; Appleman; Gaughan; Giroux; Graff; Pasternak, "Poetry" and "Combat Ready"; and Soter et al.

4. Other resources for native voice and choice in YA literature include the following: American Indians in Children's Literature (americanindiansinchildrensliterature.blogspot.com), American Indian Library Association (ailanet.org), Cooperative Children's Book Center's list "American Indian/First Nations Presses and Tribal Publishers" (ccbc.education.wisc.edu/books/pclist.asp#indian), "*SLJ*'s 2013 Focus on 'Resources and Kid Lit about American Indians'" (americanindiansinchildrensliterature.blogspot.com/2013/11/sljs-2013-focus-on-resources-and-kid.html), and "Teacher and Librarian Resources for Native American Children's and Young Adult Books" (cynthialeitichsmith.com/lit-resources/read/diversity/native-am/teaching/native_resources/).

Works Cited

Applebee, Arthur N. *Curriculum as Conversation: Transforming Traditions of Teaching and Learning.* U of Chicago P, 1996.

Appleman, Deborah. *Critical Encounters in High School English: Teaching Literary Theory to Adolescents.* 3rd ed., Teachers College P, 2015.

Atwell, Nancie. *In the Middle: New Understandings about Writing, Reading, and Learning.* 2nd ed., Boynton / Cook, 1998.

Bradford, Clare. "Reading Indigeneity: The Ethics of Interpretation and Representation." *Handbook of Research on Children's and Young Adult Literature*, edited by Shelby Wolf et al., Routledge, 2011, pp. 331–41.

Fecho, Bob. *"Is This English?": Race, Language, and Culture in the Classroom.* Teachers College P, 2004.

Freire, Paulo. *Pedagogy of the Oppressed.* Translated by Myra Bergman Ramos, Herder and Herder, 1970.

Gaughan, John. *Reinventing English: Teaching in the Contact Zone.* Heinemann, 2001.

Giroux, Henry A. *Teachers as Intellectuals: Toward a Critical Pedagogy of Learning.* Bergin and Garvey, 1988.

Golub, Jeffrey N. *Making Learning Happen: Strategies for an Interactive Classroom.* Heinemann, 2000.

Graff, Gerald. "Conflict Clarifies: A Response." *Pedagogy*, vol. 3, no. 2, Spring 2003, pp. 266–76.

Harjo, Joy, and Gloria Bird, editors. *Reinventing the Enemy's Language: Contemporary Native Women's Writings of North America.* W. W. Norton, 1997.

Hintz, Carrie, and Eric L. Tribunella. *Reading Children's Literature: A Critical Introduction.* Bedford / St. Martin's, 2013.

Jennings, Louise B., and Cynthia Potter Smith. "Examining the Role of Critical Inquiry for Transformative Practices: Two Joint Case Studies of Multicultural Teacher Education." *Teachers College Record*, vol. 104, no. 3, Apr. 2002, pp. 456–81.

Mitchell, Diana, and Leila Christenbury. *Both Art and Craft: Teaching Ideas That Spark Learning.* National Council of Teachers of English, 2000.

Noodin, Margaret. "Language Revitalization, Anishinaabemowin, and Erdrich's *The Birchbark House* Series." *Frontiers in American Children's Literature*, edited by Dorothy Clark and Linda Salem, Cambridge Scholars Publishing, 2016, pp. 123–32.

Pasternak, Donna L. "Combat Ready: Teaching Young Adult and Classic Literature about War." *SIGNAL*, vol. 34, no. 1, Fall 2010–Winter 2011, pp. 34–43.

———. "Poetry and Pop Culture: Exploring America and Norway." *English Journal*, vol. 96, no. 1, Sept. 2006, pp. 105–09.

Soter, Anna O., et al., editors. *Interpretive Play: Using Critical Perspectives to Teach Young Adult Literature.* Christopher-Gordon, 2008.

Yang, Gene Luen. "The Reading without Walls Challenge." *Gene Luen Yang: Cartoonist and Teacher*, 13 May 2016, geneyang.com/the-reading-without-walls-challenge.

Katie Kapurch

A Girls' Studies Approach to Young Adult Literature

A girls' studies pedagogy recognizes girls as active creators of culture and defines girlhood as feminine adolescence, a socially constructed period of becoming whose boundaries are not contingent on biological sex and age (Driscoll 6). Mary Celeste Kearney's scholarship, groundbreaking for theorizing girl-made media, has been influential to a field that perceives girls as cultural agents, rather than passive, spongelike consumers. An appreciation for girls' agency is also consistent with Holly Virginia Blackford's findings about girl readers, "who construct a piece of literature as an aesthetic object" and do not read for role models to emulate (*Out of This World* 19).

Seeing girls as active cultural participants is not difficult to do when teaching novels in which girl characters are heroic like Hermione Granger, Katniss Everdeen, and Esperanza Cordero; Esperanza promises to write her way out of Mango Street but to return for those she leaves behind. A girls' studies pedagogy is harder to enact when the female protagonist appears passive, as does Bella Swan, whose agency is consistently undermined by her vampire boyfriend. Introducing Blackford's thesis about girl readers early in the semester discourages role-model criticism and begins to invite more thoughtful analyses. Even with this theoretical point of view, however, many undergraduates still have trouble reconciling the seemingly antifeminist sensibilities in some YA texts with their popular appeal; students can also be distracted by their own pop culture preferences or assumptions about girls as audiences. Thus, what follows is a sequence of content that builds a theoretical foundation for complex critical engagements with the representation of girls and girlhood in YA. These summaries are not entire lesson plans for individual novels, however, because a girls' studies approach is not as simple as developing a unit about a particular girl-oriented text; rather, the pedagogy involves a theoretical vantage point informing the entire course.

The Outsiders . . . with the Beatles

YA literature is a genre historically indebted to girl authors and readers, so a girls' studies approach makes logical sense when teaching about the birth of the genre in the marketplace. Maureen Daly sounds a lot like her hesitant protagonist in the autobiographical *Seventeenth Summer* when she explains, "What I've tried to do, you see . . . is just write about the things that happened to me and that I knew about—that meant a lot to me" (Cart 11). Students need only to read the first chapter of Daly's 1942 novel, which has never gone out of print, to see how YA still upholds Daly's first-person self-consciousness, limited time frame, and detailed descriptions of appearance. Two decades after Daly, S. E. Hinton saw the saccharine middle-class drama of *Seventeenth Summer*'s ilk unrepresentative of her experiences in the teenage "social jungle" of Tulsa, Oklahoma. Although Hinton perceived her work as distinct from Daly's, Hinton also derived *The Outsiders* from her own experiences (Cart 25–26). And in spite of eschewing the minutiae of 1940s heterosexual dating rituals, Hinton did indeed craft a love story—between same-sex friends.

Both Daly's and Hinton's success among readers tracks alongside the importance of girls, who were constructed as desired consumers and trendsetters by the mid-century marketplace. The Beatles, for example, achieved radio success in the United States when fourteen-year-old Marsha Albert convinced her local disc jockey to play "I Want to Hold Your Hand" in December 1963. Teaching the birth of YA, and *The Outsiders* in particular, in the context of mid-twentieth-century pop culture is one way to emphasize the role of girls—and adolescents more broadly—in the formation of the genre. The early Beatles phenomenon and *The Outsiders* pair well together since they both show how girlishness is not particular to female youth.

Beatlemania is a phenomenon well suited to any classroom discussion of the historical rise of YA literature. The collective screams of Beatlemaniacs were a first gasp of the women's liberation movement, as girls' emotional roar signified resistance to restrictive 1950s gender and sexuality norms (Ehrenreich et al. 84). Beatles fans' screams exemplify how girls, even in their consumption of texts, take an active role as audiences; what seems like out-of-control "hysteria" is, in fact, an agential response to the freedom represented by the Beatles, who appeared to their listeners to be a group of boyfriends having fun with one another, unfettered by the kinds of social pressures girls faced (Ehrenreich et al.). This historical precedent encourages perceptions of young fans, especially those who write fan fiction or make *YouTube* videos, as cocreating texts.

The first fifteen minutes of "The British Invasion," an episode of CNN's documentary series *The Sixties*, is useful material to situate the rise of YA alongside the rise of youth culture, especially since it introduces the Beatles as working-class Liverpudlians whose rough port-city hometown resembles the Greasers' wrong side of the tracks. Like other male-dominated rock and roll criticism, however, the documentary leaves out the influence of African American girl-groups on the Fab Four. I bring this race and gender gap to students' attention to preface our listening of the Shirelles' song "Boys," which the Beatles covered on their first studio album, *Please Please Me*. After the Shirelles listening, I ask students to consider how the song might appeal to girl listeners, situating observations in relation to theories of girl-group discourse. Defining features of this discourse, as illustrated by the song, include knowledge and advice passed between women and girls (especially through call-and-response), vocables that render sexual desire innocent and childlike, a concern with romance and relationships, and matching clothes and close harmonies that further the intimacy of the singers as a homosocial group of friends (Warwick, "You're" 165; see also Warwick, *Girl*). Students often recognize these as rhetorical strategies available in *Seventeenth Summer*, whose self-conscious narrator confides about first-time romance. Students are then prepared to notice how a live performance of the Beatles' "Boys" cover maintains a girlish sensibility while adding some boyish bravado (Kapurch, "Crying" 204–06). Following this, we listen to "She Loves You," a John Lennon–Paul McCartney original whose speaker is a friend trying to resolve a relationship misunderstanding—a role typical of a girl go-between (Warwick, "You're" 165). Early Beatles music frequently invokes feminine discourse through other covers and original songs, presenting a gender-fluid image of long-haired boys speaking girls' language.

The Outsiders offers a comparable example of gender-fluid performance: as a girl author, Hinton constructs a boy protagonist who spends a great deal of his narration observing the behavior and appearance of other boys with whom he has intimate, emotional friendships. One short essay assignment that works particularly well here (especially in the beginning of the semester) asks students to explore the irony of the Greasers' rejection of the Beatles in favor of Elvis Presley, a prompt that reinforces theoretical ideas related to gender as performance, encouraging students to make connections between signs of homosocial intimacy, as well as the representation of working-class youth in a 1960s historical context. Such insight can inform the study of other novels that represent intersectional identity issues related to class, gender, and race, such as Sandra Cisneros's *The House on Mango Street* and Walter Dean Myers's *Street Love.* The latter, a verse novel based on *Romeo and Juliet*, reverses traditional gender dynamics: the Romeo character is sheltered, similar to the homebound girls of Cisneros's novel, and the Juliet character has more physical freedom than her theatrical counterpart. Students are ready to recognize this reversal in other foundational content related to mythology.

Persephone Girls in *Harry Potter and the Chamber of Secrets* and the Twilight Saga

Recognizing girlhood as a socially constructed discourse of feminine becoming, especially in Western culture, does not preclude analyses of boy characters. Reading J. K. Rowling's *Harry Potter and the Chamber of Secrets* through a mythic lens, in fact, complicates a reading of Harry as a conventional male hero and leads to an interpretation of the either-or love triangle in Stephenie Meyer's Twilight series—*Twilight*, *New Moon*, *Eclipse*, and *Breaking Dawn*—as symbolic options, not simply a literal choice between Edward and Jacob.

The Perseus and Persephone myths reveal an adolescent precedent in ancient stories told by those who did not distinguish "teenager" as a distinct life phase. These mythical journeys are prototypes for socialized boyhood and girlhood, alternately constructed as masculine-exterior-active and feminine-interior-passive. Usually a student will protest that binary with contemporary exceptions: "But Katniss is doing exterior things on a physical journey *and* her narration is focused on emotion and the interior." This is exactly the right insight, moving us to question how and why more recent texts maintain or trouble Perseus and Persephone representations. How are gender binaries blurred? Can boys be Persephone girls? These questions also help us think about power dynamics associated with gender and age.

Students read primary and supplemental material about the myths, specifically from the Oxford University Press textbook *Introduction to Mythology*, and I introduce Joseph Campbell's narrative theory alongside the myths of Perseus and Persephone; Persephone's other name, "Kore," means "girl" (Thury and Devinney 522). Perseus's adherence to Campbell's monomyth is an opportunity to emphasize Freudian parent-child dynamics, since the demigod's journey is predicated on sexual jealousy about his mother's suitor, Polydectes, who thinks he can eliminate Perseus by sending him on an impossible mission for the Gorgon's head. The basilisk slaying is reminiscent of Medusa's beheading, but students are also quick to recognize the trope of older men threatened by prophecies about boys overtaking them. This is apparent in the Harry Potter series' overarching conflict between Voldemort and Harry and specifically in *Chamber* through the actions of Gilderoy Lockhart, who, jealous of Harry's celebrity, plans to erase the chosen one's memory. This scenario reinforces Roberta Seelinger Trites's theoretical insight into adolescents' precarious agency, as they are both empowered and disempowered by the very youth that makes them so attractive in Western culture (xi).

While Perseus chooses to take up the mantle of his journey, Persephone is rendered powerless, betrothed by her father, Zeus, to his brother Hades without her mother Demeter's say-so; Hades comes to collect Persephone when she, "dazzled" by "sweet-smelling blossoms," wanders away from her girlfriends (Thury and Devinney 525). The flower imagery is a recurring symbol of emerging female sexuality (see, for instance, *Seventeenth Summer*'s gardening scene, "Little Red Riding Hood," Twilight's meadow, and many other girl-oriented texts). The Homeric Hymn to Demeter also presents inconsistencies in the account of Persephone's ultimate abduction or seduction: we are first told that she "sprang up for joy" at Hades's offer of political power as he simultaneously presented the "honey-sweet pomegranate seed" (534). But when she returns to Demeter, Persephone says she "sprang for joy" at the news of her mother demanding her release, emphasizing the "force" Hades used to coerce her "taste." Then, although Persephone promises to recount "every point," she instead lists every one of the "maidens in the delightful meadow" by name—more than twenty—before devolving into grief (535). Persephone's distracting rhetorical strategy reads like any modern teenager's excuse for being home late.

I am careful to acknowledge interpretations of the myth as one about rape and kidnapping, but the Homeric Hymn also encourages reading against the grain because the bulk of the narrative action features Demeter. Persephone, "a uniquely indeterminate and homeless girl, fated forever to cycle between worlds," is silenced, which, as Blackford argues, has led other writers to continue reimagining her (*Myth* 1). I share Blackford's thesis about the role of Persephone in girls' fantasy literature and ask students to consider the persistence of the Persephone cycling narrative. This is not an immediately answerable question; rather, students receive a writing prompt to consider how *Harry Potter and the Chamber of Secrets*, one of the novels Blackford considers, invokes the myths of both Perseus and Persephone to address contemporary adolescence. Students recognize Moaning Myrtle and Ginny Weasley as obvious Persephone girls, socially isolated and underperforming at Hogwarts, thus seduced by Tom Riddle's offer of intimacy in the diary. But they often realize that Harry experiences the same feminine desire for closeness and interior connection through disclosure and revelations, which leads to his entrapment.

The maintenance of the Persephone myth in YA literature continues to beg the question about girl characters' limitations through fictional representations of either-or options that parallel the Demeter-Hades dynamic. Does the Persephone intertext persist because girls today are told they have many options when in fact there are two narrow paths, specifically those of the can-do girl and the at-risk girl? These are constructions of postfeminist girlhood theorized by Anita Harris, who recognizes the social forces that pressure girls to "succeed" through education, consumerism, career success, and delayed motherhood—and that discipline them if they stray onto the path of "risky" behavior, including behavior driven by appetites for too much sex, food, or drugs. Through its melodramatic extremes, the Twilight Saga responds to the pressures associated with these paths, especially the postfeminist demand that women stay ever youthful, articulated through Bella's anxiety about aging (see Kapurch, *Victorian*). With the Persephone context, students better appreciate Bella's passivity as a reaction to her social constraints, symbolized by the vampire-werewolf conflict. The appeal of the Twilight Saga, especially readers' empathy for Bella, then, may signal shared frustration with postfeminist demands.

The Persephone context is a good bridge to teach literary conventions associated with melodrama, the gothic, and romance; these genres are historically appealing to girls and woman, but often marginalized because of their gendered associations. Another twenty-first-century vampire text to pair with the Twilight Saga, especially in a discussion of postfeminism, is Cynthia Leitich Smith's *Tantalize*. Informed by *Dracula* and the Pygmalion myth, this novel features a girl who is rather isolated and friendless, like Bella, but who interacts with a villainous and unredeemable vampire. An end-of-term group research assignment might involve students locating scholarly articles on teen vampire texts to find points of agreement and disagreement in criticism, especially about issues related to gender, class, and race. This assignment, which could involve any topic, novel, or series related to adolescence or girls that has a rich body of scholarship, encourages students to engage with scholarship from a theoretically informed point of view.

This essay outlines a girls' studies pedagogy for YA literature, promoting a theoretical appreciation of girl authors, characters, and readers. I have selected some well-known exemplars because they have transferrable applications to more diverse and contemporary texts. A girls' studies approach encourages students to engage with the socially constructed categories of gender and age and to challenge their assumptions about girls and popular culture. More broadly, a girls' studies pedagogy develops students' rhetorical points of view in regard to literature and other media, whereby so-called literary merit or personal preferences are not necessary to critical engagement with a text.

Works Cited

Blackford, Holly Virginia. *The Myth of Persephone in Girls' Fantasy Literature*. Routledge, 2012.

———. *Out of This World: Why Literature Matters to Girls*. Teacher's College P, 2004.

"The British Invasion." Produced by Jonathan Buss. *The Sixties*, season 1, episode 6, Playtone, 2014.

Cart, Michael. *Young Adult Literature: From Romance to Realism*. American Library Association, 2010.

Cisneros, Sandra. *The House on Mango Street*. 1984. Vintage, 2013.

Daly, Maureen. *Seventeenth Summer*. Dodd, Mead, 1942.

Driscoll, Catherine. *Girls: Feminine Adolescence in Popular Culture and Cultural Theory*. Colombia UP, 2002.

Ehrenreich, Barbara, et al. "Beatlemania: Girls Just Want to Have Fun." *The Adoring Audience: Fan Culture and Popular Media*, edited by Lisa A. Lewis, Routledge, 1992, pp. 84–106.

Harris, Anita. *Future Girl: Young Women in the Twenty-First Century*. Routledge, 2004.

Hinton, S. E. *The Outsiders*. Viking, 1967.

Kapurch, Katie. "Crying, Waiting, Hoping: The Beatles, Girl Culture, and the Melodramatic Mode." *New Critical Perspectives on the Beatles: Things We Said Today*, edited by Kenneth Womack and Katie Kapurch, Palgrave Macmillan, 2016, pp. 199–220.

———. *Victorian Melodrama in the Twenty-First Century:* Jane Eyre, Twilight, *and the Mode of Excess in Popular Girl Culture*. Palgrave Macmillan, 2016.

Kearney, Mary Celeste. *Girls Make Media*. Routledge, 2006.

Meyer, Stephenie. *Breaking Dawn*. Little, Brown, 2008.

———. *Eclipse*. Little, Brown, 2007.

———. *New Moon*. Little, Brown, 2006.

———. *Twilight*. Little, Brown, 2005.

Myers, Walter Dean. *Street Love*. HarperCollins, 2006.

Rowling, J. K. *Harry Potter and the Chamber of Secrets*. Scholastic, 1999.

Smith, Cynthia Leitich. *Tantalize*. Candlewick Press, 2006.

Thury, Eva M., and Margaret K. Devinney. "Greece: Demeter and Persephone." *Introduction to Mythology: Contemporary Approaches to Classical and World Myths*, edited by Eva M. Thury and Margaret K. Devinney, Oxford UP, 2017, pp. 519–37.

Trites, Roberta Seelinger. *Disturbing the Universe: Power and Repression in Adolescent Literature*. U of Iowa P, 1998.

Warwick, Jacqueline. *Girl Groups, Girl Culture: Popular Music and Identity in the 1960s*. Routledge, 2007.

———. "You're Going to Lose That Girl: The Beatles and the Girl Groups." *Beatlestudies 3*, edited by Yrjö Heinonen et al., U of Jyväskylä Department of Music Research Reports, 2000, pp. 161–68.

Livia Antony and Padma Baliga

"Re-Presenting" Gender in Multicultural Young Adult Literature

In the last few decades, the theory of representation introduced by Stuart Hall has reinforced the idea that representation of the oppressed will lead to political change. Hall defines representation as "the production of the meaning of the concepts in our minds through language" ("Work" 17). The presence of hitherto underrepresented communities in the political arena, the economy, and popular culture is expected to eventually lead to societal change. The underlying assumption that a change in the discourse will lead to a change in meaning production has influenced conversations around gender, sexuality, race, and other contested areas. The transition of this theory from academia to popular culture has produced various narratives in film, fiction, theater, and advertising featuring black, queer, feminist, and female characters, gradually paving the way for increased representation of diversity.

In this essay, we examine one problematic aspect of this assumption: that the representation of women in different forms of popular culture serves as a solution for the various problems faced by women on account of their gender and will lead to a change in societal norms and expectations, an assumption disseminated by popular feminism. In her book *We Were Feminists Once*, Andi Zeisler defines *popular feminism* as "a mainstream, celebrity, consumer embrace that positions it as a cool, fun, accessible identity that anyone can adopt. . . . It's decontextualized. It's depoliticized" (16).

On a related topic, Cornel West argues in "The New Cultural Politics of Difference" that black artists are unable to represent themselves outside the binary of white supremacist thought; as othered groups, they "lack the power to present themselves to themselves and others as complex human beings" because of their assimilationist attitude and homogenizing impulses (261). West's essay serves as the basis of the argument that the "invisibility and namelessness" of the minority community engendered by the majoritarian can be countered through social engineering.

Like West, Judith Butler too argues that power structures and binaries in thought and the means of production do not allow for emancipation in any form (342). She contrasts "representation the practice" to "representation the language" and says that since the subject is formed through "discursive formation," it has no universal existence. Gender, for instance, is undercut by class, race, and other social formations. Butler delves into Luce Irigaray's concept of absence, in which the woman is marked by an absence in the phallogocentric language that produces the subject (348). Language and expression lie in the hands of the dominant by their very nature. The inability to define the subject, the dominant discourse through which it is produced, and the power structures surrounding it prevent "unity" and dialogue, argues Butler (352).

In order to examine representation and inequality, we focus on YA texts from India and Japan. The Indian texts are *Two States*, by the bestselling author Chetan Bhagat, and *Nirmala and Normala*, a graphic novel with two female protagonists. The Japanese texts we have chosen are two popular manga: *Fullmetal Alchemist* and *Attack on Titan*. Both are multivolume series, with the latter being an ongoing work. We shall examine the representation of gender identity and gender performance in these YA novels from two cultures and ask if the representation allows the othered to "re-present" themselves.

Subjectivity, Agency, and Limitations of Representation

The two Indian YA novels studied here share a relation with the Bollywood film industry. *Nirmala and Normala* was written by Sowmya Rajendran and Niveditha Subramaniam in response to "all the different kinds of daft heroines" they had seen over the years on the big screen (Rajendran and Subramaniam 6). *Two States*, like several of Bhagat's novels, has been made into a film. In India, gender constructs, roles, and expectations are shaped by an unlikely combination of traditional social norms and the film and television industry, leading the audience to experience firmly entrenched conventional modes of being. With an eye on the box office and popularity ratings, film and TV producers and directors are unwilling to create subversive content, and women are generally depicted in terms of an angel-siren binary. The heroine or the female lead has to be good-looking, virtuous, virginal, and heterosexual. Financial independence does not rule out emotional dependence on the man of the family, whether he is a father or husband. Most film narratives are told from the perspective of the man.

The plot of *Two States* begins with the hero at a psychotherapist's office, because "the patient has sleep-deprivation, has cut off human contact for a week, refuses to eat, has *Google*-searched on best ways to commit suicide," following his breakup with his girlfriend (1). Nowhere in the book is the woman's subjectivity explored. After the breakup, the man pleads with the woman to spend a couple of hours with him, and her response is a formal one: "it is not good for my parents' reputation" (for her to be seen with him).

Two States focuses on the struggle Ananya and Krish face in getting their parents to approve of their plans to marry, because they belong to different communities. At first, the story appears to subvert gendered expectations. In conventional Indian society, the bride's family works hard to ensure that the groom's family approves of the bride and the arrangements for the wedding. However, in this story, it is Krish who goes to a lot of trouble to ensure that his girlfriend's parents give their consent. He takes up a job in the city where Ananya lives with her family and sets out to win their respect. He helps her younger brother with his studies, her father with his business presentations at the office, and her mother with her ambitions of building up a career in music. Finally, holding four gold rings, he goes down on his knees and proposes to each of them. Young women in India who confront traditional modes of thinking every day and have to struggle for parental approval in most matters may find such behavior from the male protagonist unique.

On the other hand, the narrative attempts to slot the female character into a stereotypical role. Ananya studies at the Indian Institute of Management Ahmedabad, supposedly the most competitive of Indian business schools, but needs help from Krish to negotiate the terrain of algebra-based microeconomics. From mentoring her, Krish soon moves on to an attempted domination of her wardrobe choices, as when he objects to the length of her shorts. Later, when Ananya moves into Krish's room at the boys' hostel, his response is "it was kind of nice. She brought her electric kettle, sweet smile, and Maggi-making abilities with her" (29). After they graduate, Krish enters the banking industry, while Ananya joins the marketing department of a detergent company. In these instances, Bhagat reifies the woman as a domestic goddess, one who can spread harmony and happiness with her ability to smile and cook simultaneously. He makes use of highly codified familial roles that dictate that the woman cooks and the man has a high-paying job; the daughter studies humanities, while the son becomes an engineer. The idea of a woman as an intellectual and autonomous being is consigned to oblivion.

A mission to parody the film industry's obsessive use of stereotypes underpins the narrative of *Nirmala and Normala*, which begins with a plotline seen in several Indian films: twins who are separated at birth and lead diametrically different lives. Nirmala is adopted by a film director called GVM, and Normala is brought up in an orphanage run by nuns. Nirmala's name symbolizes purity, while Normala was named thus because the doctor the nuns consulted assured them that she was "completely normal" (13).

Nirmala lives a scripted celluloid life, with her wardrobe, behavior, and life choices determined by GVM's script—a metaphoric reference to the patriarchal control of women's lives. If her schedule for the day dictates that she has to play the role of an "intellectual woman," she has to wear a cotton sari, although it may be more practical to wear jeans or shorts. She picks a white sari because GVM has told her "she looks stunning in white" (18). Although rain is predicted, Nirmala steps out without an umbrella, as she doesn't own one. GVM's script ensures that she looks like a traditional Indian woman; she signifies purity in her white sari and appears both helpless and seductive when she walks in the rain without an umbrella and the white fabric reveals her curves. Through the figure of Nirmala, the authors critique the hegemonic construct of the Indian woman who is expected to be the bearer of tradition, culture, and nationalism, while also being the object of male sexual desire. She wears feminine and ethnic costumes and wins the approval of her boyfriend's father (an underworld don) by being devout, preparing a healthy, delicious breakfast, and worrying about his cholesterol and blood pressure. It is an excellent parody but not an effective one, for the critical lens is not internalized by Nirmala. At different points in the narrative, like any intelligent person, she questions the logic behind an action or event, but she continues to conform to the stereotype, as when she sets out without an umbrella and her boyfriend has to perform his rescue-the-damsel-in-distress act. Butler reminds us that gender is "an identity instituted through a *stylized repetition of acts*" (519), and Nirmala creates for herself the identity of the beautiful, virtuous, and fragile woman through repetitively performing her actions.

Normala is positioned by the authors as the girl next door. While the back cover presents Nirmala as the heroine who plays with street children and is Harvard educated, it also introduces her twin with these words: "As for Normala, well, we all know her, don't we?" The blurb implies that she is neither unusual nor complex and is therefore "knowable" by all. Normala chooses her clothes according to the weather and is not taken in by lovelorn admirers. She is unimpressed by one such young man's offer to jump off a bridge to prove his love for her, asking, "And of what use will that be to anyone?" (73). She makes a conscious effort to perform gender differently when she does not do things associated with the feminine. However, she appears to be trapped within the same patriarchal structures as Nirmala. When she hears that her boyfriend, Roobesh, is in a hospital, she thinks in terms of sacrifice and is ready to donate her blood. While earlier she had scoffed at Roobesh's taste in reading as being lowbrow, she now vows to read the books he likes. The resolution of her story occurs when she finds love in a happy union with her boyfriend. The slogan "Love and only love" appears in the concluding panel of both Normala's and Nirmala's stories. The presence of female protagonists has not led to a positive change, as neither is permitted to defy the norm that a girl cannot be happy by herself or step outside the bounds of heteronormativity.

The Beautiful Fighting Girl of Japanese Manga

Some forms of Japanese manga are considered YA fiction because they are written with a teen audience in mind and are very popular among young adult readers. However, *Attack on Titan* and *Fullmetal Alchemist* have received criticism for their dark themes. Both texts are set in an alternate universe, allowing the representation of gender to deviate from conventional gender norms. Susan Napier writes that "in the world of Japanese animation and manga, . . . we can find a particularly wide variety of masculine representations, ranging from realistic reflections of contemporary society to forms of wish fulfillment, to nightmarish projections of profound gender anxiety" (121). Napier's argument can be extended to representations of female characters as well.

Attack on Titan and *Fullmetal Alchemist* belong to the subgenre of *shonen* manga, the intended audience of which is young males. Interestingly, *shonen* manga makes use of well-rounded characters of both genders: female characters do not function as love interests alone and male protagonists question their own intentions to the point of anxiety. Female characters in manga are liberated and autonomous, for they are not only highly visible but also involved in the action of the story, and most important, they have an independent existence without having to rely on their relationship with a man. Conversely, when examined within the framework of Japanese cultural studies, the female characters in Japanese manga can also be problematized.

Attack on Titan, written by Hajime Isayama, is set in a postapocalyptic world where humans live enclosed within three circular walls to avoid being eaten by a race of giants called Titans. The lead characters are Eren Yeager, Mikasa Ackerman, and Armin Arlert, whose lives are changed when the Colossal Titan attacks their district. The story follows the trio from the destruction of their district to their exploits in the Scouting Legion, a wing of the army. When Eren discovers that he can turn into a Titan at will, the trio begins to uncover the secrets behind the Titans. This analysis focuses on the character of Mikasa Ackerman, the female protagonist.

Mikasa's mother is of Asian descent and her father belongs to the banished Ackerman clan, renowned for its martial skills. Her parents were killed when human traffickers attacked them to kidnap Mikasa for her exotic looks (2: 41). In the beginning, Mikasa is depicted as a feminine, peaceful, and dainty girl; she is othered and belongs to the lower class, living near the outer walls of the human world. However, with the death of her parents, Mikasa undergoes the transformation from ultrafeminine to *sentō bishōjo*, or "beautiful fighting girl." Katharine Kittredge describes the trope of the beautiful fighting girl as "young female characters who exhibit child-associated beauty (slender, prepubescent figure, large eyes, lustrous hair, and flawless skin). . . . [They] murder adult malefactors under the direction of male mentors who, if not biologically paternal, are nonetheless father figures to whom the little girls are deeply emotionally attached" (507). This description is based on the work of the Japanese critic

Tamaki Saitō, who identified this trope in manga and anime. Mikasa too shares some of these attributes. Her depiction is in line with the mode of the beautiful fighting girl along with the other female characters of the manga. Even though these characters are adolescent, the depictions do not change with their age. Mikasa is thus prefigured as the beautiful fighting girl for the text. The transformation from peaceful, dainty child to a beautiful fighting girl occurs when Eren commands her to fight the traffickers or die (2: 56). Saitō describes this as "a metaphor for accelerated maturity" (57). At his command, Mikasa unearths the power of the Ackerman clan in an instant (2: 62). She is able to remorselessly murder the traffickers. Mikasa eventually sees the transformation as a "debt" to repay Eren (1: 110). Later, Mikasa's identity is defined through her martial skills. She is the highest-performing cadet in the Scouting Legion, easily surpassing most of her peers. The arduous task of killing Titans proves easy for her. All of this would not have been possible without Eren's command, reinforcing the link to her selfhood.

Mikasa also deviates from the trope of the beautiful fighting girl in several ways. She takes on a familial and protective role, following Eren into the Scouting Legion because "Without me, you will die an early death" (1: 110). As Angela Drummond-Mathews and Deborah Scally point out, "Unlike that of the typical *shonen* manga plotline, the focus of *Attack on Titan* is often on the helplessness of the characters in an overwhelming situation. . . . Eren, the heroic center of the piece, is similarly helpless and unable to control his emotions or power" (7–8). Here, Mikasa is depicted as a levelheaded foil to Eren's impassioned character. Mikasa is devoted to Eren and refers to him as family (2: 97), but the devotion does not take on an Oedipal attachment, nor is he the father figure Kittredge writes of.

Equally significant in terms of representation is *Attack on Titan*'s inclusion of a lesbian couple, Krista and Ymir, in a subplot. It is rare to include LGBTQ+ characters in *shonen* manga because *yaoi*, *yuri*, and *bara* manga have traditionally been the genres in which those with queer identities are represented. *Attack on Titan* walks a fine line with the inclusion of Ymir and Krista. While it does not fetishize them, it does not directly label them as lesbians either. Another exceptional character is Zoë Hange, whose gender is hotly debated among fans. The Japanese language is nongendered, and Isayama has indicated that Zoë's character will not be gendered (Romano). It is a bold move on the author's part in contemporary Japan, where gender nonconforming children are diagnosed with gender identity disorder ("'Nail'"). Nonetheless, *Attack on Titan* devotes most of its story line to Eren, eclipsing the growth of the other characters mentioned here.

Hiromu Arakawa's *Fullmetal Alchemist* is set in an alternate universe where humans practice alchemy. The protagonists of the series are the Elric brothers, Edward (a State Alchemist) and Alphonse, who live in the highly militarized land of Amestris. Our focus is on two female characters in the series, General Olivier Mira Armstrong and Izumi Curtis.

As with most manga, Olivier Armstrong is depicted as a dainty woman belying the strength and power she wields. The commander of the most dangerous fortress in Amestris, she also defeats her younger brother, Alex Louis Armstrong, to gain the family inheritance (20: 172). During the coup that ends the series, it is the political strategy and manpower wielded by Olivier that decides the battle. Similarly, Izumi Curtis is depicted as petite, and she vomits blood when she overexerts herself. Yet she is physically strong and intelligent, terrifying the Elrics as their master (5: 118). Neither Olivier nor Izumi is devoted to the Elric brothers in the manner of the beautiful fighting girl. The notion of masculine strength is questioned through the depiction of Olivier's and Izumi's partners, who are depicted as huge, strong men; yet in their partnerships, it is the woman who is dominant. Olivier despises Alex for his weakness on the battlefield and she becomes the head of the family after defeating him. Izumi's husband, Sig Curtis, is portrayed as more compassionate toward the Elrics than Izumi. These bulky men display compassion, a variation that allows the women to be heartless.

Even within the complex representations of female characters in Japanese manga, Olivier and Izumi are special in their own right. They are mature women, not created to support the male protagonists of the story. Unlike Mikasa, Olivier is not just a soldier; she is also a brilliant tactician. Izumi proudly refers to herself as "a passing housewife," a departure from the prepubescent girl (5: 170). Within the phallogocentric language built around Japanese manga, Mikasa of *Attack on Titan* and other beautiful fighting girls are crippled by their need to identify with the male protagonist, but *Fullmetal Alchemist* subverts the tropes and allows female characters a representation that Indian and other YA literature has not been able to achieve. In addition, the story of the Elric brothers does not eclipse the other characters mentioned. Unlike Eren in *Attack on Titan*, the Elric brothers do not take on the villain single-handedly. In contravention of the trope of the hero, saving the world here is a joint effort, with all characters engaged in important roles.

Each of the texts discussed here represents gender by linking it to the cultural context from which the text derives. When representations are decontextualized, the presence of female characters within a text is sometimes assumed to be feminist. However, we argue that the mere presence of othered groups and genders does not guarantee that their representations will differ from existing modes. As Hall writes, "adding positive images to the largely negative repertoire of the dominant regime of representation increases the diversity of the ways in which 'being black' is represented, but does not necessarily displace the negative" ("Spectacle" 274). Apart from making them visible in the narrative, when oppressed groups do not have a role to play, they cannot exist as complex human beings. Thus, texts that are considered liberatory by popular culture standards often do not seem to move beyond the realms of phallogocentric language. Therefore, it is necessary to deliberate on whether popular feminism's emphasis on representation contributes to societal change.

Works Cited

Arakawa, Hiromu. *Fullmetal Alchemist.* Translated by Akira Watanabe, Yen Press, 2014. 27 vols.

Bhagat, Chetan. *Two States.* Rupa, 2009.

Butler, Judith. "Subjects of Sex/Gender/Desire." During, pp. 343–53.

Drummond-Mathews, Angela, and Deborah Scally. "A Phenomenology of Americans and Anime: How Tropes Predict Experience." *The Phoenix Papers*, vol. 2, no. 1, 2016, pp. 1–9.

During, Simon, editor. *The Cultural Studies Reader.* 2nd ed., Routledge, 1999.

Hall, Stuart, editor. *Representation: Cultural Representations and Signifying Practices.* Sage, 2003

———. "The Spectacle of the 'Other.'" Hall, *Representation*, pp. 223–90.

———. "The Work of Representation." Hall, *Representation*, pp. 13–74.

Isayama, Hajime. *Attack on Titan.* Translated by Sheldon Drzka, Kodansha Comics, 2012. 23 vols.

Kittredge, Katharine. "Lethal Girls Drawn for Boys: Girl Assassins in Manga/Anime and Comics/Film." *Children's Literature Association Quarterly*, vol. 39, no. 4, Winter 2014, pp. 506–32.

"'The Nail That Sticks Out Gets Hammered Down': LGBT Bullying and Exclusion in Japanese Schools." *Human Rights Watch*, 5 May 2016, www.hrw.org/report/2016/05/05/nail-sticks-out-gets-hammered-down/lgbt-bullying-and-exclusion-japanese-schools#page.

Napier, Susan J. *Anime from* Akira *to* Howl's Moving Castle*: Experiencing Contemporary Japanese Animation.* Rev. ed., Palgrave Macmillan, 2005.

Rajendran, Sowmya, and Niveditha Subramaniam. *Nirmala and Normala*. Penguin Books, 2014.

Romano, Aja. "'Attack on Titan' Creator Gets the Last Word in Debate over Character's Gender." *The Daily Dot*, 16 Jan. 2014, www.dailydot.com/parsec/fandom/attack-titan-snk-hange-hanji-gender-debate. Accessed 5 June 2017.

Saitō, Tamaki. *Beautiful Fighting Girl*. Translated by J. Keith Vincent and Dawn Lawson, U of Minnesota P, 2011.

West, Cornel. "The New Cultural Politics of Difference." During, pp. 256–67.

Zeisler, Andi. *We Were Feminists Once: From Riot Grrrl to Cover Girl®, the Buying and Selling of a Political Movement*. PublicAffairs, 2016.

Angel Daniel Matos

Subverting Normative Paradigms: Teaching Representations of Gender and Queerness in Young Adult Literature

When considering the fraught history of issues of gender and sexuality in YA literature, one will quickly realize that developing a politically viable framework to examine these issues is tricky. The production and marketing of YA texts are steeped in rigid conceptions of gender, sexuality, queerness, and the body, and it should come as no surprise that traditional and heteronormative ideologies have had a major influence in the field. Victoria Flanagan has explored YA literature's historical conservatism, in that it "has advocated sexual abstinence for young readers," and it often represents teens being punished "for expressing or acting upon this sexual desire" (28). Although Flanagan acknowledges that the circumstances of gender and sexuality have changed in contemporary YA texts, narratives that entirely disrupt hegemonic perspectives toward gender and sexuality are rare.

Many factors influence the uneasy relation between YA literature and radical approaches to gender and queerness, including the genre's target audience, its didactic aims, and, as Roberta Seelinger Trites has pointed out, its penchant for teaching adolescents "how to exist within the (capitalistically) bound institutions that necessarily define teenagers' existence"

(19). A YA novel may depict narratives that superficially seem groundbreaking and emancipatory from a gender or queer perspective, yet these same texts can also advance frameworks that endorse normative perspectives toward kinship and identity. Here, one of the main challenges of teaching YA literature centered on themes of gender, queerness, and sexuality emerges: while these texts may contain frameworks that are conceptually radical, they are nonetheless still part of a literary tradition focused on socialization, assimilation, and normative trajectories toward adulthood. YA literature with radical gender and queer themes is thus caught in a conundrum between the emancipatory potential of its ideological frameworks and the conservative impulse of the YA literary tradition.

Because this tension is not necessarily disadvantageous, this essay focuses on the anxieties between the field's traditions and radical frameworks, leading to more nuanced discussions about issues of gender and sexuality. Examining these topics is imperative in any discussion of YA literature, especially since most texts written for adolescent audiences are in some way connected to conversations about gender and sexuality. YA texts represent sexual awakenings, the exploration of characters' emerging sexualities, an understanding of characters' gender identities, and both the formation and rupture of kinship. Furthermore, the developmental state of adolescence thrives on notions such as the malleability and fluidity of identity—elements that are the cornerstone of contemporary gender and queer methodologies. By bringing gender, sexuality, and queerness to the forefront of discussions of YA literature, educators can better help students think rigorously about the relation between texts and cultural contexts. Moreover, this approach drives students to question binary modes of thinking and to challenge ideologies that lead to hierarchical discourse, central goals for an education focused on social equity and democratic thought.

Many students grow anxious when asked to unpack the gender and queer representation in the YA field. This uneasiness stems primarily from their fear of approaching concepts in the "wrong" fashion and from having little familiarity with discourse on gender and queerness. Students, however, are not alone in their apprehension. Many educators are also hesitant to discuss these topics in the classroom and to include YA novels with explicit gender, feminist, and queer themes in their classes. This reluctance is due to fear of potential backlash from parents, students, and administrators (see Bittner and Matos 99). Two fundamental questions thus arise: How does one provide students with the critical discourse to detect and critique both the radical and socializing impulses found in YA texts centered on gender, sexuality, and queerness? What texts and sources make students and educators more amenable to discussing radical approaches to gender, sexuality, and queerness in YA literature? To address these questions, the remainder of this essay will focus on a series of thematic approaches that offer suggestions for examining gender, sexuality, and queerness in YA texts. These brief accounts of how to contextualize discussions about gender and sexuality include considerations to keep in mind when designing a course. This discussion will limit itself to these three thematic approaches: deconstructing femininity and masculinity, examining representations of queerness, and framing the discussion of trans YA literature. These approaches are not the only ways educators could approach gender, sexuality, and queerness in YA literature. Nonetheless, they do model how to explore the issues of gender and sexuality that haunt YA literature and the culture that generates these texts.

Deconstructing Femininity and Masculinity

YA literature is quite conservative in terms of maintaining a distinction between traditional gender roles. Many YA books are heavily marketed to either boys or girls, and the content of these texts often focuses on gendered and heteronormative socialization. The conservative makeup of these texts exists because of the gender binary's prominence in Western cultures and because adults and sociocultural institutions regulate "the options offered individuals by creating narrow and rigid stereotypes and expectations" (Bean et al. 269). Although YA literature is conspicuously gendered, Thomas W. Bean and his coauthors suggest that educators can exploit the binary traits of the field and expose students to a diverse range of attitudes toward gender, thus "expanding and challenging gender stereotypes, and rigid gender socialization" (269). The key in dismantling binary approaches to masculinity and femininity rests in designing a curriculum that allows students to detect a spectrum of gender performance and identity, which can be achieved by including texts with characters that embody multiple and diverging gender and sexual roles.

When guiding students in understanding and dismantling the gender binary, educators should select texts that contain rich, fluid, and complex representations of gender performance. Suzanne Collins's Hunger Games series stands out in terms of this richness, mostly because the narrative inverts many of the practices and attitudes tethered to femininity and masculinity. Furthermore, the series heavily invests in the notion of performance and how people alter their behaviors in different sociocultural contexts. For instance, although the protagonist Katniss Everdeen performs roles that align her with stereotypical femininity, such as her motherly role with her sister and her contrived romance in the Hunger Games arena, she also engages in stereotypically male practices such as hunting, fighting, and leading. She also dons a stoic attitude that pressures her attachment to stereotypical femininity. Meghann Meeusen has suggested that the Hunger Games series exemplifies multiple perspectives toward selfhood and gender construction, in that it examines the "social anxiety about breaking down binaries between constructed and embodied self by melding the cognitive with culturally constructed forces" (45), thus dismantling the divide that is often imposed between social influences and personal, embodied experiences. Similarly, Jennifer Mitchell suggests that characters such as Katniss challenge the gender binary's validity, since her ability "to negotiate, try on, and experiment with various gender roles is a testament to the lack of stable substance underneath them" (129). In other words, Katniss's embodiment of practices and attitudes that are stereotypically masculine and feminine highlights the constructed nature of these gendered associations. Here, the YA text itself mobilizes a fairly radical, antibinary gender framework that is relatively easy for students to detect.

Pairing Mitchell's and Meeusen's pieces with the Hunger Games series can help students to understand how the novel makes an overt case for the constructed and arbitrary properties associated with femininity and masculinity. Although the novel dismantles the cultural divide imposed upon masculinity and femininity, educators must nonetheless assure that students do not simply praise the text as one that is entirely emancipatory in its gender representation. Meeusen, for instance, argues that while Katniss and her counterpart, Peeta, seem to invert the binary between embodiment and external forces, the series nonetheless reinforces a traditional dynamic in YA dystopias in which a "female character must save the male made victim to cognitive manipulation" and which leads readers to potentially approach the novel's gender framework as "misguided feminism" (58). Another way to frustrate the series' gender representation would be to ask students to reflect on how *Mockingjay*'s epilogue burdens the gender malleability that Katniss embodies and how she sacrifices it entirely when becoming an adult.

The purpose of complicating a novel's gender representation works two ways. First, it provides opportunities to explore the complex merger between a radical gender framework and a narrative geared toward socialization. During discussions of gender performance, for instance, students can explore whether YA literature presents gender fluidity as a provisional practice that must be disregarded in adulthood. Second, students can be taught to recognize how a single text can be both freeing and restricting in terms of its gender politics. When approaching and dismantling binary approaches to gender, educators must push students to think through the cultural negotiations YA literature undergoes to depart, even slightly, from its assimilative tendencies. Fortunately, the field has become more amenable to disrupting binary and normative approaches to gender and sexuality, especially with the recent boom in YA novels focused on queer and trans experience.

Examining Representations of Queerness

Broadly speaking, queer approaches are antiauthoritarian: they reject the demand for social assimilation and they advocate for difference rather than sameness. This counterhegemonic tendency complicates the implementation of queer approaches in YA literature centered on lesbian, gay, bisexual, trans, and queer (LGBTQ+) experience, especially since teachers and scholars often expect LGBTQ+ youth literature to depict successful acts of normative socialization. In *The Heart Has Its Reasons*, Michael Cart and Christine A. Jenkins commend contemporary YA novels with LGBT themes for representing the "increasing opportunities for assimilation that occur after the dramatic moment of coming out" (165). This penchant for assimilation is just one of the many ways in which YA literature pushes its readership to exist within capitalistically bound institutions—in this case, the institution of heteronormativity. Thomas Crisp suggests that while queer YA texts are affirmative in that they articulate ideas about sexual orientation and desire that are frequently silenced, they also "rely on heteronormative constructions of romance" and sexuality that ultimately work "to continue the invisibility of [queer characters] by filtering queer existence" (345). There has been an obvious increase in LGBTQ+ representation in contemporary YA literature; however, this representation often champions normative and neoliberal values such as monogamy, assimilation, linear growth, financial success, and lifelong relationships, which complicate the field's queer potentialities.

This double bind can be historicized in class discussions. Contemporary queer YA texts in the United States, for instance, are being published during a moment that is seemingly progressive from an institutional perspective, especially with the declared unconstitutionality of the Defense of Marriage Act and the legalization of same-sex marriage. But despite this putative progress, there have also been a rise in trans and queer murder victims, disputes over bathroom rights and privileges, and tragic events such as the Pulse nightclub shooting of 2016. People disagree over the extent to which conditions have improved for LGBTQ+ communities in the United States. This disagreement has become even more contentious in discussions of queer youth culture and literature, especially with the prominence of efforts such as Dan Savage's *It Gets Better* project, founded in 2010, in which LGBTQ+ adults use social media to share personal narratives about how their lives improve once they cross the threshold into adulthood. While scholars such as Derritt Mason have succinctly pointed out the political failures of this project, especially in terms of its reliance on narratives of success and assimilation that ignore the oppression and violence that LGBTQ+ people face, queer YA literature still relies on disseminating narratives in which queer adolescents' lives improve with time and age.

Ethical discussions of queer YA literature in the classroom demand a framing of the field through this historical moment, one that contextualizes both the benefits and drawbacks of assimilative approaches to LGBTQ+ culture and literature. To facilitate this discussion, one must ask students to determine how a queer YA text responds to its contemporary cultural and political climate. Does the text illustrate an instance of successful socialization? If a text depicts an *It Gets Better* narrative, does it nonetheless illustrate the oppression, violence, and fear often tethered to queer experience? What are the gains and losses of narratives that focus solely on the "positive," homonormative aspects of queer life? Students develop more rigorous and complex answers to these questions if they have access to literature that addresses multiple perspectives. For instance, a narrative that focuses on the coming-out process of a middle-to-upper-class white gay teen, such as Becky Albertalli's *Simon vs. the Homo Sapiens Agenda*, might yield very different answers to these questions from a narrative focused on the experience of a queer lower-class Latinx teen, such as Adam Silvera's *More Happy Than Not*. If educators include enough texts in their curricula that address sexuality through an intersectional lens, students can detect how other domains of identity, such as race, class, and gender, inflect representations of queerness.

Offering students a singular narrative of queer experience that prioritizes successful and effortless attempts for teen characters to come to terms with their sexual orientation is too simplistic. Teaching narratives that prioritize the representation of successful acts of socialization and coming out comes at the cost of impeding access to queer narratives that more holistically tackle the tribulations attached to queer experience. The stakes of teaching multiple and diverging narratives, particularly ones that highlight the moments of oppression, discrimination, and failure, are also pressing when teaching trans YA literature in the classroom.

Framing the Discussion of Trans Young Adult Literature

In conversations about gender and sexuality in YA literature, texts with trans themes and characters provide a profound way to dismantle normative thinking. Many students find it difficult to explore trans literature, however, because they have no previous engagement with literary, cultural, or scholarly texts that represent or examine trans experience. This is partly due to the lack of trans representation in cultural productions. Further complicating this issue, many educators compartmentalize discussions of trans experience and identity, therefore leading students to approach trans issues as marginal to broader understandings of gender and sexuality in the YA field. Hilary Malatino points out how trans marginalization is a looming concern in discussions of gender and sexuality in the classroom, in that some educators believe it is "pedagogically effective to have discussed one, ostensibly paradigmatic trans life narrative, and then move on with the curriculum," which can lead to the issue of "referencing one particular narrative as the 'trans take' on certain ideas" (400). No one trans narrative is sufficient to communicate the particularities and complexities of trans life and experience (which can also be said of any character that belongs to any racial, ethnic, sexual, gender, or class minority). The line between curricular inclusivity and tokenization is a fine one.

Many authors and scholars are wary of issues of tokenization and how it can lead people to approach trans representations in a monolithic fashion. Meredith Russo, in the author's note in her trans YA novel *If I Was Your Girl*, shares her fears on this matter: "I'm worried that you might take [the protagonist's] story as gospel, especially since it comes from a trans woman" (275). Including more than one trans narrative in the curriculum is thus imperative, and these texts should have very different representations of what trans adolescence is and looks like. Educators can nuance understandings of trans experience, for instance, by pairing Russo's realist novel with Anna-Marie McLemore's magical realist novel *When the Moon Was Ours.* One of the main characters in McLemore's novel partakes in the cultural practice of *bacha posh*, where certain Middle Eastern families without a son select a daughter who temporarily lives as a boy. This character desires to continue living as a boy despite the temporal limitations of the *bacha posh* practice. By reading these novels together, students can think through differences between Western and non-Western modes of trans experience, especially in terms of how culture inflects understandings of trans identity and how there is no singular truth when it comes to trans life.

Malatino further points out that the trans narratives that are frequently included in the curriculum are "unthreatening" stories that represent "coming out as a movement toward self-acceptance and love," which risk omission of the broader, institutional forms of exclusion that affect trans lives (400). This issue is tied to the central conflict between radical queer frameworks and the socializing bent of YA literature; it can be further contextualized through discussion of the *It Gets Better* narrative in queer youth narratives. Given that contemporary trans YA literature focuses almost exclusively on neoliberal narratives of success and self-acceptance, how can one use these texts to push students to rigorously engage with radical trans thought? One of Malatino's suggestions is to implement a genealogical approach to trans texts that frames "the historical emergence of identity categories" (403). Malatino recommends David Valentine's *Imagining Transgender* as a solid foundation for discussing this genealogy. The first chapter of this book is useful for students who have little knowledge of trans issues and history, mostly because Valentine's work nuances the commonalities and tensions between trans and queer identity categories and their institutionalization.

Educators who pair trans YA literature with genealogical scholarship aid students in developing contexts that allow them to critique trans YA narratives. In reading historical and sociological accounts of trans identity and culture, students develop an awareness of how these communities have changed over the years and how they overlap and come into conflict with others placed under the LGBTQ+ umbrella. Cis students can also grow more comfortable discussing trans characters when they have a viable framework they can rely on. Last, this pairing helps students develop an awareness of the history of oppression and violence that has haunted—and continues to haunt—trans and queer lives. Grappling with this history can elevate discussions of trans YA literature and spark vital discussions about whether "unthreatening" trans coming-of-age stories are contributing to an erasure of those trans narratives that do not communicate conservative or neoliberal values. Such a discussion is useful, for instance, in examining Russo's novel. Students have a framework to explore the ideologies that inform the characterization of the protagonist of *If I Was Your Girl*, especially since this character can pass as cisgender and has access to the economic means to facilitate her medical transition. This framework can also spark important conversations in YA-centric courses, such as the extent to which trans YA novels have a responsibility to represent the oppression and violence looming in the trans community and the benefits and drawbacks of a trans YA novel that ends in a traditionally successful and happy fashion.

Subverting Paradigms

YA literature can be an effective platform for students to discuss the fraught issues of gender, sexuality, and normativity in both real and fictional worlds. Enabling these discussions, however, involves more than simply including texts that represent one perspective of these issues. Educators must be frank with students about the tensions that exist between radical queer frameworks and the assimilative, socializing traditions of the YA field. Unpacking this tension starts with curricular design, in that one must select a wide range of texts that assist students in detecting and framing the double binds that characterize YA literature. Educators should also emphasize how analyses of gender and sexuality in YA literature are rarely simple or straightforward: a text that initially seems emancipatory might ultimately be one that is harmful from a radical, antioppressive, democratic perspective.

Discussing issues of gender, sexuality, and queerness is rarely an easy task in any context. These issues are polarizing; people have different attitudes and, at times, simply do not possess the language or knowledge needed to discuss these issues in the first place. Fortunately, providing students with complex representations of gender, opportunities to historicize readings, and genealogical and ethnographic scholarship makes these conversations richer because students gain a language and theoretical framework on which to rely. Furthermore, if educators refute the tendency to default to tokenism in approaching gender and sexual identity, and instead offer students a range of literary representations that depict different prospects for existing and mattering in both real and fictional worlds, then students have the potential to grasp the complexities of gender and sexuality in YA literature. The subversion of normative paradigms is not a practice that is learned overnight. However, educators can take advantage of the didactic bent of YA literature and the tensions that it thrives on as a field to invite students to think radically and queerly—and more rigorously—about the texts they read and the world they inhabit.

Works Cited

Albertalli, Becky. *Simon vs. the Homo Sapiens Agenda*. Balzer and Bray, 2016.

Bean, Thomas W., et al. *Teaching Young Adult Literature: Developing Students as World Citizens*. Sage, 2014.

Bittner, Robert, and Angel Daniel Matos. "Fear of the Other: Exploring the Ties between Gender, Sexuality, and Self-Censorship in the Classroom." *The ALAN Review*, vol. 44, no. 1, Fall 2016, pp. 98–104.

Cart, Michael, and Christine A. Jenkins. *The Heart Has Its Reasons: Young Adult Literature with Gay/Lesbian/Queer Content, 1969–2004*. Scarecrow Press, 2006.

Collins, Suzanne. *Catching Fire*. Scholastic, 2009.

———. *The Hunger Games*. Scholastic, 2008.

———. *Mockingjay*. Scholastic, 2010.

Crisp, Thomas. "From Romance to Magical Realism: Limits and Possibilities in Gay Adolescent Fiction." *Children's Literature in Education*, vol. 40, no. 4, Dec. 2009, pp. 333–48.

Flanagan, Victoria. "Girls Online: Representations of Adolescent Female Sexuality in the Digital Age." *Gender(ed) Identities*, edited by Tricia Clasen and Holly Hassel, Routledge, 2017, pp. 28–41.

Malatino, Hilary. "Pedagogies of Becoming: Trans Inclusivity and the Crafting of Being." *Transgender Studies Quarterly*, vol. 2, no. 3, Aug. 2015, pp. 395–410.

Mason, Derritt. "On Children's Literature and the (Im)Possibility of It Gets Better." *English Studies in Canada*, vol. 38, nos. 3–4, 2012, pp. 83–104.

McLemore, Anna-Marie. *When the Moon Was Ours*. Thomas Dunne Books, 2016.

Meeusen, Meghann. "Hungering for Middle Ground: Binaries of Self in Young Adult Dystopia." *The Politics of Panem: Challenging Genres*, edited by Sean P. Connors, Sense, 2014, pp. 45–64.

Mitchell, Jennifer. "Of Queer Necessity: Panem's Hunger Games as Gender Games." *Of Bread, Blood and The Hunger Games: Critical Essays on the Suzanne Collins Trilogy*, edited by Mary F. Pharr and Leisa A. Clark, McFarland, 2012, pp. 128–38.

Russo, Meredith. *If I Was Your Girl.* Flatiron Books, 2016.
Silvera, Adam. *More Happy Than Not.* Soho Teen, 2016.
Trites, Roberta Seelinger. *Disturbing the Universe: Power and Repression in Adolescent Literature.* U of Iowa P, 2000.
Valentine, David. *Imagining Transgender: An Ethnography of a Category.* Duke UP, 2007.

Melanie Goss

Teaching Transgressive Texts

Teaching transgressive and controversial literature is a challenge at any level, as the instructor must help students overcome the sensationalism of the text and recognize its worth separate from its shock value. This essay explores teaching transgressive YA literature not only as a vehicle for the basics of literary analysis but also as a tool for illuminating and challenging those social structures that affect how people grow into adulthood. I draw on my experiences teaching a specialized course in YA literature that focused on the depiction of self-harming activities, such as disordered eating and self-cutting behaviors. Students examined texts such as Beatrice Sparks's *Go Ask Alice*, Patricia McCormick's *Cut*, and Laurie Halse Anderson's *Wintergirls*. While I specifically focus on texts that address counternormative approaches to mental health and illness, the activities and discussion points that I discuss here can also be applied to many other social issues.

For the purposes of this essay, I use *transgressive literature* as an umbrella term to describe those texts that explicitly address activities or ideologies that are widely considered to be antisocial, countercultural, or dangerous to the shared beliefs of society. Most commonly, transgressive literature directed at young adults focuses on drug and alcohol use and abuse, self-harm, nonnormative or "promiscuous" sexual behavior, and violent acts. Some texts are sensationalistic, while others are more nuanced and realistic; some characterize teens as immoral for their actions, while others interrogate larger power structures in young people's lives. Regardless of the stance these texts take, their attention to these controversial topics situates them as tools for productive classroom engagement.

Teaching Critical Literacy with Young Adult Literature

In *Empowering Education*, Ira Shor defines the values of critical literacy as those skills that move beyond "surface meaning, first impressions, dominant myths, official pronouncements, traditional clichés, received wisdom, and mere opinions, to understand the deep meaning, root causes, social context, ideology, and personal consequences of any action, event, object, process, organization, text, subject matter, policy, mass media, or discourse" (129). My goals fit seamlessly with Shor's definition of critical literacy, especially in how I teach transgressive literature, which by its very nature is teeming with the types of "dominant myths" and "traditional clichés" that Shor mentions.

What sets critical pedagogy apart from other pedagogical models that emphasize critical thinking and the basis for existing power structures is that critical pedagogy "would never find it sufficient to reform the habits of thought of thinkers, however effectively, without challenging and transforming the institutions, ideologies, and relations that engender distorted, oppressed thinking in the first place—not as an additional act beyond the pedagogical one, but as an inseparable part of it" (Burbules and Berk 52). I believe that having students put in the mental work toward understanding the behaviors presented in certain YA texts fosters respect for those conditions and helps students gain empathy, which are the first steps in creating active social change. I do not wish to make the argument that there is no value to transgressive YA literature apart from its utilitarian purpose of helping troubled young readers; the social, aesthetic, and literary qualities of these texts are important on their own merit. However, YA texts featuring characters engaged in self-destructive behavior patterns are often indicative of larger cultural trends about mental health and illness, deviancy, and ownership of the body.

I teach literature involving self-destructive behavior patterns in an effort to increase students' understanding of a pressing social problem that affects many young people. I recognize, however, that my goal is not one that is widely prioritized. Criticisms of YA trends often focus on the apparent increase in texts that graphically address the darker aspects of young people's lives. In "Darkness Too Visible," an op-ed piece published in *The Wall Street Journal* in 2011, Meghan Cox Gurdon laments that, in YA literature, "pathologies that went undescribed in print 40 years ago, that were still only sparingly outlined a generation ago, are now spelled out in stomach-clenching detail." Gurdon is certainly accurate in her assessment; YA literature, like nearly every other form of entertainment, has becoming increasingly graphic over time. But I part ways with her about the conclusions she draws based on the "darkness" of the texts. Despite arguments about morality and appropriateness that surround the field of literature for young people, I maintain that these texts are worthwhile as both artistic works and social artifacts, if they are handled in a way that does not trivialize or sensationalize their content and aims.

Establishing Student Support

In my classes, I use a disability studies framework to approach issues of mental health and illness, focusing specifically on self-destructive behavior patterns (eating disorders, self-cutting, drug abuse, and the like), as they are represented in a variety of YA media. This range of topics works especially well for my goals in engaging students with transgressive literature, as students typically enter the classroom with strong preexisting notions about "crazy" and "sane." Thus, it is useful to situate these assumptions in the larger context of culturally sanctioned or socially deviant behavior. As I consider the implications of teaching transgressive literature, especially to an audience typically consisting of preservice teachers who are hesitant to engage with material they think may be harmful to young people, I find it useful to foreground the political nature of education before moving on to discussions of such controversial texts in the classroom. In his consideration of critical pedagogy and classroom curriculum, Shor writes, "No curriculum can be neutral. All forms of education are political because they can enable or inhibit the questioning habits of students, thus developing or disabling their critical relation to knowledge, schooling, and society" (12–13). By encouraging students to verbalize their understanding of the sociopolitical agenda of teaching literature, students are better able to think critically about the ways that the literature itself may either uphold or subvert those agendas.

To better facilitate a critical approach to the material, I make my aims clear to my students at the beginning of the semester by engaging them in a discussion about their assumptions about self-destructive behaviors. By starting with an open discussion of their own experiences, prejudices, and beliefs, we can begin the semester with a careful consideration of the world as we perceive it to be, thus avoiding the common outcry against "reading too much into it" when we begin our consideration of the world as it is represented in text. Students can then see why it is necessary to be aware of the impact of stereotypes and to have a critical understanding of social issues; by viewing texts as cultural products instead of isolated entities, students become more willing to engage in careful reading of the way their fictional peers are represented. The initial discomfort that many students feel in discussing self-destructive behavior mirrors larger cultural trends about the increasing visibility of people living with mental illnesses and how this presence influences American society. Many students enter the classroom with little knowledge of the realities of mental illnesses apart from what they see in horror films and on cable news; those who do have personal knowledge of mental illness are often hesitant to speak about their experiences because of this stigma.

Transgressive literature is controversial by its very nature, but the YA author Rachel Cohn argues that controversial YA books are beneficial to readers because they must abandon passive reading in favor of learning to question the characters' actions and imagine different ways that the characters might behave. Cohn asserts, "Reading controversial YA literature . . . will get students thinking not just on a selfish level—how does this apply to me?—but just as the classics can introduce students to the great ideas that have been debated throughout history, study of YA literature allows teens access to an important developmental tool in their emotional maturity" (18). Such reading strategies, which encourage students to avoid simply reading themselves into the role of the teen character and instead to think critically about the ways the character is presented and alternatives to the character's actions, are useful in helping readers understand the construction of the text and the ideologies the author may be trying to establish, reinforce, or challenge.

Having students practice thoughtful distance from the text is especially useful in helping them question the assumptions that the author reproduces in order to create an "authentic" story. Mike Cadden posits that YA literature is ironic because it is always written by an adult mimicking, with greater or lesser degrees of success, the teen voice. Cadden writes,

"Novels constructed by adults to simulate an authentic adolescent's voice are inherently ironic because the so-called adolescent voice is never—and can never be—truly authentic" (146). Because many of the students in my survey courses for YA literature are teens or still consider themselves to be adolescents, understanding this ironic distance between the adolescent character and the adolescent reader has been helpful to me when encouraging students to read critically. Once I discuss this ironic relationship with students, they become more aware of the ways that their demographic is being presented by adults, and many of them push back against these texts that promise characters who are meant to be "just like them."

Fostering Productive Classroom Discussion

When I first designed a course on transgressive YA literature, a major learning outcome that I had in mind was for students to leave with a greater understanding of self-destructive behaviors and the purposes they serve, maladaptive though they may be. This gray area is where many people start to get uncomfortable, as many people binarize mental health in terms of sanity or insanity. I want my students to understand that texts can perpetuate or challenge dominant ideologies of mental illness and to consider what the impacts of these narratives may be.

Of course, the inclusion of intentionally subversive material in the curriculum of the literature classroom is not without its problems. The teacher is neither a psychologist nor a counselor, nor should she be. Despite the current controversy surrounding so-called trigger warnings, I find that it is not at all intrusive to simply inform students ahead of time that a text may include depictions of physical or sexual violence. In fact, being considerate of students' histories and sensitivities is a clear way to model social behaviors that are respectful of individuals' unique psychological needs, thus reinforcing the goals of the course.

Furthermore, I clearly state the aims of the course at the beginning of the semester. I want students to be aware of what they will be doing and why and the concepts that make this endeavor an appropriate one for the literature classroom. I therefore collaboratively draft ground rules for student conduct and respect early in the semester, and together, the students and I are responsible for making sure the classroom environment is one of safety and mutual respect. Two of the most basic procedures that I have in place for all class discussions are to respond to other students by name and to speak directly to other students, not just to me as the professor. This encourages students to ground their arguments in discussions of real people whom they actually know, instead of resorting to stereotypical generalizations about nonnormative behavior and the people who engage in it.

To that end, when students feel that their experiences are respected, they are more willing to speak up for themselves when those experiences are questioned. For example, a student who lived with bulimia as a young teen once expressed her frustration with the unfounded generalizations many of her classmates were making about people with eating disorders: that they were infantile, that they just needed to "get over it," or that they should "grow up." In an email to me, the student wrote, "By the end of class after listening to the responses going back and forth between people I just could not keep quiet anymore. I was not sure what to say really but I just wanted to say something to make people realize its [*sic*] real and happening to people around them[,] not just in the novels and documentaries chosen for class." In a later email, she wrote, "Sometimes I hate hearing what people have to say but I am getting better with it. I like to think that even though they may not really understand it, they are at least now more aware of the world around them." I appreciated that this student who had intimate knowledge of self-harm was able to help other students become more critical of their unquestioned assumptions.

To move students beyond their own experiences and into a complex consideration of transgressive texts, I have them begin the semester by reading *Go Ask Alice*, a novel that is advertised as the diary of an actual drug-addicted teen but is in fact a work of fiction by Sparks, a social worker with ties to the Church of Jesus Christ of Latter-Day Saints. By beginning the class with this example of blatantly didactic and sensationalized fiction, the students immediately had the experience of reading a text with a skeptical eye, alert for the places where the adult author might be trying to push her own views on teens. Students react fairly uniformly to *Go Ask Alice*, and their recognition of the text's fearmongering helps them identify and analyze its stereotypes, hyperboles, and explicit ideological aims without much assistance on my part. My students recognize the didactic voice of the teen focalizer as not only inauthentic but also intentionally deceptive.

After "warming up" with a moralistic and sensationalized narrative, students then approach more legitimately transgressive literature with greater skill. By the end of the semester, we read and discuss some very complex and challenging texts, and student opinion on the matter of self-destruction tends to become far more divided. After we complete reading Anderson's *Wintergirls*, a novel about a young woman with anorexia, I ask students to consider the ways that Western standards of beauty are shown to influence the main character's struggle with her appearance. In doing so, students must interrogate larger social distinctions between behavior characterized as "normal" and that which is "transgressive," focusing especially on those gray areas where the lines are not as clear. In one particular class, what students ultimately settled on as a class definition was that self-harm only "counts" as self-harm when it is not considered socially acceptable to the broader public. Thus, cosmetic surgery, despite its potential for severe complications, is not self-destructive because it is meant to lead to a more socially desirable body, but extreme tattooing is self-destructive because to many people, especially in older generations, it is looked upon as deviant. Students don't consider dieting to be self-harm until the dieter is no longer considered attractive, and self-cutting is always self-harm even though simple ear piercing is not. Working through the complexity of these distinctions allows my students to discuss at length the countless ways that issues of beauty, mental illness, and self-harm are culturally constructed and intertwined, and it helps my students to think deeply about the liminal spaces that abound in the consideration of such topics. In linking their previous goals and passions with their newfound understanding of YA texts, self-destructive behavior, and how texts can reinforce or subvert dominant ideologies, students gain the ability and knowledge necessary to enter the world outside the classroom as critical readers of texts and informed agents of social change.

Using Discomfort Generatively

In *Teaching against the Grain*, Roger Simon writes that critical pedagogy is "the specific task of constructing educational practices that might help students challenge and assess existing social conventions, modes of thought, and relations of power" (35). If we accept this as an appropriate goal, then pedagogical theory and practice must be inherently political, a counter-discursive activity that attempts to provoke a process through which people might engage in a transformative critique of their everyday lives. This means addressing the supposed naturalness of dominant ways of seeing, saying, and doing by provoking a consideration of why things are the way they are, how they got to be that way, in what ways change might be desirable, and what it would take for things to be otherwise.

As an undergraduate English education major, I was taught that the only way to reach my students was to ensure that they felt comfortable and secure in the classroom. As my own education progressed, however, I found that the times I learned the most were the times when my worldview and assumptions were deeply shaken. I was forced to craft a coherent argument for why I believed what I did or to rethink my beliefs altogether. These instances were profoundly uncomfortable and went against everything I had learned as a prospective teacher, but I learned to embrace these feelings of discomfort as necessary steps toward opening my eyes to what was going on around me.

Now, as an instructor, my research into pedagogical theory validates my emotional experience as a student. In their essay "Discomforting Truths: The Emotional Terrain of Understanding Difference," Megan Boler and Michalinos Zembylas theorize what they term the *pedagogy of discomfort*, which

> emphasizes the need for both the educator and students to move outside of their comfort zones. By comfort zone we mean the inscribed cultural and emotional terrains that we occupy less by choice and more by virtue of hegemony. . . . The comfort zone reflects emotional investments that by and large remain unexamined because they have been woven into the everyday fabric of what is considered common sense. (111)

This is not to say that I actively try to make my students anxious or on edge; instead, I aim to foster open conversation about topics that are rarely publicly discussed, for "issues of oppression (racial, gender, sexual or otherwise) are frequently dealt with by silence and omission that stems from ignorance or feelings of discomfort for what is different" (Boler and Zembylas 129). We talk at length about self-injury, eating disorders, and suicide, all of which are by their nature usually private acts. In class, we discuss at length the ways that narrative structure functions to convey ideologies, and students become attentive to the differences between the sensationalized problem novels and the more nuanced texts we read later in the term. Literary analysis informed by critical pedagogy is "grounded in critique as a mode of analysis that interrogates texts, institutions, social relations, and ideologies as part of the script of official power" (Giroux 4). Medical power is part of this, and students become quite adept at noting how dominant discourses of mental illnesses perpetuate diagnostic imbalances and unequal treatment.

In *Social Issues in the English Classroom*, Samuel Totten argues that a key reason to include controversial public issues in the English curriculum is "to provide the means and abilities for students to examine their lives, to assist them in pondering and thoroughly assessing why they think and believe as they do, and to engender wide-awakeness so they can act on their new-found knowledge and awareness" (11). Not only are these texts helpful in getting students to discuss and think critically about their beliefs and assumptions, but they can also serve a vital role in the development of students' identities. We owe it to our students to encourage them to think critically about social concepts of adolescents and adolescences and to shape our teaching in a way that does not ignore the issues that may affect them deeply.

Works Cited

Anderson, Laurie Halse. *Wintergirls.* Viking, 2009.

Boler, Megan, and Michalinos Zembylas. "Discomforting Truths: The Emotional Terrain of Understanding Difference." *Pedagogies of Difference: Rethinking Education for Social Change*, edited by Peter Pericles Trifonas, RoutledgeFalmer, 2003, pp. 110–36.

Burbules, Nicholas C., and Rupert Berk. "Critical Thinking and Critical Pedagogy: Relations, Differences, and Limits." *Critical Theories in Education: Changing Terrains of Knowledge and Politics*, edited by Thomas S. Popkewitz and Lynn Fendler, Routledge, 1999, pp. 45–66.

Cadden, Mike. "The Irony of Narration in the Young Adult Novel." *Children's Literature Association Quarterly*, vol. 25, no. 3, Fall 2000, pp. 146–54.

Cohn, Rachel. "Teens, Teachers, and Controversial Text." *The ALAN Review*, vol. 31, no. 3, Summer 2004, pp. 16–19.

Giroux, Henry A. *On Critical Pedagogy.* Continuum, 2011.

Gurdon, Meghan Cox. "Darkness Too Visible." *The Wall Street Journal*, 4 June 2011, www.wsj.com/articles/SB100014240527023036574045763576 22592697038.

McCormick, Patricia. *Cut.* Scholastic, 2000.

Shor, Ira. *Empowering Education: Critical Teaching for Social Change.* U of Chicago P, 1992.

Simon, Roger I. *Teaching against the Grain: Texts for a Pedagogy of Possibility.* Bergin and Garvey, 1992.

Sparks, Beatrice. *Go Ask Alice.* Simon and Schuster, 1971.

Totten, Samuel. "Educating for the Development of Social Consciousness and Social Responsibility." *Social Issues in the English Classroom*, edited by C. Mark Hurlbert and Samuel Totten, National Council of Teachers of English, 1992, pp. 9–55.

Jon M. Wargo and Laura Apol

But I Can't Use This in a *Classroom*! Teaching Risky/Risqué Young Adult Literature

As scholar-activists and teacher educators who actively seek to promote culturally sustaining pedagogies (Paris and Alim) in our prospective teachers, we see the teaching of YA literature as one tool to decolonize the imagination. We regularly start our courses with bell hooks's "Narratives of Struggle," and our syllabi communicate our intent by opening with hooks's passage:

> Critical fictions emerge when the imagination is free to wander, explore, question, transgress. . . . Thinking about the imagination in subversive ways, not seeing it as pure, uncorrupted terrain, we can ask ourselves under what condition and in what ways can the imagination be decolonized. Globally, literature that enriches resistance struggles speaks about the way individuals in repressive, dehumanizing situations use imagination to sustain life and maintain critical awareness. (55)

Although we consider YA literature a potential "critical fiction," our attempts to decolonize the imagination and interrogate the archetype of school and teaching (e.g., what should be taught, who our students are, what role English curricula has in the shaping of society) are often met with simplistic rather than deep literary engagement and are frequently overshadowed by larger social and cultural issues.

In our university teaching, we often experience a tension between our view of YA literature as critical fiction and the desire our students express to focus primarily on the pedagogical possibilities of literature. When confronted with texts that transgress perceived boundaries or subvert the status quo (and thus hold the possibility of decolonizing the imagination), students in our YA literature courses often resist deep literary engagement, insisting, "But I can't use this in a *classroom*!"

Using as a starting point these firsthand experiences, this essay raises a number of questions to emphasize both the challenge and the necessity of grounding YA literature courses in critical analysis and literary criticism, focusing specifically on the sorts of issues raised in teaching risky/risqué YA literature, bringing these experiences into conversation with youth and youth culture, and articulating the intersection of YA literature with the literary, personal, and pedagogical. First, we examine and deconstruct monolithic notions of youth and the genre of YA literature, including a discussion about the ways in which we facilitate this examination in our classes. We next unpack what we mean by risky/risqué texts, discussing the censorship of graphic material that often silences our students, whose imaginary teacher-selves grow uneasy with the notion of teaching such content to youth. We close with snapshots from Jon Wargo's teaching that highlight our methods in teaching YA literature courses that survey issues of difference and diversity (specifically genders and sexualities) in YA literature. By examining how aspects of young adult experience are silenced by our prospective teachers' sense of the imagined or implied adolescent reader (and their sense of self as future teacher of these readers), we demonstrate how educators teaching risky/risqué literature must work within the competing discourses of teaching, adolescence, and critical YA literature by asking their students (who will one day have classrooms of their own) to interrogate these contexts and representations.

Reading Risky/Risqué Subject Matter through a "Youth Lens"

The concept of the adolescent in the ever-expanding field of YA literature has made teaching YA literature a daunting task. Who *is* the intended audience for this work? Can content be divorced from readership? How do these texts stand up to scrutiny as literary texts? As historical artifacts? As cultural commodities and ideological tools?

In our course we begin by exploring the limitations of defining children's and YA literature. Using Marah Gubar's "On Not Defining Children's Literature," we collaboratively create a sense of the genre based on its origins and "family roots." We attempt to define YA literature not by qualities of the text or characteristics of the audience but by the kind of work the text is intended to do in the world. From classroom AP texts (e.g., Toni Morrison's *Beloved*) to hypermedia e-literature (Tender Claws's iOS application *Pry*), students can learn to recognize YA literature not by its literary characteristics and curricular connections but rather by its function.

We recognize that issues that arise around YA texts are complicated not only by debates over audience and purpose but also by the contexts in which these texts are encountered. Situated in departments of English, teacher education, library science, cultural studies, and the like, YA literature courses and texts are shaped by and read in light of their positions in the curriculum, along with the often discipline-specific relation between the young adult and the text itself. This is particularly true of courses in colleges of education—spaces in which students' own conceptions of the adolescent and adolescence intertwine with potential issues concerning pedagogy and praxis. This tension leads to a number of additional questions that haunt humanities-based courses offered in education programs: How is the literature we include in our courses translated by prospective teachers as they imagine students in their soon-to-be classrooms? Should we include methods for teaching YA literature or simply read literature solely as literary text?

Given that students in our courses often view literature primarily through the lens of education, how do we complicate their readings and responses? One of our central arguments here is that when teaching risky/risqué YA texts, one must first explore and read them through what Robert Petrone and others call a "youth lens," or a lens that "examines how ideas about adolescence and youth get formed, circulated, critiqued and revised" (506). Recognizing that risky/risqué subject matter often depicts experiences that lie outside what most of our students consider typical, and understanding that our own conceptions of youth have pedagogical consequences to our teaching of YA literature, we suggest that a youth lens is a viable approach to teaching YA literature in schools and colleges of education, creating a space that encourages our students to shift from "But I can't use this in a *classroom*!" to "How can I use this in classroom?"

What Do We Mean by Risky/Risqué Texts?

In examining risky/risqué texts, we follow a genealogy of others interested in examining complicated social issues in children's and YA literature (Damico and Apol; Simon and Armitage-Simon). Risk stems from the encounter with this type of literature in colleges and schools of education but also from the ways in which these texts may depict injustice, inequity, and histories of trauma on the adolescent or young person's body. In many of our YA literature courses, we collaboratively construct this working definition of risk by highlighting how, as Sherman Alexie contends, "the best kids' books are written in blood." Alexie's *Wall Street Journal Speakeasy* blog post is a regular staple in our classes and serves as an entrée in helping prospective teachers consider texts as "weapons"—a pedagogical arsenal that may simultaneously act as a "window, mirror, and/or sliding glass door" (Bishop) for students. Alexie, recounting why he writes novels for young adults, says, "I write in blood because I remember what it felt like to bleed." Hence, for our students, we hope risky/risqué topics are seen as realities that shift the "implied reader" (Nodelman and Reimer 16) from a static image of what so many think youth *were* (i.e., an image of the adolescent informed by our own histories of childhood) to a flexible and adaptive exploration of who youth *are*.

As educators who take feminist and queer lenses to our work, we think of risky and risqué literature as central concepts in deconstructing power, hegemony, and cultural injustice. For the purposes of this short essay, we pair risky with risqué and think of them synonymously (as our students often do) as texts that deal explicitly with complicated social and cultural issues, with a specific focus on gender and sexuality. From nuancing Judith Butler's construct of gender performativity in Patricia McCormick's *Sold* to problematizing key words like *diversity* and *inclusion* in Bill Konigsberg's *Openly Straight*, we see risky/risqué literature as an apparatus to illustrate and ground the theory and lenses we use throughout the course. We want to be clear: the risky/risqué texts that are included in our courses are not intended to shock students to realities that may be silent in their lives and previous histories of reading but rather to engage them in texts that fall under the "narratives of struggle" paradigm that hooks argues has the potential to decolonize the imagination.

Genders, Sex, and Football Fields: Teaching Risky/Risqué Texts as Critical Fictions

We now turn to a pair of pedagogical snapshots that highlight our own encounters in teaching risky/risqué YA texts. In providing these snapshots, we wish to connect with others' experiences in teaching critical fictions and to give voice to moments of classroom challenges and rewards in teaching risky/risqué YA literature.

Using a youth lens to read across issues of social and cultural difference is a starting point for many of the YA literature courses we teach. One course in particular, entitled Issues of Diversity in Children's and Young Adult Literature, is intentional about exploring risky issues and texts in the ten to twelve novels that are read over the fifteen-week semester. In the latter half of the course, instructors ask students to explore issues of intersectionality, paying particular attention to how gender and sexuality come to intersect with race, class, disability, and culture. Jon has included two instructional practices in the course to help students navigate risky issues of gender expression and gender identity using Ellen Wittlinger's *Parrotfish*. *Parrotfish* details a transgender teen (Grady Katz-McNair, formerly Angela Katz-McNair) who is searching for identity and acceptance. A novel that falls under the trans umbrella in YA literature, *Parrotfish* operates as an exemplary pedagogical text by including helpful metaphors to explain gender expression and sexual orientation.

At the start of class, Jon opens by having students count off by fives. He then gives each group a central character in *Parrotfish*. Prior to taking on questions concerning the particulars of Grady's transition, however, the class starts with an activity Jon calls "(em)bodied text"—an exercise in close reading where students divulge their own readerly experience through creating a poster depicting what they see as the wants and wishes of their group's character (fig. 1). Through this exercise, students regularly call into question their assumptions concerning both the author and the character, as well as their personal reading of youth and adolescence. After creating their posters, groups rotate through one another's posters, responding, questioning, and adding on with Post-it notes. The groups then take stock of what the dialogue has prompted and articulate how their reading—or how their sense of risk and risqué—may be biased or affected by attitudinal dispositions and beliefs. In short, the students start here to consider how their understanding of gender and sexuality, shaped by their histories and identities, are always already refracted through text.

Head = things the character thinks about
Eyes = things the character sees
Ears = things the character hears
Mouth = things the character vocalizes or says
Hands = things the character writes or textual quotes that are important
Legs and feet = things the character does or locations in the book

Figure 1. (Em)Bodied Text Activity Directions

The class moves on to examine notions of gender expression and self. When discussing the novel, Jon regularly has groups of prospective teachers work, as Grady does in the novel, to consider the gender continuum as a football field, in which end zones mark masculinity and femininity. Students brainstorm physical characteristics and personality traits of the novels' central protagonists. Afterward, they place these descriptors on Post-it notes on various yard lines, talking about how some are considered more "masculine" while others are more "feminine." What is central to this discussion is the ability for students to move these Post-it descriptors during the discussion. How is masculinity constructed to work in opposition to femininity? What are the risks characters take on in expressing gender? In short, prospective teachers find that these identities cannot be indexed solely by a masculine or feminine characteristic or trait.

Reflecting on the activity and applying it to her own identity, a nineteen-year-old self-identifying female described, "I chose somewhere closer to the feminine side. I wanted to choose the 10- or 20-yard line by the feminine end zone, but . . . I couldn't do it. I put mine more towards the 30 or 40; my gender expression is more different than I thought." Acknowledging the fluidity of gender and desire recognized in the text, some students experience an affective reaction to Grady's transition. They interrogate heteronormative understandings of gender (masculine/feminine), in contrast to birth sex (male/female), to better recognize their own potential biases toward others—a central feature of reading with a youth lens.

Another question that surfaces in the course is how to read against archetypes of pleasure and desire (e.g., who and what can have or hold desire) when youth sex and sexualities are so tightly controlled and often censored in schools and society. In the spring of 2013, Jon had an opportunity to create and teach a special topics version of the course with a specific focus on genders and sexualities in children's and YA literature, intended to create a context in which prospective teachers could think in extended ways about how schools and the implicit and explicit curriculum of the English language arts classroom work to shape who and what can be rendered visible as a gendered and sexed body. Easing into this course, the class first read Louisa May Alcott's *Little Women*, a classic that a local school district used in its eighth grade honors English classroom. Jon's class paired it with Lena Dunham's HBO series *Girls*. Highlighting how each text shares similar, yet dissonant, understandings of gender, race, sex, sexualities, and bodies, the pairing provided an entry point into fostering a shared language that could be used for the remainder of the course. Later examinations of desire, where sex was not necessarily a means for procreation (Francesca Lia Block's *Weetzie Bat*) or an event accompanied by deep angst (Stephen Chbosky's *The Perks of Being a Wallflower*), challenged students' previous conceptions of gender and sexuality. When novels disrupted students' sense of "normal" (e.g., classroom topics and texts turned toward sex positivity or youth desire), implicit biases concerning what was "appropriate" became ripe moments for debate.

After Jon had engaged with a few more predictable readings that foregrounded the themes and issues of the course, he decided to include R. Zamora Linmark's *Rolling the R's* (which he found being used by a gay-straight alliance during a classroom observation at a neighboring local high school). *Rolling the R's*, first published in 1997, is best known as a coming-of-age coming-out story set in 1970s Hawaii. Focusing on a group of Filipino youth, Linmark uses his own histories of immigration, race, and culture to play with literary conventions. *Rolling the R's* was Linmark's attempt to push at conventional, didactic, and exceedingly white out-of-the-closet tales. Jon selected this book because of its explicit focus on desire, childhood, ethnicity, race, and sex. As an undergraduate English major, he had first been introduced to Linmark's text in a contemporary fiction class. He believed that if prospective teachers in his YA literature course saw that this novel was being read by youth in their midwestern university town within an actual classroom space (i.e., in a school during independent reading), it would demonstrate, in a concrete way, the importance of Gubar's stance of not defining YA literature. Therefore, Jon included it as the penultimate book in the course to provide a diffractive read of youth sexuality across cultures. Teaching the text, however, was not as pedagogically helpful as he thought it would be. In fact, in class discussion of the book, Jon's own body and identity became a mentor text, reinforcing the students' sense of who could or could not use a text like *Rolling the R's* in the classroom.

Jon finds that because he is a gay cisgender multiethnic educator who regularly teaches lesbian, gay, bisexual, and transgender (LGBT) literature, his personhood and identity as a teacher are regularly under scrutiny, almost always directly in opposition to what his students in the college of education at least appear to be—that is, white cisgender and seemingly straight. As his students arrived ready to discuss Linmark's novel, quiet whispers began circulating. Finally, after several minutes of *shh*s, a student who had worked with Jon in a previous instructional methods course asked, "Why did you include this text? We could *never* teach this—I mean, a fifth grader and a high schooler? I googled why people use this, but kids shouldn't see school as promoting sex positivity." The student's comment was quickly echoed by a fellow classmate: "Yeah, sex in this book is something that should be talked about at home." Their objections seemed to focus on ways the book could not be used with YA readers in a school setting; Jon defended its inclusion because he had seen it in use in a "real" classroom with "real" students. "But you were working in like that after-school club," the student continued, "the gay-straight alliance space. They would have it there." In the moment, Jon referred the student and her classmates back to earlier conversations concerning the us-them paradigm. When teaching children's and YA literature, he explained, our job as educators is not to discount or absolve ourselves from the pedagogical responsibility of teaching risky/risqué topics but to advocate for ways to include diverse voices and experiences. Now, reflecting back on this classroom interaction, Jon remains curious when considering the student's use of the pronoun *they*. In what ways do students place certain texts, especially those we consider risky/risqué, as being and belonging to certain groups (LGBTQ or otherwise)? How does this placement disavow and divorce pedagogical responsibility from the teacher? Are all risky/risqué texts for all readers?

In considering the role of theory in reading and responding to risky/risqué YA texts with prospective teachers, we maintain that a cluster of concepts concerning sexuality, gender expression, racism, ableism, class, and youth culture remain key to teaching both literary theory and risky/risqué YA literature and that these concepts can be used to engage issues of youth as objects of desire and issues of youth desire itself (that is, the subjectivity youth have when written as gendered and sexed beings). We would argue that we need to bring together literary engagement and the lived identities and experiences of students, going beyond reductionist versions of the nuts and bolts of pedagogical new criticism and close reading, to choose texts and positions that allow for subversive stances and critical awareness. To put it simply: What could be more central to teaching YA literature than considering how one looks at youth and how youth (historically marginalized youth in particular) look at the world? What does the image of a child or young person mean from the standpoint of sexuality's relation to power? We find it most productive to link these more theoretical concepts with grounded investigations of the same issues. Amy Sonnie's *Revolutionary Voices: A Multicultural Queer Youth Anthology* and Jennifer Mathieu's novel *Moxie* make some useful steps in the direction of giving voice to these risky/risqué concepts.

Not all risky/risqué texts constitute a hypersexualized view of youth; still, it is important to speak of those moments in which racism, cisheteronormativity, and patriarchy might underlie representations of historically marginalized groups and people. The challenge for us is to look at the myriad depictions of sexuality and gender in YA literature and to ask hard questions about the relation between schools, risk, and the image of the child, as well as questions about the social construction of youth and power—that is, to consider how we might partner more theoretical literary lenses with reading YA critical fictions in order to help prospective teachers develop a decolonized image of what a more just and inclusive English curriculum may look like for their future classrooms and students.

Works Cited

Alcott, Louisa May. *Little Women*. Roberts Brothers, 1868–69. 2 vols.

Alexie, Sherman. "Why the Best Kids Books Are Written in Blood." *The Wall Street Journal*, 9 June 2011, blogs.wsj.com/speakeasy/2011/06/09/why-the-best-kids-books-are-written-in-blood.

Bishop, Rudine Sims. "Mirrors, Windows, and Sliding Glass Doors." *Perspectives*, vol. 6, no. 3, 1990, pp. ix–xi.

Block, Francesca Lia. *Weetzie Bat*. HarperCollins, 1989.

Butler, Judith. *Gender Trouble*. Routledge, 2002.

Chbosky, Stephen. *The Perks of Being a Wallflower*. Simon and Schuster, 1999.

Damico, James, and Laura Apol. "Using Testimonial Response to Frame the Challenges and Possibilities of Risky Historical Texts." *Children's Literature in Education*, vol. 39, no. 2, 2008, pp. 141–58.

Gubar, Marah. "On Not Defining Children's Literature." *PMLA*, vol. 126, no. 11, Jan. 2011, pp. 209–16.

hooks, bell. "Narratives of Struggle." *Critical Fictions: The Politics of Imaginative Writing*, edited by Philomena Mariani, Bay Press, 1991, pp. 53–61.

Konigsberg, Bill. *Openly Straight*. Arthur A. Levine Books, 2013.

Linmark, R. Zamora. *Rolling the R's*. Kaya, 1995.

Mathieu, Jennifer. *Moxie*. Roaring Brook Press, 2017.

McCormick, Patricia. *Sold*. Hyperion, 2006.

Nodelman, Perry, and Mavis Reimer. *The Pleasures of Children's Literature*. 3rd ed., Allyn and Bacon, 2003.

Paris, Django, and H. Samy Alim. "What Are We Seeking to Sustain through Culturally Sustaining Pedagogy? A Loving Critique Forward." *Harvard Educational Review*, vol. 84, no. 1, Apr. 2014, pp. 85–100.

Petrone, Robert, et al. "The Youth Lens: Analyzing Adolescence/ts in Literary Texts." *Journal of Literacy Research*, vol. 46, no. 4, Dec. 2014, pp. 506–33.

Simon, Roger I., and Wendy Armitage-Simon. "Teaching Risky Stories: Remembering Mass Destruction through Children's Literature." *English Quarterly*, vol. 28, no. 1, Fall 1995, pp. 27–31.

Sonnie, Amy, editor. *Revolutionary Voices: A Multicultural Queer Youth Anthology*. Alyson Books, 2000.

Wittlinger, Ellen. *Parrotfish*. Simon and Schuster, 2007.

Wendy J. Glenn

Addressing School Censorship in the Young Adult Literature Course

This essay describes the inclusion of anticensorship content in a YA literature course designed for preservice and practicing secondary English teachers, adding to the work of others engaged in similar efforts.[1] It addresses the reality that censorship in schools is real, that it is increasing in both scope and insidiousness, and that understanding how to combat it is essential to teacher training.[2] This piece presents lesson activities and students' engagement with and responses to a unit of study implemented in a university YA literature course during the 2017 spring semester. Although this postsecondary setting comes with unique considerations of content and pedagogy, activities and materials could be adapted by educators working in other contexts.

Gathering and Building Understandings

During the unit, each course meeting began with instructor book talks about YA titles that have come under attack, including Sherman Alexie's *The Absolutely True Diary of a Part-Time Indian*, Coe Booth's *Tyrell*, and Cris Beam's *I Am J*. This introductory sharing exposed students to titles that censors call into question and highlighted elements that might raise red flags for readers. Because any text at any time is subject to potential scrutiny, teachers must have clear rationales for selecting the texts used. This exercise reinforces the fact that these reasons need to take into consideration censorial possibilities.

The first session turned to solicitation of students' understandings of censorship and how these were informed, strengthened, or challenged by Alleen Pace Nilsen and Kenneth L. Donelson's article "Censorship: Of Worrying and Wondering," which students read prior to class. I opened with the discussion prompt "What about this reading surprised, intrigued, resonated with, frustrated you?" Student responses centered on four themes. Students first expressed concerns about anticipating what content might be subject to questioning. Robert noted that he was "surprised to learn that censors don't always share the real reasons behind their attacks. I would take parents at face value."[3] In response to this comment, we discussed Christopher Paul Curtis's *The Watsons Go to Birmingham—1963* and the purported offensiveness offered by censors: vulgar language. Given the lack of such language anywhere in the book, the novel's implication of Anglo-Americans in the bombing of an African American church might be the actual reason for the attack. Andrea noted that she realized "that it's hard to know what people will go after when they censor." She followed this with an example of a mother in the school community where she student-taught who challenged a text in which the teen character defies his father. Andrea was surprised that although the text contains no reference to sex, drugs, or any usually controversial topic, it might still come under attack.

Students also engaged in rich conversation centered on the motives of parents and guardians who challenge titles in schools. Students agreed that raising children in a world dominated by media can be daunting and might leave adults feeling that they have little control over what children see and hear. As Kaitlin noted, "Parents who challenge books come from a good place, but social media, movies, etc., are too hard to control." Lizette expanded upon this claim, saying, "I understand how parents feel like they can't control the influence of the world on their children's lives (the media, etc.). The article pointed out, however, that they do think they can control what their children experience in school." Robert highlighted the accessibility of schools to adults and how they can make their voices heard in ways they cannot when trying to influence corporate media or other large entities: "A parent isn't going to call the president of NBC to complain about programming, but he or she can easily pick up the phone and talk with the principal." This conversation allowed us to explore how censorship often results from a genuine desire to protect children, to keep them innocent as long as possible. Most parents who censor believe that schools should be safe places where children won't be exposed to views that challenge their own or raise questions they don't want or feel prepared to answer, but schools are sites of democratic education in which exposure to multiple perspectives is essential. Without opportunities to think through complication, the innocence of young people can result in misguided understandings that foster and perpetuate censorial behaviors.

Students talked at length about the relation between censorship and the professionalization of teaching. Dan, the only practicing teacher in the course, expressed reservations regarding the selection of texts that are not in the approved curricula. He explained, "Keep in mind that if you teach the curriculum, your ass is covered. The board approves. Teaching a nonapproved text is not worth losing your job." Several students respectfully pushed back, noting that for them, the risks inherent in selecting texts that help students grapple with complexity (even those not included in the approved curricula) are worth taking. They embraced the role of teachers as professionals, as experts in knowing and choosing texts for the students in their care. Suzanne, for example, stated, "It is nice for a parent to imagine having some control of his or her child's education, but a parent shouldn't be involved in choosing an alternate text, for example. That is our responsibility as teachers." Students then discussed the training that encompasses teacher preparation; several students likened this education to that required of other professionals. Anton, for instance, argued, "Doctors don't ask parents for help in making a diagnosis or writing a prescription. Insulating kids doesn't help them or really protect them." Students highlighted negative perceptions that position teachers, unlike those in other professions, unfavorably and argued that educators need to own their professional status and make decisions with care and confidence.

Our conversation concluded with the reminder that students should be at the center of decisions we make as teachers. Students argued that educators, in the selection of reading materials, should trust young people to know their own levels of comfort and when to continue or stop reading. Trevor stated that "kids will skip over what makes them uncomfortable." Jackson added, "Given the active nature of reading, a person can choose to stop at any time. This puts the kid in charge." We used this opportunity to discuss student autonomy and "The Students' Right to Read," published by the National Council of Teachers of English. To transition into the next activity, I reviewed a handout that describes the top challenged books of 2016 (Doyle).

The class meeting then centered on a whole-class exploration of three questions: Who is the typical school censor? What issues do school censors find most offensive? Why is censorship in school settings particularly complicated? This activity drew from an instructor-generated presentation in which students analyzed quotations offered by censors in their attempts to deny students access to particular authors and titles. Using material that is quoted in Joan DelFattore's *What Johnny Shouldn't Read*, and that comes from transcripts published in the archives of the *Newsletter on Intellectual Freedom* (now the *Journal of Intellectual Freedom and Privacy*), I shared various statements used by censors to support their efforts, including the following:

> "Poems by African Americans about racism reflect dishonor on the United States."
> "[Edgar Allan] Poe's works should not be used because he was a cocaine addict."
> "*Romeo and Juliet* promotes teen suicide."
> "*Diary of Anne Frank* is unacceptable because it is sad."
> (DelFattore 145)

This opened space to discuss the values, beliefs, and assumptions held by those who challenge materials. As a group, we considered the traits of the average school censor (drawn from the Nilsen and Donelson article):

> a typical citizen who believes he or she is protecting children
> a conservative in terms of family values, religion, and politics
> a liberal extremist who aims to erase uncomfortable language, stereotypical characters, or politically incorrect texts
> one who wishes to indoctrinate rather than educate young people
> one who assumes that books determine behavior
> a nonreader

We talked too about the elements of texts that school censors most often find offensive (again drawing from Nilsen and Donelson), including sex, drug use, profanity, racism, witchcraft, homosexuality, violence, suicide, evolution, and anti-American sentiment.

This conversation can be challenging, because students sometimes express anger and resort to name-calling as they begin to make sense of this content. In response, I remind students that our way is just one way and that people in other communities in the United States might hold views, beliefs, and understandings that are different but no less real or deeply felt than our own. Anton offered an insight that helped us all more readily understand the thinking and actions of those who censor: "Anti-American concern seems to encompass all the reasons listed. People have a certain view of their America, and this is imbued with certain values and beliefs. When books challenge this view of America, they are seen as dangerous to a particular way of life." Books are reflections of culture; when conservatives don't see themselves and their values in the stories their children are reading, fears about being ignored or left behind might be realized.

We ended this session by discussing the complexity of school censorship given the fact that students under the age of eighteen are legally under the governance of their parents or guardians. If parents or guardians ask that their children not read a text, we are obligated by law to honor that. However, if the same parents or guardians ask that a text be removed for all students, we have a right to challenge the challenge.

Applying Our Understandings

Our next class meeting considered censorship in the context of Sara Farizan's YA novel *If You Could Be Mine*. This novel centers on the experiences of two teenage girls growing up in Iran. Seventeen-year-old Sahar is in love with her best friend, Nasrin. The girls maintain a private relationship until they learn that Nasrin is promised to a man in marriage. Sahar believes that becoming a man herself might be the only path to winning Nasrin back in a society that will not allow the girls to be together. The novel explores the tensions between personal identity and social norms, what's wanted and what's possible.

Students worked with two or three classmates to consider diverse positions. They were first given the following task: You are a parent or guardian of a sixteen-year-old student. On what grounds might you challenge the presence of this text in your child's school classroom? Students worked together to generate a list of concerns. Across every group, students argued that adults might be concerned by the novel's inclusion of LGBTQ content, normalization of transgender identity, sex, drinking and drug use, prostitution, an Islamic-based setting, nontraditional gender roles, and teen decision-making that challenges community values and expectations. Students were then given the second task: You are a teacher who has decided to use this text in the classroom. How might you respond to the concerns raised by the parent or guardian? Again, they worked in small groups to generate reasons that substantiate the inclusion of this title in their classroom curricula. Students offered insightful, careful reasoning for selecting this title despite its potentially controversial content. Across all groups, students argued that the text exposes readers to a likely less familiar culture and invites students to consider ways of doing, thinking, and being that don't align with their own—essential for successful engagement in an increasingly global community. They also noted that the text features careful decision-making on behalf of the characters; the author invites considerations of personal and social morality without being didactic, thus allowing readers to work through complexity in a fictional world before making decisions in real life. Finally, participants explained that the text is likely to attract teen readers, given the realism and relevance to adolescence it features; if our aim is to engage students as readers, it might be effective to select texts that tackle issues to which they can relate.

Students then participated in a whole-class Walk the Line activity. In preparation, I placed a line of masking tape on the floor to divide the classroom into halves. Then, in response to a statement I read aloud, students decided whether they could "walk the line" in support of that statement. If so, they stood directly on the line. If not, they positioned themselves away from the line to indicate the extent of their disagreement. For example, if they saw some merit in the statement but could not commit entirely, they stood one to two feet away from the line. If they disagreed completely with the statement, they stood six to seven feet away. The statements included the following:

The novel features characters we don't want young people to emulate.
This novel addresses themes of value.
This novel is offensive.
This novel should be kept out of a school classroom or library.

Student positioning gave rise to lively conversation. Relative to the first statement, all students remained on the line or moved away slightly, but all agreed that the novel contains characters who are not admirable. Students' comments focused on how they would wish to raise their own children, real or imagined. "I wouldn't want my daughter to emulate Daughter [an underage prostitute in the novel]," noted Robert. Suzanne added, "Even with the main character, there are some things that are strong about her, but I thought she would go through with the gender reassignment surgery. I thought this [showed her initial decision] was rash and [I] wouldn't want a child of mine to think it's okay to do this without real consideration." To push students in their thinking, I posed the following: "If there are clearly characters we wouldn't want our students—or children—to emulate in this novel, why would we teach it?" In response, students focused on the importance of exposing young readers to complexity, even if it has the potential to show a darker side of humanity, as long as that exposure is offered with care and honesty. As Kaitlin explained, "Even though there are bad characters, what they do is shown to be less than ideal, like with the girl who is a prostitute. Her life is not glamorized or desirable." Krystal added, "The characters are not glorified." Robert took the conversation to a broader consideration of narrative, challenging classmates to "name for me a story that doesn't have a bad character. All stories have antagonists, even the Bible." And Grady reminded us that "presentation does not mean endorsement."

Relative to the second statement, all students hovered close to the line. Anton's comment reflected the overarching explanation of this choice: "All of the themes are important, even those that are controversial, especially those that are controversial." Several students framed their views in the context of identity and the importance of exposing students to titles in which characters get stronger, smarter, or better somehow by the end of the story. Suzanne argued that the main character in *If You Could Be Mine* "realized something in the end. There is growth in her character, and readers can see that." Robert added that "the novel models the universal search for identity," and Kaitlin, in conjunction with this universal theme, believed that "every student could find something of value in this novel."

Student positioning in response to the third statement was visually interesting in that three participants remained near the line, while the rest moved away widely. Anton, who remained close, noted, "There are two things I know: this novel is not offensive to me, but this novel is certainly offensive to someone else." Dan complicated this claim by stating that, for him, "no idea is offensive," highlighting his decision to position himself far from the line and argue that human values determine levels of appropriateness and that these levels can change over time and place and person. Regardless of where they stood, several students argued that the offensive nature of the text itself provides justification for teaching it. As Curtis explained, "If something isn't offensive, I don't want to teach it. I don't find this novel offensive, but I want to find something that will spark someone." Amy agreed, noting, "Anything worth teaching is offensive. I want to expose students to ideas they don't know."

These final comments provided an effective transition into conversation around the fourth statement. One student (Dan, the classroom teacher) stood on the line, and all the others moved away widely. A brief transcript for a glimpse into the conversation follows:

Dan. This book will invite trouble. Why teach something that is not in the curriculum?

Trevor. Because the curriculum isn't set in stone or sanctioned from on high. It needs to shift and change with the times.

Dan. Parents should be the ones teaching about sexuality.

Andrea. And what happens if they don't?

Kendra. I want the literature I teach to reflect the kids I have and the world in which they live. If we don't include titles like these, we deny a kid's identity.

Dan. I don't like sounding like an old codger. I guess it really does come down to balance. We need to expose students to new ideas, which might mean going beyond the curriculum, but we want to be smart about our choices and make sure we know why we choose the texts we do.

These participants expressed passion and conviction, drawing from personal and professional experiences, beliefs, and values that suggest the highly emotive nature of censorship. At the end of our Walk the Line activity, I invited students to participate in a straw poll, raising their hands to reflect whether and how they would use this title in their classrooms. All students agree that they would include the novel in their classroom library, recommend it to individual students, and use it as a literature circle title. Half the students agreed that they would use it as a whole-class text.

Anticipating Classroom Censorship

Our final class meeting featured a whole-class discussion of the practicalities of managing a classroom given the possibility of censorial attacks. We discussed maintaining a classroom library (whether to read each text entirely or whether reading reviews can suffice), deciding how to deal with controversial titles (whether to code texts to indicate controversial content or whether it is acceptable to keep some texts apart from the public library space), and determining an appropriate level of parent or guardian permission in the selection of texts.

Students expressed especially mixed feelings in our discussion of securing parent or guardian permission. Curtis drew from his student teaching experience to argue that securing permission is no big deal: "If we let students self-select books, if their options are potentially controversial, you can solicit parent permission. We did this during my student teaching, and every parent signed." Geoff agreed, adding, "I did something like this too. On the first day of student teaching, we shared a handout that was a contract for sustained silent reading. The parents had to sign to show they understood that some titles include violence, some have sex, etc." Kayla noted that her cooperating teacher implemented the same policy but that she doesn't know whether she agrees this was best. She argued for honoring students and their choices as essential elements of democratic education. This led to a conversation about the tension of involving parents and guardians versus trusting kids and warding off potential problems ahead of time versus inviting potential controversy. The conversation ended with consensus regarding the importance of having a clear policy for text challenges in place, whether or not it includes parent or guardian permission. Jasmine captured the concerns of the full class when she said, "I'm thinking now that every teacher will likely be challenged at least once in his or her career. When I interview for a job, I'm going to ask if the school has a policy like this." The class session concluded with the sharing of essential resources for teachers.[4]

Censorship affects us all—as educators and as citizens in a democracy—and we all hold differing levels of what we consider acceptable. Examining these issues explicitly can help preservice teachers better understand their own biases. Katherine Paterson, the 2010 National Ambassador for Young People's Literature, offered an insightful reminder: "All of us can think of a book that we hope none of our children or any other children have taken off the shelf. But if I have the right to remove that book from the shelf—that work I abhor—then you also have exactly the same right and so does everyone else. And then we have no books left on the shelf for any of us."

Notes

1. See McGillis; McNair; Meyer and Bradley.

2. See Boyd and Bailey; Curwood et al.; Holland.

3. Pseudonyms are used throughout, and IRB permission was secured for all participants.

4. Resources include the Intellectual Freedom Center (www.ncte.org/action/anti-censorship) of the National Council of Teachers of English (NCTE); the Office for Intellectual Freedom, American Library Association (www.ala.org/offices/oif); Speak Loudly, Assembly on Literature for Adolescents of the NCTE (www.alan-ya.org/information/speak-loudly); the Freedom to Read Foundation (www.ftrf.org); and the National Coalition against Censorship (www.ncac.org).

Works Cited

Alexie, Sherman. *The Absolutely True Diary of a Part-Time Indian.* Little, Brown, 2007.

Beam, Cris. *I Am J.* Little, Brown, 2011.

Booth, Coe. *Tyrell.* Push, 2006.

Boyd, Fenice B., and Nancy M. Bailey. "Censorship in Three Metaphors." *Journal of Adolescent and Adult Literacy*, vol. 52, no. 8, May 2009, pp. 653–61.

Curtis, Christopher Paul. *The Watsons Go to Birmingham—1963.* Delacorte, 1995.

Curwood, Jen Scott, et al. "Fight for Your Right: Censorship, Selection, and LGBTQ Literature." *English Journal*, vol. 98, no. 4, 2009, pp. 37–43.

DelFattore, Joan. *What Johnny Shouldn't Read: Textbook Censorship in America.* Yale UP, 1992.

Doyle, Robert P. "Books Challenged or Banned, 2015–2016." *American Library Association*, 2016, www.ila.org/content/documents/2016banned.pdf. Accessed 28 May 2017.

Farizan, Sara. *If You Could Be Mine.* Algonquin Young Readers, 2013.

Holland, Suzann. "Censorship in Young Adult Fiction: What's Out There and What Should Be." *Voice of Youth Advocates*, vol. 25, no. 3, Aug. 2002, pp. 176–82.

McGillis, Roderick. "Looking in the Mirror: Pedagogy, Theory, and Children's Literature." *Teaching Children's Fiction*, edited by Charles Butler, Palgrave Macmillan, 2006, pp. 85–105.

McNair, Jonda C. "'But *The Five Chinese Brothers* Is One of My Favorite Books!': Conducting Sociopolitical Critiques of Children's Literature with

Preservice Teachers." *Journal of Children's Literature*, vol. 29, no. 1, Spring 2003, pp. 46–54.

Meyer, Nadean, and Darcy Bradley. "Collaboratively Teaching Intellectual Freedom to Education Students." *Education Libraries*, vol. 36, no. 1, Summer 2013, pp. 24–30.

Nilsen, Alleen Pace, and Kenneth L. Donelson. "Censorship: Of Worrying and Wondering." *Literature for Today's Young Adults*, 6th ed., Longman, 2001, pp. 390–438.

Paterson, Katherine. Speech. American Library Association Convention, 25 June 1995, Chicago, Illinois.

"The Students' Right to Read." *National Council of Teachers of English*, 25 Oct. 2018, www.ncte.org/positions/statements/righttoreadguideline. Accessed 1 July 2019.

S. Patrice Jones

The Case for Teaching Young Adult Literature Everywhere

Some years ago, the conversation surrounding the genre of YA literature and its presence in secondary English classrooms was structured around the claim that YA literature "belongs" alongside the canon of traditional, classic literature, or it should, at the minimum, serve as a gateway to the more traditional and canonical choices for classroom literature (see Sewell; Yagelski). However, as the years have passed, that argument doesn't resonate as loudly with practicing teachers and scholars of children's and YA literature. Our conversations and scholarly contributions have moved away from whether YA texts are in fact literature and worthy of study to thinking of ways scholars can teach the genre with the same sensitivity and attention as other topics.

My initial question when considering the academic context of YA literature was to ask the following: if scholars are approaching this genre as deserving of an analysis of form, content, and response, why are we continuing to question its validity or its home? As an English education professor, I can attest that our discipline is still preoccupied with this question (see, for instance, Driscoll; Soter and Connors). But rather than spend time debating this question, I prefer to explore how the presence of YA literature in various disciplines might offer one solution to that question. If we change the perception of YA literature to a nomadic rather than a transient genre, we solve the need to classify and thereby restrict YA literature.

More than likely, each academic year, many colleges and universities offer two or even three separate courses in YA literature: one in the English department, one in education, and perhaps one in library and information sciences. Taught with different objectives and readings, students are typically designated by their chosen major into which course to take, which raises multiple points of exploration in terms of the differences between these course offerings and the benefits of having multiple departments teach YA literature. This essay unpacks those reasons, while also arguing for its extension across disciplines. My aim is to bring to this conversation other important questions that could be central to understanding our pedagogical decisions when teaching YA texts in a variety of spaces.

This essay is organized into two sections. In the first section, I provide an account of my personal subjectivity on this topic, along with how our subjectivities, as English and education scholars, influence how we are reading and teaching the genre. I discuss the need to maintain YA literature as a course in multiple disciplines and how future students, teachers, and scholars of literature would benefit from those approaches. To support this section, I have reviewed samples of YA syllabi in order to extract certain characteristics that appear to be common in the teaching of YA literature in education contexts. In the second section of the essay, I give an example of how YA books can be used as the center of multiple course offerings. I provide suggestions as to how those texts can be used to encourage dialogue about a range of topics.

Subjectivity and Teaching Young Adult Literature

Understanding our own subjectivities is important when we think about how to approach the teaching of YA texts. My primary responsibility is preparing teachers for middle and high school English language arts teaching positions. Therefore, most of the assignments and readings I give are constructed around implicit and explicit pedagogical decisions and how those decisions impact what and how students learn, as noted by Amanda Haertling Thein and her coauthors. I and other scholars (Hunt; Petrone and Sarigianides) are concerned with questions such as these: How can a teacher bring YA texts into the classroom to engage resistant readers or encourage those who are already reading YA books to continue? How can educators create a space for YA literature to illicit powerful discussions about adolescent themes and issues? Admittedly, I would not consider myself a scholar of any particular type or genre of literature, yet my position as a teacher educator is to help teachers facilitate opportunities where the work of critical, literary analysis takes place in primary and secondary classrooms. So, in my own case, when teaching a course centered in YA literature, I am concerned with how one pedagogically enters a text for the purpose of having students bring meaning to, and construct meaning from, the text through a variety of responses, and how this pedagogical method enables students to transfer these meaning-making skills to other contexts.

Based on my own subject position, then, I decided to examine how YA literature is approached in other English education courses. I hoped to delineate the specialized work that places YA literature at the center of English language arts classrooms across the United States. Methodologically, I selected a number of publicly sourced syllabi from English education courses. I distinguished between the courses by their name, department, and number. Most of the available syllabi were undergraduate-level courses, and for consistency, I decided to focus exclusively on these samples. It is important to note that English education and its aligning course work, which concentrates on preparing teachers for the primary and secondary classrooms, can sometimes be housed within English departments, while other times it is found within literacy, curriculum and instruction, or discipline-specific departments and programs. Regardless of how courses are organized across departments, the teaching of YA literature as a form and as an approach is critical.

Young Adult Literature in English Education

In English education course work, YA literature is often a required course for certification and degree completion because of the recognition of its role in teaching literature to teacher candidates. Across the sample syllabi in English education, three themes emerge: introduction to the genre, pedagogical strategies for teaching the genre, and the process of selecting literature based on sociocultural perspectives of learning. Although there is an assumption that most English educators have a degree in English, a number of prospective teachers come from outside the discipline, have taken only the required number of English courses to be admitted into a certification program, or are participants in alternative certification programs. This is important to consider in that planning a course in YA literature for prospective teachers means that our approach is not necessarily one of literary analysis initially but rather an introduction to the genre.

Most courses on YA literature include some introductory discussion about the characteristics of the genre and possibly some discussion of the history and current status of adolescence. When one thinks about popular high school novels with adolescent characters, such as *The Catcher in the Rye* or *To Kill a Mockingbird*, education professors have to make the distinction between texts written for adults that have young protagonists and texts written specifically for adolescents to read. Making this distinction is important in that future teachers will be responsible for knowing and making available literature for students of all ages. If teacher educators do not carefully highlight these differences, we run the risk of books explicitly written for teens not receiving the critical attention and analysis they deserve. A popular definition of YA literature, cited by Marci Glaus, among others, includes those texts that are marketed specifically to young adults. I agree with this definition but also want to press against it. I would also argue that YA literature can cover any literature that young adults are choosing to read. This makes room for other subgenres that young adults read but that are not necessarily written for them. Examples of these overlapping genres include graphic novels, comics, and even urban fiction, as noted by Michael Cart. Also, to reverse this premise means that YA literature is not relegated to its intended audience either. Unlike some of the resistance toward adults reading YA literature (see Graham, for instance), YA literature remains a steady fixture of postadolescent readers. What does this mean for prospective teachers? Our awareness of the nuances surrounding YA literature means that we can create a space where this genre, in all its forms, is available and privileged as literature.

A vital point for teacher educators is that we construct YA literature as a tool for reader ability and access. Some scholars have advocated for YA literature as a bridge to canonical texts and for struggling readers (Rybakova and Roccanti; Connors and Shepard). However, this commitment to accessibility seems to wane as students matriculate through high school and on to higher education. Typically, because of advanced placement testing and the perceived requirements of certain English literature course work for college acceptance, most teachers end up teaching the same traditional texts they read in high school (Bushman and Haas; Hipple). This is not necessarily a bad tradition, especially when knowledge of those texts helps to create access and advantage to standardized exams and possible college credit, but it does make it difficult for teachers to step outside those strict but imaginary boundaries of classical texts. In addition, not only are teachers repeating the same books, but, as Robert P. Yagelski points out, most future teachers will teach them using the same approach. So the aim of teaching YA texts in an English education course is to introduce YA literature as a genre for students who may have not been exposed to adolescent literature since middle school. This serves two important purposes: first, it enables preservice teachers to revisit the age group that they are proposing to interact with, and second, by encouraging them to get middle and high school students engaged in narratives that center on the adolescent, they reaffirm for their students that their lives and stories are as valid as the canonical literature that we have invested so many years in teaching.

Along with considering how YA literature can improve access for students with a range of reading levels and interests, learning to teach means understanding that there is much more involved than simply opening a book and reading. Teacher education is concerned primarily with the craft of teaching the book, modeling close reading strategies, and molding ways that students can showcase their interpretations of their readings. This is important because, oftentimes, literature courses enter into texts without divulging the how and why behind teaching literature. How a teacher moves from the introduction of a novel to building a discussion around themes and literary devices are the unspoken moves that we observe from our colleagues in literature but now have the space to examine in education courses. It is possible YA literature is more effective than other genres for examining how pedagogy functions in a classroom. The required classic texts for adolescents are often both complex and detached from adolescent experience. YA texts speak directly to a relevant adolescent experience that readers can connect to and critically interpret. Thus it may be easier for a teacher to get students to engage with literary devices when the language, metaphor, and symbolism are closely related to the narratives their students have witnessed or experienced.

Finally, YA literature education syllabi typically have a component that emphasizes how the genre can help future teachers select (and help students self-select) literature that speaks directly to their circumstances or ones they are interested in learning about. Steven Wolk posits that educators are responsible for helping students "to see that inside these provocative books are stories that help us to better understand ourselves, who we are and who we want to become" (672). In short, if we allow the literature and our students to speak, we push ourselves in the direction of understanding the societal conflicts and dilemmas our students are navigating. This means that teachers must consider that students may be interested in reading stories that are reflective of their daily experiences, rather than the obligatory readings of so-called classics. YA literature can help fill this space not solely by exclusion of canonical texts but by inclusion of texts and issues outside traditional canons that are also worthy of study and critique.

Centering Young Adult Literature in Course Work

YA literature should not be limited in terms of where and how it is being offered to students. YA texts can provide additional context, specifically in courses that are not centered on literature. Using YA books in other subject areas or disciplines is not a new phenomenon in that teachers have traditionally used novels and other nonfiction texts to teach about historical events. A typical example would be reading Chris Crowe's *Getting Away with Murder: The True Story of the Emmett Till Case* or using Markus Zusak's *The Book Thief* to discuss the Holocaust. However, those novels are still primarily taken up in English classrooms. I would suggest that in addition to providing a narrative to historical events, YA texts can also be used as a supplement to more current social events and within courses not necessarily affiliated with the study of literature. Could a high school social studies course use Angie Thomas's *The Hate U Give* as a way to discuss police killings of unarmed citizens? Could that same text also be used in an undergraduate education course to talk about school desegregation and busing? Asking a different series of questions can possibly extend how we are reading and teaching YA literature.

Extending YA literature across disciplines can start by following a simple checklist that includes questions such as the following: What specific historical events or social contexts will my course cover? What YA texts discuss these events in complex and sensitive ways? In what ways can use of a YA text strengthen the goals for this course? If the goal of education, specifically the teaching of literature, is to increase the conversation surrounding the social, cultural, and political parts of ourselves, while also bringing a sense of critical awareness to the how and why the stories told in YA literature resonate with our students, instructors can move away from arguments that present YA literature as a problem, as a gateway to "real" literature, or as belonging to one discipline. The concerns of YA books are concerns that touch all areas of our students' lives as well as our own, in ways that are immediate and engaging. Using them as sites of meaning making and as spurs for sociocultural dialogue can thus benefit all areas of the curriculum.

Works Cited

Bushman, John H., and Kay Parks Haas. *Using Young Adult Literature in the English Classroom.* 4th ed., Pearson / Merrill Prentice Hall, 2006.

Cart, Michael. "The Value of Young Adult Literature." *Young Adult Library Services Association*, Jan. 2008, www.ala.org/yalsa/guidelines/whitepapers/yalit. Accessed 22 May 2018.

Connors, Sean, and Iris Shepard. "Reframing Arguments for Teaching YA Literature in an Age of Common Core." *SIGNAL Journal*, vol. 35, no. 3, Fall 2011–Winter 2012, pp. 6–10.

Driscoll, Marc C. "In Defense of Young Adult Literature." *Learning to Teach*, vol. 5, no. 1, 2016, p. 2.

Glaus, Marci. "Text Complexity and Young Adult Literature." *Journal of Adolescent and Adult Literacy*, vol. 57, no. 5, Feb. 2014, pp. 407–16.

Graham, Ruth. "Against YA." *Slate*, 5 June 2014, www.slate.com/articles/arts/books/2014/06/against_ya_adults_should_be_embarrassed_to_read_children_s_books.html.

Hallman, Heidi L., editor. *Innovations in English Language Arts Teacher Education.* Emerald, 2017.

Hipple, Ted. "It's the THAT, Teacher." *English Journal*, vol. 86, no. 3, Mar. 1997, pp. 15–17.

Hunt, Caroline. "Theory Rises, Maginot Line Endures." *Children's Literature Association Quarterly*, vol. 42, no. 2, Summer 2017, pp. 205–17.

Petrone, Robert, and Sophia Tatiana Sarigianides. "Re-Positioning Youth in English Teacher Education." Hallman, pp. 89–105.

Rybakova, Katie, and Rikki Roccanti. "Connecting the Canon to Current Young Adult Literature." *American Secondary Education*, vol. 44, no. 2, Spring 2016, pp. 31–45.

Sewell, William C. "Entrenched Pedagogy: A History of Stasis in the English Language Arts Curriculum in United States Secondary Schools." *Changing English*, vol. 15, no. 1, 2008, pp. 87–100.

Soter, Anna O., and Sean P. Connors. "Beyond Relevance to Literary Merit: Young Adult Literature as 'Literature.'" *The ALAN Review*, vol. 37, no. 1, Fall 2009, pp. 62–68.

Thein, Amanda Haertling, et al. "Rethinking Identity and Adolescence in the Teaching of Literature: Implications for Pre-Service Teacher Education." Hallman, pp. 65–87.

Wolk, Steven. "Reading for a Better World: Teaching for Social Responsibility with Young Adult Literature." *Journal of Adolescent and Adult Literacy*, vol. 52, no. 8, May 2009, pp. 664–73.

Yagelski, Robert P. "Stasis and Change: English Education and the Crisis of Sustainability." *English Education*, vol. 37, no. 4, July 2005, pp. 262–71.

Billie Jarvis-Freeman

Surveying Fiction: Teaching Young Adult Literature across the Curriculum

At the Christian liberal arts university where I teach, all students take four semesters of a mandatory interdisciplinary sequence regardless of their major. Half my course load is devoted to this team-taught sequence. I anticipate the reader's audible gasp at the words *four semesters* and *mandatory.* I get it, so do the students; it's a large chunk of any individual's sequence of study. I also think it is an honest display of how serious my school is about the development of analytical skills in conjunction with history, philosophy, and the arts. My team of colleagues—professors in their respective fields of music, art, history, science, theology, and philosophy and myself in literature—begins with ancient Sumer and ranges far and wide over the span of Western culture, one of the program goals being to help students "formulate a Christian worldview and use that worldview to evaluate their own and other cultures both past and present"; they also learn to "explain the various ways in which ancient and modern worldviews developed and demonstrate how these worldviews are evident in religion, philosophy, politics, literature and the arts" (Jarvis-Freeman et al.). As these course objectives predate my involvement with the program by at least a decade, I content myself at present with spending a portion of each of my lectures to mention, argue, or insist that literature and the arts do not merely reflect a cultural worldview but are instead active in forming the worldviews of the purveyors and consumers of such art and literature. As I have now been invited to coordinate this program, I intend to incorporate this more precise theoretical postulate in the syllabus.

Students consistently complain about the class for the time and effort that it takes, though it just as consistently shows up in exit polls as one of the most highly valued by our graduates. Those of us who teach in the program share a love-hate relation with the class as well, valuing the chance to teach interactively with a team and correlate our passions with those of our colleagues while bemoaning the fact that the students will never get to spend as much time as we believe they should within our own respective fields. We all love the days in which it is not our turn to lecture, while also fighting for more time at the podium; we all have more to say, and particular to this essay, we all have more desired readings than we can ethically assign given the strictly limited number of hours devoted to the course. If, for instance, in the first semester, in the course Ancient Civilizations, which ambitiously starts with the culture of the ancient Sumerians and ends with Rome's Principate through Augustus, I insist that "The Story of Sinuhe the Egyptian" is necessary to understanding the worldview of ancient Egypt, I may inadvertently push out the incredibly interesting selection from the Code of Hammurabi or, worse yet, part of Plato's *Republic*. What we end up doing with the letters of Cicero is guilt inducing for all of us except the students. How then can I insist that precious required reading time be given over to Veronica Roth's *Divergent* or Suzanne Collins's *The Hunger Games*? Quite simply, within this scrabbling and scraping to find more time, I have found that the inclusion of YA literature in conjunction with traditional canonical pieces has elevated both student understanding and interest in the more classic materials and has become a staple of my teaching that my colleagues have grown to embrace rather than resist.

What we really push for in the interdisciplinary sequence is a recognition that people share much in the way of common humanity across era and place, and yet, equally, all of us are embedded within particular eras and societies that affect how we see ourselves, the world, and the purpose of things. We learn about other cultures not simply through what historians have said about these cultures but through what they have said of themselves, in documentation, in story, in song, in the practice of living, in what they held as beautiful or valuable. If we can recognize the distinctions of worldview between the ancient Sumerians and the ancient Egyptians, the hope is that we can apply this skill of perception to our own and other present cultures. In this endeavor, YA literature is as obviously important in both the formulation and expression of our culture as *Gilgamesh* was for ancient Sumer. The very popularity of YA literature says something significant about our society and how we see ourselves within the transcriptions of the Western metaethic, as described by John Stephens and Robyn McCallum in *Retelling Stories, Framing Culture.*

To be fair, what I can never do, given the necessary requirements of the course, is insist that the students read whole YA novels (at least until we hit contemporary culture in the fourth semester), though I often suggest it for their spare time, and quite a few of my students take me up on that, true joy being mine when these same students request office hours to discuss the comparisons of the suggested YA literature to the more canonical pieces. This is nearly always the case with *The Hunger Games*, of which I assign chapters 19 and 25 in Ancient Civilizations, to correlate with books 1–8 (particularly book 4) of the *Aeneid.* In both works a young hero is called upon to represent his or her individual culture, as well as lead the people into a new way of living; the pairing may be unexpected, but it works quite well. Katniss and Aeneas must both contend with journeys, unexpected leadership roles, monsters, distractions of love, personal fears, paralyzing indecision, and manipulative interference from forces beyond their control.

I can count on a majority of college students to be familiar with works that gained fame during their junior high and high school years. *The Hunger Games*, and its adaptation into film, remains popular. While some students are only minimally familiar with the story line, a majority know the book or film through direct prior reading or screening; thus, being assigned to read a chapter of a story line with which they are already familiar, and one that they perceive as "fun" reading, is never met with rejection. For my pedagogical purposes, the Hunger Game series serves as a parallel to the classic Greek and Roman epic cycles. Our overarching theme for the Roman unit is: "The Romans created a civilization that unified the Mediterranean world through the adoption and adaption of existing ideas" (Jarvis-Freeman et al.). It is remarkably easy to illustrate for students the borrowing that Virgil did from Homer within the text of the *Aeneid*, but we also look closely at the purposes of adaption. In the Homerian cycle women are of course present, but they are treated largely as possessions, their actual voices rarely heard. Helen is a trophy to be won or kept, Briseis and Andromache are warm bed companions and decent cooks, and sweet Penelope is important only insofar as she is both loyal and virtuous. Virgil's Dido in comparison is, yes, an epically necessary distraction to Aeneas as "homeward-bound" hero, but she is fascinatingly more human and complex. She has a backstory; she has passions and loyalties, sorrows and responsibilities. She is interesting. She is also suicidally sacrificed in the plot and somewhat used as a lesson by Virgil of what his hero is willing to give up in order to follow the will of the gods regarding their chosen destiny for him, as perhaps all "good Romans should do." She is thus both alike and completely different from Collins's Katniss, a young woman who merges the epic heroism of Aeneas with Dido's femininity.

Katniss and Peeta, like Aeneas and Dido, are pawns of larger forces. For the latter, it may be the classical gods, but for Katniss and Peeta, it is the fickle god of audience interest and political motivation. Like Dido, Katniss's sex appeal is part of her potential power to create peace between rival interests, and like Aeneas, she has a destiny to which she can choose to give herself over, though at a deeply personal cost. In considering both works, we spend some discussion time on the role of the love interest conflict. In the sections of focus, both protagonists are suddenly trapped in a cave with a potential romantic partner, and both protagonists end up furthering their physical relationships with said partners. In the *Aeneid* this situation is again the work of the gods, while in *The Hunger Games* it is the work of polled ratings interest. If Juno sees Dido as a way to keep Aeneas from establishing Rome, certainly the Capitol designers of the Hunger Games see Peeta as a game diversion for Katniss, a choice that she will have to make between love or survival, a way to throw her off course in pursuit of her destiny.

These comparisons of characters and story lines provide the fuel for discussing how each story reflects and informs the values of the culture within which each was created. For the Romans, the call to duty, to fulfill one's purpose as a Roman citizen, was paramount. Rome was an ideal that must be pursued, its creation and continuance easily worth any personal cost. Aeneas will eventually betray Dido to heartbreak and death in order to fulfill his duty, a decision he agonizes over, but we also see that he initially spends little time questioning his dalliance with her body and emotions. Dido's death, however, does impact Aeneas and his quest, and he will face her again in the underworld. She is not a character easily forgotten or dismissed.

What then does *The Hunger Games* say? Katniss of course is always aware that there is an audience attempting to control her actions. She weighs her physical interactions with Peeta, rarely giving in to anything akin to personal passion, instead fully engaged in her ultimate purpose. What importance is there that in this modern text the protagonist is female and the distraction male? And that this protagonist ultimately can find a way to outwit the interests of an observing godlike audience and have both survival and a love interest? What is implied to the reader in a scenario wherein a reality-show-like observation has taken the place of classical gods in determining our fate or our purpose or our actions?

There are of course no correct answers to these questions, but they provide for critically engaged, analytical conversations and display the correlation between contemporary YA fiction and classical literature. These discussions convince my students that everything that they read is forming or impacting the view of the world that they hold. Moreover, they highlight the fact that literature has always done this ideological work—that within the antique story lines of Homerian and Virgilian epics are some of the same concerns of happiness, love, hate, friendship, citizenship, duty, and meaning that we find in the most arresting fiction of today's bestsellers. I think we all love those moments in which students inform us that we have "ruined" passive entertainment for them, because they are now involved critically. I particularly relish exam essays for the course Early Church to the Renaissance in which students, who've been asked to discuss the ways in which the Protestant Reformation still impacts Western culture, not only provide evidences from reading and lecture material but also voluntarily correlate Dory's search for her lost parents (from the film *Finding Dory*) as a form of identity search and return to origin that some early Protestant reformers espoused. Humorous? Absolutely. But it also shows me that they are thinking, connecting, and really considering how narrative impacts culture and how there are multiple ways of reading a story or film. To date I've done similar readings and discussions, pairing *Gilgamesh* with both Bella Forrest's *A Shade of Vampire* and J. K. Rowling's *Harry Potter and the Deathly Hallows*, in order to examine images of the afterlife, what we owe ourselves or others in a chance to live again, and the damage of seeking immortality; *Le Morte d'Arthur* and Darren Shan's *Cirque du Freak*, to discuss the lure of power, the psychological aspects of betrayal, and the potential role of fate; Aldous Huxley's *Brave New World* and *Divergent*, to investigate not only dystopian visions of future government from two different eras but also the role of segregation ideology; and Mary Shelley's *Frankenstein* and Ransom Riggs's *Miss Peregrine's Home for Peculiar Children*, to look at the role of fearing the other. Reading and incorporating YA literature not only allows me to claim the attention and hopefully the analytical engagement of my students, but it also keeps me in touch with contemporary cultural shifts, allowing me to assess how YA texts are currently evidencing and formulating my own culture's worldview.

Works Cited

Collins, Suzanne. *The Hunger Games*. Scholastic, 2008.
Forrest, Bella. *A Shade of Vampire*. Nightlight, 2012.
Gilgamesh: The New Translation. Translated by Gerald J. Davis, Lulu, 2014.
Huxley, Aldous. *Brave New World*. Chatto and Windus, 1932.
Jarvis-Freeman, Billie, et al. Syllabus for Ancient Civilizations. Interdisciplinary Studies, Lincoln Christian University, Fall 2015.
Malory, Thomas. *Le Morte d'Arthur*. Pinnacle Press, 2017.
Riggs, Ransom. *Miss Peregrine's Home for Peculiar Children*. Quirk Books, 2011.
Roth, Veronica. *Divergent*. HarperCollins, 2011.
Rowling, J. K. *Harry Potter and the Deathly Hallows*. Scholastic, 2009.
Shan, Darren. *Cirque du Freak*. HarperCollins, 2000.
Shelley, Mary. *Frankenstein*. W. W. Norton, 2012.
Stephens, John, and Robyn McCallum. *Retelling Stories, Framing Culture: Traditional Story and Metanarratives in Children's Literature*. Garland, 1998.

Helma van Lierop-Debrauwer

Literary Education That Crosses Borders: Adolescent Fiction in the Upper Grades of Secondary Schools

In 1991 *De perfecte puber* (*The Perfect Adolescent*), an anthology of adolescent fiction, was published in the Netherlands (Müller). A quick skim through the book reveals that all the abstracts are taken from adult literature. YA books are completely absent. However, at the time, the term *young adult fiction* was not yet used in the Netherlands. The accepted term was *adolescent fiction*. Young adult fiction as a denominator for books about adolescence for adolescent readers was introduced in the Netherlands between 2005 and 2010. In the project described in this essay, I used the term *adolescent fiction* and I continued to do so afterward, because one of the aims of my research was and is to make teachers in the upper grades of secondary education aware of the fact that the distinction they make between books about adolescence for adult readers and those about adolescence for young readers is an artificial one (Lierop-Debrauwer 229). Adolescent fiction is a genre that is present in both juvenile and adult literature, whereas young adult fiction is, at least in the Netherlands, considered to be only part of juvenile literature. However, in this essay I will use the term *YA fiction* every time I refer to books about adolescence published for adolescent readers.

This separation of juvenile and adult literature in historical overviews of books about adolescence has been common practice since the introduction of the term *adolescence* at the end of the nineteenth century. However, following the literary emancipation of juvenile literature in the 1980s and 1990s, the boundary between the two literary systems has become increasingly blurred, at least in the eyes of scholars and critics working in the field of juvenile literature. More particularly, many of them consider YA books to be a prime example of crossover literature, as defined by scholars such as Sandra Beckett (*Crossover Fiction*): that is, comparable to adolescent fiction published for adults in both theme and literary strategies. These critics believe it is only natural to pay attention to the genre in the upper grades of secondary schools. However, their plea was ignored by gatekeepers in the adult literary system, such as literary critics and secondary school teachers, who disqualified YA literature as not meeting the criteria of literary quality demanded in the Dutch examination programs, though they were unable to explain what the exact criteria were.

This discussion in the Netherlands about the boundary between juvenile and adult literature continued for quite some time. Some people were not convinced of the necessity of these debates. In 1996 Bart Moeyaert, a well-known Flemish author who had already written several YA books at the time, more or less distanced himself from the discussion in a column in a Dutch newspaper. He advised his readers to just read:

> If a discussion like that flares up again, I'm going to take a pile of books to these bickering people. I'll tell them it's all theoretical hogwash, this fight about the Big Difference. You don't find out about a book's target audience if you keep droning on endlessly about the difference between young and old. Start from the Big Resemblance and then the target audience will become clear by itself, . . . if you just keep your mouth shut and read.[1]

Although I agree with Moeyaert that reading a novel before making decisions about it is important, I disagree with him in thinking that it is useful to discuss the differences and similarities between YA literature and literature about adolescents written for adult readers. Historically, the problem emerged because the debate was often based on personal experience and intuition and not supported by any academic research.

In the early 2000s I made several efforts to put flesh on the bones of the debate in the Netherlands about YA literature crossing borders. In 2003 I started with a comparative literary analysis of a corpus of mainly contemporary Dutch YA novels and novels about adolescents published for adults. This analysis led me to conclude that both types of adolescent fiction are very similar in theme, structure, and style (Lierop-Debrauwer and Bastiaansen-Harks). Based on this conclusion, I argue for the use of YA literature in the upper grades of secondary schools. Neel Bastiaansen-Harks and I developed a series of lessons about adolescent fiction for classroom use, which we tested in a small-scale project.

Toward a Longitudinal Literary Education Program

The results of my comparative analysis supported the argument of a literary emancipation of children's and YA literature since the 1980s and 1990s, as outlined by, among others, Maria Nikolajeva (*Children's Literature*; "Exit Children's Literature") and Beckett (*Transcending Boundaries*). YA literature had come of age, so including this genre in literary education seemed justified, not only in the lower grades but also in the final grades of secondary schools. It is difficult to compare the Dutch and American school systems, but the upper grades (the fourth, fifth, and sixth grades) in secondary school are more or less comparable to grades ten through twelve in American high schools. The students are between fifteen and eighteen years old. Both in YA literature and in novels about adolescents written for adults there are some books that meet the literary standards of the time period in which they were written and some that do not. With this in mind, I argued that it was time that secondary schools seriously start working on a longitudinal literary education program, by which I mean a literature curriculum that is characterized by coherence and continuity across grade levels. The objectives teachers want to achieve in their literature classes can be realized, and sometimes even better realized, when YA literature is discussed together with adult literature rather than through discussions of adult literature alone. In general, YA books reflect young people's perception of their own and other people's lives and contribute to the development of self-knowledge and empathy. Objectives like personal development as well as social awareness—important aims held by teachers of Dutch literature in the upper grades of secondary education—can thus be realized when these books are included in the curriculum. If the pedagogical goal is for teachers to improve their students' cultural literacy, their aesthetic awareness, and their literary competence by dealing with literary history and theory in the classroom, these goals can be met just as easily and effectively, and perhaps even more so, by having students read YA books in conjunction with literature about adolescents written for adults. Moreover, a comparison of YA literature with books written for adults forms a good starting point for discussions about matters of literary competence, such as attribution of literary quality, the boundary between juvenile and adult literature, and the role literary institutions play in this.

Discussing YA literature in literature classes is not linked to a specific approach to literature and literary education. The books can be studied from a literary historical, a structural analytic, a sociological, or a reader-oriented point of view. However, there are two necessary preconditions: teachers should have knowledge of YA literature and they should value paying attention to these books during literature classes. A survey among secondary school teachers (Lierop-Debrauwer and Bastiaansen-Harks) and personal observation have led me to conclude that the situation on these points in the Netherlands in the early twenty-first century was far from ideal and that the teacher of Dutch language and literature, described by the well-known Dutch YA novelist Edward van de Vendel, was no exception. Van de Vendel tells how a seventeen-year-old student, Fabian, asked his teacher if he could read Van de Vendel's YA novel *De dagen van de bluegrassliefde* (*The Days of the Bluegrass Love*) for his required reading list:

> The teacher thought awhile, skimmed through the book, read the blurbs, and then said no. "Why not?" asked Fabian. The teacher pointed at a sentence below the picture of the author: "It says here that it is a youth novel. You are not allowed to read youth novels."
>
> The next day, Fabian again went to his teacher, this time with my novel *Gijsbrecht*. The teacher looked at the book and inspected it. Fabian was allowed to read it because the publisher had been wise enough not to put the words *youth novel* on the cover. (352)

Bastiaansen-Harks and I subsequently developed, on the basis of my comparative analysis, a series of six lessons for reading and comparing and contrasting YA literature with adolescent fiction for adults, with the aim of providing teachers with a concrete tool they can use to work with these books in their classes. The lessons were meant to stimulate a discussion among students about literary quality and about the boundary between juvenile and adult literature and the consequences of the distinction for their literary education, in particular for their required reading list. Moreover, we wanted to know how students experienced and evaluated this way of working with juvenile and adult literature. We tested the lessons in the fourth grade of a gymnasium, which consisted of twenty-nine students—eighteen girls and eleven boys—aged fifteen to seventeen years old. This type of secondary school in the Netherlands is meant for the highest-achieving students.

Content of the Lessons

The first lesson was an introduction to the topic. The students got a handout with questions that invited them to reflect on the similarities and differences between the two literary systems, with information about adolescence and the adolescent novel and an explanation about possible ways to compare adolescent novels aimed at adult readers with those aimed at young adults. In order to be able to make such a comparison, students were introduced to three theories: adaptation theory, reader-response theory of the implied reader (translated for them into "the reader at work"), and theory about the poetics of the author. We discussed the content of the handout with the students, and at the end of this first lesson the students were invited to form groups of two or three and choose a pair of books to work with from a preselected list. Because we hoped that the series of lessons would appeal not only to teachers of Dutch language and literature but also to modern language teachers, we included some translated books in our selection. To make sure that the school had enough books for the students, we restricted the selection to three pairs of books: *Spookliefde* (*Ghost Love*), a novel about adolescence published for adult readers by the Dutch author Vonne van der Meer, and *Bijenkoningin* (*Queen Bee*), a YA novel written by Veronica Hazelhoff; *Gebr* (*Brothers*), a YA book by Ted van Lieshout, and *De vriendschap* (*The Friendship*), by Conny Palmen; and two translated American classics: *The Catcher in the Rye*, by J. D. Salinger, and *The Chocolate War*, by Robert Cormier. The two novels in each pair were coupled on the basis of corresponding themes.

In the second lesson we gave an example of a comparative analysis by comparing a YA novel written by the Swedish author Peter Pohl, *Vi kallar honom Anna* (*We Call Him Anna*), and an adolescent novel for adult readers written by the Dutch author Wessel te Gussinklo, *De opdracht* (*The Assignment*).

In the third, fourth, and fifth lessons, the students worked in groups, discussing and analyzing their two books and writing a paper on their results. We also asked them to end their paper with a personal evaluation, paying attention to the teamwork, the project itself, and the books selected. We were present to answer any questions and to encourage them in their work. At the end of the fifth lesson they handed in their papers. We read these and provided the students with constructive feedback.

In the sixth lesson we discussed the process and the results of the project with the students. We started by exchanging with the class some general observations with respect to the approach of the analyses and the structure and content of the papers. In the second part of the lesson we again had the students work in groups, giving them the opportunity to react to the feedback on their own papers.

After concluding this series of assignments, we evaluated the project with the teacher of the class. On the basis of this evaluation we adapted the second lesson. The students were not familiar with the two books we used as an example for comparative analysis, so it was hard for them to get a good picture. We decided that to prepare them for doing an analysis on their own, it was better instead to read passages from two books together with the students and to do some exercises in comparative analysis.

Literary Quality and the Boundary between Young Adult and Adult Literature

In the first lesson, students immediately engaged in discussions about the similarities and differences between juvenile and adult literature. The students did not take the exclusion of YA books from the required reading list for granted because they had experienced the abrupt, and for many of them unpleasant, transition from reading YA books to being allowed to read only adult books for their reading list when they entered fourth grade (comparable to the tenth grade in American high schools). However, when asked to define juvenile literature and adult literature, they made a clear distinction between the two systems in terms of simple versus complex.

In making this comparison between the two books they had chosen, students showed a preference for working with adaptation theory in combination with the theory of the implied reader. They found the adaptation perspective attractive because it allowed them to go through the text step by step, analyzing the levels of adaptation distinguished by, among others, Göte Klingberg: content, structure, style, and design of the book. Moreover, the instrument is very concrete: it enabled students to establish through random checks the average length of the sentences, the number of words in a sentence, as well as the number of main clauses, composite sentences, and sentences with direct or indirect speech. However, one of the drawbacks of the adaptation approach is that it overlooks the fact that a literary text is always more than the sum of its parts. The approach falls short when a text can be read on more than one level. Therefore, most students complemented their analysis of adaptation strategies with a search for telltale gaps, an important aspect of Aidan Chambers's use of the concept of the implied reader (102).

The students presented their analyses in papers. These papers revealed that for the most part they retained their assumptions with respect to the boundary between adult literature and juvenile literature. Although in their analyses they found that both books were complex in many respects, in their conclusion they were inclined to maintain the boundary between the two literary systems; they were used to making a distinction between adolescent novels aimed at adult readers and those aimed at readers of their age in terms of high and low literary quality. Most students did not seem to be aware of their assumptions. However, there were exceptions to the rule. Two students, for example, worked as follows. They posed questions with regard to aspects of the texts. For every question they formulated a hypothesis regarding the answer. In the next step they analyzed the text to see whether their analysis confirmed their expectations. Using this approach to the texts, they were able to discuss their assumptions about adult and juvenile literature.

Regardless of the fact that in the conclusion of their papers they still believed what they had previously been told about the boundary between two literary systems, most students expressed a preference for the YA novels they read, in part because they got more emotionally involved in them and could identify more easily with these books' protagonists. Some of the students were intrigued by both books they read, and they said that they discussed them outside of class, for example with their parents, to get more of a grip on the similarities and differences in literary complexity.

Students' Evaluation of the Project

Every student was asked to reflect on the project. Twenty-four out of twenty-nine were positive, while five were partly positive, partly negative. The negative feedback had to do mainly with logistic problems and the amount of time they had to spend on the project. The positive feedback was twofold: first, they appreciated this new approach and the room it left for a genuine discussion about the quality of the books; second, they enjoyed their reading experiences.

Students liked the comparative approach because it provided them with new insights. One of them formulated it this way: "The project took more time and preparation than a regular assignment, but you really got something in return: you were forced to really get into a book in more depth, and by comparing books you discovered new aspects that you wouldn't have noticed otherwise. You get more insight into similarities and differences" (Lierop-Debrauwer and Bastiaansen-Harks 120). Students said that they had become more aware of what to pay attention to when they reflect on a book. Some students were convinced that the project changed their future reading: "I learned to look at books differently. I think this will have an impact on other books in the future, because I like the way we read these books" (121). They also appreciated the group discussions, even if they did not agree on the books, because discussions provided them with a diversified view of the books.

"Literature Is Indifferent to Target Groups"

The project described here provides interesting options for giving the YA novel a fair chance in the upper grades of secondary education. It is in line with the recommendation offered by critics and academics regarding the boundary between juvenile and adult literature, published in *Literatuur zonder leeftijd* (*Literature without Age*), a Dutch academic periodical on children's and YA literature. They advise readers to quit thinking in terms of target groups, just like Moeyaert recommends. "Literature is indifferent to target groups," Joke Linders, a Dutch literary critic, rightly notes: "*Zwart als inkt* [*Black as Ink*; a well-known Dutch fairy tale adaptation], by Wim Hofman, is both a fairy tale that you can read to six-year-olds and a novel for adolescents about standing up for yourself, breaking away from your parents, making your own choices, and being a grown-up in life" (335). And, I would like to add, it is a novel about loneliness and neglect, a feeling readers of all ages can recognize. To come to the conclusion that literature is indifferent to age, students have to read as many different YA books and novels about adolescents targeted to adults as possible and compare them with respect to content and form; then they have to reflect on them and discuss them in literature classes. This approach can help them become critical readers who have the literary competence to distinguish between literary texts in terms of complexity, regardless of target groups.

Note

1. All translations from the Dutch are mine.

Works Cited

Beckett, Sandra L. *Crossover Fiction: Global and Historical Perspectives.* Routledge, 2009.

———. *Transcending Boundaries: Writing for a Dual Audience of Children and Adults.* Garland, 1999.

Chambers, Aidan. "The Reader in the Book." *Children's Literature: The Development of Criticism*, edited by Peter Hunt, Routledge, 1990, pp. 91–114.

Cormier, Robert. *The Chocolate War.* Pantheon Books, 1974.

Gussinklo, Wessel te. *De opdracht.* Meulenhoff, 1995.

Hazelhoff, Veronica. *Bijenkoningin.* Querido, 1992.

Klingberg, Göte. *Kinder- und Jugendliteraturforschung.* Hermann Böhlau, 1973.

Lierop-Debrauwer, Helma van. "Finally Coming Together? The Bridging Role of the Adolescent Novel in the Netherlands." *Canon Constitution and Canon Change in Children's Literature*, edited by Bettina Kümmerling-Meibauer and Anja Müller, Routledge, 2017, pp. 222–37.

Lierop-Debrauwer, Helma van, and Neel Bastiaansen-Harks. *Over grenzen: De adolescentenroman in het literatuuronderwijs.* Eburon, 2005.

Lieshout, Ted van. *Gebr.* Van Goor, 1996.

Linders, Joke. "Literatuur is wezensvreemd aan doelgroepen: Het bestaan, het bestaansrecht en bestaande literatuur voor adolescenten." *Literatuur zonder leeftijd*, vol. 53, 2000, pp. 330–35.

Meer, Vonne van der. *Spookliefde.* De Bezige Bij, 1995.

Moeyaert, Bart. "Krullen zonder betekenis." *NRC Handelsblad*, 29 Nov. 1996, www.nrc.nl/nieuws/1996/11/29/krullen-zonder-betekenis-7333812-a354871.

Müller, John, editor. *De perfecte puber: Van het* Lijden van de jonge Werther *tot* Het geheime dagboek van Adriaan Mole. De Bijenkorf, 1991.

Nikolajeva, Maria. *Children's Literature Comes of Age: Toward a New Aesthetic.* Garland, 1996.

———. "Exit Children's Literature?" *The Lion and the Unicorn*, vol. 22, no. 2, Apr. 1998, pp. 221–33.

Palmen, Connie. *De vriendschap.* Prometheus, 1995.

Pohl, Peter. *Vi kallar honom Anna.* Norstedts Förlag, 1987.

Salinger, J. D. *The Catcher in the Rye.* Little, Brown, 1951.

Vendel, Edward van de. "Help! De noodzaak van de adolescentenroman: Of het loslaten van het doelgroepdenken." *Literatuur zonder leeftijd*, vol. 14, no. 53, 2000, pp. 352–55.

Justyna Deszcz-Tryhubczak

The Pleasures and Impasses of Teaching Young Adult Literature to Polish Graduates in English Studies

In 2001 Karen Coats, reflecting on the task of teaching and researching children's literature in a university English department, saw it as a risky job: "No matter how sophisticated your theoretical commitments are, no matter how learned you are in and beyond your subject area, you suffer the bemused and patronizing smiles of peers who find the aesthetic virtues of Dr. Seuss less worthy of study than those of, say, Thomas Hardy or Emily Dickinson" ("Fish" 405). While this precarious status of children's and YA literature as a legitimate field within English studies is probably no longer the case at universities in the United States, Australia, and Western Europe, this is certainly so in Poland, where no English department offers an extensive range of undergraduate and postgraduate courses or programs in children's and YA literature studies. A quick Google search reveals only isolated mentions of courses in British children's literature (with no exact dates or other details) taught at the Institute of English and American Studies at the University of Gdańsk and several courses taught by myself in my home institution, the Institute of English Studies at the University of Wrocław. While this absence of broad academic offerings can be explained simply by the lack of scholarly interest in children's literature among the faculty of English departments in Poland, I would argue that it can also be ascribed to the underappreciation of the field as worthy of academic attention and may prove potentially attractive to English studies graduates.

The lack of interest in children's and YA literature studies is reflected in its being excluded from my home institution's didactic offer in 2017–18 of the philological specialization module Literature, Culture and the Media. Its aim is to compete with the modules offering courses in translation, linguistics, and second language acquisition, which, incidentally, incorporate no elements of children's literature either. Prospective students are encouraged to select courses on American comics, role-playing games, film adaptations of nineteenth- and twentieth-century fiction, science fiction and fantasy narratives versus their film adaptations, and contemporary theater and film and TV adaptations of drama. Although the composition of the module both reflects the elevated status of popular culture as a serious object of academic interest and testifies to the growing presence of what Rob Pope calls "interdiscipline English" (234), the omission of children's and YA literature seriously reduces the offer's potential to show students that studying youth literature and culture can be helpful in finding jobs, for example in the burgeoning publishing markets, reading promotion, or cultural program coordination.

Having worked in such a climate, I consider myself very fortunate to have been allowed to teach elective MA courses and two MA seminars on broadly understood children's and YA literature and culture since 2009. In 2012 I designed and taught a course on utopianism in children's and YA literature, one of my primary and ongoing interests, which was addressed to first-year graduate students. Among the texts I selected for the syllabus were the following YA titles: *Nation*, by Terry Pratchett; *Feed*, by M. T. Anderson; *Un Lun Dun*, by China Miéville; *Kaitangata Twitch*, by Margaret Mahy; *The Giver*, by Lois Lowry; *Fruitlands: Louisa May Alcott Made Perfect*, by Gloria Whelan; and *Harry Potter and the Deathly Hallows*, by J. K. Rowling.

In this essay I discuss the challenges and rewards of teaching YA literature in the context of English studies in Poland. My broader purpose is to use my experience as a case study to highlight a rationale for the significance of these texts for engaging students in critical thinking, cultural critique, and collaborative response in contexts where such arguments are still needed. I examine the outcomes of introducing a creative writing component as both a test of students' understanding of the conventions of YA literature and as an indication of its potential to inspire their creativity and in-class cooperation. Additionally, I propose the introduction of project-based courses as a means of transferring students' academic engagements beyond the university classroom. I argue that projects addressed to local communities and aiming to contribute to the public good can make students realize the crucial role of texts for young readers as elements of culture, shaping individual and collective lives. From such a viewpoint, YA literature may serve as especially useful material for establishing a practical and constructive connection between what students learn at university and real-life issues affecting them and people around them, which in turn may help them in shaping their future professional lives.

As noted above, one of my key interests in youth culture is how it functions as a cultural expression of utopianism. Utopianism can be understood as a "human impulse/tendency" stemming from dissatisfaction with and a critical attitude toward the present (Sargisson 9). This tendency fulfills itself through people's engagement in contemporary debates, their desire for alternatives, and the very activity of imagining them. To invite my students to explore that interest, I designed the 2012 course with the following principal goals in mind: to encourage students to identify and comment on utopian and dystopian visions of life in selected texts, and to show students how childhood and youth are frequently used to represent adult fears, dreams, and ambitions concerning the future without acknowledging that the young generation have their own hopes about what their lives will look like. The fact that the course was offered as an elective was both a drawback and an advantage. Marginal as such courses seem to students who need to focus first and foremost on completing their MA theses, they give the teacher a lot of flexibility and freedom with regard to their contents, structure, and assessment. Hence, I used this opportunity to design a course that corresponded to my research interests. Since I was not concerned with examinations or essays, it enabled me to interact with students as fellow readers who all have their reading histories and literary experiences. Of the forty students who signed up for the course, nineteen indicated genuine interest in the subject, which means that my class in fact catered to student demand.

Unfortunately, the large number of students made discussions difficult. If I had hoped that I would experience what Kevin Kienholz refers to as "[t]he unique privilege of being the teacher who occasionally gets the chance to remind students of why they fell in love with reading in the first place" (in the context of his YA literature university courses), I soon realized I was in for a huge disappointment because of my students' silence in most of the classes. While collaborative in-class discussion used to be the norm at Polish universities, and would be a typical approach to class organization in humanities departments, the poor interaction among the participants in my course was an indication of a growing mismatch between students' and academics' expectations about the very purpose of university education: as access to free tertiary education in Poland has been widened in the past twenty years—predominantly because high numbers of students garner big government subsidies—for many young people studying has come to mean an effortless and noncommittal way to obtain a graduate diploma and improve their prospects on the job market. Such an approach has inevitably made spontaneous discussion an elusive and meaningless activity not only for students but also for lecturers, who in turn are likely to use any motivation and to come up with innovative ways to counteract their students' disinterest. This in turn has resulted in an awkward situation in which both sides simply want to part ways with each other as soon as possible. Such a trend is especially visible in humanities, popularly regarded as easier to manage academically than science and technology. Hence, while it would be unfair to underestimate students' potential for and interest in intellectual inquiry, including communicating and arguing their views, the effectiveness and quality of classroom interaction at Polish universities has undoubtedly declined as a result of the massification of higher education.

Yet two in-class discussions and a serendipitous development offer potent examples of how YA texts provide opportunities for students to develop skills in critical and creative thinking. In one class the students read selected excerpts from *Feed* that contain either the most poignant elements of Anderson's critique of consumerism and technology or the most alarming representations of the young living in "a state of emptiness," where they "are offered consumerism as a substitute for participation in citizenship" (Bradford 129). The students were very keen to comment on the parallels between Anderson's dystopian vision of the future and their own lives, and they found it both disturbing and fascinating that the ten years between the publication of the novel and the spring of 2012, when we were discussing it, proved that the author's diagnosis of what awaits humanity was accurate. They were especially concerned with the young characters' obsession with shopping and brands. They also focused on Anderson's representation of a world inundated by meaningless information and entertainment, pointing out that they had already been living in it for some time, often without realizing it. Finally, they were scared by the vision of a human being turned into a cyborg whose life, or functioning, as someone in the class pointed out, could depend on corporations.[1]

While I included *Feed* on the syllabus because of its being a classical example of YA dystopia, a strategic planning decision on my part had been the inclusion of J. K. Rowling's *Harry Potter and the Deathly Hallows*, as most students were fans of the Harry Potter series. For that class, I asked the students to read excerpts from Daragh Downes's 2010 article "Harry Potter and the Deathly Hollowness: A Narratological and Ideological Critique of J. K. Rowling's Magical System," in which Downes criticizes Rowling's failure to unlock the utopian potential for transformation of Hogwarts and the wizarding community that emerged during the war against Voldemort. Downes argues that this "revolutionary sabotage and the deep chivalry of a resistance movement" (164) were written off by the return to the old order and its injustices in the "Nineteen Years Later" epilogue, with Ron's prejudice against the pure-bloods and ongoing contempt for the Muggles. Most students admitted that they had not thought of the epilogue in the context of radical political and social changes. As they eagerly discussed what new developments in the wizarding world such a transformation would entail, I decided to ask them to read sample fan fictions showing how readers extrapolated from the seeds of revolution planted by Rowling to create a critical commentary on social and political phenomena they know from their own lives. Although very few of the students admitted to reading fan fiction and none to writing it, the introduction of fans' texts into the course turned out to be another good, albeit impromptu, decision, as the students enjoyed analyzing both the literary aspects of the fictions and the fan authors' ideas about the democratization of the wizarding society.

Encouraged by the success of the class on fan fiction, I introduced an alternative final assignment. Initially, the students were asked to submit two five-hundred-word comments on selected texts. The new assignment required that the students write their own utopian, dystopian, or antiutopian short story for young readers of any age. My intention was to encourage the students to perform a "critical-creative" activity (Pope 238) that would further their understanding of both utopianism and the conventions necessary to produce a YA text. As the students were then writing the first chapters of their MA theses, I expected that most of them would not risk distracting themselves with writing a story. Yet my decision was well rewarded; eighteen students submitted their stories, ten of which could be classified as YA stories. While generalizing about YA stories cannot do justice to their thematic and generic diversity, they all centered on teenage characters' disappointment with the status quo and their resulting questioning of the social order, albeit sometimes with little success.[2]

The students' approach testifies to their understanding of the conventions of YA literature about utopianism. The final class of the course, during which the students both discussed their own stories and commented on the others' texts, turned out to be the most successful one in the whole course: the students evidently enjoyed reading one another's stories and were eager to share their thoughts. The feedback questionnaire revealed twenty-seven enthusiastic responses about the assignment: "Finally, an opportunity to do something creative at the Institute of English Studies," "More creative writing!" "Polish system of education lacks ANY creativity," and "Writing a story taught everyone a lot about themselves." Both the enthusiasm and the frustration revealed in these comments seemed to me a precious guideline for the future: it would be worthwhile to explore YA texts by designing and implementing activities and assignments that both inspire students' commitment to excellence and motivate peer collaboration.

Consequently, I have tried to develop methods, learning situations, and activities through which my students could see that while reading and talking about YA literature as an adult may be a source of pleasure insofar as it satisfies our nostalgia for childhood, it is also, as Coats rightly points out, about "a sense of responsibility toward its intended audience, making critical response a mandatory and self-motivating task" ("Fish" 409). Yet I would venture to claim that critical response as such is not enough. Hence, I have consistently designed project-centered courses bridging students' classroom knowledge of literature for young readers to the social, political, economic, and cultural realities of their own communities. Such a combination of academic, pedagogic, and activist engagements empowers students as coproducers of knowledge in the here and now of a particular project. More important, it also enables them to appreciate both the reverberations of YA literature as a vital element of culture and their own potential as cultural mediators, which in turn may be seen as developing transferable skills and competences. Finally, for me, my collaboration with students is a way to overcome the devaluation of teaching literature in higher education institutions and engage in a shared productive experience and action extending beyond the classroom and the discipline of English studies to the actual effects YA literature may have on individuals and society. All this, in my view, compensates for the academic alienation still affecting children's and YA literature studies in the context of English studies in Poland and, possibly, elsewhere.

Notes

1. Coats reports observing similar reactions to the novel in her classroom ("Young Adult" 324).

2. The stories are available at *Utopianism in Children's Literature* (childrenlitutopianism.wordpress.com/page/3). All the students who submitted written assignments received maximum grades for them. In the case of the stories, I provided feedback on style and the match between the utopian content and children's and YA literature conventions.

Works Cited

Anderson, M. T. *Feed*. Candlewick Press, 2002.

Bradford, Clare. "'Everything Must Go!': Consumerism and Reader Positioning in M. T. Anderson's *Feed*." *Jeunesse: Young People, Texts, Cultures*, vol. 2, no. 2, 2010, pp. 128–37.

Coats, Karen. "Fish Stories: Teaching Children's Literature in a Postmodern World." *Pedagogy*, vol. 1, no. 2, Spring 2001, pp. 405–09.

———. "Young Adult Literature: Growing Up, in Theory." *Handbook of Research on Children's and Young Adult Literature*, edited by Shelby A. Wolf et al., Routledge, 2011, pp. 315–29.

Downes, Daragh. "Harry Potter and the Deathly Hollowness: A Narratological and Ideological Critique of J. K. Rowling's Magical System." *International Research in Children's Literature*, vol. 3, no. 2, 2010, pp. 162–73.

Kienholz, Kevin. "Young Adult Literature in the College Classroom: A Reminder of Why We Love Literature." *Assembly on Literature for Adolescents of the NCTE*, 8 Feb. 2016, www.alan-ya.org/young-adult-literature-in-the-college-classroom-a-reminder-of-why-we-love-literature.

Lowry, Lois. *The Giver*. Houghton Mifflin, 1993.

Mahy, Margaret. *Kaitangata Twitch*. Allen and Unwin, 2005.

Miéville, China. *Un Lun Dun*. Macmillan Children's Books, 2008.

Pope, Rob. "Interdiscipline English! A Series of Provocations and Projections." *Futures for English Studies: Teaching Language, Literature and Creative Writing in Higher Education*, edited by Ann Hewings et al., Palgrave Macmillan, 2016, pp. 233–52.

Pratchett, Terry. *Nation*. Doubleday, 2008.

Rowling, J. K. *Harry Potter and the Deathly Hallows*. Scholastic, 2007.

Sargisson, Lucy. *Fool's Gold? Utopianism in the Twenty-First Century*. Palgrave Macmillan, 2012.

Whelan, Gloria. *Fruitlands: Louisa May Alcott Made Perfect*. HarperCollins, 2002.

Part II

Genres and Forms

Farah Mendlesohn

Teaching Young Adult Science Fiction

My colleague Michael M. Levy was to write this essay. Mike died in April 2017, and with him died our argument about how to select YA science fiction and how to teach it. Mike and I came from very different positions. He was a literature scholar and engaged in the education world. I am originally a historian. Our argument originated in that difference and centered on what, when we select our teaching texts, we are teaching for. For Mike and for many other specialists in YA literature, there is consensus around how young adults read that focuses on identifying with the characters (see Frevert et al.). I am not arguing that this projection is not the case for many child readers, but discussion with adult readers of science fiction about what they read for now and what they read for as children (see Mendlesohn 22–82) suggests that this is not what attracts readers to science fiction. These readers are knowledge gatherers; they would read *Little House on the Prairie* for the details of building a log cabin.

The people who are attracted to science fiction are far more likely to be motivated by a combination of fact gathering and abstract thought than by empathy with the characters. From an early age they are the people who enjoy knowledge and enjoy applying knowledge: they tend to be fascinated by science (of course) but also by history, anthropology, languages, geography, social science, and philosophy.[1] This is problematic in the classroom, because the subset of people attracted to English literature courses, or librarianship, tend to be much more character and empathy readers. You can see this in the generalist recommendation companion *Genreflecting: A Guide to Popular Reading Interests in Genre Fiction*, where the science fiction recommended is always described in terms of character, identification, or anxiety explored, not in terms of the science, philosophy, or politics that are the heart of the text.[2]

When you decide what YA science fiction to teach, you need to begin by thinking why you are teaching it and what you want students to take away. You need to consider which canon or subsection of YA science fiction you are going to teach. Will you teach the books that everyone loves, the big hitters such as *The Hunger Games*? If you do, you will have to accept that if you have students in the class who already read science fiction they are unlikely to be impressed: they may take the book apart for the ludicrousness of its political and economic setup. The students who want to empathize with the characters will probably find this a rather irritating critique.

An additional problem is that science fiction is a huge, baggy genre. More than one critic has referred to it as a mode, a way of writing (Mendlesohn 1). Science fiction encompasses near future technothrillers, far future space opera, alien encounters, experience with real developing technology and world-scale politics, and far more. It has proved a platform for political engagement with racism, sexism, and homophobia in ways difficult to manage in mimetic fiction; it has allowed authors to imagine how things might be different. It contains both optimistic and pessimistic views of the future and is often simply about how we might live very ordinary lives in a different world. It has very little plot of its own. Perhaps only the invention story is indigenous to science fiction, so you will find mysteries, romances, and exploration stories. It is a way of writing about a subject, not a subject itself. It is very difficult, if you restrict yourself to a small body of well-known texts, to represent this. Finally, science fiction has accreted a body of knowledge in the genre. Legacy texts have left a consensus around future technology, ways of writing, and naming practices (neologisms) that can confound the inexperienced, and although there are, understandably, fewer of these issues in children's and YA books, they are still there. You can find an exploration of these issues in the *Cambridge Companion to Science Fiction* (James and Mendlesohn); the best history of the field is currently Mark Bould and Sherryl Vint's *The Routledge Concise History of Science Fiction*.

Given all this, what I have done is to select and recommend not the most popular books in the genre but some of the best writers, the ones who explore what the genre can do and who take no quarter in what they expect their readers to be able to accept. All began writing in the last two decades: K. A. Applegate, Philip Reeve, Oisín McGann, Cory Doctorow, and Nnedi Okorafor. None of these authors write space opera, so I have made some other suggestions for teachers who wish to include it. Summaries of the texts appear in the middle of the essay, followed by reading strategies for these texts drawn from Istvan Csicsery-Ronay's *Seven Beauties of Science Fiction.*

Applegate writes in many genres, including romance and mystery, but she achieved her major success with the series Animorphs, a subversive superhero story in which a group of children receive the power to transmute themselves into animals in order to battle the forces of evil, alien invaders. Most stories of this kind are barely science fiction, closer perhaps to wish fulfillment fantasy, but the Animorphs sequence, which runs to fifty-four books, engages early with issues of childhood trauma, the resistance to an invader, and the nature of evil. By the end of the books the children have experienced the horrors of war and the deaths of those they love and face the difficulties that await them in peace.

Applegate's Remnants is a series told in thirteen parts, each focalized through a different character and aimed at early teens and upward. It begins as a very straightforward planetary escape. The planet is doomed to be destroyed by an asteroid, and one nation creates a spaceship that can take eighty people. These people are not a carefully selected pool of genetic perfection and beaming intelligence but are adults and the children of adults who could bribe their way onto the ship. The result is a mishmash of individuals, some with skills, some without, and a set of children who are spoiled, screwed up, concerned with their own needs, and generally dysfunctional. They are put into cold sleep and wake to find that half the passengers are already dead because their pods malfunctioned or were holed by micrometeorites or space worms. In addition, there are other refugee species on the ship, and they are not happy about the changing conditions. Over the thirteen books the party diminishes, finds new places to live, makes allies with some species, has its members picked off by circumstances, and changes as it is affected and infected by the environment. Eventually some parts of it merge with alien intelligence. The books are dark, following the shifting alliances and a world beyond the characters' control, to maximum dramatic effect. They raise issues about how we work together, what we value, what we mean by identity, and how we interact with an other with whom we can have no empathy. The thirteen-part structure is a high-interest, low-readability package, a useful reminder that reading level is not necessarily linked to the developing capacity for abstract thought

Reeve's science fiction is predominantly far future. The Hungry City Chronicles was published at a time when science fiction for teens struggled to find either publishers or an audience, despite the growing popularity of science fiction movies, and can be fairly said to have created the modern market. In the series, which begins with *Mortal Engines*, the main characters leave London in search for a new land and become involved in a climactic battle for the world and its resources. The landscapes and mise-en-scène are sublime: plains are vast, the cities are huge techno monsters, and airships are used in battle. The human characters are injured, fall in love, hurt each other, and die, but the focus is on the politics of the world, whether the perniciousness of knowledge held in hereditary clans or the much wider politics of the Green Aviators, and the threat of plague. Perhaps the most interesting character is the reclaimed soldier, the cyborg Shrike, who moves from threat to protector to eventually a golem figure watching a new world of ceramic technology emerge. The three prequels of the Fever Crumb sequence are also worth reading for their exploration of living through rapid change.

Reeve's *Railhead* is similarly far future but this time a YA novel set in a world of megacapitalism, deep poverty, and galaxy-spanning railroads. A subversion of the *Prince and the Pauper* theme, the book's protagonist, the thief Zen Cho, turns out to be a lost member of a major family, but there is no welcome back for him: once a branch is cut off, it can't rejoin the root stock. This is classic big-picture science fiction, with huge canvases, fantastical science, and complex politics through which the hero must navigate, and an excellent demonstration of the picaresque mode of writing that fuels much multivolume science fiction and positions the hero less as our emotional focus than as our tour guide.

McGann writes across the thriller, science fiction, and fantasy genres. His two most interesting series are the Archisan Tales and the Wildenstern Saga. There are two standalone novels also well worth considering: *Gods and Their Machines* and *Small-Minded Giants. Gods and Their Machines* tells of two children on opposite sides of a vicious war, forced together for survival; the novel goes beyond a simple friendship survival narrative to interrogate the nature of colonialism and propaganda. *Small-Minded Giants* explores the class politics in an isolated, domed postcatastrophe city. The Archisan Tales, which comprises *The Harvest Tide Project* and its sequel, is relatively unusual for science fiction for this age group because it is set on an alien planet with aliens as the protagonists: very little science fiction for children or teens ever really steps beyond the human. Both siblings in these novels are shape changers, caught up in national and international politics in which mining rights lie at the heart of invasion and empire. The Wildenstern Saga, set against the heated political environment of late nineteenth-century Ireland, is written for the older teen: set in an alternate Ireland where engimals (live engines) are captured and rounded up while people figure out what they do (they are often recognizable twentieth-century machines), the story is of the Wildenstern family who have the hereditary ability to heal almost any injury and who have unusually extended lives.

Doctorow is perhaps the most directly political of the writers here. Well-known for his freedom of information advocacy, in *Little Brother* he provides a handbook for teens who want to use their computers to resist the state. The title interrogates government responses to terrorism and questions the restrictions that governments like to impose in the name of preserving freedom. In the sequel, *Homeland*, Doctorow looks at the ethics of hacking and leaking and the temptation of easy admiration offered to heroes. Both books are interested in the politics and technology of resistance, but they also offer interesting discussions of the relationships among people engaged in political activity and resistance to the government and the strains that different levels of social and cultural privilege can impose on those relations. Doctorow is particularly good at demonstrating how even the personal cost of resistance can vary according to one's position in life.

Most science fiction for teens is very strongly Western oriented. Okorafor offers a counterbalance. Her first novel, *Zahrah the Windseeker*, is a planetary romance. When Zahrah is born with the long dada vines that indicate power growing in her hair, she is pushed to explore the world around her that has been largely shunned by the colonists. *Zahrah the Windseeker* gives us a Jack Vance–style sense of possibility and the sublime. *Shadow Speaker* and *Who Fears Death* are much stronger meat. In *Who Fears Death*, the action is set on an alien planet that might be that of *Zahrah the Windseeker*. Okorafor interrogates the cycle of genocide when a daughter of wartime rape seeks the father she knows exists among the aggressors. Although there is magic in the books, the magic takes place at the genetic level and is presented as science fiction.

Tie-in novels are also popular among teens: these books, often written by mainstream science fiction novelists, are far too frequently disparaged, in part because their older, pre-video manifestation meant that their primary material use was for replay and recall of the original text. The modern tie-in is an expansion and extension of a universe, sometimes with major characters, sometimes concerned with minor characters and incidents. Some of the best writers are Karen Traviss and Sean Williams (*Star Wars*), Una McCormack (*Star Trek* and *Doctor Who*), and Dan Abnett (*Warhammer*). All of these authors take on complex technological and sociological issues.

It is also worth including science fiction short stories to introduce students to interesting and challenging work by some of the best writers for adults in the field. Each year a number of editors produce anthologies, of which the best are by Ellen Datlow, Gardner Dozois, and Jonathan Strahan. If you want to give students access to a range of stories from the past one hundred years of the genre, then Ann VanderMeer and Jeff VanderMeer's *The Big Book of Science Fiction* or *The Wesleyan Anthology of Science Fiction* both provide in their selections comprehensive accounts of the diversity and breadth of the genre.

Science fiction is a literature of ideas, and it is a literature of possibilities and alternatives. It should be challenging. When done well it should leave the reader uncomfortable. In order to do so it estranges the reader from the sense of the normal, placing the reader in a world where things are done differently, and sets out to create a sense of the sublime and awe and wonder at the size of the world. There are a number of ways of doing this.

Science fiction has a narrative trajectory: science fiction begins with dissonance, a sense of the different; continues like most fiction with a rupture, a sense that something has gone wrong; and moves toward a resolution (Mendlesohn 9–21). Where it differs from mimetic fiction is that it needs to conclude with a sense of consequence and change. This is part of science fiction's *attitude*, a feeling that the world can be investigated, explored, and fixed (it shares this with crime fiction). Science fiction stories that end with a restoration of the status quo are often unsatisfying. In YA science fiction, returning from the outside world back to the safety of home and family can reduce the adventure to just that, an adventure. All the texts considered here, including Reeve's Hungry City Chronicles and especially Applegate's Animorphs and Remnants sequences, demonstrate vividly this idea. There is no going back in terms of the social and economic conditions of the world or the emotional growth of the characters. Doctorow's *Homeland* is entirely focused on this idea and on the rule of unintended consequences, as Marcus is constrained and shaped by the reputation he has acquired. Okorafor's *Who Fears Death* is a novel that is about the consequences of a previous, offstage story and its effects on the people left behind.

Science fiction has a set of techniques. Csicsery-Ronay divides science fiction into seven "beauties," and these seven make a reasonable outline for a course that avoids both the chronological approach and the difficulty of covering every single subgenre of science fiction. Illustrate these modes of science fiction and students will stand a chance of leaving the classroom with a real sense of what science fiction is, explored through fiction for children and teens and leading into the adult genres. Csicsery-Ronay's seven beauties are: fictive neology, fictive novums, future history, imaginary science, the science fictional sublime, the science fictional grotesque, and the technologiade.

The use of fictive neologisms—the play with language and invented language; the use of language to "conjure up a sense of the inevitability of a new thing" (Csicsery-Ronay 13)—is relatively rare in science fiction for teens, although it does appear in the form of invented futuristic slang in the works of Applegate, McGann, and Doctorow. Paul Kincaid argues that the use of invented language, while it does "make strange," performs the full function of "making the strange and alien seem familiar and understandable," thus clarifying the incomprehensible by giving us a clue to understanding it (3). Linguists call the process by which this works *syntactic bootstrapping*, and we can see it most obviously and effectively in the opening sentences of some of the best works of science fiction. *Zahrah the Windseeker* opens with: "When I was born, my mother took one look at me and laughed. 'She's . . . dada,' said the doctor, looking surprised" (vii). *Mortal Engines* opens with the unforgettable "It was a dark and blustery afternoon in spring, and the city of London was chasing a small mining town across the dried-out bed of the old North Sea" (3).

Both of these sentences conjure the *novum* (a term coined by Darko Suvin in *Metamorphoses of Science Fiction*): "radically new inventions, discoveries, or social relations, around which otherwise familiar fictional elements are organized in a historically plausible way" (Csicsery-Ronay 47).

The novum is a destabilizing force: in several of the works discussed here, it begins, as it often does with modern YA science fiction, with the sense of a postapocalyptic or exhausted and depleted world. In a Western world awash with luxury, many of these texts imagine what it would be like if this all came to an end. The fictive history provides flesh on this basic skeleton: "Unlike real prophecies, [science fiction's] are narrated in the past tense. They don't pretend to predict a future, but to explain a *future past*" (Csicsery-Ronay 76). This is particularly evident in Reeve's *Predator Cities* and in Okorafor's far future African novels; both of these authors are concerned in these books as much with how we got there as to what the there is, but it is rarely explained; rather it is the secret that is gradually uncovered, often to the reader far more than to the protagonists. Science fiction is a genre very much concerned with the workings of the world so that to take the back off the clock and figure out how each element fits together is one key to understanding its reading strategy (Mendlesohn 5).

Without imaginary science, science fiction would not be *science* fiction. The science in science fiction is its pretext; it creates "the illusion that sf stories are dramatizations of scientific knowledge" (Csicsery-Ronay 111). Ironically, YA science fiction is generally rather poor at this unless dealing with the consequences of climate change: the clones in YA science fiction are too often overly significant, carrying genetic memory or acting as metaphors for exploitation. Noga Applebaum has explored the uneasiness that much modern YA fiction has with modern and potential technology. Thus, compared with middle-grade science fiction of the 1950s, in the modern genre there is little invention fiction, and teens are rarely the inventors. But we can see imaginary science in the domed city of McGann's *Small-Minded Giants*, as a society struggles to survive.

The most scientifically inventive of the texts here come from Reeve, in his engine cities, the alternative pasts of the Victorian era, and the interstellar trains. Reeve uses his inventions to thrill us with the fifth beauty, the science fictional sublime. The sublime is that which makes us gasp with wonder; it can be very small or very large, but it provides the intensity and emotion of science fiction: it is "a response to a shock of imaginative expansion" (Csicsery-Ronay 146). Applegate has the same gift; Remnants continually shocks with interruptions and interventions that force the reader to step back and to wonder, sometimes at the stunningly beautiful and complex, sometimes taking you over to Csicsery-Ronay's sixth beauty, the grotesque, the sense of being fixed to the earth and denied paradise while the sublime is around you. The Remnants series, predominantly set in a space ship that is not suitable for humans and with characters who would all be the last selected in any team game, continually confronts the reader with the sheer unlikelihood of survival and the limits of the human condition, even as it forces the humans beyond their known capacities to confront and even become the sublime. In Csicsery-Ronay's terms, it is an antitechnologiade.[3]

Notes

1. In *Young People's Reading in 2005*, 24.3% of students age seven to eleven and 21.2% of students age eleven to sixteen cited "it is about your hobby" as an attractor. The authors of the report did not include "it is a subject you are interested in," a rather wider topic (Maynard et al. 12). It would also have been interesting to know how much groups intersected, to know how they intersected, and to have focused on the most pro-nonfiction group for the later discussion (63) about what topics they found interesting.

2. There is now a companion volume, *Encountering Enchantment: A Guide to Speculative Fiction for Teens*, by Susan Fichtelberg, that may be more genre appropriate in its descriptions.

3. Csicsery-Ronay defines the technologiade as the "epic of the struggle surrounding the transformation of the cosmos into a technological regime" (217). For further reading, see Bould and Vint; Evans et al.; Maynard et al.; Orr and Herald.

Works Cited

Applebaum, Noga. *Representations of Technology in Science Fiction for Young People.* Routledge, 2010.

Applegate, K. A. *Animorphs.* Scholastic, 1996. 54 vols.

———. *Remnants.* Scholastic, 2001. 14 vols.

Bould, Mark, and Sherryl Vint. *The Routledge Concise History of Science Fiction.* Routledge, 2011.

Csicsery-Ronay, Istvan, Jr. *Seven Beauties of Science Fiction.* Wesleyan UP, 2008.

Doctorow, Corey. *Homeland.* Tor Teen, 2013.

———. *Little Brother.* Tor Teen, 2008.

Evans, Arthur B., et al., editors. *The Wesleyan Anthology of Science Fiction.* Wesleyan UP, 2010.

Fichtelberg, Susan. *Encountering Enchantment: A Guide to Speculative Fiction for Teens.* 2nd ed., Libraries Unlimited, 2015.

Frevert, Ute, et al. *Learning How to Feel: Children's Literature and Emotional Socialization, 1870–1970.* Oxford UP, 2014.

James, Edward, and Farah Mendlesohn, editors. *The Cambridge Companion to Science Fiction.* Cambridge UP, 2003.

Kincaid, Paul. "What It Is We Do When We Read Science Fiction." *What It Is We Do When We Read Science Fiction*, by Kincaid, Beccon, 2008, pp. 3–12.

Maynard, Sally, et al. *Young People's Reading in 2005: The Second Study of Young People's Reading Habits.* Roehampton U, 2007.

McGann, Oisín. *Gods and Their Machines.* O'Brien Press, 2004.
———. *The Harvest Tide Project.* O'Brien Press, 2012.
———. *Small-Minded Giants.* Doubleday Children's, 2006.
———. *The Wildenstern Saga.* Open Road Media, 2015.
Mendlesohn, Farah. *The Inter-galactic Playground: A Critical Study of Children's and Teens' Science Fiction.* McFarland, 2009.
Okorafor, Nnedi. *Who Fears Death.* Penguin, 2010.
———. *Zahrah the Windseeker.* Houghton Mifflin, 2005.
Orr, Cynthia, and Diana Tixier Herald, editors. *Genreflecting: A Guide to Popular Reading Interests.* 7th ed., Libraries Unlimited, 2013.
Reeve, Philip. *Fever Crumb.* Scholastic, 2009.
———. *Hungry City Chronicles.* Scholastic, 2001. 4 vols.
———. *Railhead.* Scholastic, 2015.
Suvin, Darko. *Metamorphoses of Science Fiction.* Peter Lang, 2016.
VanderMeer, Jeff, and Ann VanderMeer, editors. *The Big Book of Science Fiction.* Vintage, 2016.

Elizabeth Marshall

Representations of Youth, Schooling, and Education in Dystopian Young Adult Novels

Scott Westerfeld writes that "dystopian literature is just like high school: an oscillation between extremes of restraint." The author of the popular Uglies series rightly points out how classrooms are spaces of surveillance, conformity, official knowledge, and discipline. Dystopian YA novels set in schools interrogate these restraints and the adolescent protagonists' efforts to overcome them.[1] Texts about school as dystopia are highly appealing to university students. They are eager to speak to and contextualize their own educations, how they were schooled through textbooks that were more propaganda than truth or how their behavior and creativity were constrained through disciplinary practices. In this essay I offer resources and strategies for teaching YA dystopian school novels.

Published during a boom in dystopian YA literature (Miller; Basu et al.; Green), the novels that I address in this essay, Joelle Charbonneau's *The Testing*, Sally Gardner's *Maggot Moon*, and Robison Wells's *Variant*, form a unique subset of texts.[2] These YA dystopian school fictions highlight the school as a key institution in which adolescent characters confront and negotiate power and identity (Trites). Students choose one of these novels to focus on in depth and meet in groups to discuss and research the book, its author, and the educational issues the text engages.

The strategy of assigning a variety of narratives rather than one book for the whole class to study allows students to compare and contrast the critiques of schooling in these novels.

Before students delve into their books, we discuss the history of YA literature (Brown; Crowe), its definitions, and its purposes, to lay the groundwork for analyzing school dystopias. I introduce students to classic YA texts such as Robert Cormier's *The Chocolate War* as well as contemporary fictions like Walter Dean Myers's *Shooter* and Marieke Nijkamp's *This Is Where It Ends*, which focus on the topic of school shootings. While not formally dystopian, these examples underscore how the school is often the setting where repression and violence occur in YA fictions. This contextualization of YA dystopian school fictions as part of a larger trend in YA literature is coupled with a clarification about genre.

The class works with the *Oxford English Dictionary*'s definition of dystopia: "[a]n imaginary place or condition in which everything is bad." Students also read secondary materials that define and provide examples of dystopian YA fiction (Spisak). To fully understand the work that these dystopian school narratives do, it is crucial for students to understand the larger history of which these contemporary novels are a part. Texts like George Orwell's *Nineteen Eighty-Four*, Aldous Huxley's *Brave New World*, and Margaret Atwood's *The Handmaid's Tale* have long been staples in the secondary school curriculum. Dystopias in picture book format are also a part of this tradition, including David Macaulay's *Baaa*, Shaun Tan's *The Lost Thing*, Gary Crew's *The Viewer* (illustrated by Tan), and Margaret Wild and Anne Spudvilas's *Woolvs in the Sitee*. Dystopian stories remain extremely popular, especially during times of political or social tension. Sales of Orwell's *Nineteen Eighty-Four*, for instance, saw a 9,500% increase in sales after the 2017 US presidential inauguration (de Freytas-Tamura).

To emphasize the key elements of this genre, we conduct an analysis of Macintosh's 1984 computer commercial (see Wright's "Decoding the Dystopian" for a full description). The commercial invites repeated viewing as students consider the narrative, the visual imagery, and how the two complement each other to create a dystopian world. This activity generates much conversation and debate about symbols and meanings and gets students thinking about the distinctive aspects of the dystopian genre that they can then apply to their YA novels.

Building on this knowledge, students consider the prevalence of dystopian stories marketed to YA readers. A particularly useful teaching resource developed by Annissa Hambouz and Katherine Schulten, entitled

"Dark Materials: Reflecting on Dystopian Themes in Young Adult Literature," can be found on *The New York Times*'s *Learning Blog*. In this activity, students consider several quotes from YA authors about why dystopian fictions are so popular with youth. After each quote is read, students are asked to position themselves into four different corners of the room that represent their opinion—strongly agree, agree, strongly disagree, and disagree. Once in their places, students discuss why they picked the position that they did. Students converse in small groups to deepen their rationale and then report to the whole class, exchanging multiple perspectives, noting disagreements, and problematizing theories offered on the blog about why youth are so interested in dystopian fictions.

Through this introduction to dystopian YA narratives, students understand that the authors of their novels deliberately chose the dystopian genre to make a critique. As Carrie Hintz articulates, dystopian YA novels "honor dissent and agitation, and action based on a prolonged and combative questioning of the society in which the protagonists find themselves" (255). Students also understand that dystopian narratives include standard features, such as constant surveillance, a figurehead, and dehumanizing conditions. Given that these features (surveillance, conformity, authority figures) map onto many of the elements of school life, it is not surprising that a subset of YA dystopias take place in educational institutions. Novels such as *The Testing*, *Maggot Moon*, and *Variant* combine YA's focus on teen protagonists and their everyday struggles with the sociopolitical punch of the dystopian genre. Charbonneau, Gardner, and Wells critique teachers, standardized testing, conformity, discipline, and violence.

Like other YA fictions, dystopian school narratives center on adolescent heros and their fight against the status quo. Students often enter into the course with preconceived (and often stereotypical) ideas about adolescents, including assumptions that teenagers are hormonal, emotionally unstable, or rebellious. To get students thinking critically about the teenager as a sociohistorical and political term, I rely on Nancy Lesko's article "Denaturalizing Adolescence: The Politics of Contemporary Representations." Lesko offers readers a list of "characterizations" commonly associated with adolescence. These include the following:

Adolescents come of age into adulthood
Adolescents are controlled by raging hormones
Adolescents are peer oriented
Adolescence is signified by age

I pair Lesko's article in the first week of readings with contemporary films based on dystopian YA novels that broadly address education, such as *The Giver*, *The Hunger Games*, *Divergent*, or *Ender's Game*. These comparative cultural texts, although not necessarily set in formal school contexts, provide a way to reiterate key concepts about dystopian narratives, to encourage students to think about popular representations of adolescence as constructions, rather than as facts, and to consider the potential blockbuster appeal (in the case of *The Hunger Games*) of YA fictions. Students write a short analytic paper. The questions that guide their response include: What specific dystopian elements do you see in the film? Where, when, and how does the adolescent protagonist "learn" crucial truths or skills? Does the film support or challenge Lesko's "characterizations" about adolescence?

The question about the location and nature of what the adolescent protagonist learns highlights an important feature of YA dystopian school novels, and it is essential for students to understand the difference between the terms *schooling* and *education*. The term *education* focuses broadly on what one "knows," whereas *schooling* refers to mechanisms of formal learning that seek to teach conformity, the sorting of students into social structures through grades and other mechanisms, and instruction in learning how to defer to authority (Gatto). In *Variant*, for instance, the Maxfield Academy curriculum covers topics like aesthetics, an area of study completely useless to the students. There are no teachers or assessments at the academy, and lessons are delivered via a computer screen. In *Maggot Moon* students with disabilities are regularly "disappeared," and the sole curriculum is obedience to the Motherland. As one group of students in the class observed, these dystopian novels expose "the mechanics of curriculum delivery and what is defined as learning." Indeed, the authors of YA dystopian school narratives chart out the limits of formal schooling, defining it as the transfer of knowledge through standardized curricula, tests, and compulsory attendance—a contrast to the more useful and radical educations that the protagonists receive outside of or in spite of formal institutional learning.

To solidify this distinction between schooling and education I show a clip from the film *The Matrix*, in which Morpheus says to Neo, "You take the blue pill, the story ends. You wake up in your bed and believe whatever you want to believe. You take the red pill, you stay in Wonderland, and I show you how deep the rabbit hole goes."[3] Discussion of this clip centers on Neo, who has accepted rather than questioned the official knowledge of his world. In this scene, Neo must decide whether he wants to receive an education in the truth from a more knowledgeable guide. Like Neo, who accepts the red pill, protagonists in dystopian YA novels face similar turning points and learn that what they have been formally taught is largely a fiction. Each confronts the violence of the schooling process and seeks out or teaches an alternative curriculum.

YA dystopian school stories are important because they offer an appraisal of current educational issues and controversies. For example, in an interview Charbonneau stated that her inspiration for writing *The Testing* grew out of a concern for her students and the testing processes they experienced. She said, "The need to be better and brighter than the other applicants has never been more keenly felt. Students are hyper aware that every answer they give could impact the quality of their future. Some handle the pressure well. Others falter" ("Author"). In *The Testing*, Charbonneau takes a familiar educational experience and gives it a dystopian twist (only 34 of the 108 candidates in her book make it to the end of the novel): "anyone who voices negative opinions about the testing either is relocated to an outpost or disappears" (256), and readers witness the characters buckling to authority and to emotional pressure. As Cia's father states early in the novel, "The testing is not always fair, and it isn't always right" (6).

Similarly, *Maggot Moon* makes a statement on the educational system's narrow definition of normal, especially its medical view of dyslexia as something to be cured or remediated. At school, students taunt the profoundly dyslexic hero, Standish Treadwell, with a rhyme: "Can't read, can't write, Standish Treadwell isn't bright" (3). Teachers also single him out, and Standish is routinely punished and beaten for his learning differences. Writing in *The Telegraph*, Gardner opined that, "[t]he word associated with dyslexia in schools, that I absolutely hate, is special needs. Our special needs are that the non-dyslexic world stop telling us how we should be learning or what magic cure they have for us. It's not a disease" ("Dyslexia"). Her dystopian YA novel intervenes publicly in larger conversations about education policies and practices. She underscores, through the use of dystopian features, the dangers of narrow definitions of literacy. Through Standish Treadwell, Gardner suggests that schools expand definitions of ability to include visual and emotional intelligence.

Likewise, *Variant* considers issues of school discipline, gang violence, and conformity within a dystopian setting. The book has been compared with William Golding's *Lord of the Flies*. Foster child Benson Fisher applies and receives a scholarship to attend the elite Maxfield Academy in New Mexico. Rather than the luxurious environment advertised online, Benson finds himself locked in a dystopian institution in which he is constantly under surveillance.[4] Maxfield Academy consists of three central factions: Society, Havoc, and Variant. Cameras are installed in every hallway and room, and students are required to wear watches, bracelets, or necklaces that track their every move. Maxfield Academy is overseen by The Iceman, who appears via a screen to mete out punishments, such as no food for the day for any student caught on camera breaking rules. As the dystopian hero, Benson constantly questions the nonsensical rules of the institution and tries to convince others around him to escape. Students in my courses point out that the violence between rival gangs in *Variant* challenges the idea that school is a safe place for adolescents and also point out how the book raises questions (or anxieties) about the possibility of computers replacing human teachers.

Wells's novel hits on one of the most familiar themes in YA dystopias set in schools: the absent, ineffective, or evil teacher. As one group of students in my course pointed out after comparing and contrasting their novels, "teachers are useless." The adolescent protagonists, like Neo in *The Matrix*, must take over their own education, sourcing out the best curriculum and finding a guide (usually an adult) to teach them what they need to survive. The education scholar Christine Jarvis argues that teachers in horror stories about school "are rarely shown as human beings with whom young people can have a relationship. They are often revealed to be dangerous" (264). This trend occurs in YA dystopias too. Teachers are often witting or unwitting agents of an oppressive regime. One of the most brutal teachers to appear in a YA dystopian novel is Mr. Gunnell from *Maggot Moon*, about whom Standish tells the reader: "He brought with him no knowledge worth learning. Just propaganda. A minor major man was Mr. Gunnell" (64). At one difficult point in the novel Mr. Gunnell beats a student to death while the class looks on and Standish unsuccessfully tries to stop him. "Little Eric Owen lying there like a twisted sack, his hair no longer bleach blond but blood red, his face raw mutton, one of his eyes hanging out of its socket" (79). Standish sees with clear eyes the ways in which the teacher is an arm of the government, more prison guard than benevolent educator. As students in the course come to understand, teachers are not only useless but often agents of violence.

Teachers more often support rather than resist the institution's efforts to experiment on or contain youth, since they teach propaganda that limits rather than expands knowledge. Kay Sambell observes the following:

> Many children's dystopias are peopled with adult teachers who imprison their child pupils with corrupting knowledge and ideas. In [Monica] Hughes's *Devil on My Back*, [G. R.] Kesteven's *The Awakening Water*, [John] Christopher's *The Guardians*, [Robert] Westall's *Futuretrack 5* and [Ann] Schlee's *The Vandal*, to name but a few, we are introduced to future schools in which children are systematically drugged, brainwashed, or otherwise forced by adult tutors to become docile and compliant. (251)

The protagonists of the YA novels considered here quickly see that something is wrong and refuse to cooperate or fold under pressure. In *The Testing* Cia learns the lessons that she needs from her father and takes help from an outsider, and Benson takes over his own education in *Variant*. Standish exposes the Motherland's ruse using knowledge that he learned from his grandfather.

YA dystopian school stories encourage students to question familiar conceits about what it means to be educated. In *The Testing*, *Variant*, and *Maggot Moon*, teachers fail to protect students or instruct them in anything of consequence. Cia and Standish learn important information from their family members, and Benson comes to know through his own curiosity and firsthand experience. Some useful questions for interrogating YA dystopian school narratives and their relation to education include the following:

What kinds of schooling do the main characters experience? Where do these lessons take place? Who teaches or enforces them?

What is the school's relation to the dystopian society in these novels?

At what point in these novels do the main characters challenge the schooling they have received? What sparks the decision to challenge or rebel?

When and how do the main characters come to know or take control of their education? How and what do they learn? Who teaches them?

The Canadian novelist and essayist Grant Allen wrote that one shouldn't "let schooling interfere with education" (17). How do authors use the dystopian genre to highlight the differences between education and schooling?

This essay offers resources, strategies, guiding discussion questions, and comparative texts drawn from television, film, and picture books. Dystopian YA fictions require readers to take seriously the representation of youth and schools and to tie the critiques in these novels to current realities. Dystopian fictions for youth are part of a larger archive of popular cultural narratives that forward a politics of education, as each raise warnings about the violence of everyday schooling environments, processes, and practices.

Notes

1. The theoretical and pedagogical approach described in this essay is the result of teaching dystopian YA fictions across three interdisciplinary undergraduate courses on the topic from 2014 to the present.

2. I focus in this essay on three exemplary titles. Others to consider include Kazuo Ishiguro's *Never Let Me Go*, Orson Scott Card's *Ender's Game*, and Rae Mariz's *The Unidentified*.

3. See Wright's very helpful lesson plan "Decoding *The Matrix*: Exploring Dystopian Characteristics through Film."

4. This is a common feature of urban school movies, such as *Blackboard Jungle*, *Dangerous Minds*, and *Freedom Writers*.

Works Cited

Allen, Grant. *The Woman Who Did*. Roberts Bros. / John Lane, 1895.

Atwood, Margaret. *The Handmaid's Tale*. McClelland and Stewart, 1985.

Basu, Balaka, et. al, editors. *Contemporary Dystopian Fiction for Young Adults: Brave New Teenagers*. Routledge, 2013.

Brown, David W. "How Young Adult Fiction Came of Age." *The Atlantic*, 1 Aug. 2011, www.theatlantic.com/entertainment/archive/2011/08/how-young-adult-fiction-came-of-age/242671.

Card, Orson Scott. *Ender's Game*. Tor, 1994.

Charbonneau, Joelle. "Author Q&A." *Joelle Charbonneau*, www.joellecharbonneau.com/about-joelle.

———. *The Testing*. Houghton Mifflin, 2013.

Cormier, Robert. *The Chocolate War*. Pantheon Books, 1974.

Crew, Gary. *The Viewer*. Illustrated by Shaun Tan, Simply Read Books, 2003.

Crowe, Chris. "Young Adult Literature: What Is Young Adult Literature?" *English Journal*, vol. 88, no. 1, Sept. 1998, pp. 120–22.

de Freytas-Tamura, Kimiko. "George Orwell's *1984* Is Suddenly a Best-Seller." *The New York Times*, 25 Jan. 2017, www.nytimes.com/2017/01/25/books/1984-george-orwell-donald-trump.html.

Gardner, Sally. "Dyslexia Is Not a Disease." *The Telegraph*, 1 Nov. 2011, www.telegraph.co.uk/culture/books/booknews/8862822/Sally-Gardner-Dyslexia-is-not-a-disease.html.

———. *Maggot Moon*. Candlewick Press, 2013.

Gatto, John Taylor. "Against School." *Harper's Magazine*, Sept. 2003, pp. 33–38.

Green, John. "Scary New World." *The New York Times*, 7 Nov. 2008, www.nytimes.com/2008/11/09/books/review/Green-t.html.

Hambouz, Annissa, and Katherine Schulten. "Dark Materials: Reflecting on Dystopian Themes in Young Adult Literature " *The New York Times*, 6 Jan. 2011, learning.blogs.nytimes.com/2011/01/06/dark-materials-reflecting-on-dystopian-themes-in-young-adult-literature.

Hintz, Carrie. "Monica Hughes, Lois Lowry, and Young Adult Dystopias." *The Lion and the Unicorn*, vol. 26, no. 2, Apr. 2002, pp. 254–64.

Huxley, Aldous. *Brave New World*. Doubleday, 1932.

Ishiguro, Kazuo. *Never Let Me Go*. Faber and Faber, 2005.

Jarvis, Christine. "School Is Hell: Gendered Fears in Teenage Horror." *Educational Studies*, vol. 27, no. 3, 2001, pp. 257–67.

Lesko, Nancy. "Denaturalizing Adolescence: The Politics of Contemporary Representations." *Youth and Society*, vol. 28, no. 2, Dec. 1996, pp. 139–61.

Macaulay, David. *Baaa*. Houghton Mifflin, 1985.

Mariz, Rae. *The Unidentified*. Balzer and Bray, 2012.

Miller, Laura. "Fresh Hell: What's Behind the Boom in Dystopian Fiction for Young Readers?" *The New Yorker*, 14 and 21 June 2010, www.newyorker.com/magazine/2010/06/14/fresh-hell-2.

Myers, Walter Dean. *Shooter*. Amistad, 2004.

Nijkamp, Marieke. *This Is Where It Ends*. Sourcebooks Fire, 2016.

Orwell, George. *Nineteen Eighty-Four*. Secker and Warburg, 1949.

Sambell, Kay. "Carnivalizing the Future: A New Approach to Theorizing Childhood and Adulthood in Science Fiction for Young Readers." *The Lion and the Unicorn*, vol. 28, no. 2, Apr. 2004, pp. 247–67.

Spisak, April. "What Makes a Good Dystopian Novel?" *The Horn Book Magazine*, May-June 2012, pp. 55–60.

Tan, Shaun. *The Lost Thing*. Hachette, 2000.

Trites, Roberta Seelinger. *Disturbing the Universe: Power and Repression in Adolescent Literature*. U of Iowa P, 1998.

Wells, Robison. *Variant*. HarperTeen 2011.

Westerfeld, Scott. "Teens and Dystopias." *Scott Westerfeld*, 13 Sept. 2012, scottwesterfeld.com/blog/2012/09/teens-and-dystopias/.

Wild, Margaret, and Anne Spudvilas. *Woolvs in the Sitee*. Front Street, 2007.

Wright, Junius. "Decoding the Dystopian Characteristics of Macintosh's '1984' Commercial." *ReadWriteThink*, www.readwritethink.org/classroom-resources/lesson-plans/decoding-dystopian-characteristics-macintosh-933.html. Accessed 4 June 2017.

———. "Decoding *The Matrix*: Exploring Dystopian Characteristics through Film." *ReadWriteThink*, www.readwritethink.org/classroom-resources/lesson-plans/decoding-matrix-exploring-dystopian-926.html?tab=3#tabs. Accessed 4 June 2017.

Mary Bricker

Teaching Genre: Fairy Tales and Their Retellings in Young Adult Literature

This essay reflects on teaching YA fairy tale remakes in my college introductory fairy tale course, Masterpieces of World Literature: The Fairy Tales of the Brothers Grimm. The course is taught at the 200 level and is open to all levels of undergraduate students. In fall 2016, I incorporated YA retellings of fairy tales through student presentations in the last month of the course. YA literature was identified in my course as literature written for and marketed to a young adult audience. Earlier readings and discussions of the Grimms' fairy tales and their secondary literature preceded the section on YA literature. The students' prior familiarity with the Grimms' fairy tale collection provided a solid basis to think critically about modern remakes encountered in popular culture, something that Antero Garcia notes is lacking among modern readers (4).

In the course each student gave a ten-minute individual presentation of a YA fairy tale remake that he or she had selected from a list that I had created prior to the semester. The YA fairy tale retellings included the subgenres of science fiction, fantasy, dystopic novels, horror, adventure, westerns, and historic fiction. The parameters set by scholars, bookstores, and YA literary Web sites helped me to identify the remake as YA when the line between YA and adult literature blurred in certain subgenres like science fiction and fantasy. Jack Zipes's scholarship was helpful in initially identifying fairy tale remakes at large.[1] To further limit the selection, I looked at the YA sections in local bookstores and the Web sites of authors, literary magazines, and literary awarding organizations for YA literature. Whereas many of the YA fairy tale remakes are novels, other genre forms, such as poetry and novellas, were also included.

Incorporating YA literature was a welcome addition for my students, who were already familiar with the genre from adolescence. The remakes added breadth to the class: reading classical fairy tales alongside mixed-genre forms of YA fairy tale retellings allowed for layered discussions. The addition of YA fairy tale remakes further allowed students to practice advanced pedagogical literary comparisons of plots, characters, settings, themes, and styles.

Genres

The Grimms' collection *Kinder- und Hausmärchen* (*Children and Household Tales*) functions as the international prototype of *Märchen* ("fairy tale") collections (Grzybek, "Märchen" 151). The Grimms believed that fairy tales continue to evolve from their initial form as myth (155). Fairy tales continue to be remade because of their resonance. YA fairy tale remakes can be seen within this larger context. In her Berkeley lectures on genres, Rosalie Colie concurred with the literary critic E. D. Hirsch, whose book *Validity of Interpretation* deems genres as "indispensable to literature." Genres have been passed down and used as models to imitate or to oppose with each new literary development (Colie 151). The Grimms' collection encompasses many kinds of tales, with the origins of the stories varying from fairy tales passed down orally to literary fairy tales that had been written with intent. YA fairy tale remakes fit into the literary fairy tale category.

Maria Tatar mapped out the differences between the closely related genres of folklore/literature and folk tale / fairy tale in order to better understand the way in which the editing choices of Wilhelm Grimm affected the genre classification of the tales within the Grimms' collection. She explains that fairy tales can be situated in relation to other like genres based on their setting, either naturalistic or supernaturalistic (34). Tatar notes that the Grimms' collection contains four types of tales: oral folk tales, oral fairy tales, literary folk tales, and literary fairy tales (35). The hybridity of these closely related genres has interested scholars for centuries. In the first third of the twentieth century, André Jolles published a seminal work on simple forms, including the folk tale, and Roman Jakobson and Petr Bogatyrev looked at the differences between literature and folklore. As early as the nineteenth century, Jacob Grimm began the inquiry into the distinction between *Naturpoesie* ("natural poetry"), which is spontaneous, and *Kunstpoesie* ("artistic poetry"), which is the result of an artistic literary creation (Grzybek, "Simple Form" 694). *Naturpoesie* is an anonymous, orally passed down tale that has a revered status, and *Kunstpoesie* is written by an author, often famous (Grzybek, "Märchen" 152).

The intentions of the literary fairy tale authors are easily discernible, given that an identifiable author is responsible for the changes. However, in general, literary tales can still be changed through oral dissemination. There is a lack of accord within folklore scholarship on the origins of the fairy tale genre, largely because of the lack of written records for the earliest tales. Further, Peter Grzybek states that fairy tales basically stop being folk tales as soon as they are recorded and altered by the documenter ("Märchen" 151). In writing about the role of gender in fairy tale narratives, Cristina Bacchilega succinctly sums up the fairy tale genre as a transitional borderline genre, given its competing hybrid history as a "*literary* appropriation of an older folk tale . . . [that] continues to exhibit and reproduce some *folkloric* features" (3).

YA fairy tale remakes are individually written texts that allude to and expand shorter fairy tale forms. As retellings of fairy tales, YA fairy tale remakes are most identifiable by iconic motifs specific to each tale, such as the glass slipper in "Cinderella." However, the YA fairy tales may subvert these motifs, thus presenting the perspective of the author. Incorporating YA literature in the class allowed a comparison of fictional fairy tale genres. To these ends, Tatar's categorical distinctions help students to understand that YA fairy tale remakes are literary fairy tales, as Tatar explains that fairy tales have "narratives set in a fictional world where preternatural events and supernatural interventions are taken wholly for granted" (33). Realism is not part of the fairy tale, which contains magical and marvelous elements (34).

Whereas the fairy tales from the Brothers Grimm are brief, YA retellings tend to be written in a longer prose form, such as the novel. Colie explains that since antiquity the size of a work has played a role in defining genre (154). The longer length of YA literature allows additional textual space for character background. In the Grimms' collection, the actors tend to be stock characters that carry out important narrative sequences similar to those carried out by the characters Propp describes in his discussions of the functions of dramatis personae (Propp 79–83). Their backgrounds are less important than the types of action that these characters experience. YA fairy tale remakes differ greatly in this sense, especially novels (and novellas) in which texts are rich with detail about the individual characters and their psychological motivations. When a character's background information is lacking in a YA fairy tale remake, suspense is created. The inclusion of YA literature allowed students to be exposed to differences within the fairy tale genre.

Student Presentations

In my course, students began their projects a month in advance of their presentations and were given deadlines for their independent preparation. Four weeks before their presentation they began a weekly journal concerning their progress as well as observations from their research. At the beginning of each week I checked their journals. The entries, along with a postpresentation follow-up worksheet, amounted to ten percent of the grade. Journals served as sounding boards for their discoveries and as a way to gather feedback for each of the categories that they would be presenting.

Students were graded on the quality of their material for each of the required parts of their presentations: background on author; synopsis, including genre and aspects of the story that they liked; the Grimms' version of the story, including context from previous class discussions; and the differences between the author's perspective and the Grimms' version. The discussion of the synopsis, genre, and aspects of the story that the student liked received the largest portion of the grade. Students were also graded on their ability to answer questions in the discussions that ensued thereafter. Students were randomly selected to ask questions after each presentation.

The students' first journal entry concerned the YA author of the fairy tale remake that they had selected. A 2004 metadata study suggests that allowing students to select texts for reading is a powerful motivational factor for academic achievement (Allington 278). The readings included, but were not limited to, Robin McKinley's *The Princess and the Frog*, Marissa Meyer's *Cinder*, and Elizabeth C. Bunce's *A Curse Dark as Gold*, each of which I draw on for examples of student observations in this section. Web sites proved to be the main source for bibliographic information about the authors. Later, in the presentations, students introduced the authors to the class. These introductions also served to raise awareness of prominent YA literary awards. For example, the William C. Morris YA Debut Award was organically introduced through Bunce's award-winning novel, and the Newbery Medal was discussed in the context of McKinley's oeuvre.

For the second journal entry, students began to read and take notes on their YA fairy tale remake. This assignment helped them prepare a synopsis of the story for the presentation and also encouraged them to take note of YA authors' adoption of iconic fairy tale motifs. What would a Cinderella tale be without an evil stepmother? A burden to her ward, Marissa Meyer's Cinder becomes domestic help to her stepfamily. The father who had agreed to raise the exiled Lunar princess Selene, also known as Cinder, dies of the plague before he can tell anyone Cinder's secret origin. The stepmother is quick to volunteer Cinder for life-threatening testing to find a cure for the plague after her youngest daughter dies from the disease. As in the Grimms' version, in *Cinder*, the stepmother is the selfish caregiver who has two other daughters whom she favors.

Literary themes also surfaced in this assignment. Students generally found that the YA fairy tale remakes can be very dark through the themes they address. In Bunce's *A Curse Dark as Gold*, the child protagonists (Charlotte and her sister Rosie Miller) are left to run the family's mill, Stirwaters, after their father's death, a situation that a long-lost uncle with a gambling problem takes advantage of to fund his destructive addiction. Bunce's "Rumpelstiltskin" remake begins at the funeral of their father, a situation that students found to be relatable. Death is a very common crisis in the Grimms' fairy tales: the death of a parent creates a void at the beginning of the tale that propels the plot forward and leaves child protagonists vulnerable.

The students were also given project guidelines to help them collect and analyze specific information from the YA fairy tale remakes. Besides an introduction to the author and a remake synopsis, the presentation also included a discussion of the genre. The presenter of Bunce's novel observed that Bunce sets the story in the industrial era of the eighteenth century, as opposed to the undefined space and time of the Grimms' tales (once upon a time in a kingdom far, far away). As a class, we talked about the role of time as a marker of genre. Grzybek calls the introductory and closing formulae of "once upon a time" and "happily ever after" genre markers that show "transitions from the reality of the story-telling situation to events presented" ("Märchen" 148). Even though the Grimms tried to remove all such markers in their tales, their inclusion does not counter fairy tale genre convention, as other fairy tale authors reference time and geographic location.

This second entry allowed students to equally highlight an aspect of the tale that they enjoyed. According to Richard Allington, "The ability to consider one's own stance as one of many—the author's stance, that of another reader, those of various characters in the book—is one of the highest-order literacies that many people consider critical . . ." (283). The presenter of Meyer's *Cinder* enjoyed the science fiction subgenre of this retelling of the Cinderella material. Cinder is a cyborg alien in disguise and is the finest information technology mechanic in New Beijing. The presentation focused on the writing style of Meyer, who in this case employed technology to modernize the tale. Technology is a key component from the beginning of the story, with Prince Kai examining the cyborg foot that Cinder had removed shortly before his arrival at her market stand after finding a new foot that fit better. The prince is at the market to elicit Cinder's help to retrieve data from an old android. Through the inclusion of a glass-slipper motif, even in its futuristic form, the remake alludes to the more classic versions of "Cinderella" while establishing the author's feminist perspective in this fantasy retelling.

In the third week, students were asked to reread the entire YA fairy tale remake or parts of the story that would allow them to finish the outline of their presentation. They were also asked to review the Grimms' version of the story as well as the class discussion in which the Grimms' version was covered. This review allowed students to recheck comparisons of plots, characters, settings, themes, and styles within each genre. Reading the Grimms' versions before the YA fairy tale remakes gave the students a natural point of comparison. For example, Meyer's child protagonist Cinder is free of the gender stereotypes that are found in the Grimms' Cinderella.

The comparative point of the presentations included a synopsis of the Grimms' original story and a comparison to the YA version. For example, in Bunce's tale, witchcraft plays a role as it does in many of the Grimms' fairy tales. The presenter gave an example from Bunce's novel in which the young Miller daughters use magic to gain financial stability. A mysterious tradesman, who goes by the name Jack Spinner, appears before the hex sign in response to Rosie's reciting from their father's book *To Summon Faerie Aid* (95). He initially makes a deal with Charlotte to spin straw into gold for her mother's ring (100). By the end of the novel the deal involves her child, William, which alludes to the Rumpelstiltskin fairy tale in which a maiden makes a deal with a magical being to spin gold from straw in exchange for material gifts and ultimately the woman's offspring. In discussion, students remarked that in YA fairy tale remakes young women use magic, whereas in the Grimms' fairy tales, magic is reserved for evil witches and other magical beings.

The presenter of McKinley's YA fairy tale remake of "The Frog King; or, Iron Heinrich," entitled *The Princess and the Frog*, spoke of the similarities between the two stories. McKinley's novella maintains the lesson that the father teaches the daughter on the importance of keeping one's word, despite the remake's pronounced differences from the Grimms' version. This kind of didactic lesson, which is typical for the Grimms, still holds credence in the twentieth century in McKinley's feminist adaptation. An interesting discussion that arose from the frog's role in the tale concerned magical space and animal characters, as the class had previously spent much time looking at magical aspects of fairy tales. In the Grimms' fairy tales, carriers of action can be man or animal from this world or the netherworld (Grzybek, "Märchen" 147). These spaces are also intertwined in the fairy tale through the enchanted frog who speaks to the princess. Mixing of worlds holds true for both the Grimms' version and the YA remake.

The happy ends were examined by several students in their presentations. From the collection of YA fairy tale remakes presented, students discovered that the tales do not consistently have happy endings. In Rumpelstiltskin-type tales, the happy end occurs once the riddle is solved. This holds true in the YA remake *A Curse Dark as Gold*, when Charlotte uses the information she uncovers at Simplecross to make her final deal with John Simple to break the curse. At the end of *The Princess and the Frog*, Princess Rana saves herself from marriage to Aliyander and saves Prince Lian's life by killing Aliyander through collecting and pouring pond water over him, which had earlier removed the dark magic of the jewels in his gift necklace. In both of the YA fairy tale remakes, the happy endings underscore the daughters' strong female agency. In the Grimms' version, happy endings typically occur once daughters are saved.

Not all YA fairy tale remakes have happy endings, though, and they are generally less pronounced than in the Grimms' fairy tales. For example, in *Cinder*, the ball scene consists of a series of mishaps that begin when Cinder appears in rags wearing her old foot that is too small. This old foot, which had initially fascinated the prince during their first encounter in the novel, makes Cinder fall on the stairs as she tries to leave. Disgusted that Cinder is not only cyborg but also Lunar, the prince turns his back to Cinder, who is then held in prison until she can be returned to her planet. In prison, Cinder is saved not by the prince but by Dr. Erland, the doctor at the castle searching for a cure for the plague. Also a Lunar in disguise, he had been conducting research at the castle only in order to find Princess Selene. The novel concludes with their romance unresolved and the traditional happy end subverted. The prince never discovers that Cinder is the exiled Lunar princess he has been in search of throughout the novel.

Final Thoughts and Journal Entry

The fourth week's entry was for any final thoughts and preparation. The majority of students found that reading the YA remakes in addition to regular class readings could be easily accomplished within the allotted time. In the final week before their presentation, students used the time to create any visuals to accompany their presentation and to practice beforehand. They were asked to consider the following questions: How will you present? Will you read your presentation? Will you use index cards? Will you create a *PowerPoint* presentation or some other visuals to help you express your ideas? Consider which of these possibilities should work best for you.

Through the presentations and ensuing discussions, students were exposed to many YA authors and their works, which allowed them to gather valuable information about the genre of YA fairy tale remakes at large. As noted by Vicki Roberts-Gassler in her article "Teaching the Fairy Tale," the benefits of teaching a fairy tale course as an introduction to literature are transferrable to later courses (250). By including YA fairy tale remakes, this transfer of knowledge occurs within the course itself to the interpretation of YA remakes of classic fairy tales. Beyond the initial plot comparison between contemporary YA adaptations and the Brothers Grimms' version, the comparison opened up a range of fruitful literary examinations.

After the completion of their presentations, students reported that they enjoyed reading fairy tale remakes from YA perspectives. One thematic conclusion was that feminist retellings are common in YA fairy tale remakes, especially compared with the Grimms' tales, in which smart women are old witches and young, beautiful princesses do not speak much. The female agency of Charlotte is especially pronounced throughout *A*

Curse Dark as Gold. Strong female agency can be seen not only in Bunce's and Meyer's novels but also in McKinley's *The Princess and the Frog*. Another class conclusion concerned the way in which the length of the majority of the YA remakes allowed flexibility to the author to include and build on characters' backgrounds to explain character development but also create subplots that added layers of complexity. In addition to the character backgrounds, many of the YA authors are more elaborate in the detail of their story lines. In the Grimms' fairy tales, there is no room for subplots, as they would only distract from the main sequence of actions. Students' familiarity with the fairy tale versions of the Brothers Grimm allowed them to analyze and appreciate the YA versions.

Note

1. Zipes, *Don't Bet*, *Fairy Tales*, *Relentless Progress*, *Sticks*, and *Why Fairy Tales*.

Works Cited

Allington, Richard L. "Effective Teachers, Effective Instruction." *Adolescent Literacy: Turning Promise into Practice*, edited by Kylene Beers et al., Heinemann, 2007, pp. 273–88.

Bacchilega, Cristina. *Postmodern Fairy Tales: Gender and Narrative Strategies*. U of Pennsylvania P, 1997.

Bunce, Elizabeth C. *A Curse Dark as Gold*. Arthur A. Levine Books, 2008.

Colie, Rosalie. "Genre-Systems and the Function of Literature." *Modern Genre Theory*, edited by David Duff, Pearson Education, 2000, pp. 148–66.

Garcia, Antero. *Critical Foundations in Young Adult Literature: Challenging Genres*. Sense, 2013.

Grimm, Jacob, and Wilhelm Grimm. *The Complete Fairy Tales of the Brothers Grimm*. Translated by Jack Zipes, Bantam Books, 1992.

Grzybek, Peter. "Märchen." *Simple Forms: An Encyclopedia of Simple Text-Types in Lore and Literature*, edited by Walter A. Koch, Universitätsverlag Dr. Norbert Brockmeyer, 1994, pp. 144–57.

———. "Simple Form." *Encyclopedia of Humor Studies*, edited by Salvatore Attardo, vol. 2, Sage, 2014, pp. 693–94.

Hirsch, E. D., Jr. *Validity in Interpretation*. Yale UP, 1967.

Jakobson, Roman, and Petr Bogatyrev. "On the Boundary between Studies of Folklore and Literature." *Readings in Russian Poetics: Formalist and Structuralist Views*, edited by Ladislav Matejka and Krystyna Pomorska, translated by Herbert Eagle, MIT Press, 1971, pp. 91–93.

Jolles, André. *Einfache Formen*. Wissenschaftliche Buchgesellschaft, 1958.

McKinley, Robin. *The Princess and the Frog*. *The Door in the Hedge*, Firebird, 2003, pp. 79–104.

Meyer, Marissa. *Cinder: The Lunar Chronicles*. Feiwel and Friends, 2012.

Propp, Vladimir. *Morphology of the Folktale.* Translated by Laurence Scott, 2nd ed., U of Texas P, 1968.

Roberts-Gassler, Vicki. "Teaching the Fairy Tale." *Die Unterrichtspraxis / Teaching German*, vol. 20, no. 2, Autumn 1987, pp. 250–60. *JSTOR*, doi:10.2307/3530086.

Tatar, Maria. *The Hard Facts of the Grimms' Fairy Tales.* Princeton UP, 1987.

Zipes, Jack. *Don't Bet on the Prince: Contemporary Feminist Fairy Tales in North America and England.* Gower, 1986.

———. *Fairy Tales and the Art of Subversion: The Classical Genre for Children and the Process of Civilization.* Wildman Press, 1983.

———. *Relentless Progress: The Reconfiguration of Children's Literature, Fairy Tales, and Storytelling.* Routledge, 2009.

———. *Sticks and Stones: The Troublesome Success of Children's Literature from Slovenly Peter to Harry Potter.* Routledge, 2001.

———. *Why Fairy Tales Stick: The Evolution and Relevance of a Genre.* Routledge, 2006.

Mary Adler

The Story behind the Story: A Cross-Textual, New Historicist Approach to Historical Fiction

Authors of historical fiction for young adults write to enlighten, inform, entertain, engage, and even persuade—a purpose sometimes made explicit for the adolescent reader. For example, Joseph Bruchac, author of *Code Talkers: A Novel about the Navajo Marines of World War Two*, includes a lengthy author's note introducing a main reason for writing the book: to correct the "lack of understanding and appreciation" for the Navajo military contributions to World War II. Bruchac also highlights his background in efforts to preserve native languages and culture, explaining that his Abenaki tribe "now has a base of less than forty fluent speakers," and he gives advice on how to interpret the text: "In some ways, this novel can be read as a parable about the importance of respecting other languages and cultures" (220–21).

Often, though, authors' goals and influences are less explicit and available to readers only through outside sources such as interviews or letters. When I ask my students whether authorial intention matters, they are often quiet or conflicted. This year I opened our historical fiction segment with a more specific question: Does it matter what's in an author's mind when the author sets out to write about war? For example, does it matter if Henry Wadsworth Longfellow, in a letter to a close friend, the abolitionist Charles Sumner, on the eve of the Civil War, indicated his intention to write "Paul Revere's Ride" to wake up a sleepy nation overlooking a grave threat (Lepore)? Together we examine Longfellow's poem, including its famous conclusion:

> In the hour of darkness and peril and need,
> The people will waken and listen to hear
> The hurrying hoof-beats of that steed,
> And the midnight message of Paul Revere. (Longfellow)

A few students (represented here with pseudonyms) expressed skepticism, wanting to review Longfellow's other work in the context of the abolitionist movement. Matt observed, "It matters. The letter that we read before this makes it impossible not to read it as something related to slavery." Cayden focused on the tense—"the people *will* waken"—observing that the awakening at the end can serve as "a significant call to action for the wars that are coming. . . . When you actually stop to think about it, you can *see* it—I can see it as more broad than just Paul Revere."

Clearly, I am arguing that authorial influence does matter, partly because this approach, originating in new historicism and now used more broadly in cultural studies, provides a valuable pedagogical method. It stimulates readers to take an active and critical stance toward historical fiction, pulling them beyond the more typical goals of engagement and empathy that are ascribed to the genre.[1] It also matters because it has a corrective effect on YA versions of history, providing an interrogation of the grand narrative so pervasive in K–12 history textbooks.[2]

In the sections that follow, I will first discuss how I use the concept of new historicism and connect it to potential problems posed by YA history and historical fiction. Then I'll examine how these ideas play out during a specific set of activities that apply new historicism to YA war novels within collaborative book groups.

Pinning Down New Historicism

In conceptualizing this essay, I owe a debt to Anna Soter, whose chapter "Looking at the Past through the Present: A New Historicist Reading of *My Brother Sam Is Dead*" inspired me to test out new historicist approaches to war novels (45–58). Pinning down new historicism, however, is a slippery business. As Sidney Li puts it, "Even [Catherine] Gallagher and [Stephen] Greenblatt, two major practitioners of the theory, admitted that the scope of New Historicism is not entirely clear. This vagueness is caused by the incorporation of many fields of theory, ranging from psychoanalysis to deconstructionism, into literary criticism" (8). In setting up my instructional focus, I concentrated instead upon the (generally agreed upon) assumptions that underlie the approach:

History and anthropology can provide powerful tools for the study of literature—and the reverse is also true. While each has a different purpose and claim on truth, all "are fictions in the sense of things made" and "are shaped by the imagination and by the available resources of narration and description" (Gallagher and Greenblatt 31).

In Soter's words, "No text is innocent" (46). Rather, new historicism understands works to be constructed, "the product of a negotiation," as authors both draw from shared societal conventions and practices and seek to create art that will be recognized and appreciated by the same (Greenblatt, "Towards a Poetics" 12).

The explicit examination of artists' societal influences, as well as our own relation to the text, can add complexity to a simplistic view of history, interrogating events that seem orderly, wherein "actions that appear to be single are disclosed as multiple" (Greenblatt, "Resonance" 15).

In light of the above, we can think of both historical fiction and history as constructed works that are filtered in the learning, again in the retelling, and again in the reading; they are "telling *a story about a story of past events*" (Soter 45).

Challenges Posed by Historical Fiction

The deliberate interrogation of a story about a story counters the seductive power of historical fiction to slip in unquestioned historical facts, concepts, and viewpoints in the guise of an engaging narrator. Such texts cultivate sympathy in readers and have the potential to create a valuable relation with history and a deeper personal understanding of historical events ranging from the Civil War to World War II and the Holocaust.[3] The study of historical fiction can also stimulate an emotional response.

Linda Levstik and Keith Barton examine the draw of YA historical fiction, highlighting the use of accessible narratives that focus on human behaviors; readers tend to believe that these narratives are "telling what actually happened" (117). Although such strong engagement provides memorable stimuli for historical thinking, narrative's power "is not an unmitigated good . . . a good story can mask bad history and blind students to other interpretations" (127).

Readers' close identification with historical fiction can create challenges to accepting alternate interpretations (Apol et al.). After reading Eleanor Coerr's compelling story *Sadako and the Thousand Paper Cranes*, undergraduate preservice teachers listened to a scholar who provided a historical account of the child Sadako, showing that details of her story had been changed, "co-opted," or "constructed" for various audiences and purposes, including as a peace symbol (437). Yet the power of fiction was such that students resisted conflicting evidence. Moreover, some quoted fictional information as fact, and nearly all expressed a desire to teach the book, insisting that the scholar show them how to make paper cranes. Researchers speculate that, in addition to a professed desire to shield children from disturbing historical details related to Hiroshima, "students may have had little practice interrogating or questioning print versions of history. They may have assumed that the historical record in print was categorically 'true'" (450).

Why War Fiction?

Historical fiction focused on war provides readers with a sense of personal agency and experience that they are unlikely to find in textbook accounts, which, "intentionally or not, create a hegemonic voice, excluding alternative views, one which infers that the war, while regrettable, was necessary, and that soldiers in the war suffered and died willingly for the cause" (Pearcy 57). Moreover, as the historian Joseph Moreau has established, accounts of historical events in American textbooks have always been sites of conflict, a sort of microcosm in which "national soul-searching" plays out as arguments over race, class, and religion "continually echo through the hallways of our schools" (16). While historical fiction on war can help break up the hegemonic narrative, a new historicist approach can help "unmask these conflicts" by questioning some of the historical representation (18).

Text Selection

The activities that follow span three rounds over about two weeks, although they could easily be expanded. Texts are selected to address different reading levels, perspectives, and subjects; this semester they ranged from the American Revolution (James Lincoln Collier and Christopher Collier's *My Brother Sam Is Dead*) and the Civil War (Paul Fleischman's *Bull Run*) to World War II (*Code Talker* and Harry Mazer's *The Last Mission*) and Vietnam (Walter Dean Myers's *Fallen Angels*), each with potential for a new historicist inquiry. *My Brother Sam* narrates a family's experience with hypocrisy and savagery at the hands of both the British and rebel armies, with a strong and explicit antiwar message. In *Bull Run*, Fleischman provides sixteen perspectives on the Civil War, of which only one comes from a historical figure; the effect is "to evoke the early course of the war and its impact on ordinary people—some beginning with dreams of glory, all forced to endure the grim reality" (review of *Bull Run*). *Code Talker*, discussed earlier, reveals the intentionally obscured story of Navajo code talkers as well as the government's complicity in nearly destroying their linguistic and cultural heritage. In *The Last Mission*, Mazer draws on his experience as a captured fighter pilot to set up a fifteen-year-old Jewish narrator who is similarly shot down and captured during World War II—and who ends the novel with an antiwar speech. Finally, in *Fallen Angels* (dedicated to Myers's brother, killed on his first day in Vietnam), an African American narrator enlists to escape poverty in Harlem and "survives racist officers, pitched battles, guerrilla raids, and multiple wounds, not all of them physical" (review of *Fallen Angels*).

ROUND ONE

First, students select one of the five novels and form a book group with others who choose the same text. For those who plan to teach, a book group approach is an important pedagogical model to experience, for students can engage as experts on a text they select at their reading and interest level.[4]

To prepare for class discussion, students read the text and consider it in light of key questions:

How did the main character's understanding about war change over time? What changed it?

How is the government depicted in the novel? Why might that be?

What larger themes, or lessons about life, are young adults to take away from this novel?
What was the author's attitude toward the war?

During class, students meet in book groups and debrief on these questions. To ease our cross-textual comparison to come, I ask them to revisit the text, looking for examples of some of the following:

Enlistment experience
Communication, news, and rumors
Friends, comrades, and people to watch your back
Thoughts of and relations to family, friends, and girls back home
Collateral damage
Chain of command, bureaucracy, and orders
Loyalty and questioning loyalty
Human drives: sex, fear, hunger, thirst, health, loneliness, anger, and hope
Encounters with the enemy
Waiting, traveling
(Dark) humor or irony
Reentry to the "real world"

The above characteristics have proven to be reliable cross-textual comparison points, allowing us in the next round to move beyond the compelling stories to seeing the genre and the authors at work.

ROUND TWO

After the groups have marked up their texts for common elements and discussed the four key questions, we regroup into a circle, with students primed for the discussion on their text. To facilitate cross-textual understandings, I distribute a page of short book reviews of all five novels and ask each group to read its book's summary aloud to the class, while an image of the book cover is projected as visual reinforcement. A group member then has a chance to clarify, correct, or add to the summary as needed.

Finally, we are ready to engage in a cross-textual, cross-group discussion. Or, as I put it to them this spring, "We have four different wars with different points of view, different narrative structures, different authors: can we pull a common thread, a common narrative about war, from these?" We start with the top of the long list of common elements, the enlistment experience, and begin to analyze across texts from there. At first students are allegiant to their novels, as in this response by Marco: "For *Fallen Angels*, the reason why he wanted to enlist was because he wanted to get away from home and all the problems that come along with home; he thought that [by] going to the military [he] would escape his problems, but quite the opposite." With encouragement, and as more anecdotes are shared, students begin to connect ideas across texts:

Chris. In *The Last Mission* . . . he was very excited to enlist . . . he's Jewish, and he wants to get back at Hitler and thinks about killing him; he wants to be a hero.

Matt. Let me reiterate. Our protagonist was also excited to join the war effort, to the point where he tried to join when he was fifteen—but his parents don't let him, and he had to wait a year.

Some students, like Elynor, venture a broader analysis: "It sounds like in the majority of these stories the people who are enlisting are either underage or just really young." I followed this with questions about the effect on young readers: Is it still that way—still sort of a way out—to be part of something, serve your country, be a hero? Are young people still invited to be part of that culture? Students described current military recruiting efforts and the possibility that these texts may make young readers more critical of modern recruitment campaigns.

Over time, the discussion becomes less a recounting of discrete war elements and more an integrated, complicated understanding of war. Below, for example, students connected the role of government with sobering encounters with the enemy:

Cody. There's one thing that happens a lot [in *Fallen Angels*]: when they kill the Viet Cong, they report a false count. The government lies to the characters throughout about the war. [Perry] becomes disillusioned.

Marco. I want to add to that. I think [Perry's] perception of the war changes when he first kills someone. Because he asks his buddy, "Hey, I could know that person"; his friend is like, "Man, you don't know that person!" He says, "It doesn't matter, I still killed someone; it's a person with a face." "You did your job." [But] he thinks, *That could have been me.*

Chantal. [In *The Last Mission*], he realizes that he's not killing Hitler, he's killing a whole lot of [civilians]. [Reads an excerpt as evidence.]

At the end of round 2, we have not yet applied new historicism, but the cross-textual methodology has already produced critical observations of the novels' antiwar themes. Moreover, students are using textual evidence in the service of a larger understanding about patterns to be found in the genre.

ROUND THREE

Students prepare for the next class by reading Soter's article, a new historicist approach to *My Brother Sam* that considers its antiwar message a possible response to the Vietnam War. Given that YA author interviews are so readily available, I also ask students to read or watch one for their author to find out more about possible motivations or influences.

After an opening discussion of Longfellow's poem, as discussed earlier, book groups meet to debrief what they have learned about their author, and then we regroup for more cross-textual analysis. Together we identify a range of authorial influences and purposes, which sometimes help to explain choices. For example, Perry's disillusionment upon his return from Vietnam appears to be constructed by Myers as part of an antiwar effort, in light of his joyful anecdote of a boy who decided not to enlist after reading *Fallen Angels*—the mother's profuse thanks were "better than every award" (Myers, "Walter Dean Myers"). Comparing insights from authorial intentions or influences seemed to cause students to analyze their original texts in a new way, viewing them less as compelling stories and more as constructed narratives.

I conclude our class conversation with clips from *Johnny Tremain*, a 1957 Disney film directed by Robert Stevenson and adapted from the 1943 novel by Esther Forbes, in which both filmmaker and author had nationalist goals. According to Neil York's article "Son of Liberty," Walt Disney sought Forbes's work as part of his effort to heighten core American values through patriotic filmmaking during the Cold War.

After a few clips of *Johnny Tremain*, students easily made the comparison: "I never knew war was so happy like that; he was invincible"; "It's just weird to see it—blinders—so patriotic, so happy"; "Touches on the propaganda thing, if you follow your country you'll get the girl"; "[War has] no effect on you as long as you survived at the end." To reveal patterns, a comparison provided insight into how the Revolutionary War seems to serve as a touchstone across time for authors seeking to redefine our national identity:

"Paul Revere's Ride"
Set in 1775; published in 1861
Rouses the nation against slavery

Johnny Tremain
Set in 1773–75; published in 1943 (Forbes) and in 1957 (Disney)
Inspires patriotism during World War II (Forbes); cements American values during the Cold War (Disney)

My Brother Sam Is Dead
Set in 1775–79; published in 1974
Sends an antiwar message in the aftermath of the Vietnam War

In conclusion, I asked, "So is [Disney] any different from your authors, who are using the war in some cases to tell their own story, promote a group that hasn't been paid attention to, or dissuade young people from enlisting?" Cayden conceded that, in her view, "[s]ome motives are better than others; it depends on how we're viewing them," adding, "they're similar in that they both have a story they want to tell, they both have a group they want to reach."

Implications

Teaching YA war fiction to undergraduates offers exposure to periods of extreme conflict in which young narrators confront death on a regular basis. Cross-textual examination of the subgenre offers a range of powerful opportunities, including self-reflection. As Roberta Seelinger Trites has argued, when YA literature tackles death, it "serves to simultaneously empower readers with knowledge and to repress them by teaching them to accept a curtailment of their power" (140). In discussing decisions made by and for these constructed narrators, students get closer to the heart of agency in YA literature.

However, these stories also risk a more "passive empathy" of the kind that Megan Boler associates with "easy identification and flattened historical sensibility" (157). Though writing in a different context, Boler's remediation for passive empathy is consistent with a new historicist approach: a self-reflective participation that challenges assumptions, questions what is true, and examines the source of emotional responses. As one of my students put it, "Understanding ideology gives us insight into history because it explains motivations and beliefs: the things that cause historical events." Taking a new historicist approach toward war fiction provides the opportunity to build empathy and understandings as an active response to the effects of literature and history at work.

Notes

1. See Baer; George and Stix; Levstik and Barton, who promote YA historical fiction as an antidote to inaccessible, dry, and fragmentary history textbooks. Marshall George and Andi Stix suggest developing thematic text sets that promote student choice, while Allison Baer advocates connecting YA historical fiction to "quality informational texts" to deliver background knowledge and historical content (285). Linda Levstik and Keith Barton provide a comprehensive guide to developing historical understandings.

2. See Pearcy for a critical analysis of the Civil War sections of six history textbooks. Among other concerns, Mark Pearcy finds that the emphasis on passive voice in such texts "denotes a lack of agency in human behavior—we do not cause events, such events *happen* to us" (57).

3. See Rodwell; Cianciolo; Raphael et al.; Ross, who study shifts in thinking that come from reading historical fiction. For example, Grant Rodwell argues that "[n]arrative is a personal engagement between the author and the reader, often embracing real and enduring social and personal contradictions" (24), while Taffy Raphael and colleagues report that such texts provided students with regular opportunities to discuss conflicting points of view, including those internal to the story and those that reflect students' values.

4. See Daniels, whose adaptable "literature circles" model incorporates student-led, temporary groups based on student choice.

Works Cited

Apol, Laura, et al. "'When Can We Make Paper Cranes?': Examining Pre-service Teachers' Resistance to Critical Readings of Historical Fiction." *Journal of Literacy Research*, vol. 34, no. 4, Dec. 2002, pp. 429–64. *Sage*, doi:10.1207/s15548430jlr3404_3.

Baer, Allison L. "Pairing Books for Learning: The Union of Informational and Fiction." *History Teacher*, vol. 45, no. 2, Feb. 2012, pp. 283–96.

Boler, Megan. "The Risks of Empathy: Interrogating Multiculturalism's Gaze." *Feeling Power: Emotions and Education*, Routledge, 1999, pp. 155–174.

Bruchac, Joseph. *Code Talker: A Novel about the Navajo Marines of World War Two.* Dial Books, 2005.

Cianciolo, Patricia. "Yesterday Comes Alive for Readers of Historical Fiction." *Language Arts*, vol. 58, no. 4, Apr. 1981, pp. 452–62.

Collier, James Lincoln, and Christopher Collier. *My Brother Sam Is Dead.* Simon and Schuster Books for Young Readers, 1974.

Daniels, Harvey. *Literature Circles: Voice and Choice in Book Clubs and Reading Groups.* Stenhouse, 2002.

Fleischman, Paul. *Bull Run.* HarperTrophy, 1993.

Forbes, Esther. *Johnny Tremain.* Houghton Mifflin Harcourt, 1943.

Gallagher, Catherine, and Stephen Greenblatt. *Practicing New Historicism.* U of Chicago P, 2000.

George, Marshall A., and Andi Stix. "Using Multilevel Young Adult Literature in Middle School American Studies." *The Social Studies*, vol. 91, no. 1, 2000, pp. 25–31.

Greenblatt, Stephen. "Resonance and Wonder." *Bulletin of the American Academy of Arts and Sciences*, vol. 43, no. 4, Jan. 1990, pp. 11–34.

———. "Towards a Poetics of Culture." *The New Historicism*, edited by H. Aram Veeser, Routledge, 1989, pp. 1–14.

Lepore, Jill. "The Hyperlore of Paul Revere." *The New Yorker*, 6 June 2011, www.newyorker.com/news/news-desk/the-hyperlore-of-paul-revere.

Levstik, Linda S., and Keith C. Barton. *Doing History: Investigating with Children in Elementary and Middle School.* 4th ed., Routledge, 2011.

Li, Sidney C. "Advancing Multicultural Education: New Historicism in the High School English Classroom." *The High School Journal*, vol. 99, no. 1, Fall 2015, pp. 4–26.

Longfellow, Henry Wadsworth. "Paul Revere's Ride." *Poets.org*, poets.org/poem/paul-reveres-ride. Accessed 8 Aug. 2019.

Mazer, Harry. *The Last Mission.* Laurel-Leaf Books, 1979.

Moreau, Joseph. *Schoolbook Nation: Conflicts over American History Textbooks from the Civil War to the Present.* U of Michigan P, 2003.

Myers, Walter Dean. *Fallen Angels.* Scholastic, 1988.

———. "Walter Dean Myers Discusses Fallen Angels." *YouTube*, uploaded by Walter Dean Myers, 9 Apr. 2014, www.youtube.com/watch?v=oe6IyKM59Zw.

Pearcy, Mark. "'We Have Never Known What Death Was Before': U.S. History Textbooks and the Civil War." *The Journal of Social Studies Research*, vol. 38, no. 1, Jan. 2014, pp. 45–60.

Raphael, Taffy E., et al. "Developing Students' Talk About Text: Analyses in a Fifth-Grade Classroom." *National Reading Conference Yearbook*, vol. 47, Jan. 1998, pp. 116–28.

Review of *Bull Run*, by Paul Fleischman. *Kirkus Reviews*, 20 May 2010, www.kirkusreviews.com/book-reviews/paul-fleischman/bull-run.

Review of *Fallen Angels*, by Walter Dean Myers. *Kirkus Reviews*, 19 Oct. 2011, www.kirkusreviews.com/book-reviews/walter-dean-myers/fallen-angels.

Rodwell, Grant. "Student Engagement through Historical Narratives." *Whose History? Engaging History Students through Historical Fiction*, U of Adelaide P, 2013, pp. 17–28.

Ross, Dianne. "A Study of How Children's Responses to Historical Fiction Are Reflected in Their Writing." Michigan State U, 1982. PhD dissertation.

Soter, Anna O. "Looking at the Past through the Present: A New Historicist Reading of *My Brother Sam Is Dead*." *Young Adult Literature and the New Literary Theories: Developing Critical Readers in Middle School*, Teachers College P, 1999, pp. 45–58.

Stevenson, Robert, director. *Johnny Tremain.* Created by Esther Forbes, Walt Disney Productions, 1957.

Trites, Roberta Seelinger. *Disturbing the Universe: Power and Repression in Adolescent Literature.* U of Iowa P, 2000.
York, Neil L. "Son of Liberty: Johnny Tremain and the Art of Making American Patriots." *Early American Studies*, vol. 6, no. 2, Fall 2008, pp. 422–47.

Cathryn M. Mercier

Taking a Second Look at First-Person Narration in Young Adult Realistic Fiction

My graduate course Contemporary Realistic Fiction for Young Adults studies the prevalence of the first-person voice to consider how first-person narrators beckon to the reader with invitations of identification and subjectivity. The course investigates ways in which YA realistic fiction scripts young adulthood and acts as a discourse invested in the knowability of young adulthood. The course is a core requirement in an MA degree program in children's literature and a genre elective for students earning an MFA in writing for children. Students come from or are headed into a multiplicity of professions, including education at all levels, librarianship, writing, publishing, criticism, and doctoral studies. The course has four epistemological movements: definition of realism, historical grounding in YA realistic novels, questions of subjectivity in first-person novels for a young adult audience, and introduction to the growing scholarship on narratology in children's and YA literature. Except for historical grounding, first-person novels published within the past twelve years delimits the primary fictional material studied. The course consistently attempts to be inclusive of race, class, gender, sexuality, and ability and overtly addresses these areas in literary and scholarly content.

Early class sessions tackle operationalizing a definition of YA literature, fictional young adults, and realism as a genre. Joanne Brown's deceptively simple essay about "the 'real' in young adult realism" (345) begins to develop a shared vocabulary, as it contests our immediate response of measuring a text's realism against the perceived realities of our lives and experiences. We unpack some of our assumptions of "common interpretations" (349) of diversely experienced events, of "a stable, identifiable meaning . . . despite the many denotations and connotations" (348) we ascribe, and of the identifiable yet too often inescapable tautology that realistic fiction has real (or real-seeming) characters, places, and plots (349). Soon enough, students begin making statements about realism as the fiction of the possible, mimetic and representational, different from reality; a genre whose exemplars adhere to linguistic codes that we recognize (350). Brown's use of Jonathan Culler's structuralist understanding of realism in terms of verisimilitude, "a text's artificial resemblance to the external world" (353–54), establishes the linguistic constructedness of realism and makes it harder to conflate fictional characters with real people. Jerome Bruner's essay "The Narrative Construction of Reality" leads us to recognize realistic narratives "as a form not only of representing but of constituting reality" (5). While one can find places for disagreement with Bruner, such as the unity of narrative and the concept of an individual self, his list of ten qualities underscoring the linguistic base of narrative and reality replaces our initial impulse to evaluate texts against our own lives with strategies to interrogate texts and their operations.

Students find examples of Bruner's concepts in James Joyce's *A Portrait of the Artist as a Young Man* and Zora Neale Hurston's *Their Eyes Were Watching God*. These two works establish today's YA realism in literary traditions that precede the psychological and sociological concept of young adulthood. Roger Sutton's "Problems, Paperbacks, and the Printz: Forty Years of YA Books" gives a neat overview of YA literature and observes its "tension between serving readers and creating readers" (232). The article begins with 1967's publication of S. E. Hinton's *The Outsiders* and tracks to 2000's inaugural Michael L. Printz Award for Excellence in Young Adult Literature, the field's own coming of age through the cultural capital of prizing.

Defining continues with close examination of two contemporary works of YA realism directly published for a juvenile audience. *The Chocolate War*, by Robert Cormier, and *I Hadn't Meant to Tell You This*, by

Jacqueline Woodson, were published twenty years apart; with Joyce and Hurston, the combined titles establish a near century of the realistic fiction now part of young adulthood to bring YA realism from the modern into the postmodern period. *The Chocolate War* serves as a literary and scholarly benchmark, as it launched the continuing trend of dark realism in YA novels and serves as the subject of past and current scholarly investigation. Sylvia Patterson Iskander's essay "Readers, Realism, and Robert Cormier" reads *The Chocolate War* as a cultural text of shared knowledge filled with recognizable moral systems, even if they aren't the reader's, that makes legible the difference between the real world and the literary world in its conformity and challenge to genre (11), that demonstrates the text's attitude toward its own artifice (13), and that uses intertextualities to create meaning. Adrian Schober's essay "Rereading Robert Cormier: Realism, Naturalism, and the Young Adult Novel" reframes our now comfortable readings of Cormier. Schober attends to Cormier's intentionality and self-aware worldview, the critical reception of his work that struggles to see its realism, and the "muddled passages" that create stresses between "Cormier's naturalism [and] romantic-humanism" (322). Even as Schober offers an appreciation forty years after Cormier's debut, he also provides a historical overview of naturalism and realism as intersecting genres. Together, Iskander's and Schober's considerations of Cormier's works trace and disrupt the historical continuity of the genre of YA realism and contextualize *The Chocolate War* within YA fiction and scholarship about it.

The opening essay of *Disturbing the Universe: Power and Repression in Adolescent Literature*, by Roberta Seelinger Trites, initiates examination of subjectivity in YA literature and contextualizes that examination within two historically foundational novels. Trites's first chapter centers on *The Chocolate War* as the emblematic YA text that "self-consciously problematizes the relationship of the individual to the institutions that contrast her or his subjectivity" (20). Just as Trites tests her theories through application to the case of *The Chocolate War*'s Jerry Renault, so our class tests her ideas against *I Hadn't Meant to Tell You This*, a text situated within institutions of racism, sexism, and classism. We consider the thresholds of moral agency, the particular nature of socially situated and intersectional identities, and questions of subjectivity—for the character in and the reader of Woodson's novel. Resistance to keeping the secrets of sexual abuse and disbelief that there are no adults to tell often characterize students' initial response to the novel. As we look at the ambiguities that texture Woodson's retrospective first-person narration, close reading exposes that when Lena tells Marie that her father loves her "too much" (42), Marie's own need for her father's unquestioning love obscures her ability to understand Lena's figurative language. Thus, Lena's and Marie's tellings are not-tellings, and the text itself remains silent on the details of incest, secreting it away from the reader. Where does our adult knowledge fill narrative gaps, and where, if, and how might young readers be asked to fill meaning-making gaps? Even though we don't attempt to define the young adult, this discussion troubles our sense of young adult readers, challenges the expectation that readers identify with characters, and questions how much we think we know about how texts construct reader subjectivity. Marie's becomes one of the first confessional narratives in this course where young adult narrators must speak their trauma to adults in order to move beyond it (McGee). However, Marie does not tell the adults in her life; instead, she addresses an unspecified "you" to whom she "hadn't meant to tell" the secrets that she doesn't quite understand and cannot speak. The text desires an adult audience who can hear this inexplicit telling, understand the figurative language that conveys it, and take action on behalf of the actual young adult reader who might be in Lena's or Marie's position.

Ultimately, these early class meetings describe more than define a realism and develop a shared, if fragile and unstable, vocabulary through which to talk about it. We've looked at four touchstone texts that chart the first ninety years of formative YA texts. A handful of critical essays provide historical information, and we have practiced with original theorizing of the particulars of YA literature. Now, we are prepared to examine some thirty novels and graphic novels published over the past decade to see what stories young adults are told and employ narratological approaches to consider how these stories are told.

The works of Andrea Schwenke Wyile ("Expanding the View"; "Value of Singularity"), Jani Barker, Mike Cadden, and Maria Nikolajeva ("Imprints") scaffold our examination. Wyile's pieces provide terms, definitions, and examples of differences between the narrator, character, and narratee to establish a paradigm through which to consider the differences between "the perceived gap between the narrated I . . . and the narrating I" and "the difference between the narrating subject and the subject of narration" ("Expanding the View" 187, 191). Definitions of retrospective, dissonant, and consonant narration; focalization; and immediate- and distant-engaging narration guide our reading of complex texts such as *Boy Toy*, by Barry Lyga; *Surrender*, by Sonya Hartnett; and *Marcelo and the Real*

World, by Francisco X. Stork. The pilot episode of *Veronica Mars* serves as an illuminating template on which to exercise Nikolajeva's observations about voice (including the language in which characters speak, the social and cultural discourses in which they participate, the attitudes they convey, how one character's focalization structures another's) and strands of narration. Cadden's discussion of "how novels that employ double-voiced discourse offer young adult readers the tools necessary for identifying and coping with that irony [of an adult author speaking through the consciousness of a young person]" (146) lends concrete ways of uncovering single-, double-, and multiple-voicedness. Cadden also initiates our consideration of how a text's ironic relationships complicate reader subjectivity as we look at works by Rita Williams-Garcia (*Jumped*), Lucy Christopher (*Stolen*), and E. Lockhart (*The Disreputable History of Frankie Landau Banks*).

The essays upset the duality of reliable or unreliable narrators inculcated since high school, as they yield questions to consider what readers think they know about what characters, like Stork's Marcelo, know or don't know. What happens when Josh's first-person immediate-engaging narration in *Boy Toy* conflicts with younger Josh's more distant-engaging narration? What worldviews account for a narrative that invests twelve-year-old Josh with sexual pleasure and awareness even as it replaces that account with a culturally accepted script that names his experience as criminal abuse? Narratological frameworks also query how telling, remembering, and retelling disclose workings of gender and class and challenge views of childhood as "unaware of and unencumbered by . . . tokens of adulthood" (Nikolajeva, "Dream" 307). The novels rattle readers' investment in Romantic innocence, desire for obvious character growth, or belief in a whole, integrated self.

With this narratological basis, we return to questions of subjectivity considered first with Cormier and Woodson and now considered in contemporary works. We complicate our earlier considerations of subjectivity with the final plank in the course architecture. Robyn McCallum's *Ideologies of Identity in Adolescent Fiction: The Dialogic Construction of Subjectivity* casts subjectivity as "that sense of personal identity an individual has of her/his self as distinct from other selves, as occupying a position within society and in relation to other selves, and as being capable of deliberate thought and action" (3). Using McCallum, we turn to detecting elements of voice, addressivity, audience position, intertextuality, polyphony, and relationships between self and others within the text. We consider the ways in which the ideology of subjectivity itself is produced and consumed in

YA fiction as we examine the discourses that operate in the literature and in our reading, writing, and discussions of it.

The first six weeks of the semester cover the foundational units defining and describing realism and combine discussions of subjectivity with reading strategies from narratology to uncover the novels' ideological operations and identify textual gestures toward subjectivity. The subsequent six weeks amplify those discussions as we expand our historical base in the "second look" section of the course. Students take a second look at a touchstone novel in YA literature published in the United States from 1942 to 1999 using different critical lenses. Admittedly, the list is idiosyncratic and varies from year to year. It includes adult titles that have made their way into the high school curriculum, such as J. D. Salinger's *The Catcher in the Rye*, Carson McCullers's *The Member of the Wedding*, Harper Lee's *To Kill a Mockingbird*, and Sandra Cisneros's *The House on Mango Street*; books published for young adults, such as Robert Lipsyte's *The Contender*, Hinton's *The Outsiders*, and Paul Zindel's *The Pigman*; others that break conventions of form and genre, for example Toni Morrison's *The Bluest Eye* and Virginia Hamilton's *The Planet of Junior Brown*; and yet others that bring once taboo or ignored topics into discussion, such as Rosa Guy's *The Friends*, Nancy Garden's *Annie on My Mind*, Walter Dean Myers's *Fallen Angels*, and Kyoko Mori's *Shizuko's Daughter*. During the first seminar meeting, each student pulls a lottery number to select one of the touchstone titles about which to write an original second-look argument for presentation. They revisit the touchstone in light of contemporary scholarship (no earlier than 1999, ideally) in YA literature *not directly about the touchstone title* and assign one essay for class reading. Not an argument for or against the touchstone's status, the paper examines the book through the scope of current academic conversations in YA literature.

Students present their second-look papers in three-person panels that imitate the format of professional conferences and require that panelists put touchstone titles into conversation with contemporary fiction assigned that week. I organize the panels according to the student-assigned scholarly essays and weave them into the strands of realism, first-person narratives, and questions of identity and subjectivity that have shaped the course so far. Thus, each panel discussion becomes a set of arguments contributing to the overarching argument of the course. Students advance a rigorous class bibliography as they assign pieces on trauma (Tribunella), abjection (Coats; Wilkie-Stibbs), gender (Marshall; Wannamaker; Chaudri), ethnicity and race (Capshaw Smith; Engles and Kory; Tuon), sexuality

(Pattee), class (Wilson and Short), disabilities (Meyer), and a host of other topics that further texture our discussion of voice and the discourse of subjectivity. As a whole, these essays uncover continuities or discontinuities in YA realism across time. The panels express uniquely authoritative student voices, and students find this section of the course demanding and deeply rewarding. The course is one of the last in their graduate program, and students leave confident in their mastery of material and in their readiness to enter and shape tomorrow's scholarly conversations.

The last weeks of the course further weave together understandings of realism as a genre, questions of subjectivity, and diverse critical approaches to imagine the future of YA realistic fiction. In debut novels, we look for intersections of the performativity of young adulthood and performative authorship, especially in a publishing industry manipulating and manipulated by social media, fan fiction, celebrity authors, and authors as celebrity. We ask how new, creative voices script young adulthood. A final assignment about an Alex Award winner from the past decade circles back to the touchstone list's incorporation of adult novels that have made their way into young adult reading to ask how they reflect, disturb, or otherwise engage YA realism, the narratological strategies we've studied, and problems of subjectivity.

Ultimately, the course queries a literary discourse that simultaneously wants the genre of realism to act subversively with its intended audience. And yet the wide range of contemporary scholarship aiding our interrogation of the literary texts exposes a problematic knowability of the reading audience. I revel in the challenges of course design that centers on students' active learning even as it attempts to offer an overarching argument about YA realism's engagement with the first-person narrator. The dynamism of this course stems from its changing literary and scholarly material. Encounters with familiar texts reframed by current scholarship and perspicacious student exegesis create liberating discomfort and welcome disturbances in our field.

Works Cited

Barker, Jani L. "Naive Narrators and Double Narratives of Racially Motivated Violence in the Historical Fiction of Christopher Paul Curtis." *Children's Literature*, vol. 41, 2013, pp. 172–203.

Brown, Joanne. "Interrogating the 'Real' in Young Adult Realism." *New Advocate*, vol. 12, no. 4, Fall 1999, pp. 345–57.

Bruner, Jerome. "The Narrative Construction of Reality." *Critical Inquiry*, vol. 18, no. 1, Autumn 1992, pp. 1–21.

Cadden, Mike. "The Irony of Narration in the Young Adult Novel." *Children's Literature Association Quarterly*, vol. 25, no. 3, Fall 2000, pp. 146–54.
Capshaw Smith, Katharine. "Trauma and National Identity in Haitian-American Young Adult Literature." *Ethnic Literary Traditions in American Children's Literature*, edited by Michelle Pagni Stewart and Yvonne Atkinson, Palgrave Macmillan, 2009, pp. 83–97.
Chaudri, Amina. "'Straighten Up and Fly Right': HeteroMasculinity in *The Watsons Go to Birmingham—1963*." *Children's Literature Association Quarterly*, vol. 36, no. 2, Summer 2011, pp. 147–63.
Christopher, Lucy. *Stolen*. Chicken House / Scholastic, 2010.
Cisneros, Sandra. *The House on Mango Street*. 1984. Vintage, 1991.
Coats, Karen. *Looking Glasses and Neverlands: Lacan, Desire, and Subjectivity in Children's Literature*. U of Iowa P, 2007.
Cormier, Robert. *The Chocolate War*. Pantheon Books, 1974.
Engles, Tim, and Fern Kory. "'What Did She See?': The White Gaze and Postmodern Triple Consciousness in Walter Dean Myers's *Monster*." *Children's Literature Association Quarterly*, vol. 39, no. 1, Spring 2014, pp. 49–67.
Garden, Nancy. *Annie on My Mind*. Farrar, Straus and Giroux, 1982.
Guy, Rosa. *The Friends*. Bantam, 1973.
Hamilton, Virginia. *The Planet of Junior Brown*. Macmillan, 1971.
Hartnett, Sonya. *Surrender*. Walker, 2005.
Hinton, S. E. *The Outsiders*. Viking, 1967.
Hurston, Zora Neale. *Their Eyes Were Watching God*. 1937. Harper Perennial, 2006.
Iskander, Sylvia Patterson. "Readers, Realism, and Robert Cormier." *Children's Literature*, vol. 15, 1987, pp. 7–18.
Joyce, James. *A Portrait of the Artist as a Young Man*. 1916. Penguin, 2003.
Lee, Harper. *To Kill a Mockingbird*. Lippincott, 1960.
Lipsyte, Robert. *The Contender*. Harper, 1967.
Lockhart, E. *The Disreputable History of Frankie Landau Banks*. Hyperion, 2008.
Lyga, Barry. *Boy Toy*. Houghton Mifflin, 2007.
Marshall, Elizabeth. "Borderline Girlhoods: Mental Illness, Adolescence, and Femininity in *Girl, Interrupted*." *The Lion and the Unicorn*, vol. 30, no. 1, Jan. 2006, pp. 117–33.
McCallum, Robyn. Introduction. *Ideologies of Identity in Adolescent Fiction: The Dialogic Construction of Subjectivity*, Taylor and Francis, 1999, pp. 3–22.
McCullers, Carson. *The Member of the Wedding*. Houghton Mifflin Harcourt, 1946.
McGee, Chris. "Why Won't Melinda Just Talk about What Happened? *Speak* and the Confessional Voice." *Children's Literature Association Quarterly*, vol. 34, no. 2, Summer 2009, pp. 172–87.
Meyer, Abbye E. "'But She's Not Retarded': Contemporary Adolescent Literature Humanizes Disability but Marginalizes Intellectual Disability." *Children's Literature Association Quarterly*, vol. 38, no. 3, Fall 2013, pp. 267–83.
Mori, Kyoko. *Shizuko's Daughter*. Holt, 1993.

Morrison, Toni. *The Bluest Eye.* Holt, Rinehart and Winston, 1970.
Myers, Walter Dean. *Fallen Angels.* Scholastic, 1988.
Nikolajeva, Maria. "'A Dream of Complete Idleness': Depiction of Labor in Children's Fiction." *The Lion and the Unicorn*, vol. 26, no. 3, 2002, pp. 305–21.
———. "Imprints of the Mind: The Depictions of Consciousness in Children's Fiction." *Children's Literature Association Quarterly*, vol. 26, no. 4, Winter 2001, pp. 173–87.
Pattee, Amy S. "Disturbing the Peace: The Function of Young Adult Literature and the Case of Catherine Atkins' *When Jeff Comes Home.*" *Children's Literature in Education*, vol. 35, no. 3, Sept. 2004, pp. 241–55.
Salinger, J. D. *The Catcher in the Rye.* Little, Brown, 1951.
Schober, Adrian. "Rereading Robert Cormier: Realism, Naturalism, and the Young Adult Novel." *The Lion and the Unicorn*, vol. 38, no. 3, Sept. 2014, pp. 303–26.
Stork, Francisco X. *Marcelo and the Real World.* Scholastic, 2009.
Sutton, Roger. "Problems, Paperbacks, and the Printz: Forty Years of YA Books." *The Horn Book Magazine*, vol. 83, no. 3, May-June 2007, pp. 231–43.
Tribunella, Eric L. *Melancholia and Maturation: The Use of Trauma in American Children's Literature.* U of Tennessee P, 2010.
Trites, Roberta Seelinger. *Disturbing the Universe: Power and Repression in Adolescent Literature.* U of Iowa P, 2000.
Tuon, Bunkong. "'Not the Same, but Not Bad': Accommodation and Resistance in Thanhha Lai's *Inside Out and Back Again.*" *Children's Literature Association Quarterly*, vol. 39, no. 4, Winter 2014, pp. 533–50.
Veronica Mars. Pilot episode, Rob Thomas Productions / Silver Pictures Television / Stu Segall Productions / Warner Bros., 2004.
Wannamaker, Annette. "Reading in the Gaps and Lacks: (De)Constructing Masculinity in Louis Sachar's *Holes.*" *Children's Literature in Education*, vol. 37, no. 1, Mar. 2006, pp. 15–33.
Wilkie-Stibbs, Christine. *The Outside Child: In and Out of the Book.* Routledge, 2008.
Williams-Garcia, Rita. *Jumped.* Harper, 2009.
Wilson, Melissa B., and Kathy G. Short. "Goodbye Yellow Brick Road: Challenging the Mythology of Home in Children's Literature." *Children's Literature in Education*, vol. 43, no. 2, June 2012, pp. 129–44.
Woodson, Jacqueline. *I Hadn't Meant to Tell You This.* Delacorte, 1994.
Wyile, Andrea Schwenke. "Expanding the View of First-Person Narration." *Children's Literature in Education*, vol. 30, no. 3, Sept. 1999, pp. 185–202.
———. "The Value of Singularity in First- and Restricted Third-Person Engaging Narration." *Children's Literature*, vol. 31, 2003, pp. 116–41.
Zindel, Paul. *The Pigman.* Harper and Row, 1968.

Don Latham and Melissa Gross

Peritext and Pedagogy: Supporting Critical Thinking through Young Adult Nonfiction

In arguing for the importance of sources in children's nonfiction, Sandip Wilson says the question many young readers ask is: "How does the author know that?" This is a key question for readers engaging in critical thinking, Wilson says, but it is a beginning rather than an end in itself (57). How such critical thinking might proceed is suggested by Joe Sutliff Sanders, who discusses two ways that nonfiction texts can present themselves: as accurate, reliable, authoritative information on the one hand and as models of inquiry on the other (379). The latter, Sanders argues, is more conducive to facilitating critical thinking about "facts" and the research process.

One could argue that, indeed, a more "reliable" nonfiction text is one that models inquiry by foregrounding the research process. Clues to an author's employment of and attitudes toward sources can often be found in a book's peritextual elements. The peritext, as defined by Gérard Genette, are those elements "around the text . . . and within the same volume" (4) but not part of the text proper. These elements serve a variety of purposes, one of which is to provide information that can help readers think critically about how the author selected information and crafted a narrative based on numerous sources.

Focusing on two award-winning books, Neal Bascomb's *The Nazi Hunters: How a Team of Spies and Survivors Captured the World's Most Notorious Nazi* and Steve Sheinkin's *Bomb: The Race to Build—and Steal—the World's Most Dangerous Weapon*, we discuss the elements of the peritext that can help readers evaluate the credibility of a work: author biography; author note; source notes; references; bibliography, webography, and discography; suggested reading; and image credits. Employing Wilson's key questions for examining the use of sources in nonfiction shows how these peritextual elements enrich the texts proper and offers a key to evaluating the works. This framework is a valuable pedagogical tool for teaching YA nonfiction.

The Nazi Hunters

What are the author's credentials to write the book?

The main sources of information about the author Neal Bascomb are found in the author biography on the inside back flap of the book jacket and in the author's note (218–19). Neither source provides information about Bascomb's education or preparation in the use of historical methods. The biography establishes the fact that he is a published writer. It lists the titles of his five other books, two of which are designated by *The New York Times* as bestsellers, and one of which is the basis for *The Nazi Hunters.*

The author's note establishes the author's credentials by sharing with the reader the extensive effort made to uncover the details of the story. Bascomb speaks of traveling to four continents to find people who had firsthand knowledge of events, visiting archives, and utilizing researchers and translators to help him in his pursuit of the story. He acknowledges by name the researchers he employed and thanks those who engaged in interviews with him. Avraham Shalom and Shaul Shaul are thanked for answering his many questions, but their expertise is not specified.

Therefore, Bascomb's authority as an author is asserted based on his use of materials, the expertise of the people who helped with the project, and the willingness of individuals to speak with him who could provide information, documents, or context.

What did the author have to learn in writing the book?

First and foremost the author had to reconstruct the story, which involved not only uncovering the sequence of events but also identifying and understanding the motivations of key persons who pursued Adolf Eichmann and brought him to justice. Since much of what happened was "undercover," it is understandable that there continues to be missing information. For this reason, the author had to identify and seek out individuals who could act as informants and who were willing to be interviewed.

There was, therefore, much to discover and to substantiate regarding the events around Eichmann's capture. The specific story also needed to be situated within its historical context, which is related to World War II, the birth of Israel, and the continuing postwar desire to bring war criminals to trial.

How does the author know?

The author's note (218–19), bibliography (220–24), notes (225–38), and photo credits (239–40) demonstrate that the author went to great lengths to track down the facts and to understand the people and events that make up the story. These peritextual elements also make clear, through the author's own admissions and his evaluation of sources, that the historical record is incomplete and that data quality and deductive reasoning informed decisions about how to talk about the means used to track down and apprehend Eichmann.

Bascomb conceptualizes these events as "a great spy tale" (218) and as a "spy story" (219), rather than as an account or report, emphasizing that "some elements of what exactly happened remain secret—and/or clouded in half-truths" (219). While this perspective promises a particular kind of reading experience and encourages speculation about what the narrative might be missing, it may also work against the understanding that this is a well-researched work of nonfiction.

What sources are used?

Knowing where the author got his facts is key to understanding how he knows what he knows and why he thinks what he thinks. The bibliography reveals that Bascomb used many archives and libraries, documentary interviews and materials, personal interviews with more than twenty-three people who had a part in this history, as well as books and articles about Eichmann, his trial, the Israeli secret service, and related topics. A list of the archives and libraries Bascomb used is provided, as are most of the names of people he interviewed. One interview set reflects discussions with "anonymous Tacuara members" (220). It is unstated how many people this represents or whether this was a group interview.

The bibliography contains books and articles published between 1960 and 2007, although some entries are not dated. There is not a one-to-one correspondence between the bibliography and the notes section, where specific sources for quotations or other references are identified. The bibliography appears to be a list of works the author has consulted. Works the author feels young adults might be interested in and able to access are marked with an asterisk.

An extensive list of photo credits is provided that identifies the source (archive, museum, personal collection, etc.) of the photo and the name of the person responsible for it, if applicable. These credits also include the page number in the book where each photo is reproduced. This format makes it easy to connect a photo with an attribution, but the sources themselves would be difficult for most readers to follow up on if they wanted to track down the original.

What does the author say about the sources?

In the notes section, Bascomb offers several insights into his opinion of his sources and how he has used them. The notes are presented in chapter order and consist of short-form citations (shortened titles, acronyms for archives and libraries, indications of personal interviews, etc.) and page numbers for print resources that point to citations provided in the bibliography. Following the citation, Bascomb comments on the source when he feels that clarification is necessary: for example, where the sources are self-contradictory, where information is missing, whether he prefers one source over another, whether the quality of data varies, and when deductive reasoning was used to make sense of multiple sources.

An example of a note indicating that sources are self-contradictory concerns his presentation of Sylvia Hermann's visit to the Eichmann family. Bascomb states that four primary sources recount this event but that none of them agree. He stresses the only known fact is that Hermann did obtain the Eichmann address and went to see if it was indeed Eichmann living there (227).

An instance of missing information is the lack of knowledge concerning who alerted Fritz Bauer to the fact that Eichmann was living in Buenos Aires. In his note, Bascomb provides information concerning who people think this might have been but underscores the fact that this question has yet to be answered (228).

In researching Eichmann's life, Bascomb preferred the biography *Becoming Eichmann*, written by David Cesarani, calling it "thorough and balanced" (226). Nonetheless, he points to a number of other sources that he consulted in researching Eichmann.

Another disputed part of the history is a conversation between Peter Malkin, a Shin Bet agent, and Eichmann after Eichmann was captured but before he was taken out of Argentina. Bascomb states that there is disagreement about this across various accounts but that Malkin's statements, in both interviews and his memoir, are consistent and the basis for the conversation presented in the book, although they have been edited to fit Bascomb's narrative (234). This is a decision about the quality of the data, choosing a reliable first-person account over speculation by others.

Bascomb illustrates the process of using deduction in his contention that Eichmann's sons turned to Carlos Fuldner, a German expatriate, when their father did not come home (234). In a printed account Klaus Eichmann talked about turning to his "father's best friend" for help. A police report of an interview with Fuldner around this time notes that the Eichmann sons came to see him. Bascomb concluded in this case that the family friend the sons sought help from was Fuldner.

These insights into the author's use of sources allow the reader to better understand the extent of his preparation to give an accurate account and of the research process that goes into the writing of history.

What does the author want us to know about the topic?

Bascomb says, "[F]irst of all, this is a spy story" (219), emphasizing that not everything that transpired around Eichmann's capture is known and that history often leaves an incomplete record. He also tells the reader that this is an important story, one that affected the lives of many people. In fact, his interest in what happened began when he met a Holocaust survivor while studying abroad. So, while this is an important part of history, the impact on and actions of individuals are at the center of his tale.

Does the author adhere to documentation standards?

The source documentation provided in *The Nazi Hunters* clearly follows a style guide that reflects how source use is taught except for when it comes to citing sources in-line. While extensive source notes are provided in the notes section, there are no parenthetical citations or footnotes provided for the reader. This means that readers are not prompted to ask how the author knows what he knows. While there are many interesting notes, it is unlikely that many readers would of their own accord peruse the notes section, either to check the veracity of statements, to learn more about the author's process, or just for fun.

Bomb

What are the author's credentials to write the book?

An author biography is included on the back flap of the dust jacket, along with a picture of Sheinkin. The author's credentials are established in two ways. First, we are told about Sheinkin's past experience with informational writing. He is described as a "former textbook writer," who is now "making up for his previous crimes by crafting gripping narratives of American history." This description not only validates Sheinkin's background in writing informational texts but also alludes to the important role the writer's "craft" plays in shaping more interesting fare. Second, the blurb provides evidence of Sheinkin's recent success as a researcher and writer of "several historical works for young readers." In particular, his book *The Notorious Benedict Arnold* is identified as the winner of two prestigious awards.

What did the author have to learn in writing the book?

Sheinkin states in the general introduction to "Source Notes" that he "had a lot to learn" in trying to tell such a complex story. He goes on, in the "Bomb Race Sources" subsection, to identify three story threads: "the Americans try to build a bomb, the Soviets try to steal it, and the Allies try to sabotage the German bomb project" (243). Each of these threads is complex enough in and of itself; the fact that Sheinkin had to weave the three together indicates just how much he had to learn in producing the book. The sheer number of sources in the bibliography also indicates how much he had to learn: seventeen in "Bomb Race Sources," twenty-one in "Character Sources," and forty-one in "Primary Sources." The author biography on the back flap of the dust jacket says that, in researching this book, the author had to play "story detective" as well as "spy." These roles also point to the set of skills Sheinkin needed in finding, evaluating, and selecting the information used in the book. As if to underscore the point, the biography goes on to state that "he combed through hundreds of pages of declassified FBI interviews in search of the men and women who stole the bomb out from under the noses of the U.S. Government."

How does the author know?

Sheinkin can claim some expertise on the subject matter because he has undertaken careful research, as is evidenced by the number of primary and secondary sources listed in "Source Notes." He cites a total of seventy-nine sources in "Source Notes" (243–48) and cites numerous quotations in "Quotation Notes" (249–59). He makes only a few explicit statements in the peritext about his perspective on the sources, his interpretation of them, and his selection process. In fact, he comments only on sources that he judged to be especially helpful. In the acknowledgments (260–61) Sheinkin describes the genesis of the book. It seems that he and his editor had both read an article on "an obscure World War II spy" (260), and this led to the idea for a book on the development of the atomic bomb. He singles out for special recognition two authors who spoke with him directly and the librarians at the New York Public Library and the Saratoga Springs Public Library.

What sources are used?

The sources Sheinkin used in producing the book are listed in two main sections of the peritext and appear after the text proper: "Source Notes" (243–48) and the photo credits (261). Sheinkin divides "Source Notes" into three parts: "Bomb Race Sources," a bibliography of secondary sources on the race itself; "Character Sources," a bibliography of secondary sources on the various people who played key roles in the development of the bomb; and "Primary Sources," a bibliography of primary sources, which Sheinkin describes as "the heart of the book" (246). All the sources listed in the "Bomb Race Sources" section are books on history. All but one of the sources listed in the "Character Sources" section are books of biography, the outlier being an interview that was included as part of a television program broadcast on PBS. The "Primary Sources" section contains a wide variety of sources, including "memoirs, interviews, articles, letters, speeches, hearings, secret recordings, and a few primary source collections" (246). Some of these sources are books, and surprisingly, only three Web resources are listed.

The photo credits identify where the images appear in the book, and the organization that owns the image and granted permission for its use in the book is provided. For example, credit for the image that appears on the back cover is listed as "Back cover: Courtesy of Los Alamos National Laboratory" (261). Captions identifying what is depicted in individual photographs are provided elsewhere near the photograph itself—for example, within the text or on the back flap of the dust jacket.

What does the author say about the sources?

Sheinkin does not explain why he selected the sources he did, although he does say that the primary sources are "the heart of the book" (246). This indicates the importance of firsthand accounts in Sheinkin's research, as is typically the case with historical research. In "Source Notes" he provides a brief, general introduction to the section and then a brief introduction to each of the three subsections. In his introductions to all three subsections, Sheinkin identifies sources that he considers to be outstanding or particularly helpful. For example, in the introduction to "Bomb Race Sources," he writes, "The bible on this whole subject, by the way, is [Richard] Rhodes's *The Making of the Atomic Bomb*" (243). He identifies three especially useful sources in the introduction to "Character Sources." In "Primary Sources" he not only highlights particularly helpful sources but also describes the various kinds of primary sources he consulted (as noted above).

What does the author want us to know about the topic?

Sheinkin makes very few explicit statements in the peritext about what he wants his readers to know about the topic, other than saying that it is a "big story" (243) and, presumably, it constitutes one of the "gripping narratives of American history" (back flap).

Does the author adhere to documentation standards?

The book employs what is no doubt a house style for documenting sources. However, much is lacking, especially when compared with a standard documentation format such as that of the Modern Language Association (MLA). There are no parenthetical citations, footnotes, or endnotes. Complete citations for the various sources used are provided in the "Source Notes" section in MLA format. But, with material that Sheinkin has summarized or paraphrased, it is impossible to know which information comes from which sources. The situation is a bit better with direct quotations, but not much. The extensive "Quotation Notes" section follows the "Source Notes" section. Here quotations from the chapters are provided in chronological order, along with basic information about the source (typically the author's last name and an abbreviated title). For example, in the chapter "Skinny Superhero" a young Robert Oppenheimer is quoted as asking his date, Melba Phillips, "Are you comfortable?" (7). That quotation is documented in the "Quotation Notes" section as follows: "'Are you comfortable': Kelly, *Manhattan Project*" (249). By searching the "Source Notes" section, we learn that the quotation was taken from Cynthia C. Kelly's edited volume *The Manhattan Project: The Birth of the Atomic Bomb in the Words of Its Creators, Eyewitnesses, and Historians.* However, we are given no page number reference, so it would be difficult to track down the quotation in Kelly's book. Interestingly, a quotation, presumably from Oppenheimer—"Mind if I get out and walk for a few minutes?" (8)—that appears in the same chapter is not listed at all in the "Quotation Notes" section. Is the quotation taken from Kelly or an extrapolation on Sheinkin's part? It is hard to know.

Promoting Critical Thinking

Evaluating the credibility of a nonfiction work involves assessing the authority of the writer and the reliability of the sources used. Examining peritextual elements can help readers make these assessments. As the works discussed here demonstrate, the author's credentials are typically included in the author biography, but this information is somewhat limited. In both cases, the authority of the writers is established primarily by listing previous books published and, in the case of Sheinkin, awards won. Neither book provides information about the author's education or training in history or historical methods. Admittedly, this omission is somewhat ameliorated by descriptions of the research and writing processes, information typically found in the author's note or the acknowledgments, although it can be found in the author biography.

In both books, information is provided about the research process and the writing process, and both authors use terms to suggest the amount of work and excitement involved. Bascomb describes his research process as "an incredible journey" (218) in his quest to uncover "a spy story" (219). Sheinkin likens his research process to that of being "a story detective" and his writing process as "crafting gripping narratives of American history" (back flap). By describing their research and writing processes, the authors demonstrate, in general terms, their proficiency in tracking down sources and compiling them to create engaging narratives.

In judging the credibility of sources used, readers rely on what authors say about their sources and where they found the information they include in their books. Bascomb admits that some parts of the story he investigated are "clouded in half-truths" (219) and that some of his interviewees provided contradictory accounts. Sheinkin limits himself to stating which sources he found particularly helpful or authoritative, although he does not explain why. Citations to sources are more problematic. As both examples demonstrate, while complete citations may be provided, citations at the level of page number within individual sources are usually lacking. This practice makes it difficult for readers to verify information cited in the book and may also cause ethical confusion for readers who have been taught a more complete citation style to use in their own research papers. Why, they may wonder, do they need to be exact in documenting information gathered from sources when published writers do not have to meet the same standards? Image credits can be even more problematic, as images are often cited only at the level of the institution where the original images are held.

Close examination of peritextual elements in nonfiction for young adults promotes critical thinking by providing insight into the credibility of the information, as well as the joys and challenges of the research and writing processes. It can also generate much discussion based on what is included—and what is missing—in the documentation of sources.

Works Cited

Bascomb, Neal. *The Nazi Hunters: How a Team of Spies and Survivors Captured the World's Most Notorious Nazi*. Arthur A. Levine Books, 2013.

Genette, Gérard. *Paratexts: Thresholds of Interpretation*. Translated by Jane E. Lewin, Cambridge UP, 1997.

Sanders, Joe Sutliff. "*Almost Astronauts* and the Pursuit of Reliability in Children's Nonfiction." *Children's Literature in Education*, vol. 46, no. 4, Dec. 2015, pp. 378–93.

Sheinkin, Steve. *Bomb: The Race to Build—and Steal—the World's Most Dangerous Weapon*. Roaring Brook Press, 2012.

Wilson, Sandip. "Getting Down to Facts in Children's Nonfiction Literature." *Journal of Children's Literature*, vol. 32, no. 1, Spring 2006, pp. 56–63.

Karen Coats

Teaching the Young Adult Verse Narrative

YA novels and memoirs in verse have proliferated on publishers' lists and garnered significant awards in recent years, earning them a place on syllabi that include YA literature. As many critics and even publishers have noted, these books are often considered a boon for teachers trying to reach emergent or reluctant readers. Saddleback Educational Publishing, for instance, advertises its verse novels in this way: "The varying lengths of the chapters are ideal for a struggling reader, giving them breaks to collect their thoughts, to imagine the characters in their mind's eye, and to set the scene—like a frame in a movie. The structure of poetry makes the books appear less intimidating, with plenty of airy white space" ("Gravel"). But as works that combine poetry, narrative, and sometimes even drama, they can be challenging to both read and teach (Cadden). In fact, Laura Apol and Janine L. Certo claim that

> verse novels are generally *more* rather than less difficult to read and comprehend. The multilayered nature of the verse novel encourages readers to explore what is implied rather than what is simply described or stated in any single poem; as a result, there is not only density of meaning within each poem, but also in the novel sequence that allows for meaning to lie between (or across) the poems. (285)

Verse narratives offer up their stories in fragments, frequently deploying multiple first-person voices to craft tales wherein any action is narrated in retrospect and is more often internal and psychological than physical or event driven. Tracking these voices and the actions on which they may be reflecting thus requires a high level of engagement and the ability to make inferences based on limited descriptive exposition. Hence basic comprehension can be extremely challenging in itself; add to that the professorial goal of helping students analyze these texts as literary artifacts where the poetic forms contribute to the content and themes of the story, and instructors are faced with an even greater challenge. Indeed we might say that if verse novels are more difficult to read and comprehend than prose novels, they may also be more difficult to teach as well.

This essay focuses on methods I have used to teach this hybrid form, considering how to choose an appropriate YA verse narrative for various contexts, how to read for story, how to approach the poetry, and, finally, how to theorize the form itself in light of contemporary cultural theory. While there are myriad novels in verse for young readers to which these same methods can apply, my examples are drawn from verse narratives for ages fourteen and older based on my own, rather than the publishers', determination.

Choosing a Verse Novel to Teach

The first things an instructor needs to consider when assigning a verse novel are, of course, the reasons for teaching it and the context in which it will be taught. In addition to the emergent popularity of the form, there are many reasons to include a verse novel on various types of syllabi. Despite my general agreement that the verse novel is not necessarily easier for students to understand, I am sympathetic to the fact that, as preservice teachers, many of my students will need apprentice texts for emerging teen readers. Depending on my students' goals and anxieties about their capabilities to teach poetry in particular, I might introduce a verse novel from Saddleback's Gravel Road series. These realistic novels in verse are part of a publishing category called "Hi-Lo," meaning that they are high-interest, low-readability-level texts. My experience as a high school teacher has led me to understand that struggling teen readers can improve their literary competencies only if they are engaged by the books they read, and that often means hard-hitting, melodramatic, contemporary realism. Books like *A Heart Like Ringo Starr* and *Teeny Little Grief Machines*, both by Linda Oatman High, not only feature stories many teen readers will find compelling but also enable teachers to explore poetic devices like easily identifiable internal and end rhyme, accessible visual and verbal metaphors, and effective lineation, phrasing, and segmentivity in ways that give readers (and the future teachers themselves) much-needed confidence in their ability to approach poetry as well as longer narratives.

Verse narrative can also be taught in interdisciplinary contexts as well as in literature courses, and this is why I try to consistently use the word *form* rather than *genre* to describe them. While realism predominates, verse narratives appear in both fiction and nonfiction subgenres. Works like Melanie Crowder's *Audacity*, Marilyn Nelson's *Carver: A Life in Poems* and *A Wreath for Emmett Till*, and Jeannine Atkins's *Finding Wonders: Three Girls Who Changed Science* can be tied to history, civics, life writing, and science to engage and energize students committed to one side or the other of such disciplinary divides, making them appropriate for upper-division courses that contain mostly education majors as well as general education classes focused on various topics. I have also been asked by my colleagues in criminal justice, health, and psychology to recommend YA books appropriate to their fields, and I always include verse novels in my recommendations, given that many of these narratives engage topics of criminality, disability, and trauma. While I haven't taught a class in classical literature, I would certainly include David Elliott's *Bull*, which reimagines the story of Theseus and the Minotaur in multiple voices, and Nikki Grimes's *Dark Sons*, which brilliantly links the Genesis story of Ishmael with a contemporary narrative of a boy facing a parallel situation. For my YA literature classes, verse novels such as *The Sound of Letting Go*, by Stasia Ward Kehoe, which explores a sister's conflicted responses to her brother's profound autism spectrum disorder; *Freakboy*, by Kristin Elizabeth Clark, which focuses on gender fluidity; *Zane's Trace*, by Allan Wolf, where a boy's personal identity is related to the multiethnic legacy of America; and Jacqueline Woodson's *Brown Girl Dreaming* enable us to discuss identity as an intersectional construct both enabled and burdened by family relationships and intergenerational memory.

I also introduce the verse novel late in my courses on poetry for young people. By the time we turn our attention to the form, we have already explored different types of poems and figurative language, and we have developed a working theory of some of the major differences between poetry for children and poetry for young adults. Specifically, we have analyzed the conventions of various forms of lyric poetry, examined the history of narrative and dramatic poetry for young people, and traced the conditions for metaphoric understanding as these develop from early childhood through the teenage years. In more general terms, after reading and discussing a range of poems for various ages, we have concluded that while children's poetry tends to be focused on containing and transforming the physicality of emotional excess into more socially acceptable verbal forms (for instance, even a taboo emotion seems clever when expressed in a poetic form, and rhythmic language alleviates physical and emotional distress), YA poetry is more likely to court and codify excess emotion. It does this by elevating garden-variety mood swings, frustrating dissatisfactions, and transient lusts into cleverly aestheticized protests and vaulted passions and, often, links them to broader cultural frameworks. When we approach the verse novel, we put our prior learning to work and our theories to the test by comparing a YA verse novel with one for younger readers. Because of our focus on poetry in that class, I choose verse novels that use or play with recognizable forms, such as Elliott's *Bull*, or self-consciously invent new forms, such as those by Helen Frost, and stay away from ones that rely on "non-rhyming free verse," which is what Joy Alexander refers to, with some regret, as the "house-style" of the YA verse novel (270).

I have listed many titles thus far because I believe that making a good choice is critical to teaching the verse novel; alas, not all verse novels offer the opportunity to address a topical need while also providing an exemplar of the form at its best—that is, when it is a successful hybrid of a good story and poetry crafted in a recognizably intentional way. In fact many do earn the criticism of being "simply prose hacked into lines . . . [that] would not pass muster as poetry in an undergraduate creative writing class" (Rosenberg 377) or "free of poetry rather than free verse" (Cadden 309). While many Web sites offer lists of popular verse novels, most have little to say about their teachability, which, for me, refers to a combination of literary quality, relevant subject matter, formal interest, and affective appeal. The question remains of where to find such teachable works. I have the advantage of encountering many in my capacity as a staff reviewer for *The Bulletin of the Center for Children's Books*, and I can say that reviews in that journal, though brief, always attend to the quality of the poetry as well as the content of the story, and if a text has curricular uses, we say so. In addition, *The Lion and the Unicorn* features an annual assessment of the year's best poetry in its fall issue, which occasionally includes attention to verse novels. While the judgments of reviewers and critics needn't be read as the last word, they are useful guides and often provocative enough to open interesting, discussable questions with your students.

Reading for the Story

Once you have chosen the text you want to teach, the challenge shifts to helping your students navigate and engage the hybridity of the genre. Despite the stated hope of Saddleback that readers will take the breaks they need to collect their thoughts and imagine the scenes and characters, my experience is that most of my students take advantage of the form's short segments and abundant white space to read quickly, focusing on what is happening with the plot and characters rather than lingering over the language. Though the assumption might be that this activity is lower on Bloom's taxonomy of critical thinking skills, reading for the plot in many verse novels isn't as straightforward as it might seem; in fact, it may require analysis, synthesis, and creativity rather than mere comprehension skills. Verse novels most often consist of impressionistic reflections on events that have happened "offstage," requiring readers to fill in gaps of what exactly happened between the poems. Some, like Mel Glenn's *Jump Ball: A Basketball Season in Poems*, do not present their plot in a linear way. Multiple narrators also prove difficult to track for some readers. David Levithan's *The Realm of Possibility* comprises multiple, sometimes interconnected stories told through the voices of twenty students at one high school. While each section is headed by the names of five students, the individual poems aren't labeled with who is voicing them, so readers have to figure out who is speaking and how the various characters in one section are involved with the ones in other sections.

The method that I have found most effective for enabling students to weave together the plot threads so that they have a deep understanding of character motivations is one David Ball developed for reading plays, and that is to read the book backward after you have read it in the usual way. That is, he suggests that you start at the end and figure out what immediately preceded each movement of the plot. In the case of a verse novel, this is an especially effective method because it forces readers to construct any events that may not be immediately evident or spelled out in detail in the narration but have nevertheless precipitated a change in a character's relationship status or self-awareness, which is more likely to be evident in the first-person poetry. Ball argues, "Examining events backwards ensures you will have no gaps in your comprehension of the script. When you discover an event you cannot connect to a previous event, you know there is a problem for either reader or writer to solve" (16). But he also concedes that such work takes a lot of time, so I do this as a group activity; that is, I assign a set of pages to each small group and ask the students to determine which event caused each effect, and then, starting with the last page, we cover the whiteboard with the backward sequence. In the case of a verse narrative like Levithan's with multiple speakers, we have to construct multiple sequences and add arrows to show connections among characters. This method ensures that if there are problems with the sequence, it is not due to the reader's lack of understanding, and it clears the way for us to discuss how the poetry not only depicts but also supports the character development throughout the unfolding of the plot.

Approaching the Poetry

Given that most of us are accustomed to teaching prose, it is all too easy to focus, like our students, on the movement of the narrative rather than the poetry in verse novels. And, in fact, as many critics have noted, not all the poetry in such works is worth attending to; this is the chief complaint against many contemporary YA verse novels. The poet and verse novelist Nikki Grimes, for instance, laments that "there are too many so-called verse novels you get fifty pages into without finding a single metaphor" ("Interview" 283). However, I think an enhanced understanding of different types of metaphor and how teens process them can nuance our understanding of the poetic quality, or lack thereof, of a verse novel under study.

The developmental psychologist Ellen Winner identifies several different types of metaphor, and her research, confirmed and supplemented by others, suggests that a metaphor is not a metaphor is not a metaphor, at least in terms of the ability of young readers to produce and understand them. She has found that while even very young children can both understand and produce metaphors wherein both the tenor and the vehicle are apprehended by the senses (for instance, a toy ring might be called a doughnut because it looks like one), it is not until early adolescence that they can understand metaphors based on functional relations, such as when a girl with a congenital heart defect longs for "a heart like Ringo Starr" because of the drummer's ability to keep a steady beat. In addition, it is only when adolescents have a sense of their own interiority—that is, an unseen psychological domain separate from the physical domain—that they can understand what Winner calls "physical-psychological" metaphors (67). In the case of a well-made verse novel, we may see all of these types of metaphors in the verbal imagery itself, but we must also look at the forms and typography of the words on the page to see the connections being made between the physical or material domain and the psychological one in terms of character creation. For instance, in *Bull*, Daedalus the architect does not use metaphoric language to describe his predicament of having to create structures that he finds abhorrent, but his entire poetic form is a metaphor for the way he thinks; it consists of four-line stanzas with a regular rhyme scheme. In *The Realm of Possibility*, the character with an eating disorder writes poems that consist of only one or two words per line, creating the impression of someone who is very concerned with keeping the slimmest profile and making the barest impression on the world possible, while another character, who perceives herself as cut off from others, writes one haiku per page, thus emphasizing her physical containment and isolation. The teen characters in Frost's *Keesha's House* write in sestinas, suggesting a fluid, unfinished quality at this stage in their identities but also the obsessive practice of turning the same ideas in their heads over and over as they seek new ways to think about their situations. Her adults, on the other hand, are isolated in their rigid one-off sonnets, reflective of their adherence to social rules and appearances that drive their teens away. The book ends with the teens themselves composing a crown of sonnets, suggesting the possibility of entering into adult roles within an interconnected community of support and care. Thus, the forms of the poetry don't necessarily contain metaphors as much as they become metaphors in themselves, linking their physical appearance on the page with the psychological qualities of the characters.

Of course, we also look for motifs, symbols, and various types of figurative language within the verbal imagery, and I lead students through a note-taking exercise where, again working in groups, they are asked to find examples of particular elements that we then assemble on the board. From there, we cocreate multiple possible thesis statements for a written analysis and pick and choose which details would serve each thesis best. They are then instructed to go and do likewise on a verse narrative of their choice, only this time, they actually have to write the paper.

Theorizing the Emergence of the Form in Contemporary Culture

Ultimately, though, it is the form-as-metaphor quality that, for me, marks the most important reason YA verse novels can be particularly effective as texts that speak to contemporary YA audiences. As Alexander notes, the verse novel form takes advantage of a larger cultural emphasis on the "'eye and ear' communication" (270) on which millennials have cut their teeth. For general education as well as literature courses, a strong rationale can be made for the appeal and value of verse novels from a multiliteracies standpoint. That is, students whose preferred literacy modalities are aural, kinesthetic, spatial, and visual rather than oriented to print text will benefit from a form that responds to these modalities with its beats, font styles, and arrangement on the page. Offering students the opportunity to create or find images that correspond to the text they are reading, compile playlists inspired by the sounds and settings, or even construct multidimensional models such as story boxes or sculptures from found objects relevant to the texts enhances their ability to make arguments in forms and genres that are becoming increasingly persuasive given contemporary multimedia environments. But such activities can also enhance their ability to fill in the gaps within and across the poetic sequences. Such teaching for multiliteracies may seem a bit juvenile until we realize that asking students to both use and explore multiple sensory domains in their analysis of texts actually facilitates a greater understanding of the way ideas are expressed across different sign systems. As Marjorie Siegel notes, "the act of translating meanings from one sign system to another" (455) forces students to think about the way meanings are communicated metaphorically. In fact, learning to track the story and figure out how the poetic imagery metaphorizes embodiment and psychological states in a verse novel can make students better critical readers of multimedia texts in general. As I have led my students in discussions of their choices for such projects, they find themselves better able to understand and talk about the effects of the author's choices; in other words, by engaging their multiliteracy modalities, I am able to meet my goal of teaching them to think about words and images on pages and screens more effectively.

Finally, then, we theorize what we have learned. As a follow-up activity after they have analyzed the features of a verse novel of their choice in a paper and multimodal project, I ask students to draft a "walk poem" of a typical day, encouraging them to record quick impressions of moments in rich sensory detail—the feel of waking up, the smell of coffee, the snatches of media and conversations they hear as they pass through various spaces, the colors and shapes of those environments, the taste of foods, the drifts and snaps of attention. I ask them to look at their fragments, to think about how these bits add up to a day, and to reflect on what noticing these things and not others says about what they care about and what they take for granted. I have them place these reflections in conversation with their first draft impressions and ask: What if every day were like this day? What kind of life would these days add up to; what kind of person am I in the process of becoming? How does my fragmented, messy, utterly ordinary life take on the contours and themes of a YA narrative in verse?

Works Cited

Alexander, Joy. "The Verse-Novel: A New Genre." *Children's Literature in Education*, vol. 36, no. 3, Sept. 2005, pp. 269–83.

Apol, Laura, and Janine L. Certo. "A Burgeoning Field or a Sorry State: U.S. Poetry for Children, 1800–Present." S. Wolf et al., pp. 275–87.

Atkins, Jeannine. *Finding Wonders: Three Girls Who Changed Science*. Atheneum, 2016.

Ball, David. *Backwards and Forwards: A Technical Manual for Reading Plays*. Southern Illinois UP, 1983.

Cadden, Mike. "Genre as Nexus: The Novel for Children and Young Adults." S. Wolf et al., pp. 302–13.

Clark, Kristin Elizabeth. *Freakboy*. Farrar, Straus and Giroux, 2013.

Crowder, Melanie. *Audacity*. Philomel Books, 2015.

Elliott, David. *Bull*. Houghton Mifflin Harcourt, 2017.

Frost, Helen. *Keesha's House*. Farrar, Straus and Giroux, 2003.

Glenn, Mel. *Jump Ball: A Basketball Season in Poems*. Lodestar Books / Dutton, 1997.

"Gravel Road Verse Sample Set." *Saddleback Educational Publishing*, www.sdlback.com/gravel-road-verse-sample-set.

Grimes, Nikki. *Dark Sons*. Zondervan, 2010.

———. "An Interview with Poet Nikki Grimes." By Sylvia Vardell and Peggy Oxley, *Language Arts*, vol. 84, no. 3, Jan. 2007, pp. 281–85.

High, Linda Oatman. *A Heart Like Ringo Starr*. Saddleback Educational Publishing, 2015.

———. *Teeny Little Grief Machines*. Saddleback Educational Publishing, 2014.

Kehoe, Stasia Ward. *The Sound of Letting Go*. Viking, 2014.

Levithan, David. *The Realm of Possibility*. Knopf, 2004.

Nelson, Marilyn. *Carver: A Life in Poems*. Front Street, 2001.

———. *A Wreath for Emmett Till*. Houghton Mifflin Harcourt, 2005.

Rosenberg, Liz. "Reviewing Poetry." *The Horn Book Magazine*, vol. 81, no. 3, May-June 2005, pp. 375–78.

Siegel, Marjorie. "More Than Words: The Generative Power of Transmediation for Learning." *Canadian Journal of Education / Revue canadienne de l'éducation*, vol. 20, no. 4, Autumn 1995, pp. 455–75.

Winner, Ellen. *The Point of Words: Children's Understanding of Metaphor and Irony*. Harvard UP, 1997.

Wolf, Allan. *Zane's Trace*. Candlewick Press, 2007.

Wolf, Shelby A., et al., editors. *Handbook of Research on Children's and Young Adult Literature*. Routledge, 2011.

Woodson, Jacqueline. *Brown Girl Dreaming*. Penguin, 2014.

Gwen Athene Tarbox

Integrating Comics into an Undergraduate Young Adult Literature Course

Ten years ago, when I assigned Gene Luen Yang's award-winning graphic novel *American Born Chinese* in my Adolescent Literature course, I felt as if I were taking a risk, given the lack of pedagogical resources on children's and YA comics[1] that I could use to support my lesson planning. Adding *American Born Chinese* also meant dropping a traditional text-only narrative from my booklist in a course that served as a requirement for our secondary English education majors and was mandated, by state guidelines, to cover poetry, realistic fiction, fantasy novels, nonfiction texts, and film. However, over the last decade, as children's and YA comics have proliferated and educational researchers have demonstrated the importance of visual literacy, the situation surrounding comics instruction has altered significantly. In this new environment, college instructors would be remiss if they did not include at least one comics text in their YA literature courses, yet many instructors lack confidence in their ability to teach comics, and they often must convince undergraduate students that the medium is worth consideration. Many of the secondary education majors who took Adolescent Literature in spring 2017 remarked in their course evaluations that prior to the comics unit, they would never have picked up a comics text on their own, because they had doubts about the medium's viability in a language arts curriculum. In order to reach education students such as these, as well as those English majors who might be inclined to view any type of popular literature with suspicion, I have sought out resources and developed teaching assignments designed to enhance my students' understanding of the comics medium.

Defining Contemporary Young Adult Comics

Perhaps the best-known contemporary comics creator for young people is Raina Telgemeier, whose graphic novel *Ghosts* debuted in 2016 with an initial print run of half a million copies and whose middle-grade and YA novels earned nearly $10 million in 2016 (Griepp). That same year, another well-publicized YA comics text, John Lewis, Andrew Aydin, and Nate Powell's graphic memoir *March: Book Three*, was released to widespread critical acclaim, going on to win a National Book Award for Young People's Literature, as well as an unprecedented sweep of four American Library Association accolades, including the Michael L. Printz Award for Excellence in Young Adult Literature and the Coretta Scott King Book Award. Although marketing information can be difficult to quantify in a category that ranges from monthly comic book releases to graphic novels, the industry analyst Milton Griepp estimates that nearly twenty percent of texts published for young readers are now released in the comics format.

Selecting YA comics from such an extensive pool of potential titles can be challenging, given the variety of editorial and distribution models that move texts from the creative stage out into the marketplace. Unlike traditional text-only YA narratives released by publishers that have a long track record of producing young people's literature, YA comics texts are frequently issued by firms that work within the comic book industry's monthly release and direct distribution model. Thus, while Telgemeier's work comes with specific age designations and has been reviewed by Scholastic editors who work from the assumption that they are shaping literary culture, G. Willow Wilson and Adrian Alphona's *Ms. Marvel* series is the product of the Marvel business model that attempts to reach both teenage and adult readers on a monthly basis. To expand my students' understanding of the comics marketplace, I usually assign an award-winning text from a traditional publisher, such as Yang's *Boxers and Saints*, released by First Second Books, and pair it with a comic along the lines of Jillian Tamaki's *SuperMutant Magic Academy*, released by Drawn and Quarterly, a Canadian firm best known for producing high-art graphic novels.

In terms of its creation, publication, and reception, Tamaki's text provides an instructive introduction to the complexities that exist when it comes to defining the category of contemporary YA comics. In December 2010 Tamaki began drawing a daily webcomic that focused, in a mild parody of the Harry Potter and *X-Men* series, on the lives of boarding school students who possess inconvenient, and sometimes even wearisome, magical abilities. Readers were introduced to the somber musing of Everlasting Boy, a young man trapped in the body of a teenager for eternity, as well as to the lighthearted exploits of Wendy, Marsha, and Trixie, friends who use their powers to steal boys' underwear from the dorms, only to regret their decision after realizing the deplorable hygiene habits of their male classmates (70). As this subject matter suggests, Tamaki saw herself writing *about* teenagers, not *for* them, and in 2015, when Drawn and Quarterly commissioned a graphic novel version of the webcomic, its marketing staff placed the text alongside its other high-art comics releases without labeling it specifically as a YA offering.

However, from the series' inception, young readers flooded Tamaki's Tumblr page to express their engagement with the story lines. At North American comics conventions, teenagers displayed cosplay costumes of many of the SuperMutant characters, and at the 2015 San Diego Comic Con, the graphic novel version of the series won an Eisner Award in the category of "Best Publication for Teens (Ages 13–18)." As the production and reception history of *SuperMutant Magic Academy* suggests, YA comics are a vastly diverse category—one in which a text can simultaneously be labeled as adult and YA and can be distributed digitally and in print. In order to teach these texts effectively, an instructor needs to keep informed about mainstream, independent, and mass-produced comics, while also grasping the formal properties that set comics apart from text-only narratives.

Developing a Background in Young Adult Comics

When I made the decision to begin teaching YA comics, I knew that I would have to spend time reading widely in comics theory. I also benefited from learning about the experience of established scholars who had already made the move from studying illustration to studying comics. For instance, in "Picture Book Guy Looks at Comics: Structural Differences in Two Kinds of Visual Narrative," Perry Nodelman emphasizes that knowing the way illustrations work in the picture book category does not provide a sufficient basis for interpreting comics. Nodelman observes that

> when readers look at a picture in a picture book, they tend to expect a variation of it in the text, and vice versa—something that is different enough from it but related enough to it to help account for its significance. Having tried to puzzle out how, readers can then turn the page in expectation of a development that draws from, but also continues to build bilaterally upon, the information found previously in earlier words and pictures. (442)

However, when it comes to comics, Nodelman notes that they are less "insistently dual, and most usually suggest a much less contrapuntal rhythm" (443), because readers must remain aware of visual repetitions that may be spaced in irregular intervals across the entirety of a comic.

Like most North American comics scholars, I began my comics studies by reading Scott McCloud's *Understanding Comics: The Invisible Art*, a text that focuses on the formal aspects of comics, including the way that sequential art compels the reader to work toward closure by filling in gaps between panels (60). In addition to recommending this text to beginning scholars, I also suggest Barbara Postema's *Narrative Structure in Comics*, Thierry Groensteen's *Comics and Narration*, Jan Baetens and Hugo Frey's *The Graphic Novel: An Introduction*, and Paul Karasik and Mark Newgarden's *How to Read* Nancy*: The Elements of Comics in Three Easy Panels*, all of which extend McCloud's ideas in important ways. While McCloud focuses primarily upon how a series of panels operate on the comic page, Postema and Groensteen draw readers' attention to how each panel in the comic is in dialogue not only with the other panels on a page but with panels across the entirety of the comic text. Baetens and Frey consider the process of visual rhetoric as well, arguing that the spatial aspects of comics impact the narrative in ways that go beyond the traditional analysis of a text's action and plot (167), and Karasik and Newgarden put forward a model of close reading that encourages readers to pay attention to detail. Finally, to round out the preparation process, I suggest Randy Duncan and Matthew Smith's *The Power of Comics: History, Form, and Culture*, an overview that provides a detailed history of the medium and offers exercises that focus specifically on comics interpretation.

Over the last decade, a number of scholars, including Charles Hatfield, Carol Tilley, Philip Nel, and Joe Sutliff Sanders, have produced well-researched scholarship on children's and YA comics, with subjects ranging from the institution of the Comics Code Authority in the 1950s to the role that digitalization has played in changing reading practices. In

2017 Michelle Ann Abate and I coedited *Graphic Novels for Children and Young Adults: A Collection of Critical Essays*, which includes articles on more than twenty popular comics, including the *Lumberjanes* series, Telgemeier's *Drama*, and Vera Brosgol's *Anya's Ghost*. Additionally, essays on YA comics can also be found in comics-specific journals such as the *Journal of Graphic Novels and Comics* and *Inks*, the newly revived periodical sponsored by the Comic Studies Society.

Structuring a Comics Unit for an Undergraduate Young Adult Literature Course

Before I introduce my students to a YA comic—or even to elements of comics form—I offer a unit on a hybrid comic such as Keshni Kashyap and Mari Araki's *Tina's Mouth: An Existential Comic Diary*. Hybrid comics, which include a mixture of text and image, help ease students into the realm of visual interpretation, and Kashyap and Araki's decision to intersperse handwritten diary text with frequent illustration offers a good example of word-image interaction. Another excellent transition text would be the graphic novel version of Laurie Halse Anderson's *Speak*. This 2018 variant, written by Anderson and drawn by Emily Carroll, includes both traditional comics panel sequences and full-page illustrations. Pairing the text-only novel with the graphic adaptation offers students the opportunity to discuss the segments of the origin text that are rendered solely in visual imagery as well as the dialogue and narration that are carried over.

For the comics unit, my learning objectives include making sure that my students are able to place the medium of comics within the context of YA literature as a whole and that they are able to define terminology associated with comics interpretation. I also expect students to feel comfortable discussing the context and form of key scenes within a YA comic and to write short interpretative essays based upon their analysis of comics sequences. The comics unit for Adolescent Literature comprises three one-hour-and-fifteen-minute class sessions centered around an award-winning graphic novel such as Yang's *American Born Chinese* or Lewis, Aydin, and Powell's *March: Book One*. Selecting an award-winning graphic novel ensures that there will be journal articles and book chapters that focus on the comic, as well as an abundance of critical reviews and publisher-sponsored lesson plans.

During the initial class session, I provide a brief lecture on the history and origins of YA comics. This process introduces basic comics terminology (*panel*, *borders*, *breakdown*, *gaps*, and *closure*), while demonstrating to students that they already possess many of the skills necessary to interpret visual narratives. For homework, I provide students with a handout that includes comics terms, short secondary readings about the terms, and interpretative questions. In the version of the handout below (appendix 1), I have included interpretative questions for a variety of the comics that I teach in the course, rather than just focusing on one text.

At the beginning of the second class session, I ask students to recall the critical ideas that we have been discussing all semester in relation to text-only YA narratives, such as Karen Coats's observation that YA literature mirrors many of the tensions "that preoccupy the physical bodies and emotional lives of its intended audience," including the "tensions between growth and stasis, between an ideal world we can imagine and the one we really inhabit, between earnestness and irony, [and] between ordinary bodies and monstrous ones" (316). I prompt students to think about how the comic text they have read reflects these concepts, and almost immediately, students move to a discussion of how form impacts their understanding of the content. They recognize that for comics creators, whose work involves articulating characters into being, categories such as class, gender, and ethnicity can never be masked. They point out places in the narrative in which image and text seem to conflict or where point of view, something rendered in text-only narratives through pronoun use, has to be denoted through visual cues in the comics medium. At this point I turn to the terminology handout and ask students to discuss specific scenes from the comic, either as a class or in groups, and for homework between sessions two and three, I prepare students to write about comics by giving them a brainstorming handout (appendix 2) that they fill out and bring with them to the next class meeting. In addition to asking students to practice the terminology they have just learned, this assignment emphasizes the important role that description plays in effective comics interpretation. I invite two or three students to share their brainstorming document so that the entire class can offer feedback, and I ask students to write a short interpretative essay on their comic spread so that we can share those responses, an activity that extends our discussion of content and helps students link close reading and focused writing as part of their interpretative process.

Discussing Censorship

To conclude the comics unit, I provide students with information on the Comic Book Legal Defense Fund (CBLDF), a nonprofit organization that defends the First Amendment rights of comics creators, assists teachers and librarians in fighting censorship, and offers excellent educational materials, including detailed reading guides and course plans for a number of popular YA comics. As the CBLDF points out, "In theory, dealing with challenges to graphic novels is no different than dealing with challenges to print material. In practice, however, it is important to keep in mind that many people consider an image to be far more powerful in its impact than any written description of that image" ("Why Comics"). As such, I want my preservice students in the Adolescent Literature course to be prepared not only to interpret and teach comics but to defend their use in K–12 curricula. What is heartening is finding that by the end of their very brief introduction to the comics medium, the overwhelming majority of my students want to learn more.

Note

1. In this essay, I refer primarily to YA comics but identify individual texts that have been marketed as "graphic novels." For a discussion of the evolution of comic terminology, see Hatfield.

Appendix 1: Comics Terminology and Interpretation Handout

Panels

DEFINITION: Panels, whether alone or in a sequence, form the building blocks of comics. A panel represents one discrete moment in a comic.

RELEVANT SCHOLARSHIP: Postema 1–7; Baetens and Frey 103–07

INTERPRETIVE PRACTICE: On page 189 of Tamaki's *SuperMutant Magic Academy*, how does panel composition create both the humor in the sequence as well as commentary on upsetting the status quo?

Breakdown

DEFINITION: The choices a comic creator makes about how panels should be arranged is called the *breakdown*. The term *spread* refers to two facing comic pages.

RELEVANT SCHOLARSHIP: Duncan and Smith 131–32

INTERPRETIVE PRACTICE: In *March: Book One*, the spread on pages 76–77 features Lewis looking back on the moment he decided to dedicate his life to social justice. How does the breakdown of panels on these pages convey Lewis's visualization of Lawson's words?

Bubbles

DEFINITION: Speech bubbles convey dialogue within a comic. Thought bubbles refer to a character's inner monologue.

RELEVANT SCHOLARSHIP: McCloud 134

INTERPRETIVE PRACTICE: In *American Born Chinese*, Yang depicts Jin's crush on Amelia and his struggle to gain her acceptance. On page 98, how does Yang's use of thought bubbles contribute to a reader's understanding of Jin's inner struggle?

Captions

DEFINITION: Text-based narration in a comic is usually set out in captions. Sometimes these captions appear in rectangular boxes; other times, they are allowed to float across a panel or a page.

RELEVANT SCHOLARSHIP: Duncan and Smith 128–31

INTERPRETIVE PRACTICE: As a memoir, *March: Book One*, relies heavily upon Lewis's narration of his coming-of-age experience. Describe how the narration is integrated into the pages and panels.

Gaps and closure

DEFINITION: When readers move from one panel to the next, they are filling in gaps and performing an act referred to as *closure*.

RELEVANT SCHOLARSHIP: McCloud 68–73

INTERPRETIVE PRACTICE: On the first page of *The Arrival*, Tan presents a traditional three-by-three waffle panel, and at first it is difficult to discern the connections among the panels on the page. What occurs on the next page that encourages a reader to reach closure?

Page layout

DEFINITION: Most comics are often arranged using what is known as a waffle pattern, with three or four panels per row and three to four rows per page. Changing this pattern can draw attention to important elements in the story.

RELEVANT SCHOLARSHIP: Duncan and Smith 139–41

INTERPRETIVE PRACTICE: At key moments in *March: Book One*, Powell varies the sizes and layout of panels. Locate one such scene and consider how panel size helps express the seriousness of the situation Lewis wishes to convey.

Line style

DEFINITION: The thickness of lines and the use of shading can help to set the mood and direct readers as to where they should be placing their attention. When the lines of a comic are uniform in size and contain little shading, the mood may seem lighter than if the lines of the comic are varied in thickness and are jagged.

RELEVANT SCHOLARSHIP: Gardner 53–69

INTERPRETIVE PRACTICE: Yang employs what is referred to as a "clear line" style in which his lines are uniform in size and his images are free from shadow and shading, effects that cartoonists often employ to depict dramatic situations. The clear line style is often associated with adventure and humor comics; however, in a couple of scenes, including the attack on Wong Lao-Tsai, how does Yang manage to convey the seriousness of the situation, even though his line style remains the same?

Color choice

DEFINITION: When the comics industry was in its infancy, publishers used basic primary colors because they were less expensive to replicate. Beginning in the 1970s, as many comic creators hoped to distinguish their work from that of the traditional comic book, they turned to limited color palettes in order to express serious subject matter.

RELEVANT SCHOLARSHIP: Baetens

INTERPRETIVE PRACTICE: Lewis, Aydin, and Powell elected to use black, white, and gray tones for the March series. In the spread on pages 82–83, how does color, shading, and light combine to create a sense of the struggle that Lewis and his friends face as they try to practice the principles of nonviolent resistance?

Braiding

DEFINITION: Repetition of images, panel shapes, page layouts, colors, and other visual features in a comic help to create continuity within a text. *Braiding* refers to the repetition of highly significant visual features across an entire comic.

RELEVANT SCHOLARSHIP: Postema 69–71

INTERPRETIVE PRACTICE: The theme of transformation is central to Yang's *American Born Chinese.* What images attach to this theme and are repeated across the comic?

Appendix 2: Writing about Comics: From Brainstorming to Composition

When writing about comics, beginning scholars can summarize the significance of the spread first and then discuss how the author creates meaning through the content of the panels and their relation to one another. Or they can write about the content of the panels and their relation to one another while simultaneously discussing the significance. Either way, brainstorming in advance is an important first step.

When writing about a comic panel, place the page in parentheses, add a period, and then place the panel number or numbers, as in: (66.1–3) or (67.1). Select a spread from the comic we are reading for this unit. Answer the following questions, paying attention to the word count minimums.

Look carefully at the panels, paying attention to layout, spacing, lines, color, shapes, and style. What are the features that seem to stand out in terms of these aspects of the segment you are reading? (200 words)

How do words and images coexist in the panels? Do the words back up the image or contradict it? (150 words)

What do you feel to be the overall significance of this spread in relation to the text as a whole? (250 words)

Works Cited

Abate, Michelle Ann, and Gwen Athene Tarbox, editors. *Graphic Novels for Children and Young Adults: A Collection of Critical Essays.* UP of Mississippi, 2017.

Anderson, Laurie Halse. *Speak.* Farrar, Straus and Giroux, 1999.

———. *Speak: The Graphic Novel.* Artwork by Emily Carroll, Farrar, Straus and Giroux, 2018.

Baetens, Jan. "From Black and White to Color and Back: What Does It Mean (Not) to Use Color?" *College Literature*, vol. 38, no. 3, Summer 2011, pp. 111–28.

Baetens, Jan, and Hugo Frey. *The Graphic Novel: An Introduction.* Cambridge UP, 2014.

Coats, Karen. "Young Adult Literature: Growing Up, in Theory." *Handbook of Research on Children's and Young Adult Literature*, edited by Shelby A. Wolf et al., Routledge, 2011, pp. 315–29.

Duncan, Randy, and Matthew J. Smith. *The Power of Comics: History, Form, and Culture.* Continuum, 2009.

Gardner, Jared. "Storylines." *Substance*, vol. 40, no. 1, 2011, pp. 53–69.

Griepp, Milton. "ICv2 Presents White Paper at New York Comic Con Event." *ICv2*, 8 Oct. 2015, icv2.com/articles/news/view/32738/icv2-presents-white-paper-new-york-comic-con-event.

Groensteen, Thierry. *Comics and Narration.* Translated by Ann Miller, UP of Mississippi, 2013.

Hatfield, Charles. *Alternative Comics: An Emerging Literature.* UP of Mississippi, 2005.

Karasik, Paul, and Mark Newgarden. *How to Read* Nancy*: The Elements of Comics in Three Easy Panels.* Fantagraphics Books, 2017.

Kashyap, Keshni, and Mari Araki. *Tina's Mouth: An Existential Comic Diary.* Houghton Mifflin Harcourt, 2012.

Lewis, John, and Andrew Aydin. *March: Book One.* Illustrated by Nate Powell, Top Shelf Productions, 2013.

McCloud, Scott. *Understanding Comics: The Invisible Art.* Morrow, 1994.

Nodelman, Perry. "Picture Book Guy Looks at Comics: Structural Differences in Two Kinds of Visual Narrative." *Children's Literature Association Quarterly*, vol. 37, no. 4, Winter 2012, pp. 436–44.

Postema, Barbara. *Narrative Structure in Comics: Making Sense of Fragments.* RIT Press, 2013.

Tamaki, Jillian. *SuperMutant Magic Academy.* Drawn and Quarterly, 2015.

"Why Comics Are Banned." *CBLDF*, cbldf.org/why-comics-are-banned.

Meghann Meeusen

Teaching Adolescent Film: A Cultural-Historical Activity-Theory Approach

Teaching YA literature necessarily involves consideration of many genres and medias, for in order for students to develop a rich understanding of adolescent texts, such study must address what Margaret Mackey calls the "exponential increase in the re-spinning of stories for young people" (496). Films adapted from YA novels offer particularly rich interrogation of such respinning, but teaching YA film often requires pedagogical approaches that take into account not only theoretical, cultural, and ideological underpinnings of such texts but also the rich and complex contextual webs in which they are embedded. This pedagogy challenge can be met by building from cultural-historical activity theory (CHAT) to help students conceptualize the contextual and material factors inherent to the production and reception of adolescent film adaptations. Furthermore, a CHAT approach to adolescent film pedagogy also encourages students to consider their own textual productions in a similar way, utilizing a meta-analysis of literate activity to think more critically about adolescent films and also about how to write about them in more proficient and purposeful ways.

For these reasons, a CHAT approach to literary analysis has widespread usefulness to the teaching of a variety of genres and media. However, CHAT is particularly applicable to teaching YA film for three reasons.

First, film pedagogy is often limited to a study of either plot and thematic elements or more technical elements; a CHAT approach merges these for a richer understanding of both, also integrating cultural and historical considerations that are sometimes overlooked. Second, CHAT applies even more specifically to adolescent adapted film because these texts stand at the center of a wide range of analytical contexts. CHAT allows for a merging of these elements as well, combining literary analysis techniques and theoretical frameworks with adaptation and film studies pedagogical approaches. Third, the crossover nature and complexity of competing contextual factors in YA film also makes it a strong pedagogical pairing with CHAT. Adolescent films are exceptionally liminal, not only speaking to liminal spaces between adulthood and childhood but also bridging other gaps. Such movies are often seemingly timeless while also culturally and historically bound, enjoyed by both teens and adults, simultaneously hated and beloved, and considered both popular and literary. While the same might be said for children's films or other texts, I believe YA film's position in this space of intersectionality makes it a great fit for a CHAT pedagogical approach.

YA films are "cultural products of their historical moments" (Cobb 23), simultaneously a "formal entity or product," "a process of creation," and "a process of reception" (Hutcheon 7–8). As a result, studying such works requires "full investigation of the economic, political, historical, cultural, cinematic, and artistic reasons for a text's adaptation" (Jeffers 123). CHAT creates this framework, examining what Anis S. Bawarshi and Mary Jo Reiff call the "dialectical relationships between genres, individuals, activities and contexts" in order to "more fully describe tensions within genres as individuals negotiate multiple competing goals" (102). Such multiple and various competing objectives are perhaps evident nowhere more fully than in YA film.

Furthermore, CHAT is useful not just to study texts but also to produce them more deftly. As David Russell describes, teachers can help students better grasp how to use the tools of writing to produce texts that meet certain objectives by asking them to develop a meta-awareness of their own writing practices as literate activity. This is a key tenet of CHAT: understanding the contextual factors of the situations in which textual productions are embedded can help individuals adapt to new writing situations in productive ways.

Thus my YA film pedagogy includes two key objectives: students explore contextual and material factors inherent to the production and reception of adolescent adapted film, and they also research and analyze how scholars, teachers, and other individuals talk, think, and write about films marketed to young adults. Moreover, these two elements intertwine, so that while students consider the social, cultural, and historical factors that affect the decisions that filmmakers make, they also apply this same principle to the study of various genres used to write about film. This leads them to develop a meta-awareness of their own writing and to produce more purposeful analytical work. As a result, students come to understand textual production—both their own writing and the films that they study—in remarkable ways.

To explain the potential of this approach, this essay uses a representative example—the 2012 film adaptation of Suzanne Collins's *The Hunger Games*—to explore how students might begin to think about the social, cultural, and historical factors that affect film production and reception. I begin by explaining how students might map the contextual factors of this film and go into several of these areas of inquiry more specifically in order to highlight what kinds of research students might conduct. I end by articulating some specific course objectives and related assessment opportunities that can support students in taking a meta-analytical approach to their own work, providing a template that can work in tandem with the kinds of class discussions of a film's cultural-historical web that I articulate with relation to *The Hunger Games.*

CHATing about *The Hunger Games*

When explaining CHAT to students, I often speak about a web of contextual factors. In fact, I frequently begin by writing a film's title on the board and deriving subtopics from it, asking students to identify social, cultural, and historical factors that affect production and reception. These, then, will be the topics we study in more depth, for while we might know only a little about each factor to start, research and close reading can enrich this understanding as students develop their critical thinking skills. Moreover, starting with a visual map or web showcases interactions of factors and helps facilitate a discussion of the materiality of film by highlighting that textual production is mediated through the use of particular tools, not in isolation but as part of a system influenced by countless diverse factors that are all "laminated"—imbricated, layered, fused, blended, and simultaneously at play in any activity (Prior et al.). This idea is useful in studying YA film because it provides an avenue to discuss materiality, activity, situation, genre, context, media, and ideological concerns as well as how these factors affect the ways we might understand, talk, and write about adapted texts.

When making a CHAT web for *The Hunger Games* film, for example, students often start by mentioning gender dynamics or other dystopia films they know, and these two ideas become nexuses on our map, each with more specific subtopics. When I ask students to broaden their thinking to any key elements of film (again placing a node on the map), students will add terms like *sound track*, *actors*, or *adaptive cuts or changes*, and sometimes this spawns even more subtopics, such as *romantic chemistry* or *Jennifer Lawrence*, in the case of the actors nexus. Or I ask students to narrow their ideas, and perhaps someone will bring up how difficult it is to portray violence against children on-screen, a news media discussion about race, or a negative review posted online. Each new element is added to the web, which grows more and more complex as the richness of context emerges.

Something I especially stress when building a web for this film with students is that we are not simply considering the story on the screen. By focusing on the film as a cultural artifact, we think about meaning but also materiality—how a film is made, what tools are used in production, what factors shape reception, and other situational factors of filmmaking and movie viewing as a historically and culturally bound activity. Identifying such factors can take practice, but by combing through a variety of elements to build a discussion of context, students develop a rich understanding of textual meaning as well as the culture within which a text is embedded.

Once we have a map in place, I ask students to delve into these various contextual elements, sometimes as a class, but more often individually or in groups. For example, I might start by modeling how one might dig into a line of inquiry by using film clips and quotes to share adult dystopian texts like George Orwell's *Nineteen Eighty-Four* or Aldous Huxley's *Brave New World*, canonical predecessors like Thomas More's *Utopia*, and even children's dystopia such as Lois Lowry's *The Giver*. I ask students to think about how *The Hunger Games*—a YA movie—approaches dystopia differently from adult, classic, or children's books, which begins a discussion of medium, genre, audience, and purpose. Why position teenage Katniss, for example, as motivated by an urge to protect her young sister rather than tending toward politics of rebellion like her friend Gale? What power does Katniss hold or lack as a teenager and a young woman, and how does this differ from the power held by Orwell's, Huxley's, or Lowry's protagonists?

I also model ways of researching particular lines of inquiry by introducing terminology or incorporating adolescent literature theory, and I find that Roberta Seelinger Trites's domination-repression model works especially well with *The Hunger Games.* Students debate what parts of the story fit Trites's model of "dynamic of (over)regulation → unacceptable rebellion → repression → acceptable rebellion → transcendence-within-accepted-limits" (38), asking whether Katniss's threat to kill herself and Peeta with the berries is her first act of acceptable rebellion and questioning if she ever reaches transcendence.

Once they are ready to branch out, students take on more responsibility for research and discussion of various nexuses on the map. For example, students might explore subtle aspects of the film to interrogate the terminology I introduce, questioning whether Jennifer Lawrence's movements and facial expressions in the film seem more a purposeful act of rebellion than the novel's description and whether the staging and music in her subsequent discussion with Haymitch allows the film to uniquely employ or challenge this domination-repression model.

Such questions of context and intertexutality allow students to delve into the story and also the nature of film, prompting additional focus on materiality. How, for example, might filmmakers who saw the success of *The Hunger Games* in 2012 have made similar choices in other dystopian film adaptations? Still, as students delve into research, they realize that even this question is too simple, for filmmaking takes time, and thus many subsequent films were already in production before *The Hunger Games*'s release. Do these films represent a trend not based on the film's success but other factors, and if so, what are these factors? Furthermore, what do we have to understand about adolescent publishing in order to investigate how this trend began? These are just a few of the questions students might ask, each opening a chance for research and discussion.

Reception is an equally important part of CHAT. In *The Hunger Games*, this includes considering visual representation of violence, especially as it relates to children and teens. Students can analyze scenes shot by shot to consider how the film relays the story's gravity while maintaining the PG-13 rating, since many teens cannot see an R-rated film in a theater without parental supervision. For example, during the cornucopia scene, camera angles show teens holding weapons and falling, but the speed of shots prevents significant focused attention, as when Cato strikes down a very young curly-haired boy. Viewers see Cato's face and arm movement, then a splatter of blood on another surface, but the position of the figures limits seeing the blade strike the boy. When slain bodies are shown later, this boy's body is crumpled and obscured. This analysis leads to a conversation about the nature of adolescent literature, especially when considering the controversial film adaptation of the Japanese novel *Battle Royale.* Remarkably similar in textual premise to *The Hunger Games*, drawing a connection to this earlier movie allows students to ask (and research) whether Japanese culture opens and perhaps also closes different filmic roads from those in American culture.

Perhaps the detail my students most enjoy researching when discussing *The Hunger Games* is Collins's screenwriting background. Getting her start writing for television series like *The Mystery Files of Shelby Woo*, *Generation O!*, and *Oswald*, Collins has unique insight into visual media. I ask students to seek examples of Collins's writing techniques that seem to reflect this, and they then explore how this writing approach translates to the actual film. Again, this inquiry requires research, not just into the text but also into television clips and screenplays, putting close comparative analysis in context. This is perhaps what I like most about a CHAT-based pedagogy: it highlights culture and situation in a way that also pairs with traditional literary approaches and close reading.

Another great example of close reading paired with material or technical factors is a consideration of point of view. While the *Hunger Games* novel is told in first person, highlighting some of Katniss's internal struggles and teen angst, the film inherently eliminates internal dialogue and thus significantly changes characterization. For example, when Rue is dying in the novel, Katniss expresses her difficulty in trying to be brave, noting, "Her hand reaches out and I clutch it like a lifeline. As if it's me who's dying instead of Rue" (233). Then, after decorating Rue's body with flowers, she directs her three-fingered salute toward Rue. Conversely, after Rue dies in the film and Katniss adorns her, Katniss directs a glare right into the camera, toward the film's audience, then angles her salute toward an arena camera, which viewers see projected on a screen in District 11. The next scene is a significant addition: unlike readers' limited first-person view of the arena, film viewers are privy to an eruption of violence led by a heavily African American crowd against the peacekeepers.

This scene opens discussion of perspective, but it also speaks to reception, especially concerning racist online response to the filmmakers' casting both Rue and Thresh with African American actors. As the *New Yorker* writer Anna Holmes summarizes, "In addition to offering object lessons in bad reading comprehension, Hunger Games Tweets—there are now more than two hundred up on the blog—illuminated long-standing racial biases and anxieties" surrounding casting. This situation, as well as news media response, provides an excellent opportunity for discussion of a cultural and historic context—not only in terms of what adaptation and visual media can do to illuminate specific elements of a text but also in terms of how social media outlets like Twitter have redefined textual reception. As part of this discussion, I also introduce students to S. R. Toliver's article "Alterity and Innocence: *The Hunger Games*, Rue, and Black Girl Adultification." Toliver explains how critical discourse analysis and systemic functional linguistics can help students "examine intertextual connections between the text and society, acknowledging the text's role in mirroring, constructing, constituting, reifying, and dismantling social identities," and she suggests that such analysis can help readers "move beyond levels of alterity that make reading about nuanced Black girlhood an unfamiliar space" (13). This critical reading, like all the factors I describe, adds to an increasingly complex web of inquiry, creating an in-depth way to research and discuss the film.

I use *The Hunger Games* as a representative example, but this approach works with a variety of YA film adaptations. For example, examining the film adaptations of Stephenie Meyer's Twilight series could include a study of vampire fiction, both historic and contemporary, as well as Meyer's religious background or the ways E. L. James began writing *Fifty Shades of Grey* as Twilight fan fiction. Students can research critical conceptions related to gender and power, doing close readings to think about how a visual medium changes problematic depictions, then compare this to the graphic novel adaptation to consider how medium affects message. Twilight also opens a unique discussion of music, and students can explicate both the score and marketing of sound track collections of "related" tracks.

The contextual production and reception factors are endless here, as they would be for a study of a classic film like *The Outsiders*, the John Green films *Paper Towns* and *The Fault in Our Stars*, or even the zombie romance *Warm Bodies*. In each of these cases, CHAT can form a base for students to study the film as both a literary and cultural artifact, pursuing countless lines of inquiry to understand both the text and the context within which the text is embedded.

Analyzing Productions and Producing Analysis

While I utilize CHAT to provide students the opportunity for a multifaceted analysis of texts, composition instructors more often use CHAT to help students analyze context in order to produce texts. Angela Rounsaville and her coauthors suggest this approach enables students to transfer classroom learning into new situations outside of the classroom, because the "ability to seek and reflect on connections between contexts, to abstract from skills and knowledge, to know what prior resources to draw on and what new resources to seek, and to be rhetorically astute and agile are all hallmark strategies that effective writers bring with them to any new writing context" (98).

Based on this principle, I ask students to apply the same methods we utilize to research and discuss movies to the writing they do for my class. First, I establish our twofold objective: analyzing and researching the factors that affect the production of movies for teens and researching how scholars, teachers, and other invested individuals write or communicate their ideas about YA film. Moreover, I also require documentation of both kinds of research: an in-depth reporting of what they have learned about a film's production or reception and a similarly detailed report about the kind of writing they produce to share their analysis.

I implement this approach via a three-part individual project in which students study a YA film of their choosing alongside our study of *The Hunger Games* (which we view together in class). First, I use a familiar genre as a "starter"—their CHAT appetizer. Most students have read a movie review, and I ask them to bring two to three examples to class. We then map all the qualities they notice about this kind of writing, digging into how and why reviews are produced, who writes them, how credibility is established, where they are posted or published, and other material factors. Then students write a review, evaluating an adolescent film of their choosing. Evaluation is a skill I want students to be able to transfer to new situations, but students also practice writing about their writing, submitting a "rationale" describing how their review reflects our CHAT-based discussion of reviews as a literate activity. This document acts as more than a reflection, for students must present an argument for why their textual production—the review—fits within the activity system in which reviews are embedded.

Next, students continue to research their chosen film's context (studying elements like those we work on collectively for *The Hunger Games*), and we hold a classroom symposium, wherein each student shares what he or she discovered in a short conference presentation. Again, we map the activity system in which conference papers are embedded, discussing the purpose and audience of an academic conference and what factors presenters must consider, including audience engagement, how panels are chosen or led, how to present one's self professionally, and so forth. This acts as another CHAT study, unpacking the context of this forum for sharing research, and they again produce a rationale describing how the decisions they make in preparation for the event match our discussions of the situation.

These two assignments build to a final project, wherein I give students the freedom to submit a multimodal or creative project, selecting any genre or medium that critics, writers, teachers, filmmakers, scholars, or others create. This time, they conduct a CHAT analysis of the activity system independently, and they create the artifact with another rationale to explain how their production choices match their literate activity research. Some students produce a film pitch, researching how writers sell a movie to producers. Others create a blog, expanding on their evaluative skills by reviewing a set of related films. Some prefer an academic route, studying academic writing and composing a journal article. Still others produce a film, write a screenplay, or create a fan video that comments on a film they enjoy. Whatever students choose, the objectives are the same: learn more about an adolescent film and share what they have learned in a purposeful way by studying the contextual factors of the method they will use to share their ideas.

CHAT sets up this pedagogical approach, wherein students learn to be more purposeful creators of texts while they also think about adolescent movies in new ways. By considering YA film adaptations as literary and cultural artifacts entrenched in a web of contextual factors, CHAT illuminates the remarkable complexity of textual production and reception. As a result, students not only come to learn to delve into adolescent literary respinnings but also find meaning in complexity—a notion that lies at the heart of my pedagogical objectives.

Works Cited

Bawarshi, Anis S., and Mary Jo Reiff. *Genre: An Introduction to History, Theory, Research, and Pedagogy*. Parlor Press / WAC Clearinghouse, 2010.

Cobb, Shelley. "Canons, Critical Approaches, and Contexts." *Teaching Adaptations*, edited by Deborah Cartmell and Imelda Whelehan, Palgrave Macmillan, 2014, pp. 11–25.

Collins, Suzanne. *The Hunger Games*. Scholastic, 2008.

Holmes, Anna. "White until Proven Black: Imagining Race in *Hunger Games*." *The New Yorker*, 30 Mar. 2012, www.newyorker.com/books/page-turner/white-until-proven-black-imagining-race-in-hunger-games.

Hutcheon, Linda. *A Theory of Adaptation*. Routledge, 2006.

Jeffers, Jennifer M. "Life without a Primary Text: The Hydra in Adaptation Studies." *The Pedagogy of Adaptation*, edited by Dennis R. Cutchins et al., Scarecrow Press, 2010, pp. 123–38.

Mackey, Margaret. "Spinning Off: Toys, Television, Tie-Ins, and Technology." *Handbook of Research on Children's and Young Adult Literature*, edited by Shelby Wolf et al., Routledge, 2011, pp. 495–506.

Prior, Paul, et al. "Re-situating and Re-mediating the Canons: A Cultural-Historical Remapping of Rhetorical Activity, a Collaborative Webtext." *Kairos*, vol. 11, no. 3, 2007, kairos.technorhetoric.net/11.3/topoi/prior-et-al/index.html.

Rounsaville, Angela, et al. "From Incomes to Outcomes: FYW Students' Prior Genre Knowledge, Meta-Cognition, and the Question of Transfer." *WPA*, vol. 32, no. 1, Fall-Winter 2008, pp. 97–112.

Russell, David R. "Rethinking Genre in School and Society: An Activity Theory Analysis." *Written Communication*, vol. 14, no. 4, Oct. 1997, pp. 504–54.

Toliver, S. R. "Alterity and Innocence: *The Hunger Games*, Rue, and Black Girl Adultification." *Journal of Children's Literature*, vol. 44, no. 2, Fall 2018, pp. 4–15.

Trites, Roberta Seelinger. *Disturbing the Universe: Power and Repression in Adolescent Literature*. U of Iowa P, 2000.

Part III

Assignments

Melissa Sara Smith

Theorized Storytelling: A Tool for Practicing Reader-Response Criticism

College students love to tell stories. In almost any classroom on any college campus, students will raise their hand to tell a personal anecdote during class discussion or will write about their own experiences as part of a written assignment. It seems that this is particularly true in YA literature courses for two reasons: literature courses tend to be smaller than large lecture-hall classes, allowing students the time and space to share their stories, and the very nature of studying narratives about adolescence encourages students to talk about their own teen experiences in relation to the novels we are reading.[1] While these stories might initially seem like a distraction from class, I have found that the key to making this storytelling productive is to make sure these stories are contextualized and analyzed in such a way that they build upon the texts and theories being studied.

Theorized Storytelling

I encourage my students to practice what I call *theorized storytelling.*[2] Theorized storytelling is a tool to implement reader-response criticism in the classroom, and it is a strategy that asks the reader to examine the narration of their personal stories and see themselves as characters within a narrative. Theorized storytelling utilizes two tactics:

Readers as narrators. Students tell stories that connect to the literature they are reading, but in doing so they are tasked with questioning their own narrative choices and reliability. This narrative criticism of their own storytelling (and the stories of their peers) will encourage them to think more critically about the authors and narrators of the texts they are reading.

Readers as characters. Students question and engage with characters as peers and equals, investigating their own motivations for actions and beliefs as well as those of the characters.

Rather than merely having students respond to texts with their subjective reactions and opinions (which is often how reader-response pedagogy is enacted in the classroom), theorized storytelling takes this process one step further by asking students to then think critically about their own narratives in relation to the texts being read and studied. Asking students whether they like or can relate to a text can create an imbalance wherein the reader is privileged within the reader-text transaction. On the other hand, asking students to tell their own stories challenges this imbalance and brings the focus of a literature class back to literary analysis.

Louise M. Rosenblatt's approach to reading as a *transaction* between reader and text establishes a framework for the way individuals, in this case students, construct meaning and interpretation when they read. She argues that "the literary work exists in the live circuit set up between reader and text: the reader infuses intellectual and emotional meanings into the pattern of verbal symbols, and those symbols channel his thoughts and feelings" (*Literature* 24).[3] This is an important pedagogical approach for literature classrooms of all types. For instance, Nicholas J. Karolides argues that only Rosenblatt's transactional reader-response theory allows for the balanced interaction between author, reader, and text; and Geoff Bull posits storytelling as a method to increase critical thinking and analysis. When professors utilize this approach in the classroom, they encourage students to use their own experiences as a way of filling in the gaps and connecting to the readings. Unfortunately, however, many educators interpret Rosenblatt's ideas for reading as mere personal response, or they use this strategy solely to foster engagement and enthusiasm for the literature being assigned. While I don't disagree with this approach as a potential starting place, I do think that there exists a gap between student engagement and literary analysis. Student engagement is grounded in subjective enjoyment of texts, while literary analysis investigates the construction and meaning of a text within historical and social contexts. Encouraging students to theorize their lived experiences actually bridges the gap between student subjectivity and literary analysis.

Readers as Narrators

In my experience, theorized storytelling often happens organically in class discussion. For instance, students in many of my classes have used their experiences from high school to better understand Jerry Spinelli's *Stargirl*, a coming-of-age novel narrated by an adult, Leo, looking back at his high school relationship with a newcomer, Stargirl. A great deal of our class conversation revolves around ideas of conformity, since Stargirl is ignored and bullied (but eventually welcomed) because of her idiosyncrasies. Many of my students connect their own lives to the novel. For instance, I had two students in a recent course who responded to this book by explaining that there were two distinctive cliques in their high school.[4] They claimed that there were no similarities between the two groups, but I encouraged the rest of the class to compare their claims to Leo's assertion that his high school "was not exactly a hotbed of nonconformity. There were individual variants here and there, of course, but within pretty narrow limits we all wore the same clothes, talked the same way, ate the same food, listened to the same music" (10). Rather than moving past their story quickly and returning to the lesson I had planned for the day, I asked the class to theorize the story they had just told. In this scene in the novel, Leo is commenting on his high school's social cliques from an adult perspective, demonstrating the way time can change the way a person views his or her environment. I asked these two students to think about how much time had passed since they were in high school. Were they remembering their environment accurately? Or would greater distance from their high school experiences lead them to conclude, like Leo, that there weren't as many differences between these two groups as they thought? More important, hearing these two classmates tell this story helped the rest of the class to consider how Leo's role as an adult narrator (rather than a teen narrator) changed the construction of Spinelli's text. In this instance, the entire class began to see the two classmates as authors and narrators of their own story, and this helped the students to think critically about the author and narrator of the book we were reading.

Similarly, another student in the same course asserted that everyone in her high school got along; she claimed there were no outcasts like Stargirl. Without prompting, her classmates immediately questioned whether this was actually true or whether she was simply unable to recognize those students who felt like outsiders. Both were viable options, and this student later conceded that her experiences were subjective. In both of these examples, students told their stories first as a way to relate to the text, but they later became a way to analyze the text. These discussions helped students investigate the role of Leo as narrator and Stargirl as outsider, and the act of storytelling helped the class think critically about the social dynamics found within the novel.

Readers as Characters

Personal response to a character's personality or actions can be an excellent starting point for conversation, but it often leads to students limiting their understanding to whether they do or do not like something. Traditionally, reader-response theory has asked students to respond to the text, but what actually occurs is that students take a text and interject it into their own lives. For instance, when my students read J. D. Salinger's *The Catcher in the Rye*, I find they are often trapped by their dislike of Holden. It doesn't matter why they dislike him or why Salinger may have created a dislikable character. For many students, characters are story elements to be liked or disliked, and students remain in a subject position to discuss how a text or a character does or does not relate to their own experience.

Character motivations and complexities are, for me, some of the more interesting aspects of a novel, so asking students to see themselves as characters in their own stories helps them to unpack this dichotomy. They know that they themselves have complicated motivations, so once they start talking about their complicated motivations or backstories, they are able to see them in the novel. To help students make this connection and to implement the practice of theorized storytelling, I recently changed my approach to *The Catcher in the Rye*, offering this prompt instead: "Think about the way you might fit into Holden's world. What would he think of YOU? Would he call you a phony? Could he relate to your life (family, education, hobbies, etc.)? What would he think about the world we live in today?" Students are eager to respond to this question, and while it may seem student-centered, it actually prompts students to think more critically about Holden as a character and as a reflection of Salinger's world, because it asks them to consider themselves as a character as well. For instance, one student responded to this prompt by arguing that he and Holden would get along because they would both hate the popularity of reality television. The student started by talking about his own experiences and dislikes (his story), but the prompt forced him to think about Holden's decisions as well. Moreover, this student was able to think about Holden's dislike of Hollywood "phonies" within the historical context of the novel by comparing it to contemporary culture. His answer evolved from personal story to textual analysis, and this happened only once he saw himself as a character in Salinger's fictional world. Students know that real people have complex emotions and reasonings, so theorizing themselves as characters helps them to then theorize the characters of the texts being studied.

Rosenblatt argues that literature should do more than simply help us understand our own lives and stories. She writes that "[w]hen concern with the human elements in literature has become confused with the purely practical approach to those elements in life itself, distortion and critical confusion have followed" (*Literature* 29). Literature is not merely a resource for better understanding the world around us. The examples I have given here demonstrate how theorized storytelling can actually invert this relation, thus becoming a tool for fostering a transaction where both reader and text contribute to meaning making. Students may read stories to help them understand the world around them, but they also tell stories to help them understand the complexities of textual production and meaning.

Personally, I encourage the practice of theorized storytelling most often in my YA literature courses because the concept of adolescence serves as an entry point into literary discussion. For most of my students, adolescence is something they are, or have just recently been, experiencing.[5] Typically, about half the students in my YA literature courses identify as adolescents, and for this reason, reading texts concerned with the anxieties surrounding this stage of life (emerging sexuality, independence, etc.) gives many students a "way in" to the texts. Students may feel a connection with these characters that they don't have with traditional adult protagonists—characters with spouses, children, full-time jobs, or aging parents. I would argue, then, that YA novels also have a place in non-YA literature courses, as they can serve as starting points for literary analysis. I have taught both of these texts, *Stargirl* and *The Catcher in the Rye*, in a variety of literature courses, not just YA ones. Students reading texts by John Green or Suzanne Collins may be more inclined to share their own stories than students studying traditional literature because they feel like they have something in common with the text. While I do not believe that students have to be able to identify with a character in order to critically engage with a text (and, in fact, sometimes such a connection can hinder analysis), these connections are incredibly useful as a starting point for literary analysis. However, this pedagogy, though particularly applicable to YA literature, can work with adult texts as well. Students can and will tell their own stories whether they are studying Harry Potter or *Hamlet*.

Rosenblatt, and those scholars like Karolides and Bull who build upon her ideas, sees reader response as more than just a way for students to use texts to better understand their lives; it does the opposite as well. As Jane Gallop claims, "Anecdotal theory, it turns out, is not a one-way street from story to theory, but a busy two-way traffic" (20). Student storytelling can do much more than engage reluctant readers or help encourage students' interest in literature; the practice discussed here posits storytelling as a way for students to use the world they live in to better understand the texts they read. By theorizing their own stories, students can shift their focus to the text and become better scholars of the literature they are reading. In this way, they become more critical readers of the literature, their own stories, and the world they live in.

Notes

1. I use the terms *adolescent* and *adolescence* to refer to the social and biological stage of life, while *young adult* refers to the genre of literature.

2. I first employed this phrase in my dissertation, "The Anxiety of Time in Young Adult Literature: Writing the Adolescent Body." Meem and her coauthors use the phrase in a similar manner in *Finding Out: An Introduction to LGBTQ Studies*.

3. See *Literature as Exploration* and *The Reader, the Text, the Poem: The Transactional Theory of the Literary Work* for a thorough exploration of her ideas.

4. These two students attended the same high school before coming to college as best friends and roommates. Though I am certain their individual experiences were quite different, they presented a united front when telling this story, even finishing each other's sentences as they told it.

5. Of course, not all students identify as an adolescent, but even those who don't because of age or life experiences are able to talk about this stage of life in some way. The physical and emotional maturation process that takes place between childhood and adulthood seems to be, at least anecdotally, universal.

Works Cited

Bull, Geoff. "Children's Literature: Using Text to Construct Reality." *Australian Journal of Language and Literacy*, vol. 18, no. 4, Nov. 1995, pp. 259–69.

Gallop, Jane. *Anecdotal Theory*. Duke UP, 2002.

Karolides, Nicholas J. *Reader Response in Secondary and College Classrooms*. 2nd ed., Lawrence Erlbaum, 2000.

Meem, Deborah T., et al. *Finding Out: An Introduction to LGBTQ Studies*. Sage, 2010.

Rosenblatt, Louise M. *Literature as Exploration*. 1938. Modern Language Association of America, 1995.

———. *The Reader, the Text, the Poem: The Transactional Theory of the Literary Work*. Southern Illinois UP, 1978.

Salinger, J. D. *The Catcher in the Rye*. 1951. Bantam Books, 1967.

Smith, Melissa Sara. "The Anxiety of Time in Young Adult Literature: Writing the Adolescent Body." Illinois State U, 2010. PhD dissertation.

Spinelli, Jerry. *Stargirl*. Scholastic, 2000.

Roxanne Harde

Team-Based Learning and Young Adult Literature

This essay discusses the effectiveness of team-based learning (TBL) in enabling students to better understand and analyze the contents, contexts, and forms of YA literature. In the 1990s Larry Michaelsen developed TBL for use in business and professional programs. Because of TBL's overwhelming effectiveness in enabling students to learn deeply and apply their learning quickly, instructors in the pure and applied sciences, including entire medical faculties, quickly adopted this set of learning strategies. The cornerstones of TBL—heterogeneous permanent learning teams and frequent teamwork, regular readiness assessment tests with prompt feedback, and applications of theory through appropriate exercises and assignments—have proved just as effective in the social sciences and humanities classrooms.

A decade ago, I chose TBL as the pedagogical tool kit best suited for teaching literary theory and subsequently used it with great success in courses on feminist theory and women's writing, ecofeminist theory and women's nature writing, and Indigenous women's writing. I should note that for a small (1,200 students), rural liberal arts undergraduate faculty, the students I teach are quite diverse: the University of Alberta, Augustana, has a small majority of female to male students, a solid minority of both international (twelve percent) and Indigenous (ten percent) students, and a thriving LGBTQ community. With TBL, my students' learning outcomes were stellar; their ability to understand and apply theory in textual analysis went far beyond my high expectations. I then incorporated TBL into my freshman English survey and my children's and YA literature survey, courses I had taught several times previously. My studies of learning outcomes in three of these courses are cited below, and they uniformly demonstrate the benefits of TBL: deeper learning, increased confidence and accountability, higher grades (in that the range of grades stays the same but they increase across the board), better attendance, and demonstrable preparation for every class.

Because a large portion of the final grade depends on students' commitment to working with their teams, my students are uniformly willing to engage fully with their teammates in all aspects of teamwork. TBL's effectiveness can best be explained in the terms of Lev Vygotsky's work on the zone of proximal development: peers more successfully scaffold one another into deeper learning because language mediates thought in a dynamic and interactive way and social interaction is essential for learning and development. If knowledge acquisition occurs best in relation, when a subject (text, theory, concept) requires concentrated efforts to clarify, analyze, and evaluate, then that subject can best be learned in collaboration. TBL insists that all voices are heard, and as each member of a team makes individual contributions to a collective effort, the dialogic aspect of peer learning becomes essential for both mastery of a subject and richer intellectual development. Or, as one student noted, "understanding these concepts on my own . . . would not have become a part of the way I understand literature (and life) without the discussions with my team." While this comment makes clear that TBL facilitates learning content, it also offers insight into why TBL works in facilitating the teaching of YA fiction, particularly those texts that are emotionally and ideologically challenging: as they engage in daily discussions and frequent team assignments, students come to rely upon and trust their teammates. They first acquire a heightened level of comfort and then increased confidence; their voices are heard and their opinions matter. More important, their questions and concerns often inspire the whole team to work through difficult subject matter in a collaborative and supportive manner.

I include at least one YA text in all my first-year and most of my senior courses, not just the children's and YA literature survey, and I am currently building a thematic first-year seminar on the body and embodiment and the ways two YA novels (Louise O'Neill's *Only Ever Yours* and John Green's *The Fault in Our Stars*) encourage readers to explore their understanding of subjectivity and the body. YA literature, though "easier" to read, often presents my students with an array of challenges; students face emotional and intellectual struggles when analyzing narratives that make them confront issues of sexuality, racial and other biases, or cultural misunderstandings and misconceptions. When required to detail how form and content enhance each other, such as in poems or comics and graphic novels, they find it difficult to navigate among the literary and thematic aspects of the texts. As a cornerstone of TBL, their learning teams support their explorations of YA literature and enable, indeed challenge, them to make deeper analyses of and wider connections among the works they study in my classrooms and the "texts" of their lives. I turn now to a few examples of TBL's effectiveness in facilitating meaningful discussions of YA texts.

Most of my TBL classes begin with a readiness assessment test (RAT), taken individually. Students are given the topic of the RAT in the previous class and are expected to have read the assigned text closely before coming to class. The RATs focus on a particular passage, chapter, or poem, and students have to address specific features of the reading, such as theme, form, figurative language, character, or scene. Questions on the RATs will direct them to, for example, closely read the inclusion of baby girls in Richard Van Camp's *Path of the Warrior*, form an argument about Laurie Halse Anderson's thematic use of trees in *Speak*, or discuss how poetic form helps uncover the meaning in the paired poems in Lesléa Newman's *October Mourning*. They complete the test individually, then again with their team (as I move among the conversations), and then offer their team's answers in a whole-class discussion, during which I offer short lectures to help address lingering questions or offer additional information to enrich the discussion and their readings. By the time the session ends, students have solid understandings of the material and topic, theme, or theory covered and can incorporate this knowledge into wider contexts.

In the case of a book like *October Mourning*, Newman's poem cycle about the murder of Matthew Shepard, students face real difficulties in analyzing and discussing the poems. Whether part of or outside the LGBTQ community, they must face prejudices and hatred, their own or that of others. Their emotional responses to the book can be overwhelming; one student asked her team, "[W]ill I ever be able to read these poems and not cry?" In addition, students often feel inadequate to the challenge of reading poetry, which is where I use TBL to give them an opening into the text. Knowing that they must unpack three of the poems through considerations of how poetic form enables or enhances the poems' meaning, students sketch their thoughts individually and then delve more deeply with their teams. Newman's paired villanelles—one about antigay protesters outside the trial; the other about the Angel Action activists who blocked them—meant more as students contextualized the form and the ways in which it allowed the first to express hatred, anger, and fear, while the other works with the dignity and grace of Dylan Thomas's canonical villanelle "Do Not Go Gentle into That Good Night." Aside from the comfort and confidence given to these students by their teams, the freedom to concentrate first on poetic forms allowed them to move more gradually into the details of Newman's language and the incident that inspired these poems. Their resulting readings were sophisticated and nuanced, but their growing ability as literary and cultural critics also enabled them to stand back from the text and criticize Newman's appropriation of other cultures' spiritual practices: as one team noted, "it's one thing to model poems after William Carlos Williams but quite another to pull apart a Navajo poem and insert lines from the colonizer's sacred texts in its middle." The students could scaffold each other past their myriad difficulties into analyses that considered the entire poem cycle even as they were performing close readings of select poems.

Anderson's *Speak* poses similar challenges to students as they grapple with issues of sexual violence and consent, belonging and identity, and constructions of masculinity and femininity. They often feel overwhelmed by this novel, and I am aware that given current statistics (and there is no reason to believe my campus is an outlier), about one-quarter of the members of every class has been or will be sexually assaulted by the time they graduate. Again, in the security of their teams, students work with and around the acquaintance rape that is central to the plot and find ways to engage deeply with the thematic aspects of the novel: Melinda's art class and her tree project alongside the plethora of other trees in the book; Anderson's humor alongside the grimmer realities of high school; Melinda's self-harming behaviors alongside her strength and will to survive. Teamwork on the RATs and in directed discussions regularly enables students to develop research questions and answers that become the foundations of strong term papers. They have seemed especially eager to help one another on these essays through stages of peer review, and private conversations have helped me to understand that working together on *Speak* allows them to come to terms as individuals with their knowledge or experiences of sexual violence. I am convinced of the necessity of the team in enabling them to rise to the challenges of this text.

YA literature by and about Indigenous peoples presents its own set of challenges. *The Grass Dancer*, by Susan Power (Sioux), features the intertwined stories of several young adults on a Sioux reservation. As it demonstrates how these young people are the products of Native and colonial histories, it offers extremely difficult scenes, including one in which a female protagonist uses her grandmother's dark magic to seduce six of her high school classmates. Given the full context, this scene should not be considered rape. Rather students must trace the workings of magic, sexual and otherwise, through the novel. Discussions of this scene and others in the text tend to be polarized and raucous, in part because even with my campus's proximity to four First Nations, and even with our large number of Indigenous students, most students have had little exposure to these cultures, their worldviews, and their spiritual practices. I watch teams move from consensus that Charlene Thunder is "just a slut" to consideration that "sexual magic might work to heal a person" to an acceptance that, once "ideas about promiscuity" are set aside, "Charlene's magic was the only way she could break free from a bad situation." Tellingly, as they come to accept that other cultures understand sexuality in different ways, students working on this novel come to accept and learn from its ghosts even as they make efforts to fully understand the Sioux cultural codes and customs at play.

If team learning consistently supports my students as they face challenging YA literature, then at times it also seems to force them into confronting their own assumptions and biases. Much depends on the composition of the team, and I find building the most heterogeneous teams possible to be one of the most stressful parts of using TBL. However, I've also found that once students commit to their teams, which happens surprisingly early on, they uniformly resist changes to team rosters. A recent experience teaching the Indigenous comic *The Path of the Warrior* (Van Camp is Dene and the illustrator Steven Keewatin Sanderson is Cree) led to some of the most contentious teamwork I've seen. The comic, about a young man breaking away from his gang on a reserve, begins with a child getting shot during a gang war, something that happens almost annually in our neighboring Cree Nations. I posed questions on the RATs that would help students to look past their assumptions as they traced the role of sport in the narrative, attended to both text and illustrations to determine the ages of the characters (and come to some distressing conclusions about the reserve system and teenage pregnancy), looked to the ways in which traditional practices can heal as the protagonist follows "the red road," and placed this story in the wider contexts of Canada's colonized First Nations. Where a student on his or her own might shy away from this text and retreat into the safety of the dominant discourse about why Indigenous peoples have these problems, these teams generally disallowed the "easy out." One team member insisted on deeper and more encompassing readings; someone invariably had taken other Indigenous studies courses; another called into question assumptions and judgments about single mothers. They ultimately scaffolded one another into reading the comic as a method of decolonization as they thought through the meanings of the red road it describes.

When I began using TBL, I wanted no more than that my students could apply literary theories and thereby enrich their understanding and appreciation of a given text. The nature of the permanent learning team, without fail, grounds and deepens their ability to navigate the challenges of YA literature. Regardless of the course, as one student noted, "YA books hit me where I live, but the teamwork helped me go where I needed to go."

Note

Student comments are used with permission and with University of Alberta Research Ethics Board approval.

Works Cited

Anderson, Laurie Halse. *Speak*. Farrar, Strauss and Giroux, 1999.

Harde, Roxanne. "Team-Based Learning in the Humanities Classroom: 'Women's Environmental Writing' as a Case Study." *The Canadian Journal for the Scholarship of Teaching and Learning*, vol. 6, no. 3, 2015, dx.doi.org/10.5206/cjsotl-rcacea.2015.3.11.

———. "'The Union of Theory and Practice': Using Team-Based Learning in the Feminist Literary Theory Classroom." *Feminist Teacher*, vol. 22, no. 1, 2011, pp. 60–75.

Harde, Roxanne, and Sandy Bugeja. "Team-Based Learning in the First-Year English Classroom." *Team-Based Learning in the Social Sciences and Humanities: Group Work That Works to Generate Critical Thinking Engagement*, edited by Michael Sweet and Larry K. Michaelsen, Stylus, 2012, pp. 143–58.

Michaelsen, Larry K., et al., editors. *Team-Based Learning: A Transformative Use of Small Groups in College Teaching*. Praeger, 2002.

Newman, Lesléa. *October Mourning: A Song for Matthew Shepard*. Candlewick Press, 2012.

Power, Susan. *The Grass Dancer*. Berkley Books, 1994.

Van Camp, Richard. *Path of the Warrior*. Illustrated by Steven Keewatin Sanderson, Healthy Aboriginal Network, 2009.

Vygotsky, Lev S. *Mind in Society: The Development of the Higher Psychological Processes*. Edited by Michael Cole et al., Harvard UP, 1978.

Camille Buffington, Beverly Lyon Clark, and Eric Esten

On Curating Online Anthologies: Not the Traditional Term Paper

"Cool," "inventive," "current," "a fun twist to a lit review"—these were some student responses to the term project in an upper-level undergraduate class on YA literature.[1] Since students were already doing close readings of texts during the semester, Beverly Lyon Clark, the instructor, had decided against the traditional term paper. Instead of zeroing in on theses, students created anthologies: they aimed for variety while also making informed choices of the best, most provocative, or most characteristic pieces responding to or contextualizing a work of YA literature. And unlike anthology assignments that Bev had tried in the past, these projects appeared online.

Perhaps most obviously, curating an online anthology prepares undergraduates for future work in researching and presenting digital projects. "To curate," as Anne Burdick and others note, "is to filter, organize, craft, and, ultimately, care for a story composed out of the infinite array of potential tales, relics, and voices" (34). Such curating—in our case, gathering sources that respond or correspond to a YA novel—is becoming increasingly important in this time of information overload.

More generally, working on such a project can broaden students' repertoires of analytical skills, as it fosters divergent thinking. Students accustomed to writing thesis-driven essays may find the kind of divergence that this project endorses challenging. While components of the project may make traditional convergent arguments, the various components are not collectively arguing a thesis, nor are they necessarily linked logically. Instead, digital media projects allow "refractory elements" that might be neglected or subordinated in a traditional term paper to "be given weight in their own right" (Hayles 4). Digital anthologies rely more on implication and juxtaposition (38–39), giving the reader more scope to make meaning. The result is what Eric Esten, a student in the class, calls "purposeful divergence."

The online anthology consists of an introduction, clusters of items with brief contextualizations, and a bibliography. These appear in *Google Blogger*, in a subsection called Pages, where students can arrange the pieces. The fifteen to twenty items that each student chooses are clustered in half a dozen or more categories, or sections, each of which gets a page. Categories might include a relevant type of literary criticism, such as posthumanism, or issues of censorship, for instance. Within the categories, the student incorporates source information for each item and a brief contextualization (50–200 words) that outlines the item's key features, justifies its inclusion, and evaluates it. The overall introduction page (1,000–2,000 words) addresses such matters as whether the book has crossover appeal, why it might be marketed differently in different countries, whether it does justice to its historical setting or to any trauma it may depict, and whether the located responses raise questions about the nature of YA literature.

The goal is to include a diverse range of material, such as fan fiction and other fan items, *Amazon* and *Goodreads* reviews, professional reviews, reviews of adaptations, book and movie trailers, international cover images and other illustrations, blog posts, author or other interviews, and scholarly criticism of the book and of relevant genres or themes (such as historical fiction or depictions of trauma). Two students addressing Libba Bray's *Beauty Queens*, for instance, included their interview with a beauty contestant; a student addressing Todd Strasser's *Give a Boy a Gun* contextualized its disparate covers in America and Germany, where Strasser is better known than in his native United States; one addressing the cult classic *Go Ask Alice*, by Beatrice Sparks, explored the curious relation between the book and *Go Ask Alice!* (goaskalice.columbia.edu), a health information Web site for adolescents. Students are also encouraged to address controversies, preferably including at least one item with which they disagree. A student focusing on Julie Anne Peters's *Luna* could examine how literary critics received the novel, the ways that members of the LGBT+ community reacted to Peters's depiction of a transgender woman, objections to the novel, and more general responses to transgender identity, such as a video interview with transgender children. In a project on Elizabeth Wein's *Code Name Verity*, another student, Carly Lewis, included a *New York Times* review, two historical accounts of women pilots in the 1940s, a scholarly consideration of the way that Wein portrays feminine intimacy, an interview with the author, and professional and fan-made trailers. In any case, the student should not attempt to approach the work with an active thesis in mind but rather should try to capture a plurality of opinions, thoughts, and feelings about the chosen text.

At the beginning of the semester students received instructions outlining each stage. They also received a sample student anthology on Markus Zusak's *The Book Thief* and Bev's partial sample on Louisa May Alcott's *Little Women* (see clarklittlewomen.blogspot.com) to refer to as they scavenged the Internet and the brick-and-mortar library, keeping in mind that each YA book would raise different issues and pose different difficulties. Their first task was to find a novel. If a student did not fancy any of the titles from a list Bev provided, he or she could petition for another one, giving a rationale for that book. After a couple of weeks for exploratory research, students reported back through an informal blog entry. Here and throughout the semester Bev provided instruction regarding how to research and evaluate online materials.

An expert in library and information services also visited the class to explain how to use *Google Blogger*. Among other things, he showed students how to set up restricted access to their blogs. Although some advocates of digital humanities encourage making students' projects public—to participate in the "real" world and to get "real" feedback[2]—we did not do so. Many of the items that students would want to include in their projects are protected by copyright, so they made their anthologies private, accessible only to the instructor and fellow classmates for teaching and feedback purposes. Fair use of materials under copyright allows "multiple copies for classroom use" in a nonprofit setting to be made by or for the teacher ("Subject," secs. 107, 110). Library of Congress guidelines that more specifically address Internet resources suggest that limiting access to student projects to a local area network is more consistent with fair use than public availability ("Copyright").[3] Restricted access means that students can incorporate articles, reviews, or fan art directly into their anthologies without having to rely on potentially faulty links. Having items incorporated directly into the blog also makes the reader's job easier: there is less chance that he or she will have to resort to a *Google* search or scroll through a long file to find what a student meant to include. So we consider it important to find a hosting service, such as *Google Blogger*, that allows for privacy settings to limit the audience to the professor and the students in the class.

We also sought a service that is free and makes the privacy settings free. *Google Blogger* was completely free and permitted students to post virtually any kind of item, from videos to Word files, while remaining simple to navigate. There were, however, a couple of problems, including difficulty in formatting entries and also heavy use of cookies, which tends to slow the processor. In addition, although it's easy to upload Word files, videos, and JPEGs and other images to *Blogger*, it's more complicated to upload pdfs (the easiest way is to upload to *Google Drive* and create a link). For these reasons, Camille Buffington, a student, researched alternative hosting services, specifically *Weebly*, *Omeka*, *Jimdo*, and *SimpleSite*. She found that, as a general rule, free Web sites must be open to the public and that each of the services comes with its own problems regarding privacy and additional costs for shared access. For these reasons, *Google Blogger* is our current choice for a hosting service.[4]

Midsemester, students e-mailed Bev an annotated bibliography of ten items they might use in their final projects, and they made a brief oral presentation explaining their progress. They could thus reflect on their research as a whole and gain feedback, including information other students had discovered.

Also midsemester, students created at least one page in their blogs, to make certain they knew how to use *Blogger* and to encourage them to put part of their research into some semblance of a finished form. Shortly afterward, they submitted an item from their anthology with its draft contextualization. Bev's feedback ensured that their contextualizations would be sufficiently analytical and thoughtful. For example, Margaret Frothingham's discussion of the American cover of Laurie Halse Anderson's *Wintergirls* began:

> Aesthetically, this cover is the best out of all four. The colors accent each other, and the title is well incorporated into the image so that it almost becomes a part of it. The girl's face is almost entirely obstructed by frost, reflecting how Lia is trapped by her illness. The designer calls to the viewer to crack the ice and free her just by simply opening the book.

A week before the final deadline, students undertook peer review of drafts of their introductions. In the future, students will hand in a table of contents as well. This is also when students tested one another's blogs to make sure the links and other technical aspects were working correctly. Afterward, they had the option to meet with Bev individually to voice any last concerns, and they made finishing touches on their projects.

Students found the project challenging in a number of ways. The most significant conceptual challenge was the focus on purposeful divergence. Unlike assignments to which they had become accustomed, this project required attending to too many perspectives to consolidate into one thesis. For most papers, students need to focus on a single point; the anthology project, however, leads to what Eric called a mosaic. A reader has to piece together a final impression, while a student compiler has to appreciate others' viewpoints—and thus more fully enrich his or her own. This process makes the project an exercise in creativity. In their explorations, students often find something they might otherwise never have imagined. Camille, for instance, couldn't find anything useful in the college's humanities databases (e.g., *JSTOR*) about beauty standards as she researched her anthology on Scott Westerfeld's *Uglies*. When she turned to alternative resources, however, she found an article in a medical journal about teenage plastic surgery, connecting the novel's conflict with real-world issues. Then in exploratory Web searching, she found two videos illustrating women's and men's intercultural standards of beauty over time.

Other aspects that students found challenging included time management for an unfamiliar assignment; creating a project that was visually pleasing, or at least not cluttered; being selective given the wealth of material available online; being concise in the contextualizations; and finding suitable angles to foreground as pages, since not all novels would have, say, a fandom. Because of the many challenges of the project, especially the conceptual one of aiming for divergence and thus stretching their research skills in ways that they hadn't before, Camille and Eric, along with other students, recommend even more early guidance during the semester, as well as more structure and more deadlines.

Yet students' overall responses have been quite positive. Carly Lewis felt that "the blog incorporated information in a very modern and relevant way." Evelyn Fisher reported that mentioning the anthology helped her to get a summer internship. Taylor Bardsley appreciated the opportunity to research multimedia sources and found the project "a very current lens through which to view Young Adult literature, much of which is discussed and shared online by young readers themselves." Indeed, a number of students have stressed that in fan fiction, customer reviews, and blogs, one can learn the responses of actual young adults. Thus, the project can be useful in gaining an understanding of the diverse ways in which young adults read YA literature—while also learning more about audience in general. Camille, a creative writing and psychology major who hopes to publish in one or both fields, found this aspect especially helpful. For Eric, an English major, the project raised theoretical questions about the literary authority held by scholars or other readers, including young readers, given the democratizing effect of the wealth of information accessible on the Internet.

Curating an online anthology is one of many ways of performing digital humanities; it enables students to develop not only online skills but also new skills in analysis. Some years ago, Bev asked students in a different course to create hard-copy anthologies, imitating published ones. Amassing and analyzing these collections of scholarly criticism did foster divergent thinking, but not to the extent that these digital projects have. Indeed, creating an online collection is especially valuable when working with YA literature, given the dearth of scholarly criticism for many works and the profusion of online responses and other materials, both textual and multimedia, which often provide glimpses of the responses of young adults themselves.

Notes

We are grateful for research funding for this project from a Clemence Faculty-Student Research award. We are also grateful for insights from the students who took Young Adult Literature in 2014 and 2015, especially Taylor Bardsley, Sarah Creese, Kaela Feit, Evelyn Fisher, Margaret Frothingham, Kelsey Goodwin, Kelly Jochems, Carly Lewis, Allie Lizotte, Olivia McGrath, Meghan Roberts, and Jenna Tramonti. Bev is likewise grateful to Kathleen Vogt for long ago planting the seed of the idea of an anthology project.

1. The students in the class have been primarily juniors and seniors and mostly English majors, although majors in nine other programs have also been represented. Some of the students are also working toward secondary education certification.

2. See, for example, McGrath. For discussion of the desirability of making students' projects public versus students' rights to privacy under the Family Educational Rights and Privacy Act, see Dougherty, pp. 115–24.

3. See the "Fair Use" subsection of "Copyright." Case law and copyright law are murky about what exactly constitutes fair use in a nonprofit educational set-

ting, especially for user-generated content created by students. The best general, unbiased guidelines we've located are in "Code."

4. Our second choice would have been *Weebly*, specifically *Weebly for Education* (education.weebly.com), which allows an educator to create a master Web site, under which each student can create his or her own site. The free service offers suitable privacy settings and relative ease in formatting posts and in uploading pdfs, Word documents, and JPEGs and other images (some videos, though, entail a fee). But it's not free for large classes or for projects with more than five pages, and it restricts copyrighted material.

Works Cited

Burdick, Anne, et al. *Digital Humanities.* MIT Press, 2012.

"Code of Best Practices in Fair Use for Media Literacy Education." *Center for Media and Social Impact*, cmsimpact.org/code/code-best-practices-fair-use-media-literacy-education.

"Copyright and Primary Sources." *Library of Congress*, www.loc.gov/teachers/usingprimarysources/copyright.html#fair.

Dougherty, Jack. "Public Writing and Student Privacy." *Web Writing: Why and How for Liberal Arts Teaching and Learning*, edited by Dougherty and Tennyson O'Donnell, U of Michigan P, 2015, pp. 115–24. *Web Writing*, epress.trincoll.edu/webwriting/chapter/dougherty-public.

Hayles, N. Katherine. *How We Think: Digital Media and Contemporary Technogenesis.* U of Chicago P, 2012.

McGrath, Jim. "Digital Public Humanities: Reflections on Teaching a Graduate-Level Course in Digital Humanities and Public History." *Jim McGrath, PhD*, 8 June 2016, jimmcgrath.us/teaching/digital-public-humanities-reflections-on-teaching-a-graduate-level-course. Accessed 3 Aug. 2016.

"Subject Matter and Scope of Copyright." *Copyright Law of the United States (Title 17)*, www.copyright.gov/title17/92chap1.html.

Virginia Zimmerman

The Young Adult Critical Edition Project

Some years ago, in a seminar for first-year students, I taught the Norton Critical Edition of Harriet Beecher Stowe's *Uncle Tom's Cabin*. As we discussed a scholarly article included in the edition, it became clear that a small group of students believed all the material in the book—the introduction, criticism, and so forth—had been written by Stowe. Dismayed, I determined to include in all my classes a guided exploration of assigned texts, aimed at teaching students how scholarly editions work and what they offer. This exploration prompts students to make better use of critical editions and to reflect on their own editorial processes. However, critical editions do not exist for the more contemporary texts I assign in Young Adult Fiction.[1] In fact, almost no scholarship has been produced on many of these recent publications. These limitations, along with the need to teach writing and information literacy, led me to design, as the final assignment for Young Adult Fiction, the critical edition project (CEP).

The assignment requires each student to create a critical edition of a contemporary novel on the syllabus. Recent selections include Suzanne Collins's *The Hunger Games*, Neil Gaiman's *The Graveyard Book*, and Rebecca Stead's *When You Reach Me* (a sample table of contents for CEPs on each of these novels is included in the appendix). The CEP has five components: an introduction; a chronology of the author's life; excerpts from three scholarly pieces, with introductory paragraphs written by the student; excerpts from three supplementary items, such as interviews, other primary works, and so forth, also with introductory paragraphs; and thirty pages from the novel with footnotes. Each component requires a different type of textual analysis, research, and writing, and the completed project ensures a robust engagement with the primary text. In the sample CEP on *When You Reach Me*, for instance, the student investigates mother-daughter relationships in the genre of YA literature and advances an argument about the novel that goes into much more depth than is possible in a ninety-minute class discussion or a short essay.

Unlike a standard research paper, the CEP requires three different kinds of writing. The introduction is a traditional five- to seven-page literary analysis on a focused topic—a topic that is bolstered throughout the CEP. For instance, in the sample project on *The Hunger Games*, the student argues that Collins's dystopian Panem reflects many of the difficulties of coming of age, such as recognizing the limits of one's power. In the introduction, she supports her argument with close reading and evidence drawn from secondary sources, and she uses the other components of the CEP to set her analysis in a broader conversation about YA literature.

In the footnotes and the introductions to the scholarly and supplementary materials, students must extend their arguments into very concise forms of writing—paragraphs and even short sentences and phrases. The paragraphs introducing scholarly and supplementary material must both summarize the content of the included pieces and concisely explain how those pieces are germane to the CEP. The footnotes are usually informative, including definitions, connections to the author's life, and explanations of cultural or literary references. For example, the sample CEP on *The Graveyard Book* includes notes for *ifrit*, "a fire demon from Islamic mythology," and *sleer*, the "mysterious guardian of an ancient, presumably Celtic burial site and treasure, based partly on Kipling's cobra from 'The King's Ankus.'"[2] Both of these footnotes support the student's focus on globalization and identity.

With its varied elements, the CEP also promotes information literacy. Students research scholarly works, biography, and popular culture, each requiring different resources. Moreover, students must become adept at assessing information from the Internet. While some contemporary authors have already made their way into authoritative biographies, such as the *Dictionary of Literary Biography*, many have not. Students must therefore collect information for the chronology of the author's life from author and publisher Web sites, interviews, and articles in the popular media. In the sample CEP on *The Hunger Games*, the student assembled the chronology from Collins's and Scholastic's Web sites, an article from the Indiana University Web site, and text from the California Young Readers Medal Web site. Students must assess the reliability of each source and, wherever possible, verify information with multiple sources. They undertake this same process of evaluation and cross-checking with the supplementary materials they select and sometimes use the introductory paragraph to describe ways in which the information in the source may be problematic. The business of evaluating and effectively framing information garnered from the Internet has taken on special urgency and is a form of literacy beneficial well beyond the world of YA literature.

Even the traditional scholarly research required for the CEP comes with a special challenge: because so little has been published on these contemporary works, students must often select material that doesn't address their primary text at all and then do the work themselves of applying the scholars' arguments to their chosen novel. For instance, all the scholarly articles selected for the sample CEPs of *The Hunger Games* and *When You Reach Me* predate publication of the novels. As a result, the students could not rely on the scholars to apply their arguments to the primary texts; they had to do that work themselves. The author of the CEP on *The Graveyard Book* included two articles on the novel, but his third source is one that required him to make his own connection. After briefly describing the argument of "Myth and Nihilism in the Discourse of Globalization," the student writes, "This battle between the desire for myth and the realization of its illusory nature seems to be where Gaiman has placed himself. . . ." Students often enter more wholeheartedly and productively into a scholarly conversation when they engage with a piece that does not directly address the primary text in question. They must assume the authority to extend the argument beyond its bounds, thus advancing scholarly discourse as well as their critical thinking.

The CEP is not without challenges. First, with its five components, the project is quite time consuming. Since it comes at the end of the semester and the majority of students in Young Adult Fiction are nonmajors for whom this final project may not be a top priority, students often find the work overwhelming. This can result in cut corners and a less valuable experience. Assigning components throughout the semester would alleviate the end-of-semester burden, but earlier deadlines would discourage students from selecting the most contemporary texts assigned late in the course. Making the assignment a group project might be a more viable way to reduce the workload. However, I fear students would divide up the sections, and thus individuals would not experience the range of writing and information literacy components or the comprehensive nature of the whole project. Having discarded the solutions of staggering due dates and making the CEP a group project, I'm left with frequent reminders to get started in a timely fashion and morale-boosting speeches about how wonderful it is to work so intensely on a favorite book.

Another problem is environmental. As hard copy, the CEP is often more than one hundred pages, including printouts of the supplementary and scholarly materials. Multiplied by twenty-five students, this is an extraordinary amount of paper.[3] To alleviate the environmental impact, I once required students to create online CEPs, simple Web sites in WordPress, but the technological skills required were not central to the mission of the course and were frustrating for some students. I've settled on a compromise: I give students the option of creating a Web site, submitting a pdf electronically, or handing in a hard copy. They can work in the medium with which they are most adept, and though some still choose to print the CEP, the volume of paper is reduced. It's worth noting that students sometimes express a great sense of accomplishment when handing in a nearly book-length assignment, which might make the reams of paper worthwhile.

The CEP has proven to be a rigorous assignment that allows students to pursue topics of interest with a focus on a contemporary YA text. It requires short- and long-form writing, and it offers robust training in information literacy, including different types of research and the evaluation of sources. Students come away experts on their chosen texts but also informed participants in scholarly and popular discourse on YA literature. Because the final assignment comes after students fill out course evaluations, I have only anecdotal feedback; however, I will conclude with the words of the student who gave me permission to quote from his CEP on *The Graveyard Book*. Several years after completing the assignment, he wrote, "I really enjoyed working on that project and thought it was one of the more unique and productive experiences in my studies."

Notes

1. I teach Young Adult Fiction at Bucknell University, a medium-sized liberal arts institution with strong preprofessional programs in engineering, management, and education. Young Adult Fiction is an elective for English majors, an

elective in the general education curriculum, and a required class for students seeking certification to teach at the secondary level. It also fulfills a university-wide writing requirement. Students thus come to the class for a range of reasons and with a range of backgrounds. Some students are advanced English majors; for some, Young Adult Fiction will be their only college-level English course.

2. Thanks to Steven Belskie for permission to quote from his CEP.

3. At institutions that charge students for printing, this is also a financial burden.

Appendix

The Hunger Games

Introduction: Protagonist growth through dystopia
Chronology of author's life: Suzanne Collins

Scholarly Sources

Kennon, Patricia. "'Belonging' in Young Adult Dystopian Fiction: New Communities Created by Children." *Papers: Explorations into Children's Literature*, vol. 15, no. 2, Sept. 2005, pp. 40–49.

Sambell, Kay. "Presenting the Case for Social Change: The Creative Dilemma of Dystopian Writing for Children." *Utopian and Dystopian Writing for Children and Young Adults*, edited by Carrie Hintz and Elaine Ostry, Routledge, 2003, pp. 163–78.

Totaro, Rebecca C. N. "Suffering in Utopia: Testing the Limits in Young Adult Novels." *Utopian and Dystopian Writing for Children and Young Adults*, edited by Carrie Hintz and Elaine Ostry, Routledge, 2003, pp. 127–38.

Supplementary Sources

Collins, Suzanne. "A Conversation: Questions & Answers." *Scholastic*, www.scholastic.com/thehungergames/media/qanda.pdf.

King, Stephen. Review of *The Hunger Games* by Suzanne Collins. *Entertainment Weekly*, 8 Sept. 2008, ew.com/article/2008/09/08/hunger-games.

Miller, Laura. "Fresh Hell: What's behind the Boom in Dystopian Fiction for Young Readers?" *The New Yorker*, 7 June 2010, www.newyorker.com/magazine/2010/06/14/fresh-hell-laura-miller.

Annotated text (thirty pages): From chapters 3–4

The Graveyard Book

Introduction: Identity and globalization
Chronology of author's life: Neil Gaiman

Scholarly Sources

Camus, Cyril. "The 'Outsider': Neil Gaiman and the Old Testament." *Shofar: An Interdisciplinary Journal of Jewish Studies*, vol. 29, no. 2, Winter 2011, pp. 77–99.

Robertson, Christine. "'I Want to Be Like You': Riffs on Kipling in Neil Gaiman's *The Graveyard Book*." *Children's Literature Association Quarterly*, vol. 36, no. 2, Summer 2011, pp. 164–89.

Shershow, Scott Cutler. "Myth and Nihilism in the Discourse of Globalization." *CR: The New Centennial Review*, vol. 1, no. 1, Spring 2001, pp. 257–82.

Supplementary Sources

Edinger, Monica. "Raised by Ghosts." *The New York Times*, 13 Feb. 2009, www.nytimes.com/2009/02/15/books/review/Edinger-t.html.

Fleming, Mike, Jr. "Henry Selick to Direct Neil Gaiman's 'The Graveyard Book' in Disney Deal." *Deadline*, 27 Apr. 2012, deadline.com/2012/04/disney-scares-up-deal-for-neil-gaimans-the-graveyard-book-263157.

Gaiman, Neil. Interview by John Krewson. *AV Club*, 3 Feb. 1999, www.avclub.com/neil-gaiman-1798207974.

Annotated text (thirty pages): From chapters 7–8

When You Reach Me

Introduction: Gender and the mother-daughter relationship
Chronology of author's life: Rebecca Stead

Scholarly Sources

Bennett, Barbara. "Gender Understanding in Young Adult Literature: Reading Jill McCorkle's *Ferris Beach*." *North Carolina Literary Review*, no. 15, 2006, pp. 64–72.

Schneebaum, Katherine. "Finding a Happy Medium: The Design for Womanhood in *A Wrinkle In Time*." *The Lion and the Unicorn*, vol. 14, no. 2, Dec. 1990, pp. 30–36.

Seelinger Trites, Roberta. "Refuting Freud: Mother/Daughter Relationships." *Waking Sleeping Beauty: Feminist Voices in Children's Novels*, by Trites, U of Iowa P, 1997, pp. 100–21.

Supplementary Sources

Gootman, Elissa. "Pen Down, Brain Off." *The New York Times*, 5 Mar. 2010, www.nytimes.com/2010/03/07/nyregion/07routine.html.

"Rebecca Stead at Reading Matters 2011." *Vimeo*, uploaded by SLVictoria, 15 June 2011, vimeo.com/25167661.

Stead, Rebecca. "Don't Think. Write." *Children and Libraries*, vol. 8, no. 2, Summer-Fall 2010, pp. 6–8.

Annotated text (thirty pages): From pages 1–30

Works Cited

Collins, Suzanne. *The Hunger Games*. Scholastic, 2008.

Gaiman, Neil. *The Graveyard Book*. HarperCollins, 2008.

Stead, Rebecca. *When You Reach Me*. Wendy Lamb Books, 2009.

Jan C. Susina

Sound Tracks of Our Lives: Mix Tapes and Playlists in the Young Adult Literature Classroom

While many teenagers, as well as more than a few adults, might ironically summarize the three major preoccupations of adolescence as "sex, drugs, and rock 'n' roll," there is a bit of truth behind that broad generalization. I would like to focus on the third of those hot-button topics, since popular music has become the sound track for the lives of many American teens. Teens in the United States spend a significant amount of time listening to music. According to the Kaiser Family Foundation study *Generation M^2: Media in the Lives of 8- to 18-Year-Olds*, released in 2010, the typical American teenager spends, on average, seven hours and thirty-eight minutes using entertainment media per day. Factoring in multitasking, teens are actually consuming ten hours and forty-five minutes per day of entertainment (Rideout 2). Given this media activity occurs seven days a week, year-round, it also means adolescents spend more time listening to music and consuming other entertainment media than they spend attending high school and even than most teenagers spend sleeping. According to *Generation M^2*, listening to music is American teens' second most popular media activity. They spend, on average, two hours and nineteen minutes listening to music a day (28) compared with the twenty-five minutes a day they spend reading books (30). When it comes to multitasking, four percent of teens reported that they combine listening to music with another activity most of the time (29).

Music is an essential part of contemporary adolescent culture and ought to be included and examined in the YA literature classroom. Song lyrics are a form of poetry, and students bring a deep knowledge and appreciation of specific songs and bands that are personally meaningful to them. Unlike some texts that instructors assign students to discuss in class and analyze in writing assignments, popular music is a literary art form that many students are willing and eager to examine. While students in my university-level YA literature courses write dutifully and often perceptively on the novels, plays, and poetry assigned in the course, they write passionately and with great insight on the music they know and admire.

Few things evolve as quickly as young adult popular culture. While sex and drugs continue to hold great fascination for teens, instructors ought to consider the increasing number of categories of popular music beyond rock 'n' roll, including indie, country, rap, hip-hop, electronic, and jazz. Because of the influence of films such as *High School Musical* and *Pitch Perfect*, the success of *Hamilton*, and the many Disney films that have been adapted into musicals, Broadway show tunes are extremely popular. Given that musicals, like mix tapes, use a series of songs to construct a longer narrative and employ individual songs to provide insights into characters' emotions, musicals and movie sound tracks are a useful model for mix tapes. Robert Lopez and Jeff Marx's *Avenue Q* even features the song "Mix Tape," in which Princeton gives a mix tape to Kate, who sings that such a gift can mean the giver "[h]as a crush on you. . . ." Lin-Manuel Miranda's *Hamilton* was originally developed as a mix tape, which he subsequently expanded into his innovative Broadway musical.

In my college-level YA literature courses, I use the construction and analysis of mix tapes in conjunction with the reading of three popular adolescent novels: Stephen Chbosky's *The Perks of Being a Wallflower*, Rachel Cohn and David Levithan's *Nick and Norah's Infinite Playlist*, and Rainbow Rowell's *Fangirl*. The first two novels feature teens constructing a mix tape as a gift that reveals their personality and helps to establish friendships with other characters. The examples of mix tapes are "One Winter," the mix tape that Charlie creates for Patrick as a Christmas present in *The Perks of Being a Wallflower* (61–62), and the "(T)rainy/Dreamy" playlist of dreamy songs that feature the word *train* or *rain* that Norah works out in her head for Nick in *Nick and Norah's Infinite Playlist* (168). In *Fangirl*, Cath has created an "Emergency Kanye [West] Party" playlist (109) that she plays whenever she is stressed out, as when her creative writing professor accuses her fan fiction of being a form of plagiarism.

Like youth culture, technology quickly evolves, and most adolescents now produce playlists on and download playlists from MP3 devices such as smartphones and post playlists on such services as *Spotify* or Web sites as *YouTube*. The term *mix tape*, or *mixtape*, is still used when referring to compilations of songs, despite the different formats that are used to create them. Older practitioners of the form, such as Michele Catalano and Thurston Moore, lament the loss of "meticulously recording song after song off of albums and the radio in order to make a perfect musical love letter" (Catalano). I use the terms *mix tapes*, *mixes*, and *playlist* interchangeably, although Chbosky uses the term *mix tape*, Cohen and Levithan use *mixes* and *playlist*, and Rowell uses *playlist*.

A successful mix tape combines and reorders preexisting songs in original and innovative ways to create a new narrative. A well-designed mix tape allows the individual to craft a musical narrative that evokes a specific mood and feeling through the lyrics or music of songs. It becomes a site of memories and it is often intensely personal. The intended audience for a mix tape is usually specific, often just an audience of one, unlike a party mix, which is more public.

For the assignment in my YA literature course, students construct a personal mix tape in the manner of those featured in *The Perks of Being a Wallflower*, *Nick and Norah's Infinite Playlist*, and *Fangirl*. While these adolescent novels work well for this assignment, there are other adolescent novels that focus on the importance of music in the lives of teenagers and feature mix tapes, as well as those texts that are referred to by the critic Sophie Brookover and others as "new adult" novels (42), such as Nick Hornby's *High Fidelity* and Rob Sheffield's memoir *Love Is a Mix Tape: Life and Loss, One Song at Time*. Although most college students are familiar with the construction of mix tapes, I encourage them to visit Web sites and services—such as *Art of the Mix*, *8tracks*, and *Spotify*—where individuals post their mix tapes. Mix tapes are no longer the purview of teenagers and college students. In the summer of 2015 President Barack Obama posted his first "Summer Playlist" on *Spotify* (Schulman). These resources show students the immense range of possibilities for mix tapes, with categories as varied as romantic or breakup mixes to motivational or road trip mixes. I ask students to select a specific category and eight to twelve songs (citing the song titles and performers), construct the order of the playlist, provide a title for the compilation, and design the cover art. Students receive handouts of "The Art of the Mix: 15 Foolproof Rules for Creating the Perfect Mixtape" from the *GetFrank* Web site and Sheffield's "Top Ten Tape Tips," which discuss the aesthetic decisions to consider when creating a mix tape. "The Art of the Mix" suggests that creating a mix tape is more art than science. Song selection becomes the vocabulary for a good mix tape. Like effective writing, a good mix requires a rich and varied vocabulary to convey the mood and the message ("Art").

In addition to curating and designing the mix tape, students are also asked to then write an essay analyzing their mix and explaining how the selected songs and their placement work together to create a cohesive musical narrative. Since many students have already created mix tapes, they are encouraged to use or revise an existing mix tape and bring in information gleaned from Web research to reflect on and analyze their compilation.

This mix tape assignment allows the students to explore the role that music plays in the adolescent novels read in class and, by extension, allows them to reflect on the significance of music in their own lives. As Hornby writes in *High Fidelity*, "To me, making a tape is like writing a letter—there's a lot of erasing and rethinking and starting again" (88). Students are frequently surprised with the amount of time that goes into creating a mix tape, but they also report the mix tape is the most enjoyable assignment in the YA literature course. The mix tapes create passionate class discussion. The analysis of the mix tape encourages the students to consider their reasons for song selection and placement in the compilation. This creative assignment successfully combines reading, writing, and organization skills and encourages students to build from their own knowledge base.

Given the autobiographical and often self-revealing nature of a mix tape, I offer students the option to create a sound track for one of the novels read in the course rather than creating one based on personal experiences. Students have provided compilations that are insightful musical companions to J. D. Salinger's *The Catcher in the Rye*, S. E. Hinton's *The Outsiders*, and Ray Bradbury's *Fahrenheit 451*. Rowell, in an interview with *The Hub*, said of her writing process, "I build soundtracks for each book in my head, and I associate each scene with a specific song. The song gives me an emotional anchor for the scene" ("One Thing"). Rowell then posts the playlists for her novels and specific characters on *Spotify*.

The process of creating a mix tape and writing the accompanying essay encourages students to extend their analysis of adolescent novels to the larger world of adolescent culture and their own lives. The mix tapes have become a creative and analytical assignment that combines aspects of the personal essay with student knowledge and appreciation of music that I have found successful and that students find challenging but worthwhile.

Works Cited

"The Art of the Mix: 15 Foolproof Rules for Creating the Perfect Mixtape." *GetFrank*, www.getfrank.co.nz/lifestyle/music/the-art-of-the-mix-15-foolproof-rules-for-creating-the-perfect-mixtape.

Bradbury, Ray. *Fahrenheit 451*. Simon and Schuster, 1951.

Brookover, Sophie, et al. "What's New about New Adult?" *The Horn Book Magazine*, vol. 90, no. 1, Jan.-Feb. 2014, pp. 41–45.

Catalano, Michele. "The Lost Art of the Mixtape." *Medium*, 31 Mar. 2015, medium.com/cuepoint/the-lost-art-of-the-mixtape-9ca967be0cd0.

Chbosky, Stephen. *The Perks of Being a Wallflower*. MTV Books, 1999.

Cohen, Rachel, and David Levithan. *Nick and Norah's Infinite Playlist*. Alfred A. Knopf, 2006.

Hamilton: An American Musical. Created by Lin-Manuel Miranda, Atlantic Records, 2015.

High School Musical. Directed by Kenny Oretga, First Street Films / Salty Productions, 2006.

Hinton, S. E. *The Outsiders*. Speak, 1967.

Hornby, Nick. *High Fidelity*. Riverhead Books, 1995.

Lopez, Robert, and Jeff Marx. "Mix Tape." *Avenue Q: The Musical*, Masterworks Broadway, 2003.

Moore, Thurston. *Mix Tape: The Art of Cassette Culture*. Universe Publishing, 2004.

Pitch Perfect. Directed by Jason Moore, Gold Circle Films / Brownstone Productions, 2012.

Rideout, Victoria J., et al. *Generation M^2: Media in the Lives of 8- to 18-Year-Olds*. Kaiser Family Foundation, Jan. 2010.

Rowell, Rainbow. *Fangirl: A Novel*. St. Martin's Griffin, 2013.

———. "One Thing Leads to Another: An Interview with Rainbow Rowell." By Julie Bartel, *The Hub*, 27 Feb. 2014, www.yalsa.ala.org/thehub/2014/02/27/one-thing-leads-to-another-an-interview-with-rainbow-rowell.

Salinger, J. D. *The Catcher in the Rye*. Little, Brown, 1951.

Schulman, Kori. "The White House Just Joined Spotify: Listen to the President's Summer Playlist." *The White House*, 14 Aug. 2015, www.whitehouse.gov/blog/2015/08/14/white-house-just-joined-spotify-listen-presidents-summer-playlist.

Sheffield, Rob. *Love Is a Mix Tape: Life and Loss, One Song at a Time*. Three Rivers Press, 2007.

———. "Top Ten Tape Tips." *Independent*, 14 July 2008, www.independent.co.uk/artsentertainment/music/features/top-ten-tape-tips-866786.html.

Katherine Bell

The Politics of Realism: Interdisciplinary Explorations of Adolescent "Storm and Stress"

For several years I taught a capstone course titled Adolescence: Constructions, Realities, Regulations in a youth and children's studies program. This course offered an interdisciplinary exploration of the role youth plays in the social imaginary. I began by providing a history of youth, noting that the term *adolescent* had little currency before the early twentieth century. It was then that a host of factors, such as the increased visibility of young people in industrial cities and the emergent middle class, led to the most vigorous articulation of this new, exploratory stage of life. We would then spend the next few weeks of the course exploring the interlocking discourses of psychoanalysis (Anna Freud), psychology and pedagogy (G. Stanley Hall), sociology (Margaret Mead), and criminal justice, which have competed to label and explain this stage. This exploration allowed students to see that adolescence is deeply bound up in an interest in modernity. Aaron Esman argues that though puberty has always been with us, the process of *adaptation* to puberty has changed; Kent Baxter adds that, in the twentieth century, this became an endlessly monitored process of adaptation to the modern world. Leading theorists such as G. Stanley Hall and Margaret Mead may have been disparate in their definitions of this stage of life, but, as Baxter notes, they were "united in the rehabilitative nature of their work, which claimed to provide objective observations of adolescence, but really outlined methods to deal with members of this demographic if they got out of control" (5). For Baxter, the delineation and explanation of adolescence have been linked to the treatment of it.

It is within this context that we approach the YA novel, which emerged during the social unrest of the 1960s as a response to the monitoring and foregrounding of this stage of life—and as a response to the monitoring and foregrounding of modernity—though, as Roberta Seelinger Trites notes, the genre itself is another institution complicit in the monitoring of youth (xii). I now teach a course on YA literature as part of my regular teaching load in an English department, but an interdisciplinary pedagogical approach remains vital in this course. This approach redresses something I've noticed in my many years of teaching: it is easy to see any troubles adolescents might have as naturally endemic to youth, even as youth are, paradoxically, deployed to channel anxieties about social and political futures.

Facilitating Exploration of Context

The following assignment has helped to foster a critical inquiry into representations of youth. I have used this assignment in the interdisciplinary capstone course described above (twenty-four students) and in a YA literature course (capped at fifty). This assignment may be modified in courses with larger class sizes, where group seminars are not possible or feasible. In lieu of presentations, instructors might simply ask each student to hand in a small assignment that links the novel to a cultural artifact (explained below).

At the beginning of the semester, I ask students to form in groups of six. At six points throughout the semester, this group meets and one student presents a seminar to the five other group members. The seminar leader discusses a five-page written response to the following questions:

> How is youth represented in this novel? Is adolescence characterized as deviant, idealized, a "problem" to be solved, or is it nuanced and fully humanized? Are adolescent characters afforded agency? What specific moments or scenes in the novel lead to your conclusions?
>
> How does literary form, style, or narrative structure affect the representation of youth?

What is the sociohistorical context of the primary reading, and how does this inform the representation of youth?
How do you think the sociocultural moment underpins how we read youth struggles and concerns?

This last question links nicely to a second component of the assignment. For this component, the presenter introduces a cultural artifact to the group that relates to a topical issue, social problem, or modern trend in the novel. The cultural artifact may be an alternate representation of the particular thematic concern (i.e., youth and technology or youth and sexuality) from a news source, film, television show, popular book, video game, or other media platform or a tool designed for or by youth culture that relates to the thematic concern. This tool is expressive rather than utilitarian, and it should provide inroads for considering the traits of its young users.

I provide examples in the course outline, but I encourage students to choose their own artifacts. Even in small seminar classes, there are at least a handful of students discussing different cultural artifacts at one time. Toward the end of class, I facilitate a large-class discussion where we juxtapose the cultural artifacts alongside the literary text.

Examples

To illustrate, I turn to some artifacts students have discussed in their presentations on M. T. Anderson's dystopian novel *Feed*. The title of this text refers to a device that is implanted in people's brains to connect them to a "feednet"—an advanced version of the Internet that allows for telepathic communication with others on closed channels, personalized shopping preferences based on previous consumption patterns, and unlimited access to a shared knowledge base. While *Feed* positions its readers to recognize and critique the processes of consumerism and technology in American society, the following artifacts are points of reference for conversations about youth and technological change.

The Dumbest Generation

One student brought in a text titled *The Dumbest Generation*. Written by the Emory University professor Mark Bauerlein, this well-known text is almost dystopian in tone, but its temporal reference is the present and Bauerlein argues that adults have done youth a disservice by extolling the virtues of the digital world. He finds that "many generations ago, adolescent years meant preparation for something beyond adolescence, not authentic selfhood but serious work, civic duty, and family responsibility, with parents, teachers, ministers, and employers training teens in grown-up conduct" (168). Now, however, technology has allowed adolescents to fold into a narcissistic world of instant gratification, constant social interaction, and a false sense of confidence in knowledge that has little to do with sustained thought or problem solving. Rather than rising above the generations that precede them, youth "can't climb out of adolescence on their own" (161). This stunted period threatens "the vitality of democracy in the United States" (203).

Another artifact that frames youth technology usage as a widespread social concern is the *Frontline* documentary "Digital Nation." A few students have shown excerpts that feature the policing of technology users, such as large Internet detox boot camps for youth in South Korea and the school-wide surveillance of laptop activity at an intermediate school in the Bronx, where the vice principal remotely monitors the students; he can see the students, "but they can't see him," and he occasionally snaps pictures of them with their laptop cameras when they need reminders to get back to their schoolwork ("Digital Nation" 33:06).

"From Teenager to Teenagent"

For the very same class, another student brought in an article, "The Transformation of American Youth: From Teenager to Teenagent," by Marian Salzman. For Salzman, technology endows youth with the tools they need to be on the cutting edge of change; they are currently "changing the world of marketing, altering communications, inventing new lexicons and adopting still-embryonic innovations." Furthermore, the Internet allows youth to live in virtual urban meccas, accessing trends from New York City to Japan. Hypermobility produces a tacitly different teen who has acquired an "always-on, interactive dynamic [that] can be both exhausting and exhilarating." The student presenter observed this dynamic in *Feed*, where characters grow weary of trips to the moon and tend to their outfits several times throughout the day to keep up with trends. Yet this student appreciated Salzman's ardent support of "teenagents" around the world who employ technology to be agents of change and innovation; she positioned the article as a refreshing antidote to the dystopian bleakness of *Feed*. Salzman reminds us that, in reality, it is possible for characters like Violet, the strongest-dissenting figure in *Feed*, to break old rules and create change.

DeviantArt

At one point in *Feed*, the main character struggles to interpret a painting: "One of [the walls] had a picture of a boat on it. The boat was on a pond or maybe lake. I couldn't find anything interesting about that picture at all. There was nothing that was about to happen or had just happened. I couldn't figure out even the littlest reason to paint a picture like that" (45). One student was particularly struck by this passage but insisted that regular use of technology need not result in a loss of aesthetic sensibility. This student argued that participatory culture was a big part of her life and that technology—in itself a neutral medium—can be a useful tool for youth despite what adults might think. Her cultural artifact was the large online artistic community *DeviantArt*, which features various pieces of artwork and fan fiction created largely by youth. She focused specifically on several samples of original artwork inspired by Anderson's novel ("Traditional Art") and a short story, "To Those Who Resist" (Pailei), that borrows its title from Anderson's dedication. This fan fiction features dissenting figures and uses the technology-inflected lingo rampant in *Feed*.

Discussing Context

Hall, a pioneer of the child study movement, scrutinized the adolescent body and brain and ultimately argued that the "powers of acquisition are increased and deepened" during adolescence, and while "the point of departure for higher and more evolved forms is adolescence and not adulthood," any changes to thinking "best occur now" (1: 49). Hall's tenacious logic—that adolescence is a make-or-break period—sheds light on how our culture continues to hold youth in such paradoxical regard long after some of his research has been disproven. Many cultural artifacts fall into one of two camps: youth are either feared to be dupes of mass consumption or admired as agents of change who resist and rebel against prevailing social norms. They are either pitied for being dumbed down by the digital world that whisks them away from tradition or envied for the imagined virtual metropolis to which they belong. When students see the extent to which youth is scrutinized in popular news sources and institutional discourse, some begin to question if it is the surveillance itself, the anxiety over youth—in short, youth's fraught relation to the larger body politic—that helps position adolescence as what Hall dubbed a period of "storm and stress."

Cultural artifacts such as the images and fan fiction on *DeviantArt* remind students that, unlike the youth in *Feed*, contemporary youth can use technology to their advantage in their singular, everyday creative pursuits. Furthermore, Anderson's text allows students to refute the binary positioning of youth in our society. Anderson actually refuses to cordon youth off as the "dumbest generation"; both the teen narrator Titus and his father are intellectually stunted by the feed, and all culture is presented as both hyperstimulated and vapid. In like manner, Violet and her father are concerned with how to be human in their posthumanist world. The novel doesn't position youth as markedly other to adults in their logic and their use of technology, but Anderson's fictional society persecutes the female adolescent alone for her attempts to use the technology subversively. The novel and the cultural artifacts work together, then, to help students understand the ways in which youth bear the brunt of society's highly charged efforts to manage the effects of modernization.

Works Cited

Anderson, M. T. *Feed*. Candlewick Press, 2002.

Bauerlein, Mark. *The Dumbest Generation: How the Digital Age Stupefies Young Americans and Jeopardizes Our Future*. Tarcher/Penguin, 2008.

Baxter, Kent. *The Modern Age: Turn-of-the-Century American Culture and the Invention of Adolescence*. U of Alabama P, 2008.

"Digital Nation: Life on the Virtual Frontier." Produced by Rachel Dretzin and Douglas Rushkoff, *Frontline*, Feb. 2010, www.pbs.org/wgbh/pages/frontline/digitalnation.

Esman, Aaron H. *Adolescence and Culture*. Columbia UP, 1990.

Freud, Anna. "Adolescence." *The Psychoanalytic Study of the Child*, vol. 13, no. 1, 1958, pp. 255–78.

Hall, G. Stanley. *Adolescence: Its Psychology and Its Relations to Physiology, Anthropology, Sociology, Sex, Crime, Religion, and Education*. D. Appleton, 1904. 2 vols.

Mead, Margaret. *Coming of Age in Samoa: A Psychological Study of Primitive Youth for Western Civilisation*. Quill, 1928.

Pailei. "To Those Who Resist . . ." *DeviantART*, 30 Mar. 2009, www.deviantart.com/art/To-Those-Who-Resist-117641634. Accessed 5 May 2017.

Salzman, Marian. "The Transformation of American Youth: From Teenager to Teenagent." *HuffPost*, 12 May 2010, www.huffpost.com/entry/the-transformation-of-ame_b_573486.

"Traditional Art: MT Anderson Feed." *DeviantArt*, www.deviantart.com/traditional/newest/?q=MT+Anderson+feed. Accessed 5 May 2017.

Trites, Roberta Seelinger. *Disturbing the Universe: Power and Repression in Adolescent Literature*. U of Iowa P, 2000.

Lauren Byler

Teaching Young Adult Girls' Books: Why Bother?

Girls' Books?—what's the justification for teaching a course with this title? Even with the bait of the question mark—suggesting the category of girls' books and perhaps even the meaning of the word *girl* will be interrogated—imagining objections to this course isn't hard. However, given the number of popular YA books that feature girls as protagonists, analysis of what purposes the girl serves in popular culture is warranted, especially because the girl often signifies a preciousness necessarily removed from serious social issues. For instance, while the initial concern about diversity in a girls' books class would likely involve the question of whether it would be a no-boys-allowed club, two topics I believe such a course should address are the pejorative use of the term *girl* to shame men and boys for failures in normative masculinity and the tendency of popular culture to associate girlhood with extreme blondness and whiteness. My syllabus attempts to account for the ways that girls and the word *girl* signify across terrains of gender, age, race, and sexuality, as well as less identity-based fields of cultural value.

Girls weigh inconsistently on scales of cultural value, simultaneously the apotheosis of cherished innocence and nauseatingly trivial objects. On the first day of class, I ask students what the word *girl* means to them.

Their responses are perhaps predictably negative. Girls are naive, silly, and incapable. The label "girl" is embarrassing: feminizing when applied to men or boys, and less appropriate than "woman" for females who have reached puberty. If girls are idealized, this valuation involves suspicious purification or intensification of their sexuality or utopian excursions into fantasy genres. Though most students dislike such definitions of *girl*, they often feel stuck with them. This terminological and ideological state of affairs can make us eager to get beyond derogatory images of girls; however, I urge students to contemplate the possibility of not rushing to recuperate negative images but rather pinpointing how they intersect with and facilitate other systems of cultural value, particularly structures of inequity. As a label for classifying and demeaning persons and things, the term *girl* names a category so elastic that even the most normative man can be swallowed by it. Thus the girl's expansive triviality makes her significant as a topic, but we can't see her significance if we erase this triviality.

As part of resisting the impulse to deny the girl's triviality by revealing her true substance, I emphasize the readability and conventionality of many literary texts on the syllabus by linking them with challenging critical reading from the fields of feminist theory, critical race theory, and cultural studies. Additionally, I try to illustrate continuities of the girl's signification in literature and culture through the transnational and long historical arc of the syllabus. My course begins in the early nineteenth century with Jane Austen, to establish the dominance of the marriage plot in the girl's story and to examine a key author who captured the simultaneous exultation and abjection of the girl. These themes carry through to the most recently published text on the syllabus, Suzanne Collins's *Mockingjay*. I also pair literary texts that explicitly or serendipitously rewrite each other, such as Austen's *Northanger Abbey* and Ian McEwan's *Atonement*, Elizabeth Barrett Browning's *Aurora Leigh* and L. M. Montgomery's *Emily of New Moon*, and Collins's *Mockingjay* and Melba Pattillo Beals's *Warriors Don't Cry*—the final pair being the focus of this essay.

There are three major types of assignment in my course. The first is a series of one-page critical reading assignments in response to prompts that assess students' effectiveness in writing about critical theory *before* they deploy it in formal papers. One prompt, for instance, asked, "Why does Diana Fuss title her essay 'Reading Like a Feminist'? How is reading *like* a feminist different from reading *as* one?" The other two assignments are a short "defining the girl" paper and a final research paper. The former assignment asks one student per week to perform a close reading of a scene from her or his text that delineates the girl's meaning or role in that text; students must present their papers as a means of opening class discussion. The final research paper may be on any topic.

Girls' Books? wasn't designed primarily as a YA literature class, because the course is premised upon the belief that classifying the girl only as an identity position inhabited by female human beings of a certain age range limits our understanding of the work the girl does as a figure of remarkably flexible signification in literature and culture. That said, we talk a lot about the differences between children, adolescents, and adults, asking in particular why girls of specific ages appear to be crucial to certain tasks set for them by the texts we read. Such questions are especially pressing in relation to *Mockingjay* and *Warriors Don't Cry*, since each book features a high school–aged girl who becomes a figure of political change in her world. Both books are marketed as YA literature, though Beals wrote *Warriors* for an adult audience and authorized an abridged "youth edition" (Beals, interview). As measured by the number of papers written on these two books, they were the most popular in the class.

While Collins writes fantasy, and Beals, a memoir about the integration of Little Rock Central High School in 1957–58, their protagonists bear a strong resemblance by belonging to oppressed communities, being objects of intense media scrutiny, and experiencing frustration with being powerful icons but relatively powerless individuals. These books might not seem to fit my course's directive of examining rather than recuperating the girl's triviality, since their heroines appear anything but trivial in risking their lives to participate in major civic events. However, I have students read these books along with Lauren Berlant's work on the politics of citizenship in the United States to help them see the ways in which the books provoke distrust of collective politics by depicting girls as damaged by engaging in them. According to Berlant, in the late twentieth century in the United States, matters that counted as public politics were reduced to a set of concerns about private life: this "intimate public sphere . . . renders citizenship as a condition of social membership produced by personal acts and values, especially originating in or directed toward the family sphere" (5). Collins's and Beals's narratives uphold this model of citizenship insofar as each heroine has a romantic decision to make between two boys, and this decision becomes the overriding telos of her story, shrinking its concluding image of political progress to the intimate space of a love triangle resolved. Though there are significant sexual politics in these love triangles—one of which involves an interracial relationship—I would emphasize how the love triangle supplants concern for collective enfranchisement with the isolating intimacy of a love story. The girl is the ideal citizen for a politics suspicious of collectivity because of her persistent propulsion into the marriage plot that makes the world vanish in the euphoria of romantic pairing. Neither Collins nor Beals explicitly attempts to write a narrative resistant to exploring public politics, yet their placement of teenage girls in love triangles and depictions of them as innocent children mutilated by civic demands generate wariness of public politics and distaste for its physical dangers and emotional difficulties.

In the style of the Twilight series and the later books and films in the Harry Potter series, both *Mockingjay* and *Warriors* generate fervor over the question of which romantic partner the heroine will choose. The aim of this excitement appears to be providing a means for heroine and reader to escape the difficult realm of civic politics. Rejecting Gale and his violent, retributive politics, Katniss repairs her relationship with Peeta and has two children with him. Though we might read her choice of Peeta as an embrace of his investment in sustaining a livable, civic world, there is nothing public about the politics of this trilogy's conclusion, which focuses on personal healing and nurturing a nuclear family. Katniss and Peeta live in a private world of ghosts, and we hear nothing about the new government of Panem or its policies beyond the fact that "memorials" have been built to commemorate the Hunger Games—more specters of the past rather than operational modes of the present (389).[1]

Unsurprisingly, Beals's nonfiction memoir is more complex in its representation of a teenager's political knowledge than Collins's novel, but it also evaluates political progress by assessing its heroine's love life. *Warriors* includes a love triangle that's unusual because it goes unacknowledged until it's resolved. Early in the book, Beals introduces the African American teenager Vince, who serves as an index of young Melba's desire to be a normal teenager, outside of the civil rights spotlight, but their relationship falls apart because of the demands of integration. Later, we meet Melba's white classmate Link, who helps her escape many segregationist attacks. Only in the book's final chapter do we learn that Link repeatedly asked Melba to be his girlfriend and to run away with him to Harvard, where he would "take care of [her] until [she got] a job" (305). Link supersedes Vince in importance to Melba because he can aid her in ways few African American men can, a conclusion Beals draws in her epilogue when describing her failed marriage to another white man: "Later I would come to understand that [John Beals] represented Danny, my 101st guard; Link, my protector; the power of those who held sway over me at Central High; and the safety that my black uncles and father could not provide in the South" (311). This analysis is incredibly honest as well as insightful about the knotty dynamics of psychic life produced by American apartheid. It also offers a nonfictional account of national politics being turned inward and confined to the privatized spaces of sexual desire and marriage.

One means I found to highlight the retreat from civic politics in these texts was to ask students whether episodes in them were public, private, or both. This tactic was useful in discussing how Beals's assessment of the ways integration affected her sexual object choice overlooks a significant event in her adolescence: a white man's attempt to rape her as a reprisal against the *Brown v. Board of Education* ruling.[2] Students initially wanted to read this event through the lens of personal trauma, but I pressed them to consider the publicness of the attack and its indication of desire and power being constructed through both private familial and public cultural conventions. Robin Bernstein's book *Racial Innocence* also helped us to postulate how the man who tried to rape Melba might be seeing her through the image of the pickaninny, "an imagined, subhuman black juvenile who was typically depicted outdoors, merrily accepting (or even inviting) violence," a figure "always resistant if not immune to pain" (34, 35). Because postslavery culture detached African American children from the vulnerable innocence of childhood—which became a purely white category—the man could see twelve-year-old Melba walking home from school through public space as "inviting" his attentions and as a durable body on which to inscribe his rejection of *Brown*.

Though intolerable racist and sexist violence may provoke the urge to reinforce innocence, *Warriors* and *Mockingjay* also display the dubious influences of innocence that shape girls and girls' books. At times, insistence on innocence belittles the girl, reducing her to a symbol and dismissing her ideas and emotions. Relatedly, attachment to girlish innocence serves as an impetus to nostalgia and retreat into fantasized domestic security, such as when a nearly eighteen-year-old Katniss, who wasn't safe in childhood, laments, "[I]t's been a long time since I've been considered a child in this war" (360). Beals becomes similarly sentimental about the "children" at the center of her story, despite the facts that they are nearly old enough to vote and freely chose to participate in integration. While the first and final chapters of *Warriors* emphasize that "My eight friends and I paid for the integration of Central High with our innocence," Beals recounts earlier losses of innocence, including the attempted rape and being kicked off a whites-only merry-go-round at age five (2). These competing narratives about the primal scene of racial knowledge counterpoise an adult Beals—so badly wanting to restore childhood innocence that she finds it in teenagers—against the child Melba, who knows her innocence was lost long before high school. Maudlin expressions of regret for the harm done to a girl's delicate naïveté when she enters public life help to account for the prominence of girls as icons of puerile politics. Reverence for girls' innocence trivializes them and makes them a powerful excuse for truncating various kinds of public acts. Though children of both sexes are associated with innocence, girls retain this tie much longer, carrying it into adolescence when innocence is the thing they must keep and boys must lose. Thus we may be more prone to view adolescent girls as in need of protection from public politics no matter what fictional and nonfictional girls are saying and doing in that lively realm.

Why bother teaching YA girls' books? Because the obvious negative and positive answers to this question both take the girl's triviality for granted, whether by dismissing the books' value or granting it in an inclusionary gesture. Yet, read with nonidealizing scrutiny, YA books like those discussed above can show us the political risks of underestimating the power of the artlessness attributed to girls and books associated with them.

Notes

Completion of this essay was supported by a College of Humanities faculty fellowship from California State University, Northridge.

1. Broad makes a similar assessment of *Mockingjay*'s epilogue, though her critique focuses on Katniss as a feminist icon, while I wish to problematize the book's meager representation of politics more generally.

2. As Berg likewise notes, Beals "remain[s] silent on what effect her childhood encounter with a would-be white rapist had on her association of white men with safety" (95).

Works Cited

Beals, Melba Pattillo. Interview by Brian Lamb. *Booknotes*, C-SPAN, 28 Oct. 1994, www.c-span.org/video/?61780-1/warriors-cry.

———. *Warriors Don't Cry: A Searing Memoir of the Battle to Integrate Little Rock's Central High*. Washington Square Press, 1994.

Berg, Allison. "Trauma and Testimony in Black Women's Civil Rights Memoirs: *The Montgomery Bus Boycott and the Women Who Started It, Warriors Don't Cry*, and *From the Mississippi Delta*." *Journal of Women's History*, vol. 21, no. 3, Fall 2009, pp. 84–107.

Berlant, Lauren. *The Queen of America Goes to Washington City: Essays on Sex and Citizenship*. Duke UP, 1997.

Bernstein, Robin. *Racial Innocence: Performing American Childhood from Slavery to Civil Rights*. New York UP, 2011.

Broad, Katherine R. "'The Dandelion in the Spring': Utopia as Romance in Suzanne Collins's *The Hunger Games* Trilogy." *Contemporary Dystopian Fiction for Young Adults: Brave New Teenagers*, edited by Carrie Hintz et al., Routledge, 2013, pp. 117–30.

Collins, Suzanne. *Mockingjay*. Scholastic, 2010.

Fuss, Diana. "Reading Like a Feminist." *The Essential Difference*, edited by Naomi Schor and Elizabeth Weed, Indiana UP, 1994, pp. 98–115.

Part IV

Resources

General Criticism

Aronson, Marc. *Exploding the Myths: The Truth about Teenagers and Reading.* Scarecrow Press, 2001.

Austin, Ralph A. "Struggling with the African Bildungsroman." *Research in African Literatures*, vol. 46, no. 3, Fall 2015, pp. 214–31.

Baxter, Kent. *The Modern Age: Turn-of-the-Century American Culture and the Invention of Adolescence.* U of Alabama P, 2008.

Bezhanova, Olga. *Growing Up in an Inhospitable World: Female Bildungsroman in Spain.* Asociación Internacional de Literatura y Cultura Femenina Hispánica, 2014.

Boes, Tobias. *Formative Fictions: Nationalism, Cosmopolitanism, and the Bildungsroman.* Cornell UP, 2012.

Bright, Amy. "Writing Homer, Reading Riordan: Intertextual Study in Contemporary Adolescent Literature." *Journal of Children's Literature*, vol. 37, no. 1, Spring 2011, pp. 38–47.

Brisson, Genevieve, and Theresa Rogers. "Reading Place: Bodies and Spaces in Quebecois Adolescent Literature." *Children's Literature in Education*, vol. 44, no. 2, June 2013, pp. 140–55.

Buckley, Jerome Hamilton. *Season of Youth: The Bildungsroman from Dickens to Golding.* Harvard UP, 1974.

Butler, Catherine. "Critiquing 'Calypso': Authorial and Academic Bias in the Reading of a Young Adult Novel." *Children's Literature in Education*, vol. 44, no. 3, Sept. 2013, pp. 264–79.

Cadden, Mike. "Genre as Nexus: The Novel for Children and Young Adults." Wolf et al., pp. 302–13.

———. "The Irony of Narration in the Young Adult Novel." *Children's Literature Association Quarterly*, vol. 25, no. 3, Fall 2000, pp. 146–54.

Campbell, Patty. *Spirituality in Young Adult Literature: The Last Taboo.* Rowman and Littlefield, 2015.

Carroll, Virginia Schaefer. "Re-reading the Romance of *Seventeenth Summer*." *Children's Literature Association Quarterly*, vol. 21 no. 1, Spring 1996, pp. 12–19.

Cart, Michael. *From Romance to Realism: 50 Years of Growth and Change in Young Adult Literature.* HarperCollins, 1995.

Chambers, Aidan. "Finding the Form: Toward a Poetics of Youth Literature." *The Lion and Unicorn*, vol. 34, no. 3, Sept. 2010, pp. 267–83.

Coats, Karen. *The Bloomsbury Introduction to Children's and Young Adult Literature.* Bloomsbury Academic, 2017.

———. "Young Adult Literature: Growing Up, in Theory." Wolf et al., pp. 315–29.

Crowe, Chris. *More Than a Game: Sports Literature for Young Adults.* Scarecrow Press, 2004.

Daniels, Cindy Lou. "Literary Theory and Young Adult Literature: The Open Frontier in Critical Studies." *The ALAN Review*, vol. 33, no. 2, 2006, pp. 78–82.

Day, Sara K. "Power and Polyphony in Young Adult Literature: Rob Thomas's *Slave Day*." *Studies in the Novel*, vol. 42, nos. 1–2, Spring-Summer 2010, pp. 66–83.

Engel, Manfred. "Variants of the Romantic 'Bildungsroman.'" *Romantic Prose Fiction*, edited by Gerald Gillespie et al., Benjamins, 2008, pp. 263–95.

Engles, Tim, and Fern Kory. "Incarceration, Identity Formation, and Race in Young Adult Literature: The Case of *Monster* versus *Hole in My Life*." *English Journal*, vol. 102, no. 4, Mar. 2013, pp. 53–58.

Ewers, Hans-Heino, and J. D. Stahl. "The Limits of Literary Criticism of Children's and Young Adult Literature." *The Lion and the Unicorn*, vol. 19, no. 1, June 1995, pp. 77–94.

Flanagan, Victoria. *Technology and Identity in Young Adult Fiction: The Posthuman Subject*. Palgrave Macmillan, 2014.

Garcia, Antero. *Critical Foundations in Young Adult Literature: Challenging Genres*. Sense, 2013.

Gubar, Marah. "Species Trouble: The Abjection of Adolescence in E. B. White's *Stuart Little*." *The Lion and the Unicorn*, vol. 27, no. 1, Jan. 2003, pp. 98–119.

Hall, G. Stanley. *Adolescence: Its Psychology and Its Relations to Physiology, Anthropology, Sociology, Sex, Crime, Religion, and Education*. D. Appleton, 1904. 2 vols.

Hateley, Erica. "Canon Fodder: Young Adult Literature as a Tool for Critiquing Canonicity." *English in Australia*, vol. 48, no. 2, Sept. 2013, pp. 71–78.

Head, Patricia. "Robert Cormier and the Postmodernist Possibilities of Young Adult Fiction." *Children's Literature Association Quarterly*, vol. 21, no. 1, Spring 1996, pp. 28–33.

Hill, Crag, editor. *The Critical Merits of Young Adult Literature: Coming of Age*. Routledge, 2015.

Hilton, Mary, and Maria Nikolajeva, editors. *Contemporary Adolescent Literature and Culture: The Emergent Adult*. Ashgate, 2012.

Hogan, Walter. *Humor in Young Adult Literature: A Time to Laugh*. Scarecrow Press, 2005.

Hunt, Caroline. "Young Adult Literature Evades the Theorists." *Children's Literature Association Quarterly*, vol. 21, no. 1, Spring 1996, pp. 4–11.

Isaac, Megan. *Heirs to Shakespeare: Reinventing the Bard in Young Adult Literature*. Boynton/Cook, 2000.

Iskander, Sylvia Patterson. "Readers, Realism, and Robert Cormier." *Children's Literature*, vol. 15, 1987, pp. 7–18.

Kapurch, Katie. "'Unconditionally and Irrevocably': Theorizing the Melodramatic Impulse in Young Adult Literature through the Twilight Saga and

Jane Eyre." *Children's Literature Association Quarterly*, vol. 37, no. 2, Summer 2012, pp. 164–87.

Khorana, Meena, editor. *Critical Perspectives on Postcolonial African Children's and Young Adult Literature*. Greenwood Press, 1998.

Kidd, Kenneth B. *Freud in Oz: At the Intersections of Psychoanalysis and Children's Literature*. U of Minnesota P, 2011.

Kidd, Kenneth B., and Joseph T. Thomas, Jr., editors. *Prizing Children's Literature: The Cultural Politics of Children's Book Awards*. Routledge, 2016.

Koss, Melanie D. "Young Adult Novels with Multiple Narrative Perspectives: The Changing Nature of YA Literature." *The ALAN Review*, vol. 36, no. 3, 2009, pp. 73–80.

Kümmerling-Meibauer, Bettina. "Emotional Connection: Representation of Emotions in Young Adult Literature." Hilton and Nikolajeva, pp. 127–38.

Lawrence-Pietroni, Anna. "*The Tricksters*, *The Changeover*, and the Fluidity of Adolescent Literature." *Children's Literature Association Quarterly*, vol. 21, no. 1, Spring 1996, pp. 34–39.

Lerner, Richard M., and Laurence Steinberg, editors. *Handbook of Adolescent Psychology*. 2nd ed., Wiley, 2004.

Martens, Marianne. "Consumed by Twilight: The Commodification of Young Adult Literature." *Bitten by Twilight: Youth Culture, Media, and the Vampire Franchise*, edited by Melissa A. Click et al., Peter Lang, 2010, pp. 243–60.

McCallum, Robyn. *Ideologies of Identity in Adolescent Fiction: The Dialogic Construction of Subjectivity*. Garland, 1999.

Mills, Claudia. Introduction. *Ethics and Children's Literature*, Ashgate, 2014, pp. 1–12.

Mintz, Steven. *Huck's Raft: A History of American Childhood*. Belknap Press, 2004.

Miskec, Jennifer, and Chris McGee. "My Scars Tell a Story: Self-Mutilation in Young Adult Literature." *Children's Literature Association Quarterly*, vol. 32, no. 2, Summer 2007, pp. 163–78.

Nel, Philip, and Lissa Paul, editors. *Keywords in Children's Literature*. NYU P, 2011.

Nikolajeva, Maria. *Power, Voice and Subjectivity in Literature for Young Readers*. Routledge, 2012.

Nikolajeva, Maria, and Carole Scott. *How Picturebooks Work*. Garland, 2001.

Nilsen, Don L. F. "Northrop Frye Meets Tweedledum and Tweedledee: Adolescent Literature as Comedy, Romance, Tragedy, and Irony." *Journal of Evolutionary Psychology*, vol. 19, nos. 1–2, Mar. 1998, pp. 10–20.

Nodelman, Perry. *Alternating Narratives in Fiction for Young Readers: Twice upon a Time*. Palgrave Macmillan, 2017.

———. *Words about Pictures: The Narrative Art of Children's Picture Books*. U of Georgia P, 1988.

Pattee, Amy. "Between Youth and Adulthood: Young Adult and New Adult Literature." *Children's Literature Association Quarterly*, vol. 42, no. 2, Summer 2017, pp. 218–30.

———, editor. *Critical Survey of Young Adult Literature.* Grey House, 2016.

———. "Disturbing the Peace: The Function of Young Adult Literature and the Case of Catherine Atkins' *When Jeff Comes Home.*" *Children's Literature in Education*, vol. 35, no. 3, Sept. 2004, pp. 241–55.

Prain, Vaughan, et al. "Getting Real in Literature for Adolescents: The Cases of Cormier, Almond and Hartnett." *Journal of Children's Literature Studies*, vol. 8, no. 3, 2012, pp. 1–21.

Reeve, Philip. "The Worst Is Yet to Come." *School Library Journal*, vol. 57, no. 8, Aug. 2011, pp. 34–36.

Rokison, Abigail. *Shakespeare for Young People: Productions, Versions and Adaptations.* Bloomsbury, 2013.

Schober, Adrian. "Rereading Robert Cormier: Realism, Naturalism, and the Young Adult Novel." *The Lion and the Unicorn*, vol. 38, no. 3, Sept. 2014, pp. 303–26.

Small, Robert C., Jr. "The Literary Value of the Young Adult Novel." *Journal of Youth Services in Libraries*, vol. 5, no. 3, Spring 1992, pp. 277–85.

Spacks, Patricia Meyer. *The Adolescent Idea: Myths of Youth and the Adult Imagination.* Basic Books, 1981.

Starr, Carol. "Brief History of the Young Adult Services Division." *YALSA*, www.ala.org/yalsa/aboutyalsa/history/briefhistory. Accessed 22 Jan. 2016.

Stephens, John. "Cognitive Maps and Social Ecology in Young Adult Fiction." *International Research in Children's Literature*, vol. 8, no. 2, 2015, pp. 142–55.

Stewart, Susan Louise. "In the Ellison Tradition: In/Visible Bodies of Adolescent and YA Fiction." *Children's Literature in Education*, vol. 40, no. 3, Sept. 2009, pp. 180–96.

Stover, Lois Thomas, and Connie S. Zitlow. *Portrait of the Artist as a Young Adult: The Arts in Young Adult Literature.* Scarecrow Press, 2013.

Stringer, Sharon. *Conflict and Connection: The Psychology of Young Adult Literature.* Boynton/Cook, 1997.

Sutton, Roger. "Problems, Paperbacks, and the Printz: Forty Years of YA Books." *The Horn Book Magazine*, vol. 84, no. 3, May 2007, pp. 231–43.

Tarr, Anita. "The Absence of Moral Agency in Robert Cormier's *The Chocolate War.*" *Children's Literature*, vol. 30, 2002, pp. 96–124.

Tarr, Anita, and Donna R. White, editors. *Posthumanism in Young Adult Fiction: Finding Humanity in a Posthuman World.* UP of Mississippi, 2018.

Thein, Amanda Haertling, and Mark A. Sulzer. "Illuminating Discourses of Youth through the Study of First-Person Narration in Young Adult Literature." *English Journal*, vol. 104, no. 3, Jan. 2015, pp. 47–53.

Trites, Roberta Seelinger. *Disturbing the Universe: Power and Oppression in Adolescent Literature.* U of Iowa P, 2000.

———. "Growth in Adolescent Literature: Metaphors, Scripts, and Cognitive Narratology." *International Research in Children's Literature*, vol. 5, no. 1, July 2012, pp. 64–80.

———. "The Harry Potter Novels as a Test Case for Adolescent Literature." *Style*, vol. 35, no. 3, Fall 2001, pp. 472–85.

———. *Literary Conceptualizations of Growth: Metaphors and Cognition in Adolescent Literature.* John Benjamins, 2014.

———. "Theories and Possibilities of Adolescent Literature." *Children's Literature Association Quarterly*, vol. 21, no. 1, Spring 1996, pp. 2–3.

———. *Twain, Alcott, and the Birth of the Adolescent Reform Novel.* U of Iowa P, 2007.

Vitto, Cindy L. "*Sir Gawain and the Green Knight* as Adolescent Literature: Essential Lessons." *Children's Literature Association Quarterly*, vol. 23, no. 1, Spring 1998, pp. 22–28.

Waller, Alison. *Constructing Adolescence in Fantastic Realism.* Routledge, 2011.

Walsh, Jill Paton. "The Writer's Responsibility." *Children's Literature in Education*, vol. 10, 1973, pp. 30–36.

Wasserman, Emily. "The Epistolary in Young Adult Literature." *The ALAN Review*, vol. 30, no. 3, 2003, pp. 48–51.

Wayland, Nerida. "Representations of Happiness in Comedic Young Adult Fiction: Happy Are the Wretched." *Jeunesse: Young People, Texts, Cultures*, vol. 7, no. 2, Winter 2015, pp. 86–106.

Wickham, Anastasia. "It Is All in Your Head: Mental Illness in Young Adult Literature." *The Journal of Popular Culture*, vol. 51, no. 1, Feb. 2018, pp. 10–25.

Wissman, Kelly. "'Spinning Themselves into Poetry': Images of Urban Adolescent Writers in Two Novels for Young Adults." *Children's Literature in Education*, vol. 40, no. 2, June 2009, pp. 149–67.

Wolf, Shelby, et al., editors. *Handbook of Research on Children's and Young Adult Literature.* Routledge, 2011.

Yampbell, Cat. "Judging a Book by Its Cover: Publishing Trends in Young Adult Literature." *The Lion and the Unicorn*, vol. 29, no. 3, Sept. 2005, pp. 348–72.

Zeegers, Margaret. "A Clash of Chronotopes: Adult Reading of Children's and Young Adult Literature." *International Journal of the Book*, vol. 7, no. 4, 2010, pp. 89–97.

Pedagogy

Bixler, Phyllis. "*I Am the Cheese* and Reader-Response Criticism in the Adolescent Literature Classroom." *Children's Literature Association Quarterly*, vol. 10, no. 1, Spring 1985, pp. 13–16.

Bond, Ernest L. *Literature and the Young Adult Reader.* Pearson, 2010.

Boyd, Ashley S., and Taylor Bereiter. "'I Don't Really Know What a Fair Portrayal Is and What a Stereotype Is': Pluralizing Transgender Narratives with Young Adult Literature." *English Journal*, vol. 107, no. 1, Sept. 2017, pp. 13–18.

Bucher, Katherine T., and KaaVonia M. Hinton. *Young Adult Literature: Exploration, Evaluation, and Appreciation*. Pearson, 2013.

Bushman, John H., and Kay P. Bushman. *Using Young Adult Literature in the English Classroom*. Merrill / Maxwell Macmillan, 1993.

Cole, Pam B. *Young Adult Literature in the 21st Century*. McGraw-Hill Higher Education, 2009.

Elliott, Joan B., and Mary M. Dupuis, editors. *Young Adult Literature in the Classroom: Reading It, Teaching It, Loving It*. International Reading Association, 2002.

Herz, Sarah K., with Donald R. Gallo. *From Hinton to Hamlet: Building Bridges between Young Adult Literature and the Classics*. Greenwood Press, 1996.

Kaywell, Joan F. "Using Young Adult Literature to Develop a Comprehensive World Literature Course with Several Classics." *Adolescent Literature as a Complement to the Classics: Addressing Critical Issues in Today's Classrooms*, edited by Joan F. Kaywell, Christopher-Gordon, 2010, pp. 109–81.

Latrobe, Kathy H., and Judy Drury. *Critical Approaches to Young Adult Literature*. Neal-Schuman, 2009.

Mathison, Ymitri, editor. *Growing Up Asian American in Young Adult Fiction*. UP of Mississippi, 2017.

Matos, Angel Daniel. "'Without a Word or Sign': Enmeshing Deaf and Gay Identity in Young Adult Literature." *Lessons in Disability: Essays on Teaching with Young Adult Literature*, edited by Jacob Stratman, McFarland, 2015, pp. 221–43.

Metcalf, Eva-Maria. "Children's and Young Adult Books in the Intermediate and Advanced German Class: Two Projects." *Die Unterrichtspraxis / Teaching German*, vol. 31, no. 2, Autumn 1998, pp. 148–53.

Metzger, Kenan, et al. "Embracing Intercultural Diversification: Teaching Young Adult Literature with Native American Themes." *English Journal*, vol. 102, no. 5, May 2013, pp. 57–62.

Miller, S. J. "'Speaking' the Walk, 'Speaking' the Talk: Embodying Critical Pedagogy to Teach Young Adult Literature." *English Education*, vol. 40, no. 2, Jan. 2008, pp. 145–54.

Monseau, Virginia R. *Responding to Young Adult Literature*. Boynton/Cook, 1996.

Monseau, Virginia R., and Gary Salvner, editors. *Reading Their World: The Young Adult Novel in the Classroom*. Boynton/Cook, 1992.

Nicosia, Laura. "Adolescent Literature of Witness: Testimonies from the American Margins." *Transformations: The Journal of Inclusive Scholarship and Pedagogy*, vol. 17, no. 1, Spring 2006, pp. 85–97.

Nilsen, Alleen Pace, and Kenneth L. Donelson. *Literature for Today's Young Adults.* 4th ed., HarperCollins, 1993.

Parsons, Linda T. "Learning from Preservice Teachers' Responses to Trans-Themed Young Adult Literature: Improving Personal Practice in Teacher Education." *Discourse: Studies in the Cultural Politics of Education*, vol. 37, no. 6, 2016, pp. 933–47.

Reed, Arthea J. S. *Reaching Adolescents: The Young Adult Book and the School.* Merrill/Maxwell Macmillan, 1994.

Schulz, Renate A. "Using Young Adult Literature in Content-Based German Instruction: Teaching the Holocaust." *Die Unterrichtspraxis / Teaching German*, vol. 31, no. 2, Autumn 1998, pp. 138–47.

Stover, Lois Thomas. *Young Adult Literature: The Heart of the Middle School Curriculum.* Boynton/Cook, 1996.

Sulzer, Mark A., and Amanda Haertling Thein. "Reconsidering the Hypothetical Adolescent in Evaluating and Teaching Young Adult Literature." *Journal of Adolescent and Adult Literacy*, vol. 60, no. 2, Sept.-Oct. 2016, pp. 163–71.

Thein, Amanda Haertling, and Mark A. Sulzer. "Illuminating Discourses of Youth through the Study of First-Person Narration in Young Adult Literature." *English Journal*, vol. 104, no. 3, Jan. 2015, pp. 47–53.

Tomlinson, Carl M., and Carol Lynch-Brown. *Essentials of Young Adult Literature.* Pearson, 2007.

Trupe, Alice. *Thematic Guide to Young Adult Literature.* Greenwood Press, 2006.

Van Hart, Rachel F. "A Case for the Autistic Perspective in Young Adult Literature." *English Journal*, vol. 102, no. 2, Nov. 2012, pp. 27–36.

Wolk, Steven. "Reading for a Better World: Teaching for Social Responsibility with Young Adult Literature." *Journal of Adolescent and Adult Literacy*, vol. 52, no. 8, May 2009, pp. 664–73.

Crossover Writing

Beckett, Sandra L. *Crossover Fiction: Global and Historical Perspectives.* Routledge, 2008.

———. *Crossover Picture Books: A Genre for All Ages.* Routledge, 2012.

———, editor. *Transcending Boundaries: Writing for a Dual Audience of Children and Adults.* Garland, 1999.

Falconer, Rachel. "Crossover Literature and Abjection: Geraldine McCaughrean's *The White Darkness.*" *Children's Literature in Education*, vol. 38, no. 1, Mar. 2007, pp. 35–44.

———. *The Crossover Novel: Contemporary Children's Fiction and Its Adult Readership.* Routledge, 2008.

Galef, David. "Crossing Over: Authors Who Write Both Children's and Adults' Fiction." *Children's Literature Association Quarterly*, vol. 20, no. 1, Spring 1995, pp. 29–35.

Knoepflmacher, U. C., and Mitzi Myers. "'Cross-Writing' and the Reconceptualization of Children's Literary Studies." *Children's Literature*, vol. 25, 1997, pp. vii–xvii.

Phillips, Michelle H. "Along the 'Paragraphic Wires': Child-Adult Mediation in *St. Nicholas Magazine*." *Children's Literature*, vol. 37, 2009, pp. 84–113.

Talley, Lee A. "Susan Cooper's *Dawn of Fear*: Cross-Writing, the Uncanny, and a Childhood in Wartime." *The Lion and the Unicorn*, vol. 37, no. 3, Sept. 2013, pp. 238–56.

Thum, Maureen. "Misreading the Cross-Writer: The Case of Wilhelm Hauff's *Dwarf Long Nose*." *Children's Literature*, vol. 25, 1997, pp. 1–23.

Genre and Form

Fantasy

Abbruscato, Joseph, and Tanya Jones, editors. *The Gothic Fairy Tale in Young Adult Literature: Essays on Stories from Grimm to Gaiman*. McFarland, 2014.

Blackford, Holly Virginia. *The Myth of Persephone in Girls' Fantasy Literature*. Routledge, 2014.

Bodart, Joni Richards. *They Suck, They Bite, They Eat, They Kill: The Psychological Meaning of Supernatural Monsters in Young Adult Fiction*. Scarecrow Press, 2011.

Chappell, Shelley. "Contemporary Werewolf Schemata: Shifting Representations of Racial and Ethnic Difference." *International Research in Children's Literature*, vol. 2, no. 1, July 2009, pp. 21–35.

Kokorski, Karin. "Death Is but the Next Great Adventure: Representations of Death and the Afterlife in Fantastic Literature for Children and Young Adults." *Death: Representations in Literature: Forms and Theories*, edited by Adriana Teodorescu, Cambridge Scholars Press, 2015, pp. 340–58.

Latham, Don. "The Cultural Work of Magical Realism in Three Young Adult Novels." *Children's Literature in Education*, vol. 38, no. 1, Mar. 2007, pp. 59–70.

Silva, Roberta. "Representing Adolescent Fears: Theory of Mind and Fantasy Fiction." *International Research in Children's Literature*, vol. 6, no. 2, Dec. 2013, pp. 161–75.

Sutliff Sanders, Joe. "'*Blatantly* Coming Back': The Arbitrary Line between Here and There, Child and Adult, Fantasy and Real, London and UnLondon." *China Miéville: Critical Essays*, edited by Caroline Edwards and Tony Venezia, Gylphi, 2015, pp. 119–38.

Graphic Narrative

Abate, Michelle Ann, and Gwen Athene Tarbox, editors. *Graphic Novels for Children and Young Adults: A Collection of Critical Essays.* UP of Mississippi, 2017.

Connors, Sean P. "Altering Perspectives: How the Implied Reader Invites Us to Rethink the Difficulty of Graphic Novels." *The Clearing House: A Journal of Educational Strategies, Issues and Ideas*, vol. 85, no. 1, 2012, pp. 33–37.

Gilmore, Leigh, and Elizabeth Marshall. "Trauma and Young Adult Literature: Representing Adolescence and Knowledge in David Small's *Stitches: A Memoir.*" *Prose Studies*, vol. 35, no. 1, 2013, pp. 16–38.

Hatfield, Charles. *Alternative Comics: An Emerging Literature.* UP of Mississippi, 2005.

Keen, Suzanne. "Fast Tracks to Narrative Empathy: Anthropomorphism and Dehumanization in Graphic Narratives." *Substance*, vol. 40, no. 1, 2011, pp. 135–55.

McCloud, Scott. *Understanding Comics: The Invisible Art.* William Morrow, 1994.

Musgrave, Megan L. "Gamer Girls, Gold Farmers, and Activism *In Real Life.*" *Children's Literature in Education*, vol. 47, no. 2, 2016, pp. 161–76.

Historical Fiction

Barnhouse, Rebecca. "Books and Reading in Young Adult Literature Set in the Middle Ages." *The Lion and the Unicorn*, vol. 22, no. 3, Sept. 1998, pp. 364–75.

Brown, Joanne, and Nancy St. Clair. *The Distant Mirror: Reflections on Young Adult Historical Fiction.* Scarecrow Press, 2006.

Cross, Amy. "The (Im)Possibility of Objectivity: Narrating the Past in Young Adult Historiographic Metafiction." *The ALAN Review*, vol. 42, no. 3, 2015, pp. 12–21.

Dean-Ruzicka, Rachel. "Representing 'The Great Devouring': Romani Characters in Young Adult Holocaust Literature." *Children's Literature in Education*, vol. 45, no. 3, Sept. 2014, pp. 211–24.

Henderson, Laretta. "The Black Arts Movement and African American Young Adult Literature: An Evaluation of Narrative Style." *Children's Literature in Education*, vol. 36, no. 4, Dec. 2005, pp. 299–323.

Philpott, Sarah Lewis. "Girls Like Us: Looking at History through the American Girl Series." *Social Studies and the Young Learner*, vol. 26, no. 3, Jan.-Feb. 2014, pp. 24–27.

Poetry

Johnson, Angela Beumer, et al. "Gender Representation in Poetry for Young Adults." *The ALAN Review*, vol. 26, no. 3, 1999, pp. 39–44.

Lipsett, Laura R. "No Need to 'Duck, Run and Hide': Young Adult Poetry That Taps into You." *The ALAN Review*, vol. 28, no. 3, 2001, pp. 58–64.

Rudd, Lynn L. "Just 'Slammin!': Adolescents' Construction of Identity through Performance Poetry." *Journal of Adolescent and Adult Literacy*, vol. 55, no. 8, May 2012, pp. 682–91.

Thomas, Joseph T., Jr. *Poetry's Playground: The Culture of Contemporary American Children's Poetry*. Wayne State UP, 2007.

Science Fiction

Cadden, Mike. *Ursula K. Le Guin beyond Genre: Fiction for Children and Adults*. Routledge, 2005.

Campbell, Joseph. *The Order and the Other: Young Adult Dystopian Literature and Science Fiction*. UP of Mississippi, 2019.

———. "'The Treatment for Stirrings': Dystopian Literature for Adolescents." *Blast, Corrupt, Dismantle, Erase: Contemporary North American Dystopian Literature*, edited by Brett Josef Grubisic et al., Wilfrid Laurier UP, 2014, pp. 165–80.

Day, Sara K., et al., editors. *Female Rebellion in Young Adult Dystopian Fiction*. Routledge, 2016.

Hintz, Carrie, et al., editors. *Contemporary Dystopian Fiction for Young Adults: Brave New Teenagers*. Routledge, 2013.

Mendlesohn, Farah. *Diana Wynne Jones: Children's Literature and the Fantastic Tradition*. Routledge, 2005.

———. *The Inter-galactic Playground: A Critical Study of Children's and Teens' Science Fiction*. McFarland, 2009.

———. "Is There Any Such Thing as Children's Science Fiction? A Position Piece." *The Lion and the Unicorn*, vol. 28, no. 2, Apr. 2004, pp. 284–313.

Oziewicz, Marek C. *Justice in Young Adult Speculative Fiction: A Cognitive Reading*. Routledge, 2015.

Tarr, Anita, and Donna R. White. *Posthumanism in Young Adult Literature*. UP of Mississippi, 2018.

Verse Narrative

Abdur-Rahman, Samira. "Spaces of the Ancestor: Jacqueline Woodson and the Long Civil Rights Movement." *The Lion and the Unicorn*, vol. 42, no. 2, Apr. 2018, pp. 180–97.

Addison, Catherine. "The Verse Novel as Genre: Contradiction or Hybrid?" *Style*, vol. 43, no. 4, Winter 2009, pp. 539–62.

Alexander, Joy. "The Verse-Novel: A New Genre." *Children's Literature in Education*, vol. 36, no. 3, Sept. 2005, pp. 269–83.

Anatol, Giselle Liza. "*Brown Girl Dreaming:* A Ghost Story in the Postcolonial Gothic Tradition." *Children's Literature Association Quarterly*, vol. 41, no. 4, Winter 2016, pp. 403–19.

Cadden, Mike. "Rhetorical Technique in the Young Adult Verse Novel." *The Lion and the Unicorn*, vol. 42, no. 2, Apr. 2018, pp. 129–44.

———. "The Verse Novel and the Question of Genre." *The ALAN Review*, vol. 39, no. 1, 2011, pp. 21–27.

Campbell, Patty. "The Sand in the Oyster: Vetting the Verse Novel." *The Horn Book Magazine*, vol. 80, no. 5, Sept.-Oct. 2004, pp. 611–16.

Coats, Karen. "Form as Metaphor in Middle Grade and Young Adult Verse Novels." *The Lion and the Unicorn*, vol. 42, no. 2, Apr. 2018, pp. 145–61.

Farish, Terry. "Why Verse?" *School Library Journal*, vol. 59, no. 11, 2013, p. 32.

Flynn, Richard. "Why Genre Matters: A Case for the Importance of Aesthetics in the Verse Memoirs of Marilyn Nelson and Jacqueline Woodson." *The Lion and the Unicorn*, vol. 42, no. 2, Apr. 2018, pp. 109–28.

Friesner, Brenna. *The Verse Novel in Young Adult Literature*. Rowman and Littlefield, 2016.

Frost, Helen. "Michael L. Printz Honor Speech." *Young Adult Library Services*, vol. 3, no. 1, 2004, pp. 29, 31.

Glenn, Wendy. "Form Follows Function: The Relationship between Structure and Content in Three of Karen Hesse's Novels." *The ALAN Review*, vol. 31, no. 2, 2004, pp. 27–32.

Hill, Rebecca. "Taking a Closer Look: Ellen Hopkins and Her Novels." *The ALAN Review*, vol. 38, no. 2, 2011, pp. 77–82.

Howard, Krystal. "Collage, Confession, and Crisis in Jacqueline Woodson's *Brown Girl Dreaming*." *Children's Literature Association Quarterly*, vol. 42, no. 3, 2017, pp. 326–44.

Mallan, Kerry, and Roderick McGillis. "Textual Aporias: Exploring the Perplexities of Form and Absence in Australian Verse Novels." *The Looking Glass: New Perspectives on Children's Literature*, vol. 7, no. 2, 2003, www.lib.latrobe.edu.au/ojs/index.php/tlg/article/view/208/206.

O'Neal, Amy. "Calling It Verse Doesn't Make It Poetry." *Young Adult Library Services*, vol. 2, no. 2, 2004, pp. 39–40.

Rebellino, Rachel Rickard. "'I'll Write What Needs to be Remembered': The Use of Verse in Children's and Young Adult Historical Fiction about the Vietnam War." *The Lion and the Unicorn*, vol. 42, no. 2, Apr. 2018, pp. 162–79.

Ruwe, Donelle. "Dramatic Monologues and the Novel-in-Verse: Adelaide O'Keeffe and the Development of Theatrical Children's Poetry in the Long Eighteenth Century." *The Lion and the Unicorn*, vol. 33, no. 2, Apr. 2009, pp. 219–34.

Sullivan, Ed. "Fiction or Poetry? A Librarian Looks at the Profusion of Novels Written in Verse." *School Library Journal*, vol. 49, no. 8, 2003, pp. 44–45.

Thomas, Joseph T., Jr. "Mel Glenn and Arnold Adoff: The Poetics of Power in the Adolescent Voice-Lyric." *Style*, vol. 35, no. 3, 2001, pp. 486–97.

Van Sickle, Vikki. "Subcategories within the Emerging Genre of the Verse Novel." *The Looking Glass: New Perspectives on Children's Literature*, vol. 10, no. 3, 2006, www.lib.latrobe.edu.au/ojs/index.php/tlg/article/view/74/88.

Wissman, Kelly. "'Spinning Themselves into Poetry': Images of Urban Adolescent Writers in Two Novels for Young Adults." *Children's Literature in Education*, vol. 40, no. 2, 2009, pp. 149–66.

Wolff, Virginia Euwer. "An Interview with Virginia Euwer Wolff." By Roger Sutton. *The Horn Book Magazine*, vol. 77, no. 3, May-June 2001, pp. 280–86.

Censorship Texts

Batycki, Donna M. F. "Systemic Censorship: The Myth of Freedom and the Place of the Child." *Para-doxa*, vol. 2, nos. 3–4, 1996, pp. 318–27.

Bosmajian, Hamida. "Children's Literature and Censorship." *Para-doxa*, vol. 2, nos. 3–4, 1996, pp. 313–17.

Davis, Kenneth C. "The Lady Goes to Court: Paperbacks and Censorship." *Publishing Research Quarterly*, vol. 11, no. 4, Winter 1995–96, pp. 9–32.

DelFattore, Joan. *What Johnny Shouldn't Read: Textbook Censorship in America*. Yale UP, 1992.

Denby, David. "Buried Alive: Our Children and the Avalanche of Crud." *The New Yorker*, 15 July 1996, pp. 48–58.

Donelson, Ken. "Censorship and Adolescent Literature." *Para-doxa*, vol. 2, nos. 3–4, 1996, pp. 472–79.

Foerstel, Herbert N. *Banned in the U.S.A.: A Reference Guide to Book Censorship in Schools and Public Libraries*. Greenwood Press, 1994.

Reichman, Henry. *Censorship and Selection: Issues and Answers for Schools*. American Library Association, 1988.

Gender and Sexuality

Abate, Michelle Ann. "'Soda Attracted Girls like Honey Draws Flies': *The Outsiders*, the Boy Band Formula, and Adolescent Sexuality." *Children's Literature Association Quarterly*, vol. 42, no. 1, Spring 2017, pp. 43–64.

Abel, Elizabeth, et al., editors. *The Voyage In: Fictions of Female Development.* UP of New England, 1983.

Bilz, Rachelle Lasky. *Life Is Tough: Guys, Growing Up, and Young Adult Literature.* Scarecrow Press, 2004.

Cart, Michael, and Christine A. Jenkins. *The Heart Has Its Reasons: Young Adult Literature with Gay/Lesbian/Queer Content, 1969–2004.* Scarecrow Press, 2006.

Clasen, Tricia, and Holly Hassel. *Gender(ed) Identities: Critical Readings of Gender in Children's and Young Adult Literature.* Routledge, 2016.

Cleveland, Erika, and E. Sybil Durand. "Critical Representations of Sexual Assault in Young Adult Literature." *The Looking Glass: New Perspectives on Children's Literature*, vol. 17, no. 3, 2014, www.lib.latrobe.edu.au/ojs/index.php/tlg/article/view/545/487.

Crisp, Thomas. "From Romance to Magical Realism: Limits and Possibilities in Gay Adolescent Fiction." *Children's Literature in Education*, vol. 40, no. 4, Dec. 2009, pp. 333–48.

———. "It's Not the Book, It's Not the Author, It's the Award: The Lambda Literary Award and the Case for Strategic Essentialism." *Children's Literature in Education*, vol. 42, no. 2, June 2011, pp. 91–104.

Crisp, Thomas, and Suzanne M. Knezek. "'I Just Don't See Myself Here': Challenging Conversations about LGBTQ Adolescent Literature." *English Journal*, vol. 99, no. 3, Jan. 2010, pp. 76–79.

Dalsimer, Katherine. *Female Adolescence: Psychoanalytic Reflections on Works of Literature.* Yale UP, 1986.

Day, Sara K. *Reading Like a Girl: Narrative Intimacy in Contemporary American Young Adult Literature.* UP of Mississippi, 2013.

Fraustino, Lisa Rowe, and Karen Coats, editors. *Mothers in Children's and Young Adult Literature: From the Eighteenth Century to Postfeminism.* UP of Mississippi, 2016.

Gillis, Bryan, and Joanna Simpson. *Sexual Content in Young Adult Literature: Reading between the Sheets.* Rowman and Littlefield, 2015.

Gross, Melissa, et al. *HIV/AIDS in Young Adult Novels: An Annotated Bibliography.* Scarecrow Press, 2010.

———, et al. "What Do Young Adult Novels Say About HIV/AIDS? A Second Look." *The Library Quarterly*, vol. 78, no. 4, Oct. 2008, pp. 397–418.

Gruner, Elisabeth Rose. "Telling Old Tales Newly: Intertextuality in Young Adult Fiction for Girls." *Telling Children's Stories: Narrative Theory and Children's Literature*, edited by Mike Cadden, U of Nebraska P, 2010, pp. 3–21.

Guanio-Uluru, Lykke. "Female Focalizers and Masculine Ideals: Gender as Performance in Twilight and The Hunger Games." *Children's Literature in Education*, vol. 47, no. 3, Sept. 2016, pp. 209–24.

Hartley-Kroeger, Fiona. "Silent Speech: Narration, Gender and Intersubjectivity in Two Young Adult Novels." *Children's Literature in Education*, vol. 42, no. 4, Dec. 2011, pp. 276–88.

Holt, Jenny. *Public School Literature, Civic Education and the Politics of Male Adolescence.* Ashgate, 2008.

James, Kathryn. *Death, Gender, and Sexuality in Contemporary Adolescent Literature.* Routledge, 2009.

Jarvis, Christine. "The Twilight of Feminism? Stephenie Meyer's Saga and the Contradictions of Contemporary Girlhood." *Children's Literature in Education*, vol. 45, no. 2, June 2014, pp. 101–15.

Jones. Caroline E. "From Homoplot to Progressive Novel: Lesbian Experience and Identity in Contemporary Young Adult Novels." *The Lion and the Unicorn*, vol. 37, no. 1, Jan. 2013, pp. 74–93.

———. "'Jesus Loves Me, This I Know': Finding a Rainbow God in Contemporary Adolescent Literature." *Children's Literature in Education*, vol. 43, no. 3, Sept. 2012, pp. 223–41.

Kertzer, Adrienne. "Reclaiming Her Maternal Pre-text: Little Red Riding Hood's Mother and Three Young Adult Novels." *Children's Literature Association Quarterly*, vol. 21, no. 1, Spring 1996, pp. 20–27.

Kneen, Bonnie. "Neither Very Bi nor Particularly Sexual: The Essence of the Bisexual in Young Adult Literature." *Children's Literature in Education*, vol. 46, no. 4, Dec. 2015, pp. 359–77.

Kokkola, Lydia. *Fictions of Adolescent Carnality: Sexy Sinners and Delinquent Deviants.* Benjamins, 2013.

Kokkola, Lydia, et al. "'Who Does What to Whom and How': 'Knowing Children' and Depictions of Prostitution in Anglophone Young Adult Literature." *Children's Literature Association Quarterly*, vol. 38, no. 1, Spring 2013, pp. 66–83.

Labovitz, Esther Kleinbord. *The Myth of the Heroine: The Female Bildungsroman in the Twentieth Century: Dorothy Richardson, Simone de Beauvoir, Doris Lessing, Christa Wolf.* Peter Lang, 1987.

Matos, Angel Daniel. "'Without a Word or Sign': Enmeshing Deaf and Gay Identity in Young Adult Literature." *Lessons in Disability: Essays on Teaching with Young Adult Literature*, edited by Jacob Stratman, McFarland, 2015, pp. 221–43.

Mitchell, Jennifer. "'A Girl. A Machine. A Freak': A Consideration of Contemporary Queer Composites." *Bookbird: A Journal of International Children's Literature*, vol. 52, no. 1, Jan. 2014, pp. 51–62.

Munson-Warnken, Megan. "The High Cost of 'Girl Books' for Young Adolescent Boys." *The Reading Teacher*, vol. 70, no. 5, Mar.-Apr. 2017, pp. 583–93.

Myers, Mitzi. "The Dilemmas of Gender as Double-Voiced Narration; or, Maria Edgeworth Mothers the Bildungsroman." *The Idea of the Novel in the*

Eighteenth Century, edited by Robert W. Uphaus, Colleagues Press, 1988, pp. 67–96.

Nash, Ilana. *American Sweethearts: Teenage Girls in Twentieth-Century Popular Culture*. Indiana UP, 2006.

Pfeiffer, Julie. "The *Backfisch* and Stories of Female Adolescence." *Tulsa Studies in Women's Literature*, vol. 36, no. 2, Fall 2017, pp. 295–321.

Pratt, Annis. *Archetypal Patterns in Women's Fiction*. Indiana UP, 1981.

Putzi, Jennifer. "None of This 'Trapped-in-a-Man's-Body Bullshit': Transgender Girls and Wrong-Body Discourse in Young Adult Fiction." *Tulsa Studies in Women's Literature*, vol. 36, no. 2, Fall 2017, pp. 423–48.

Sciurba, Katie. "Texts as Mirrors, Texts as Windows: Black Adolescent Boys and the Complexities of Textual Relevance." *Journal of Adolescent and Adult Literacy*, vol. 58, no. 4, Dec. 2014–Jan. 2015, pp. 308–16.

Seymour, Jessica. "'Murder Me . . . Become a Man': Establishing the Masculine Care Circle in Young Adult Dystopia." *Reading Psychology*, vol. 37, no. 4, 2016, pp. 627–49.

Stein, Katy. "'My Slippery Place': Female Masturbation in Young Adult Literature." *Children's Literature Association Quarterly*, vol. 37, no. 4, Winter 2012, pp. 415–28.

Storer, Heather L. "A Year of Bad Choices: The Postfeminist 'Restorying' of Teen Dating Violence in Young Adult Literature." *Affilia: Journal of Women and Social Work*, vol. 32, no. 3, 2017, pp. 292–307.

Trites, Roberta Seelinger. "Material Feminism, Adolescent 'Becoming,' and Libba Bray's *Beauty Queens*." *Tulsa Studies in Women's Literature*, vol. 36, no. 2, Fall 2017, pp. 379–400.

———. *Twenty-First-Century Feminisms in Children's and Adolescent Literature*. UP of Mississippi, 2018.

Wilson, Lucy. "Dialogic Interplay in Coming-of-Age Novels by West Indian Women Writers." *Children's Literature Association Quarterly*, vol. 18, no. 4, Winter 1993, pp. 177–82.

Younger, Beth. *Learning Curves: Body Image and Female Sexuality in Young Adult Literature*. Rowman and Littlefield, 2009.

Diversity and Inclusion

Abate, Michelle Ann. "'The Capitol Accent Is So Affected Almost Anything Sounds Funny in It': The Hunger Games Trilogy, Queerness, and Paranoid Reading." *Journal of LGBT Youth*, vol. 12, no. 4, 2015, pp. 397–418.

Baer, Allison L., and Jacqueline N. Glasgow. "Negotiating Understanding through the Young Adult Literature of Muslim Cultures." *Journal of Adolescent and Adult Literacy*, vol. 54, no. 1, Sept. 2010, pp. 23–32.

Becnel, Kim. "Holding Out Hope: Homelessness in Children's and Young Adult Literature." Naidoo and Dahlen, pp. 129–38.

Brown, Joanne. *Immigration Narratives in Young Adult Literature: Crossing Borders.* Scarecrow Press, 2010.

Cadden, Mike. "'But You Are Still a Monkey': *American Born Chinese* and Racial Self-Acceptance." *The Looking Glass: New Perspectives on Children's Literature*, vol. 17, no. 2, 2014, www.lib.latrobe.edu.au/ojs/index.php/tlg/article/view/477/427.

Chaudhri, Amina. "Growing Mixed/Up: Multiracial Identity in Children's and Young Adult Literature." Naidoo and Dahlen, pp. 95–104.

Cummins, Amy. "Border Crossings: Undocumented Migration between Mexico and the United States in Contemporary Young Adult Literature." *Children's Literature in Education*, vol. 44, no. 1, Mar. 2013, pp. 57–73.

Cummins, June. "What Are Jewish Boys and Girls Made Of? Gender in Contemporary Jewish Teen and Tween Fiction." *Children's Literature Association Quarterly*, vol. 36, no. 3, Fall 2011, pp. 296–317.

Curwood, Jen Scott. "Redefining Normal: A Critical Analysis of (Dis)Ability in Young Adult Literature." *Children's Literature in Education*, vol. 44, no. 1, Mar. 2013, pp. 15–28.

Dean-Ruzicka, Rachel. "Combating Hate through Young Adult Literature." *Journal of Hate Studies*, vol. 10, no. 1, 2012, pp. 199–220.

———. *Tolerance Discourse and Young Adult Holocaust Literature: Engaging Difference and Identity.* Routledge, 2016.

Dunn, Patricia. *Disabling Characters: Representations of Disability in Young Adult Literature.* Peter Lang, 2015.

Gangi, Jane. *Genocide in Contemporary Children's and Young Adult Literature.* Routledge, 2015.

Gates, Pamela S., and Dianne L. Hall Mark. *Cultural Journeys: Multicultural Literature for Children and Young Adults.* Scarecrow Press, 2006.

Henderson, Laretta, editor. *The Américas Award: Honoring Latino/a Children's and Young Adult Literature of the Americas.* Lexington Books, 2016.

———. "The Black Arts Movement and African American Young Adult Literature: An Evaluation of Narrative Style." *Children's Literature in Education*, vol. 36, no. 4, Dec. 2005, pp. 299–324.

Hughes-Hassell, Sandra. "Multicultural Young Adult Literature as a Form of Counter-Storytelling." *The Library Quarterly: Information, Community, Policy*, vol. 83, no. 3, July 2013, pp. 212–28.

Jans-Thomas, Susie. "Beyond Tamales, Tacos, and Our Southern Neighbors: Exploring Latino Culture in Child and Young Adult Literature." *Making Connections: Interdisciplinary Approaches to Cultural Diversity*, vol. 11, no. 1, Sept. 2009, pp. 33–39.

Johnson, Dianne. "African American Women Writers of Children's and Young Adult Literature." *The Cambridge Companion to African American Women's Literature*, edited by Angelyn Mitchell and Danille K. Taylor, Cambridge UP, 2009, pp. 210–23.

LeSeur, Geta. *Ten Is the Age of Darkness: The Black Bildungsroman.* U of Missouri P, 1995.

Molin, Paulette F. *American Indian Themes in Young Adult Literature.* Scarecrow Press, 2005.

Naidoo, Jamie Campbell, and Sarah Park Dahlen, editors. *Diversity in Youth Literature: Opening Doors through Reading.* American Library Association, 2013.

Pérez, Ashley Hope, and Patricia Encisco. "Decentering Whiteness and Monolingualism in the Reception of Latinx YA Literature." *Bilingual Review / Revista Bilingüe*, vol. 33, no. 5, 2017, pp. 1–14.

Reynolds, Nancy Thalia. *Mixed Heritage in Young Adult Literature.* Scarecrow Press, 2009.

Smart, Graham, and Richard Thompson. "'Someone Just Like Me': Narrative, Figured World, and Uptake in Therapeutic Books for Youths with Mental Health Disorders." *Written Communication*, vol. 34, no. 1, Jan. 2017, pp. 5–29.

Smith, Karen Patricia, editor. *African-American Voices in Young Adult Literature: Tradition, Transition, Transformation.* Scarecrow Press, 1994.

Suhr-Sytsma, Mandy. "Jeannette Armstrong's *Slash* and the Indigenous Reinvention of Young Adult Literature." *Studies in American Indian Literatures*, vol. 28, no. 4, Winter 2016, pp. 25–52.

Van Hart, Rachel F. "A Case for the Autistic Perspective in Young Adult Literature." *English Journal*, vol. 102, no. 2, Nov. 2012, pp. 27–36.

Wickens, Corrine M. "Codes, Silences, and Homophobia: Challenging Normative Assumptions about Gender and Sexuality in Contemporary LGBTQ Young Adult Literature." *Children's Literature in Education*, vol. 42, no. 2, June 2011, pp. 148–64.

Yenika-Agbaw, Vivian, and Mary Napoli, editors. *African and African American Children's and Adolescent Literature in the Classroom: A Critical Guide.* Peter Lang, 2011.

Organization Web Sites

American Library Association (www.ala.org)

Children's Literature Association (www.childlitassn.org)

International Board on Books for Young People (www.ibby.org)

International Literacy Association (www.literacyworldwide.org)

International Research Society for Children's Literature (www.irscl.com)

National Center for the Study of Children's Literature (childlit.sdsu.edu/)

National Centre for Research in Children's Literature (www.roehampton.ac.uk/research-centres/national-centre-for-research-in-childrens-literature)

National Council of Teachers of English (www2.ncte.org)

Young Adult Library Services Association (www.ala.org/yalsa)

Other Online Resources

Amelia Bloomer Project (www.ameliabloomer.wordpress.com)

Booktoss (www.booktoss.blog)

Dr. Bickmore's YA Wednesday (www.yawednesday.com)

Forever Young Adult (www.foreveryoungadult.com)

Goddess Librarian: Young Adult Literature Reviews and Usborne Books and More Services (www.goddesslibrarian.blogspot.com)

Guys Lit Wire (www.guyslitwire.blogspot.com)

Historical Fiction for Children and Young Adults (bookgirl3.tripod.com/historicalfiction.html)

KidLitosphere Central: The Society of Bloggers in Children's and Young Adult Literature (www.kidlitosphere.org/bloggers)

Nerdy Book Club (www.nerdybookclub.wordpress.com)

Nine Kinds of Pie (www.philnel.com)

Queer Books for Teens (www.queerbooksforteens.com)

Readergirlz (www.readergirlz.com/)

Reading Rants (www.readingrants.org)

Romance Novels for Feminists (www.romancenovelsforfeminists.blogspot.com)

Social Justice Books: A Teaching for Change Project (socialjusticebooks.org)

Teenreads (www.teenreads.com)

Theoretical Approaches to Young Adult Literature (www.readingya.blogspot.com)

Urban Epics: Dark Fantasy, Tragic Romance and Epic Adventure (www.urbanepics.com)

The Verse Novel Review (www.versenovelreview.blogspot.com)

VOYA Magazine (www.voyamagazine.com)

YA Books Central (www.yabookscentral.com)

YA Lit: The Good, the Bad, and the Ugly (www.yalitgoodbadugly.wordpress.com/about)

YA Pride (www.yapride.org)

The Ya Ya Yas (www.theyayayas.wordpress.com)

"Young Adult Bloggers, Sites and More," *The YA Bookshelf* (www.theyashelf.com/young-adult-bloggers-sites-and-more)

"Young Adult Literature," *Book Riot* (www.bookriot.com/category/young-adult-literature)

"Young Adult Literature," *The Literary Link* (www.theliterarylink.com/yalink.html)

Journals That Publish Articles on Young Adult Literature

The ALAN Review (www.alan-ya.org/publications/the-alan-review)

Bookbird: A Journal of International Children's Literature (www.ibby.org/bookbird)

The Bulletin of the Center for Children's Books (bccb.ischool.illinois.edu)

CCL/LCJ: Canadian Children's Literature / Littérature canadienne pour la jeunesse (www.ccl-lcj.ca/index.php/ccl-lcj)

Children's Literature (www.childlitassn.org/children-s-literature)

Children's Literature Association Quarterly (www.childlitassn.org/chla-quarterly)

Children's Literature in Education (link.springer.com/journal/10583)

English Journal (www2.ncte.org/resources/journals/english-journal)

First Opinions, Second Reactions (docs.lib.purdue.edu/fosr)

The Horn Book (www.hbook.com)

International Research in Children's Literature (www.euppublishing.com/loi/ircl)

Journal of Adolescent and Adult Literacy (ila.onlinelibrary.wiley.com/journal/19362706)

Language Arts (www2.ncte.org/resources/journals/language-arts)

The Lion and the Unicorn (www.muse.jhu.edu/journal/201)

The Looking Glass: New Perspectives on Children's Literature (www.lib.latrobe.edu.au/ojs/index.php/tlg/index)

Magpies: Talking about Books for Children (www.magpies.net.au)

Marvels and Tales: Journal of Fairy-Tale Studies (digitalcommons.wayne.edu/marvels)

Papers: Explorations into Children's Literature (paperschildlit.com)

Publishers Weekly (www.publishersweekly.com/pw/by-topic/childrens/index.html)

Red Feather Journal: An International Journal of Children in Popular Culture (www.redfeatherjournal.org)

School Library Journal (www.slj.com)

Study and Scrutiny: Research on Young Adult Literature (journals.shareok.org/studyandscrutiny)

Awards

American Library Association (ALA) Awards

Alex Award ("given to ten books written for adults that have special appeal to young adults, ages 12 through 18") (www.ala.org/yalsa/alex-awards)

American Indian Youth Literature Award ("honors the very best writing and illustrations by and about American Indians") (ailanet.org/activities/american-indian-youth-literature-award)

Coretta Scott King Book Awards ("outstanding books for young adults and children by African American authors and illustrators that reflect the African American experience") (www.ala.org/awardsgrants/coretta-scott-king-book-awards)

Margaret A. Edwards Award ("for significant and lasting contribution to young adult literature") (www.ala.org/yalsa/edwards-award)

Michael L. Printz Award ("an award for a book that exemplifies literary excellence in young adult literature") (www.ala.org/yalsa/printz-award)

Nonfiction for Young Adults Award (www.ala.org/yalsa/nonfiction-award)

Odyssey Award ("given to the producer of the best audiobook produced for children and/or young adults") (www.ala.org/yalsa/odyssey-award)

Schneider Family Book Award ("honor an author or illustrator for a book that embodies an artistic expression of the disability experience for child and adolescent audiences") (www.ala.org/awardsgrants/awards/1/all_years)

Stonewall Book Awards ("for exceptional merit relating to the gay/lesbian/bisexual/transgender experience") (www.ala.org/rt/glbtrt/award/stonewall)

William C. Morris YA Debut Award ("honors a book published by a first-time author writing for teens and celebrating impressive new voices in young adult literature") (www.ala.org/yalsa/morris-award)

Other Awards

Américas Award (Consortium of Latin American Studies Programs) ("quality children's and young adult books that portray Latin America, the Caribbean, or Latinos in the United States") (www.claspprograms.org/americasaward)

Andre Norton Award for Young Adult Science Fiction and Fantasy (Science Fiction and Fantasy Writers of America) (nebulas.sfwa.org/award/andre-norton-award)

Arab American Book Award (www.arabamericanmuseum.org/bookaward)

Asian/Pacific American Award for Literature (Asian/Pacific American Librarians Association) ("honor and recognize individual work about Asian/Pacific Americans and their heritage, based on literary and artistic merit") (www.apalaweb.org/awards/literature-awards)

Astrid Lindgren Memorial Award (www.alma.se/en)

The *Boston Globe–Horn Book* Awards (www.hbook.com/?detailStory=boston-globe-horn-book-awards)

Children's and Young Adult Bloggers' Literary Awards (Cybils) (www.cybils.com)

CODE Burt Award for First Nations, Inuit, and Métis Young Adult Literature (a Canadian literary award and readership initiative that recognizes excellence in Indigenous-written literature for young adults) (www.burtaward.org/burt-award-canada)

Database of Award-Winning Children's Literature (www.dawcl.com/search.asp)

Lambda Literary Awards ("Lammys"; "to celebrate excellence in LGBTQ publishing") (www.lambdaliterary.org/awards)

Los Angeles Times Book Prizes (events.latimes.com/festivalofbooks/bookprizes-history)

Mystery Writers of America's Edgar Allan Poe Awards (www.theedgars.com/index.html)

National Book Award for Young People's Literature (www.nationalbook.org)

Sydney Taylor Book Award (Association of Jewish Libraries; "presented annually to outstanding books for children and teens that authentically portray the Jewish experience") (www.jewishlibraries.org/content.php?page=Sydney_Taylor_Book_Award)

United States Board on Books for Young People (www.usbby.org/awards--lists.html)

Notes on Contributors

Michelle Ann Abate is professor of literature for children and young adults at Ohio State University. She is the author of five books of literary criticism on topics including the history of tomboyism, murder in children's literature, and classic American comics. She has also published more than thirty peer-reviewed journal articles on subjects ranging from *The Outsiders* and *The Muppet Show* to *Calvin and Hobbes* and lesbian pulp fiction.

Mary Adler serves as professor of English at California State University, Channel Islands. She specializes in classroom discourse, writing processes, and literacy practices. She is the author of *Writers at Play: Making the Space for Adolescents to Balance Imagination and Craft* and of *Building Literacy through Classroom Discussion* (with Eija Rougle). Adler is past codirector and frequent contributor to an NEH Summer Institute focusing on the life and work of John Steinbeck.

Livia Antony is an independent researcher in the field of science fiction and young adult literature. She holds a master's in English from St. Joseph's College, Bangalore, and is pursuing a PhD in science fiction. She has cowritten papers on young adult fiction for various publications.

Laura Apol is associate professor at Michigan State University, where she teaches children's literature and poetry writing. Apol has published scholarly articles on historical children's literature, the intersection between children's literature and literary theory, the pedagogy of children's and young adult literature and international children's literature, and facilitating creative writing for children and adults, and she conducts creative writing workshops and classes for teachers and students on all levels.

Carey Applegate, associate professor of English education at the University of Wisconsin, Eau Claire, teaches courses in education methods, adolescent literacies, young adult literature, and critical studies. Her current research examines social justice literacies and education activism. Her previous scholarship has appeared in *The International Journal of Critical Pedagogy*, *Intercultural Education*, *English Journal*, and several edited collections, including *Exploring Teachers in Fiction and Film: Saviors, Scapegoats and Schoolmarms*.

Padma Baliga has taught English to high school, undergraduate, and graduate students for more than twenty years. Her doctoral thesis was on gender theory and contemporary Indian children's literature. Her research and teaching interests include children's and young adult literature, women's studies, language pedagogy, Indian literatures, and Dalit writing. She cotranslated

Alice in Wonderland into Konkani and is engaged in a critical and sociological study of children's books in Konkani.

Katherine Bell is associate professor in the Department of English and Film Studies at Wilfrid Laurier University, where she teaches courses in children's, tween, and young adult literature. Her most recent research focuses on representations of adolescents in contemporary Canadian literature and culture. Her research has been published in journals such as *Children's Literature Association Quarterly*, *Jeunesse*, *Children's Literature in Education*, and *The ALAN Review*.

Mary Bricker earned her doctorate from the University of Illinois, Urbana-Champaign. She is assistant professor of German at Southern Illinois University, Carbondale. She regularly teaches the introductory fairy tale course Masterpieces of World Literature: The Fairy Tales of the Brothers Grimm. Her research spans eighteenth-, nineteenth-, and twentieth-century German literature. Her fairy tale scholarship has appeared in *Neophilologus*, *PsyArt*, and *Bakhtiniana*. She is a member of the *Bakhtiniana* editorial board.

Camille Buffington graduated from Wheaton College in Massachusetts with a double major in creative writing and literature and psychology in 2017. She works at Hachette Book Group in Boston. Her poetry has been featured in the America Library of Poetry's *The Gold Edition* as well as in the literary magazines *Rushlight* and *Kaleidoscope*. She edited a children's book series on imagination and creativity and is composing a picture book about the structures of the brain.

Lauren Byler is associate professor of English at California State University, Northridge, where she teaches courses on Victorian literature, the novel, critical theory, and girls' books. Her work has appeared in *Novel*, *Victorian Literature and Culture*, *Children's Literature*, and *Texas Studies in Literature and Language*. She is currently completing a monograph titled "Everything Nice: Contingencies of Value and the Figure of the Girl in the Nineteenth-Century British Novel."

Mike Cadden is professor of English and the director of childhood studies at Missouri Western State University, where he teaches children's and young adult literature. He is the author of *Ursula K. Le Guin beyond Genre: Fiction for Children and Adults* and the editor of *Telling Children's Stories: Narrative Theory and Children's Literature*. He is a former president of the Children's Literature Association.

Beverly Lyon Clark is professor of English and women's and gender studies at Wheaton College in Massachusetts. She is the author of *Kiddie Lit: The Cultural Construction of Children's Literature in America* and *The Afterlife of* Little Women, and she has edited or coedited works by or about

Louisa May Alcott, Mark Twain, Flannery O'Connor, Carson McCullers, and Evelyn Sharp. She is currently researching juvenile captivity narratives.

Karen Coats is professor of education and director of the Centre for Research in Children's Literature at the University of Cambridge. She publishes widely on youth literature and literary and cultural theory and is the coeditor of the *Handbook of Research on Children's and Young Adult Literature*; *Mothers in Children's and Young Adult Literature: From the Eighteenth Century to Postfeminism*; and *The Gothic in Children's Literature: Haunting the Borders*. Her most recent book is *The Bloomsbury Introduction to Children's and Young Adult Literature.*

Amy Cummins is associate professor of English in the Department of Literatures and Cultural Studies at the University of Texas, Rio Grande Valley. She teaches children's and young adult literature, and she works to prepare future teachers of English language arts and reading.

Justyna Deszcz-Tryhubczak is associate professor of literature and director of the Center for Young People's Literature and Culture at the Institute of English Studies, University of Wrocław, Poland. She is the author of *Yes to Solidarity, No to Oppression: Radical Fantasy Fiction and Its Young Readers* (2016). Her research focuses on speculative fiction, utopianism, and child-led approaches. She has taught courses on children's and young adult literature and culture. She is a Fulbright, Kosciuszko, and Marie Skłodowska-Curie fellow.

Eric Esten studies education policy and management at Harvard Graduate School of Education. He graduated from Wheaton College in Massachusetts in 2016. His research interests include literacy, education reform, and minority representation.

Wendy J. Glenn is professor of literacy studies, cochair of teacher education, and chair of secondary humanities in the School of Education at the University of Colorado, Boulder. Her research centers on literature and literacies for young adults in the context of sociocultural analyses and critical and culturally affirming pedagogies. She has been named a university teaching fellow and Fulbright scholar. She is the former president of the Assembly on Literature for Adolescents of the National Council of Teachers of English and former senior editor of *The ALAN Review*.

Melanie Goss is assistant professor of English at Waldorf University. Her research interests include representations of disability and neurodivergence in contemporary young adult texts, and she is working on a project about depictions of mental illness in graphic narratives.

Melissa Gross is professor in the School of Information at Florida State University. She teaches and researches in the areas of information-seeking behavior, resources for youth, research methods, information literacy, and teacher and librarian collaboration. She has published extensively in peer-reviewed journals, including *Children's Literature in Education*, *Library and Information Science Research*, *Library Quarterly*, and others. Her most recent book, edited with Shelbie Witte and Don Latham, is *Literacy Engagement through Peritextual Analysis* (2019).

Roxanne Harde is professor of English at the University of Alberta, Augustana, where she also serves as associate dean of research. A Fulbright Scholar, Harde researches and teaches American literature and culture, focusing on children's literature and popular culture. She is coeditor of *The Embodied Child* (with Lydia Kokkola, 2017). Her disciplinary and pedagogical essays have appeared in dozens of journals and essay collections. An award-winning teacher, Harde has been invited to present team-based learning workshops in Canada and Europe.

Billie Jarvis-Freeman is associate professor of English studies and director of elementary education at Lincoln Christian University, where she teaches narratives as vehicles of truth and meaning whether or not the events actually happened. Her research interests include the works of George MacDonald and Dorothy L. Sayers.

S. Patrice Jones is assistant professor of education at Grinnell College, a private liberal arts college in the Midwest. She teaches methods courses for prospective English teachers along with special topics courses, such as Reading and Writing Youth Cultures, Risky Texts, and Critical Literacy for Diverse Learners. Her research interests are situated in black girls' literacy practices within urban, contemporary young adult literature and also the ways in which racial trauma is embedded in classroom spaces and curricula.

Katie Kapurch is associate professor of English at Texas State University. Her publications include *Victorian Melodrama in the Twenty-First Century:* Jane Eyre, Twilight, *and the Mode of Excess in Popular Girl Culture* (2016) and the coedited collection *New Critical Perspectives on the Beatles: Things We Said Today* (2016) and also include chapters and journal articles that address youth gender, sexuality, and race in pop culture. Her forthcoming books include *Black America Remixes the Beatles*, supported by a grant from the National Endowment for the Humanities, and *Sex and Gender in Rock from the Beatles to Beyoncé*, cowritten with Walter Everett.

Don Latham is a professor in the School of Information at Florida State University, where he teaches courses on children's resources, young adult resources, and graphic novels. His research on information behavior of young adults, digital literacies, and young adult literature has been published in such journals as *Children's Literature*, *Children's Literature Association Quarterly*, *Children's Literature in Education*, and *Journal of Research on Libraries and Young Adults*. He is coauthor of *Young Adult Resources Today: Connecting*

Teens with Books, Music, Games, Movies, and More and coeditor of *Literacy Engagement through Peritextual Analysis.*

Helma van Lierop-Debrauwer is professor of children's literature at Tilburg University in the Netherlands, where she coordinates the children's and adolescent literature master's program. With four European partners she developed the Erasmus Mundus International Master in Children's Literature, Media and Culture. Her research interests are adolescent literature and life writing. In 2005 she published a book in Dutch about adolescent literature in literature education. In 2017 she published *Canon Constitution and Canon Change in Children's Literature.* She is a member of International Research in Children's Literature and of the academic advisory board of the Yearbook of the German Society of Children's Literature Research.

Elizabeth Marshall is associate professor of education at Simon Fraser University in Vancouver, British Columbia. Her interdisciplinary research on contemporary children's literature, feminist theory, and constructions of childhood has been published in *Children's Literature in Education*, *Reading Research Quarterly*, *Gender and Education*, *College English*, and *Women's Studies Quarterly.* She is the coeditor of *Rethinking Popular Culture and Media* (2016) and the author of *Graphic Girlhoods: Visualizing Education and Violence* (2018).

Angel Daniel Matos is assistant professor of English and comparative literature at San Diego State University who specializes in children's and young adult literature and queer studies. His primary research explores how queer experiences, histories, and emotions are shaped and narrativized in LGBTQ+ youth fiction, specifically how queer narrative and aesthetic practices foster political and affective frameworks that complicate current understandings of young adult literature. His research and teaching interests also include space and place, the history of adolescence, digital fan production, and teen film.

Meghann Meeusen teaches children's and adolescent literature at Western Michigan University, where she works to develop innovative pedagogy approaches centering around the contextual nature of literature, as well as how individuals can become stronger critical thinkers through reading and research. She earned her PhD from Illinois State University, and her research explores ideology and binary patterns in film adaptations of children's texts. Meeusen has broader research interests in children's visual culture, representation in young adult fantasy, and film pedagogy.

Farah Mendlesohn's previous work includes *The Inter-galactic Playground: A Critical Study of Children's and Teens' Science Fiction*; *Diana Wynne Jones: The Fantastic Tradition and Children's Literature*; and *Children's Fantasy Literature: An Introduction*, cowritten with Michael Levy, which won the

World Fantasy Award in 2017. She won a Hugo with Edward James in 2005 for *The Cambridge Companion to Fantasy Literature*. She is currently working on a book on children's historical fiction of the English Civil War.

Cathryn M. Mercier is professor of children's literature and director of the Center for the Study of Children's Literature, as well as the MA, MFA, and dual degree programs in literature for children and young adults, at Simmons University in Boston. She has published three biocritical studies, contributed to *Keywords for Children's Literature*, and coedited the Children's Literature Association newsletter. Her leadership in the Association for Library Service to Children includes Newbery, Caldecott, and Geisel committee membership, and she chaired the Sibert and Legacy (former Wilder) committees. She serves on the board of trustees of the Eric Carle Museum of Picture Book Art in Amherst, Massachusetts.

Margaret Noodin is professor of English and American Indian studies at the University of Wisconsin, Milwaukee, where she also serves at the director of the Electa Quinney Institute for American Indian Education. She is the author of *Bawaajimo: A Dialect of Dreams in Anishinaabe Language and Literature* and *Weweni*, a collection of poems in Ojibwe and English. In addition to publishing research about literature, language, and teaching, she has published poetry in *Poetry*, *Michigan Quarterly Review*, and *Yellow Medicine Review*, among others.

Melek Ortabasi is associate professor and director of the World Literature Program at Simon Fraser University in Vancouver, British Columbia. She is a comparatist who specializes in modern Japanese literature. Her teaching and research interests include translation practice and theory, popular culture and transnationalism, and internationalism in children's literature. Her latest book, *The Undiscovered Country: Text, Translation, and Modernity in the Work of Yanagita Kunio*, was published in 2014. She is working on a comparative modern historiography of world children's literature tentatively entitled "The World Republic of Childhood: Transnationalism and Children's Literature, 1870–1930."

Donna L. Pasternak is professor of English education and director of the National Writing Project at the University of Wisconsin, Milwaukee. She studies the integration of technology into English and English language arts teacher education in urban contexts. Pasternak's scholarship has been published in a variety of journals and edited volumes. In 2018 she was a corecipient of the National Council of Teachers of English's ELATE Richard A. Meade Award for her cowritten book *Secondary English Teacher Education in the United States* (2018).

Melissa Sara Smith earned her PhD from Illinois State University and is an associate professor of English at Ferris State University in Big Rapids,

Michigan. She serves as both the assistant chair and the assessment coordinator of the English, Literature, and World Languages Department. She teaches courses in children's, young adult, and women's literature, and her research is focused on narrative and embodiment theory.

Jan C. Susina is professor of English at Illinois State University, where he offers courses in children's and young adult literature. He is the former editor and book editor of *The Lion and the Unicorn* and author of *The Place of Lewis Carroll in Children's Literature.* His articles and reviews have appeared in *Children's Literature, Children's Literature Association Quarterly, The Lion and the Unicorn*, and others. He has served on the executive committee of the MLA Forum on Children and Young Adult Literature and the executive board of the Children's Literature Association.

Lee A. Talley is professor of English and founding dean of the Bantivoglio Honors Concentration at Rowan University's Honors College. She has published in *Children's Literature, Keywords for Children's Literature*, and *The Lion and the Unicorn*, among other academic venues. She is working on a book-length project about the World War II evacuation of British children.

Gwen Athene Tarbox is a professor of children's and young adult literature and comics studies in the Department of English at Western Michigan University, where she is also an affiliate faculty member in gender and women's studies. She coedited *Graphic Novels for Children and Young Adults: A Critical Collection* (with Michelle Ann Abate, 2017), and she has a monograph on the same subject, *Children's and Young Adult Comics* (2020).

Ebony Elizabeth Thomas is associate professor in the Literacy, Culture, and International Educational Division at the University of Pennsylvania's Graduate School of Education. A former Detroit public school teacher and National Academy of Education/Spencer Foundation postdoctoral fellow, she was a member of the NCTE Cultivating New Voices among Scholars of Color program (2008–19) and the NCTE Conference on English Education's Executive Committee (2013–17) and the chair of the NCTE Standing Committee on Research. She serves as coeditor of *Research of the Teaching of English*, and her most recent book is *The Dark Fantastic: Race and the Imagination from Harry Potter to the Hunger Games* (2019).

Roberta Seelinger Trites is distinguished professor of English at Illinois State University, where she has taught children's and adolescent literature since 1991. She is the author of *Waking Sleeping Beauty: Feminist Voices in Children's Novels* (1997); *Disturbing the Universe: Power and Repression in Adolescent Literature* (2000); *Twain, Alcott, and the Birth of the Adolescent Reform Novel* (2007); *Literary Conceptualizations of Growth: Metaphors and Cognition in Adolescent Literature* (2014); and *Twenty-First Century Feminisms in Children's* *and Adolescent Literature* (2018). She also coedited *A Narrative Compass: Stories That Guide Women's Lives* (with Betsy Hearne, 2009).

Laurie Barth Walczak served as the eighth grade American studies English teacher and middle school English department chair at University School of Milwaukee for twelve years before moving to the upper school to teach sophomore and junior English. She also teaches courses in children's and young adult literature in the Department of Curriculum and Instruction at the University of Milwaukee, Wisconsin. Her other areas of expertise include cultural competency and diversity in English language arts, culturally responsive teaching, and capstone programs.

Jon M. Wargo is assistant professor of literacy in the Lynch School of Education and Human Development at Boston College, where he teaches qualitative research methods, teaching with technology, and arts-based methods for teaching English language arts. His research uses feminist, queer, and poststructural modes of inquiry to explore how children and youth use literacy, and technologies of composition in particular, to design more just social futures.

Michael Zimmerman, Jr., is an enrolled member of the Pokagon Band of Potawatomi Indians of Michigan and Indiana. He has served as Tribal Historic Preservation Officer, tribal historian, and lead Native American Graves Protection and Repatriation Act consultant for the Pokagon Band. He is also a consultant on Potawatomi language for his band as well as the lead Ojibwe language and culture instructor at the Indian Community School of Milwaukee, where he teaches students in K4 through eighth grade.

Virginia Zimmerman is professor of English at Bucknell University. Her publications include *Excavating Victorians* (2008) and essays in *Configurations*, *Journal of Literature and Science*, *Victorian Periodicals Review*, and others. Most recently, she published "Excavating Children: Archaeological Imagination and Time Slip in the Early 1900s" in *Excavating Modernity* (2018). Zimmerman is also a children's author; her debut novel, *The Rosemary Spell*, was published in 2015. Both her fiction and her scholarly work address material culture and time.